Key Ideas in Linguistics and the Philosophy of Language

Key Ideas in Linguistics and the Philosophy of Language

Edited by

Siobhan Chapman and Christopher Routledge

Edinburgh University Press

© in this edition Edinburgh University Press, 2009
© in the individual contributions is retained by the authors

Edinburgh University Press Ltd
22 George Square, Edinburgh

Typeset in 10/12pt Sabon
by Servis Filmsetting Ltd, Stockport, Cheshire, and
printed and bound in Great Britain by
CPI Antony Rowe, Chippenham, Wilts

A CIP record for this book is available from the British Library

ISBN 978 0 7486 2618 2 (hardback)
ISBN 978 0 7486 2619 9 (paperback)

Contents

CONTENTS

Preface

The ideas described in this book have been developed in linguistics and the philosophy of language, as well as in some related disciplines such as mathematics, logic and psychology. They necessarily represent only a very small proportion of the long tradition of the serious study of language; we have chosen them because of their impact on current work in linguistics and the philosophy of language. These two disciplines are subdivided into many different branches. Linguistics, for example, includes work undertaken in semantics, pragmatics, phonology, syntax, sociolinguistics and many other fields. In general we have not treated these individual fields as key ideas in their own right. You will not, for instance, find an entry here on 'Pragmatics', but you will find topics from the field of pragmatics discussed under entries such as 'Implicature', 'Relevance Theory' and 'Speech Act Theory'. The names of different branches of linguistics and the philosophy of language do, however, appear in the index. Similarly, we have avoided allocating entries to descriptive categories such as 'adjective', 'phrase' or 'conjunction'.

The entries are arranged in simple alphabetical order, and aim to elucidate each key idea, offering a succinct definition followed by a more discursive account of the development of the idea and of its impact and current relevance. The book can therefore be used as a stand-alone reference work. However, it is also designed to be used in conjunction with our *Key Thinkers in Linguistics and the Philosophy of Language* (2005). The coverage of these two volumes is similar: broadly, the study of language in the Western tradition from antiquity to the present-day, with an emphasis on work that has been influential on linguistics and the philosophy of language as they are practised in the early part of the twenty-first century. However, the two are complementary in that they arrange and present the material in different ways. *Key Thinkers* considers different ways of thinking about language in the context of the work of the particular figures with which they are most closely associated, drawing out continuities and developments of thought in their particular historical and social context. *Key Ideas* focuses on the development of specific ways of thinking, sometimes across many decades or centuries, considering the influences on these ways of thinking, the relationships between them, and their overall significance.

Each entry is cross-referenced both internally within this book and externally to *Key Thinkers*. The internal cross-references ('*See also*') draw attention to other key ideas that are relevant to the particular entry. These may be ideas that are concerned with similar or related issues (such as the reference from 'Deduction/Induction' to 'Empiricism/Rationalism); ideas that form a specific topic within a more general approach (such as the reference from 'Speech Act Theory' to 'Performative'); or conversely ideas that provide a broader framework for the discussion of the specific issue in question (such as the reference from ('Adequacy' to 'Transformational-Generative Grammar'). Within each entry, any term that is itself a key idea with its own entry is marked with an asterisk on first use. The external cross-references ('*Key Thinkers*') point the reader towards relevant entries in *Key Thinkers*.

The entries are all concerned with encouraging the reader to find out more, and therefore with pointing outside these two volumes to other and more detailed reading. Each entry concludes with a list of suggested readings, divided into '*Primary sources*' and '*Further reading*'. Between them these sections give the full references of any works mentioned or quoted in the entry, along with details of other particularly salient works. The section of '*Further reading*' may also include suggestions of useful introductions to or overviews of the relevant key idea.

Acknowledgements

A book of this kind depends on the cooperation and goodwill of a large number of people and it has been a privilege to work with all of them. We would like to take this opportunity to thank all of our contributors to this book and its companion volume *Key Thinkers in Linguistics and the Philosophy of Language* (2005) for their diligence and professionalism. Two individuals deserve special mention. We would like to thank Sarah Edwards and her team at Edinburgh University Press for their enduring enthusiasm and support over the course of two lengthy book projects. Jeremy Kaye, whose father Alan S. Kaye was working on entries for this book when he died in May 2007, generously gave his time searching for material that Alan was preparing for us and delivered the one entry his father had managed to complete before becoming too ill to continue. Alan was passionately committed to the study of language and a valuable contributor to these books. We dedicate this volume to his memory.

Notes on Contributors

Varol Akman, Chair, Department of Philosophy Bilkent University, Turkey.

Salvatore Attardo, Professor, English Department, Youngstown State University, USA.

Annalisa Baicchi, Professor of English, Department of Theoretical and Applied Linguistics, University of Pavia, Italy.

Jennifer A. Baldwin, freelance translator (http://jenniferbaldwin.com).

Alex Barber, Department of Philosophy, The Open University, UK.

Philip Carr, Professor of Linguistics, Department of English, Montpellier University, France.

Siobhan Chapman, Senior Lecturer in English Language, University of Liverpool, UK.

Billy Clark, Lecturer in English Language, Middlesex University, UK.

John Collins, Department of Philosophy, University of East Anglia, UK.

Yousif Elhindi, Associate Professor, Department of English, East Tennessee State University, USA.

Iván García Álvarez, Lecturer in Linguistics, School of Languages, University of Salford, UK.

Agustinus Gianto, Professor of Semitic Philology and Linguistics, Pontifical Biblical Institute, Rome, Italy.

Hans Götzsche, Associate Professor and Director, Centre for Linguistics, Aalborg University, Denmark.

Eva Herrmann-Kaliner, computational linguist, Germany.

Patrick Honeybone, Lecturer in Linguistics and English Language, University of Edinburgh, UK.

Asa Kasher, Laura Schwarz-Kipp Professor of Professional Ethics and Philosophy of Practice, Tel Aviv University, Israel.

Alan S. Kaye (1944–2007), Professor of English, California State University Fullerton, USA.

Stavroula-Thaleia Kousta, Research Fellow, Department of Psychology, University College London, UK.

Guy Longworth, Assistant Professor, Department of Philosophy, University of Warwick, UK.

Stephen McLeod, Department of Philosophy, University of Liverpool, UK.

Marie Nilsenová, Assistant Professor, Department of Communication and Information Sciences, Tilburg University, Netherlands.

Ingrid Piller, Professor of Linguistics, Macquarie University, Australia.

Geoffrey Poole, Lecturer in Linguistics, School of English Literature, Language, and Linguistics, University of Newcastle upon Tyne, UK.

Kanavillil Rajagopalan, Professor of the Semantics and Pragmatics of Natural Languages, State University at Campinas (UNICAMP), Brazil.

Christopher Routledge, freelance writer and editor (http://chrisroutledge.co.uk).

Karl Simms, Senior Lecturer, School of English, University of Liverpool, UK.

Jürg Strässler, Universities of Berne and Zurich, Switzerland.

Marina Terkourafi, Department of Linguistics, University of Illinois at Urbana-Champaign.

Geoff Thompson, Senior Lecturer in Applied Linguistics, School of English at the University of Liverpool, UK

Dominic Watt, Lecturer in Forensic Speech Science, Department of Language and Linguistic Science, University of York, UK.

David Witkosky, Professor of German and International Studies, Auburn University, Montgomery, USA.

NOTES ON CONTRIBUTORS

ACCEPTABILITY/ GRAMMATICALITY

Acceptability is the extent to which a sentence allowed by the rules to be grammatical is considered permissible by speakers and hearer; grammaticality is the extent to which a 'string' of language conforms with a set of given rules. It is assumed that a native speaker's grammar generates grammatical strings and that the speaker has the ability to judge a certain string to be either acceptable or not in her language. In practice, the two notions are frequently confounded and speakers are typically asked to give their 'grammaticality judgements' instead of 'acceptability judgements'.

See also: Innateness; Mentalism; Transformational-Generative Grammar
Key Thinkers: Chomsky, Noam

In prescriptive grammar books employed in language teaching, a string is considered to be grammatical if it conforms with a set of prescribed norms. These norms are usually based on conventionalised rules that form a part of a higher/literary register for a given language. For some languages, these norms are defined and periodically updated by an appointed body of experts whose rulings are occasionally questioned by the frustrated members of the public.

In theoretical linguistics it has become customary to utilise the term 'grammaticality' in line with Noam Chomsky's generative approach. In generative grammar, a string is grammatical – or well formed – if it could be generated by a grammar internalised by a native speaker. A grammatical string is not necessarily meaningful, as exemplified by Chomsky's famous sentence 'Colorless green ideas sleep furiously'. However, it is assumed that even nonsensical grammatical sentences can easily be pronounced with a natural intonation and that speakers are able to recall them more easily than ungrammatical sentences. Speakers also supposedly have intuitions about grammaticality (or grammaticalness; these two terms appear to be interchangeable), determined by their competence (in other words, knowledge of a language).

Acceptability, on the other hand, is related to speaker's performance, that is the actual use of her language in concrete situations. As stressed by Chomsky, acceptability should not be confused with grammaticality: while an acceptable sentence must be grammatical, not just any grammatical sentence is necessarily acceptable. For a sentence to be judged acceptable, it must also appear natural and appropriate in a given context, be easily understood and, possibly, be to a certain extent conventionalised.

Both grammaticality and acceptability are considered to be gradient properties by Chomsky and in the linguistic literature they are typically expressed with a combination of '?' and '*' for grammaticality – a sentence marked with '**' being strongly ungrammatical, a sentence marked with a '?*' being questionable, and so on – and '#' for acceptability.

It has been observed that although speakers may have intuitions about grammaticality, they cannot be expected to translate their intuitions

1

into judgements; hence, a categorisation task can only rely on their ability to judge the acceptability of a string (Schütze 1996). This assumption is often violated in the process of data collecting and speakers are typically encouraged to give grammaticality judgements of marginally sounding sentences independently of an actual discourse situation.

Primary sources

Chomsky, N. (1957). *Syntactic Structures*. The Hague: Mouton.

Chomsky, N. (1965). *Aspects of the Theory of Syntax*. Cambridge, MA: MIT Press.

Further reading

Schütze, C. (1996). *The Empirical Base of Linguistics*. Chicago and London: The University of Chicago Press.

Marie Nilsenová

ADEQUACY

In the theory of transformational-generative grammar* generative grammars are said to be evaluated with respect to three levels of adequacy: observational adequacy, descriptive adequacy and explanatory adequacy.

> *See also*: Acceptability/
> Grammaticality; Intuition;
> Transformational-Generative
> Grammar; Universal Grammar
> *Key Thinkers*: Chomsky, Noam

In *Syntactic Structures* (1957) Noam Chomsky defined a language as a set of sentences. Generative grammars were taken by Chomsky to be formal grammars, based on a branch of mathematics known as formal language theory. The idea was that one could formulate a finite set of rules which generated the set of sentences which constituted a specific language, such as English. The set of sentences constituting a language was said to be infinite. That infinitude is guaranteed by the recursive nature of the rules. Recursion is the phenomenon whereby a given syntactic category can be embedded within a category of the same type. For instance, relative clauses in English can be embedded within relative clauses, as in the sentence 'I know the woman who shot the man who held up the bank'. The relative clause 'who shot the man who held up the bank' contains the relative clause 'who held up the bank'. Recursion is widely believed to be a universal feature of human languages.

One of the aims of early generative grammars was to generate all and only the sentences which constitute a specific language. A grammar was said to be observationally adequate if it did this. The aim was to construct grammars which did not generate sequences which were ill-formed, such as '*The house have might been built', where the asterisk denotes ungrammaticality. Sequences are judged to be grammatical or ungrammatical on the basis of the intuitive grammaticality judgements of native speakers of the language. In making such judgements, native speakers are said to be accessing a mind-internal grammar, which is taken to constitute largely unconscious linguistic knowledge, known as competence.

A given generative grammar will generate not only strings of words, but also structural descriptions of those strings. For instance, one grammar might generate a structural description of the phrase 'The old man' in which there are only three constituents: 'the', 'old' and 'man', in a flat linear string. Another grammar could generate a structural description in which there are two intermediate constituents: 'the' and 'old man'. The two grammars differ in the structural descriptions they generate. In *Aspects of the Theory of Syntax* (1965), Chomsky argued that a generative grammar is justified to the extent that the structural descriptions it generates correspond to the intuitive grammaticality judgements of the native speaker. He also suggested that linguists should seek explanatory adequacy: they should go further than descriptive adequacy, devising generative grammars which were embedded within a general theory of human language. The theory in question was Chomsky's universal grammar*.

Primary sources

Chomsky, N. (1957). *Syntactic Structures*. The Hague: Mouton.
Chomsky, N. (1965). *Aspects of the Theory of Syntax*. Cambridge MA: MIT Press.

Further reading

Sampson, G. (1979). 'What was transformational grammar?' *Lingua* 48: 355–78.
Smith, N. (2004). *Chomsky: Ideas and Ideals*. Cambridge: Cambridge University Press.

Philip Carr

AMBIGUITY/ VAGUENESS

Ambiguity and vagueness are related but distinct concepts. Ambiguity, the property of having more than one linguistically encoded meaning, is an important notion in several areas of linguistics (including syntax, semantics and pragmatics) as well as in philosophy of language. Vagueness, the property of having no uniquely determinable value or interpretation, has been discussed by philosophers since ancient times and is still a focus of attention for philosophers, semanticists and pragmatists.

See also: Connotation/Denotation; Conventional Meaning; Nonnatural Meaning; Implicature; Indeterminacy; Logic; Logical Form; Sense/Reference; Signs and Semiotics
Key Thinkers: Frege, Gottlob; Grice, H. P.; Peirce, C. S.; Quine, W. V. O.; Russell, Bertrand; Wittgenstein, Ludwig

Ambiguity is the property of having more than one linguistically encoded meaning. Lexical ambiguity is a property of words (or lexemes) and syntactic ambiguity is a property of phrases, clauses or sentences.

The English noun 'seal' is an ambiguous lexical item referring, among other things, to a particular kind of sea creature or a device for making sure an opening is fully closed. The sentence 'I've brought the seal' is ambiguous because of the presence of this lexical item.

A syntactically (or 'structurally') ambiguous expression is one which can be associated with more than one syntactic structure. For example, one reading of the expression 'grey seals and walruses' refers to seals which are grey and to walruses which are grey, while on another reading it refers to seals which are grey and to walruses regardless of colour. Each of these options is associated with a different structure which can be represented by bracketing:

(a) [grey] [seals and walruses]
(b) [grey seals] and [walruses]

A full understanding of human language requires an account of knowledge about the ambiguity of linguistic expressions, the processes by which we understand utterances containing them and what happens when we fail to disambiguate them.

Vagueness is the related but distinct property of failing to determine a unique value or interpretation. Vagueness can be understood as a very general, and fairly informal, notion or as a more systematically understood property of concepts, propositions or utterances. Informally, all linguistic expressions are vague since they have more than one possible interpretation. The expression 'He has brought the seal', for example, could have several interpretations depending on who is understood as the referent of 'he', which sense of 'seal' is intended and what is the referent of 'the seal'. In most contexts, this kind of vagueness is relatively easily resolved and a unique interpretation can be determined. On the more systematic sense, vagueness is understood as the property of not having a uniquely determinable meaning. Concepts such as 'heap' or 'painful' are inherently vague since there is no way to say for certain how much of a particular substance we need to create a heap nor exactly how much discomfort is required for an experience to be painful.

Primary sources

Williamson, T. (1994). *Vagueness*. London: Routledge.

Further reading

Atlas, J. (1989). *Philosophy Without Ambiguity*. Oxford: Oxford University Press.
Hurford, J. R., B. Heasley, and M. B. Smith (2007). *Semantics: A Coursebook*. Second edition. Cambridge: Cambridge University Press.
Saeed, J. (2003). *Semantics*. Second edition. Oxford: Basil Blackwell.

Billy Clark

ANALYTIC PHILOSOPHY

Analytic, or analytical, philosophy can be any of many things. The term is used to describe philosophy that proceeds via analysis, broadly by seeking to understand the composition of its subject matter (or concepts of that subject matter) out of simple (or simpler) components. In a prominent but secondary sense, 'analytic philosophy' applies to most philosophy carried out in the mainstream of Anglo-American university philosophy departments together with philosophy that bears a suitable family resemblance to it: work within the so-called analytic tradition.

See also: Analytic/Synthetic;
Compositionality; Definite
Descriptions; Holism;
Indeterminacy; Logical Positivism;
Ordinary Language Philosophy;
Sense/Reference; Truth Theories;
Truth Values
Key Thinkers: Arnauld, Antoine;
Austin, J. L.; Carnap, Rudolf;
Frege, Gottlob; Moore, G. E.;
Pierce, C. S.; Quine, W. V. O.;
Russell, Bertrand; Ryle, Gilbert;
Strawson, P. F.; Wittgenstein,
Ludwig

Although the two senses of 'analytic philosophy' described above are quite different, it is not an accident that the same expression is used for both. The type of philosophy that now dominates the Anglo-American mainstream began its rise to prominence in the very late nineteenth century at the same time as the emergence of analysis as the central method of that type of philosophy. Analysis, broadly construed, has continued to play a large role in much work in that tradition.

The method of analysis is the method of seeking to understand a subject matter by coming to understand its composition. The aim is to understand the behaviour of a whole by tracing its behaviour to the influences of its parts and their organisation. In philosophy, the aim has often been to understand the inferential behaviour of a concept, to understand what may be inferred from a judgement involving the concept and what a judgement involving the concept may be inferred from. For example, analytic philosophy has attempted to understand the behaviour of the concept of propositional knowledge (knowledge that X is the case) by viewing it as composed of other concepts: belief, truth, and justification. Such analysis attempted to explain the apparent inferential behaviour of the concept, for example the apparent fact that if someone knows that the sun is shining then it may be inferred that they believe that the sun is shining and that their belief is both true and justified. The success of the method is dependent both upon the correctness of the analysis and upon its capacity to deepen understanding by explaining the less well understood – the whole – on the basis of what is better understood, the simpler components and the effects of their configuration in the whole. But the analysis of the concept of knowledge arguably fails on both counts. It has been argued that the concept of knowledge is a simple concept and so not composed of other concepts; and that the concept of justification (and perhaps also the concept of belief) is no simpler, or easier to understand, than is the concept of knowledge.

The method of analysis played a role in early Greek philosophy (see, for example, Plato's *Theaetetus*) and reappeared to take a major part in the early modern period, in the work of René Descartes and his followers. However, the method began gradually to lose its centrality during the rise of German idealism, as philosophers responded to the work of Immanuel Kant by seeking to develop grand systematic theories. Although it was a central tool of some other important thinkers in the nineteenth century, most notably Franz Brentano and C. S. Peirce, its rise to prominence as the central method in twentieth-century Anglo-American philosophy was due mainly to the work of G. E. Moore and Bertrand Russell.

In the very late nineteenth century, Moore began a revolt against German idealism. There were four main areas of dissent. First, Moore felt that Idealism – according to which mind and world are interdependent – was an erroneous metaphysical view and that, where possible, there should be a return to realism, according to which there is an external world that is constituted independently of operations of mind (except, of course, where the external world contains individual minds). Second, Moore felt that grand system building should be suppressed in favour of careful attention to detail and rigorous argumentation. Third, he objected to what he saw as unnecessary obfuscation in the writings of German idealists. He felt that philosophical theories and arguments for those theories should be open to objective assessment and so should be stated as clearly and sharply as possible. In Moore's view, work in the sciences at the time offered better models of philosophical methodology and this belief also motivated the fourth source of his dissent, his negative reaction to the Idealist suppression of the method of analysis. Calling for a return to the method, Moore wrote that 'a thing becomes intelligible first when it is analysed into its constituent concepts' (Moore 1899: 182).

Inspired by Moore and enamoured in particular with the science of mathematics, Russell began systematically to develop the programme of analysis. He was helped by his discovery (or rediscovery) of modern quantificational logic (see, in particular, Russell 1905). A very similar logic was developed in the medieval period, but the discovery of quantificational logic in its modern form is usually attributed to Gottlob Frege (1879) and (independently) Peirce (1885). This logic enables the systematic treatment of the inferential behaviour of a very large range of the statements that can be made in natural language (and so the thoughts expressible by the use of those statements) as well as the sharp statement of complex positions and arguments. Of special importance was Russell's treatment of definite descriptions* in sentences of the form 'The F is G'. Using the example 'The present King of France is bald', Russell represented sentences of that form as conjoining three claims:

(1) There is at least one F (there is at least one present King of France).
(2) There is at most one F (there is at most one present King of France).
(3) Whatever is F is G (what/who is the present King of France is bald).

In modern logical notation, the analysis becomes:

(4) $(\exists x) [Fx \mathbin{\&} (\forall y) (Fy \supset x = y) \mathbin{\&} Gy]$.

By systematising a statement's inferential (or, more broadly, logical) behaviour, the representation of the statement in a favoured logical system shows the (or, perhaps, a) logical form* of the statement. Russell's treatment provided a model on which a definite description that fails to apply to exactly one individual may be meaningful, and so provided a potential solution to old problems about the functioning of talk that purports to make reference to particular non-existents. On Russell's account, the fact that there is no present King of France makes the sentence 'The King of France is bald' false, rather than meaningless, because it makes false the first clause in his analysis. His treatment also made especially evident that the logical form of a statement might not be obvious from its superficial form. However, the space between logical and superficial form involved in Russell's treatment of 'The F is G' via (4) is an artefact of Russell's favoured logic. An alternative, though slightly less perspicuous, treatment is given in (5):

(5) ([The x: Fx] (Gx).)

Russell's treatment of definite descriptions showed that philosophical progress could be made by discerning the (or a) logical form of a philosophically problematic range of statements and that some philosophical disputes are usefully viewed as at least in part concerning how best to represent the logical forms of statements involved in those disputes. Together with the new treatment of quantification more generally, this became a model for a variety of approaches to philosophical problems that involved attention to the forms of language used in the statement of those problems. It supported the view that philosophical problems can arise due to the misleading superficial forms of the language we use, and it provided a model for how problems that arise in that way might be solved through uncovering the true logical forms of the statements involved.

Ludwig Wittgenstein was the most famous pupil of Russell and Moore. Wittgenstein's *Tractatus Logico-Philosophicus* (1922) further developed the analysis of statements, and of representation more generally, in the direction of *logical atomism*. According to logical atomism, the most fundamental level of representation involves point-by-point connections between simple representational elements – representational atoms – and simple represented elements – represented atoms. This paradigm of analysis was driven by the view that 'A proposition [i.e. the content of a statement] has one and only one complete analysis' (1922: 3.25). The work's major conclusion was that there are two types of statement: those that represent the world, and so can be either true or false depending upon how the world in fact is – the synthetic truths and falsehoods – and those that either cannot be true or cannot be false – the logical or analytic truths and falsehoods – that fail to represent the world as being one way or another. Since genuinely philosophical statements, derived by analysis, were taken to fall on the non-representational (analytic) side of this divide, they were taken to be devoid of real content and to have a role other than that of conveying information. And since a core sense of meaningfulness was identified with representational significance, such statements were taken to be – in that core sense – meaningless. (For an introduction to Wittgenstein's early work, see Mounce 1989. For a discussion that relates logical atomism with Plato's *Theaetetus*, see Burnyeat 1990.)

7

Members of the Vienna Circle – including especially Rudolf Carnap – were inspired by Wittgenstein's work and sought to embed its central themes in an approach to philosophy, known as logical positivism*, shaped by epistemological concerns. They replaced Wittgenstein's distinction between statements whose truth value* depends upon worldly contingency and statements whose truth value is fixed independently of such contingency with a distinction between statements that admit of verification or falsification on the basis of experience and statements that cannot be so verified or falsified. The task of philosophy was taken to be the analysis of statements into experientially significant components, an analysis that would either indicate precisely the course of experience that would verify or falsify the statement or show it to be beyond verification or falsification. In that way, philosophy would either show how a statement can be assessed on the basis of scientific observation, or show the statement to be (in the Circle's proprietary sense) meaningless. Since the only properly cognitive activity was taken to be the collection of observations, the programme of the Vienna Circle was shaped by the view that 'what is left over for *philosophy* . . . is only a *method*: the method of logical analysis' (Carnap 1932: 77).

In the early post-1945 period, many philosophers retained the Vienna Circle's animus towards traditional metaphysics but viewed its approach to analysis as overly restrictive. They sought to replace what they saw as an empirically unmotivated fixation upon a very narrow conception of empirical content with a more expansive view of philosophical analysis. According to the more expansive view, the analysis of statements was to include the tracing of their roles within larger systems of language driven by careful attention to the way those statements are actually used in ordinary contexts. The more expansive view therefore involved a partial return to the sort of holistic approach involved in German idealism. Wittgenstein's work within the more expansive paradigm developed his earlier view that the role of philosophical analysis should be largely therapeutic: that it should serve the removal of philosophical perplexity by uncovering and excising the sources of confusion in the misleading superficial forms of language. But many other philosophers working within the new paradigm of analysis, including J. L. Austin, Gilbert Ryle, and P. F. Strawson – the so-called 'ordinary language' philosophers – returned to the view that some philosophical questions might be genuine and hoped that the analysis of language would deliver answers to those questions.

W. V. O. Quine took a different path away from the Vienna Circle. Quine was strongly influenced by the work of Carnap and retained the Circle's view that scientific observation is the only source of cognitive significance. However, he thought that Carnap had failed fully to draw out the consequences of that view. Quine (1953, for example) argued that it served to undermine the distinction between statements that can be verified or falsified on the basis of experience and those that cannot be so verified or falsified: that is, the Circle's version of the distinction between statements that are analytic and those that are synthetic. Quine therefore took the range of statements that are up for scientific assessment to include statements in logic and mathematics. He took our total theory of the world to form an interconnected web of statements that can only be assessed as a whole on the basis of the range of predictions it makes about the course of experience. Quine's work involved in particular a rejection of the goal of atomist analysis that formed the impetus for the earliest work in modern analytic philosophy.

Quine's rejection of the existence of a category of analytic truths went hand in hand with a general rejection of the philosophical utility of appeals to unreconstructed notions of linguistic meaning. In particular, Quine argued for the indeterminacy* of translation, the claim that for any translation from one language into another (including translation from a language into itself), there will be other translations that have equally good empirical credentials. Famously he argued that evidence that an expression is to be translated by the English expression 'rabbit' can be equally good evidence that the expression is to be translated by the English expression 'un-detached part of a rabbit' (Quine 1960: 1–79). When conjoined with Quine's rejection of a principled distinction between analytic and synthetic statements, acceptance of Quine's views has seemed to many to undermine the possibility of a philosophy based upon methods of analysis. The rejection of an analytic-synthetic* distinction appears to undermine a distinction between the analysis of statements and the empirical assessment of those statements. And the rejection of determinate translation appears to undermine the assumption that there is such a thing as *the* analysis of a statement.

The main effects of Quine's work have involved the further broadening of the analytic horizon. Many contemporary analytic philosophers who are influenced by Quine's rejection of an analytic-synthetic distinction allow their work to be shaped by the findings of empirical science. Similarly, many contemporary analytic philosophers allow that philosophy – even when approached from the armchair – can be a source of discovery about the world. Thus the culmination, through Quine, of the Vienna Circle's anti-metaphysical empiricism has led to the reinstatement of metaphysics as a legitimate area of cognitive inquiry. Finally, many contemporary philosophers have followed Quine in relegating the study of meaning from its central place in the analytic philosophers' armoury, and have sought a more direct approach to answering philosophical questions.

The postwar period of intense focus upon language and linguistic meaning coincided with Frege's work becoming widely available in translation and led to a re-evaluation of his place in the development of analytic philosophy. In particular, Michael Dummett (1993) has claimed that it is criterial of modern analytic philosophy that it approaches the study of thought through a study of the way language is used to express thought and that, from that perspective, Frege should be assigned priority over Russell as its progenitor. Dummett's claim is controversial for several reasons, not least that it appears to place many contemporary philosophers who work within the analytic tradition outside the bounds of analytic philosophy proper, and it also seems to exclude the early work of Russell and Moore. Second, it is controversial that Frege would himself count as an analytic philosopher by Dummett's own standard, since he distrusted natural language and sought to construct artificial systems better able to capture the nature of thought. Third, although Frege's work now occupies a central place in the curriculum of analytic philosophy, there is little consensus concerning its precise role in shaping the initial development of the modern analytic tradition. Other philosophers, for example, also played important roles in the development of Russell, Wittgenstein and Carnap. What is uncontroversial, however, is that Frege's work possesses many of the qualities associated with analytic philosophy, including narrow focus, clarity, rigour and depth, and exhibits all those qualities to a very high degree. To that extent, no education in analytic philosophy would be complete that did not involve a careful study of his work.

Primary sources

Burnyeat, M. F. (1990). *The Theaetetus of Plato*. Trans. M. J. Levett. Indianapolis: Hackett.

Carnap, R. (1932). 'Überwindung der Mataphysik durch logische Analyse der Sprache'. *Erkenntnis* 2: 219–41. Reprinted as 'The elimination of metaphysics through logical analysis of language' trans. A. Pap, in A. J. Ayer (ed.) (1959), *Logical Positivism*. Glencoe, IL: The Free Press.

Dummett, M. A. E. (1993). *Origins of Analytical Philosophy*. Cambridge MA: Harvard University Press.

Frege, G. (1879). *Begriffsschrift: eine der arithmetischen nachgebildete Formelsprache des reinen Denkens*. Halle. Reprinted in Frege (1972), *Conceptual Notation and Related Articles*. Trans. and ed. T. W. Bynum. Oxford: Oxford University Press.

Frege, G. (1884). *Die Grundlagen der Arithmetik. Eine logisch mathematische Untersuchung über den Begriff der Zahl*. Frege (1950) *The Foundation of Arithmetic. A Logico-mathematical Enquiry into the Concept of Number*. J. L. Austin. Oxford: Basil Blackwell.

Moore, G. E. (1899). 'The nature of judgement'. *Mind* 8: 176–93.

Mounce, H. O. (1989). *Wittgenstein's Tractatus: An Introduction*. Chicago: University of Chicago Press.

Peirce, C. S. (1885). 'On the algebra of logic; a contribution to the philosophy of notation'. *American Journal of Mathematics* 7: 180–202. Reprinted in Peirce (1933), *Collected Papers*, ed. C. Hartshorne and P. Weiss. Cambridge MA: Harvard University Press.

Quine, W. V. (1953). 'Two dogmas of empiricism'. In *From a Logical Point of View*. Cambridge, MA: Harvard University Press.

Quine, W. V. (1960). *Word and Object*. Cambridge, MA: MIT Press.

Russell, B. (1903). *The Principles of Mathematics*. London: Allen & Unwin.

Russell, B. (1905). 'On denoting'. *Mind* 14: 479–93. Reprinted in Russell (1956), *Logic and Knowledge*, ed. R. Marsh. London: Allen & Unwin.

Wittgenstein, L. (1922). *Tractatus Logico-Philosophicus*. Trans. C. K. Ogden and

F. P. Ramsey. London: Routledge and Kegan Paul.

Further reading

Arnauld, A. and P. Nicole (1683). *La logique ou L'art de penser: contenant outre les regles communes, plusieurs observations nouvelles, propres à former le jugement.* Second edition. Paris: G. Desprez. Reprinted as Arnauld, A. and P. Nicole (1996). *Logic or The Art of Thinking.* Trans. and ed. J. V. Buroker, K. Ameriks, and D. M. Clarke. Cambridge: Cambridge University Press.

Descartes, R. (1701). *Rules for the Direction of the Mind.* Amsterdam: P & J. Blaeu. Reprinted in Descartes (1985), *The Philosophical Writings of Descartes,* vol. 1. Trans. and ed. J. Cottingham, R. Stoothof and D. Murdoch. Cambridge: Cambridge University Press.

Hylton, P. (2007). *Quine.* London: Routledge.

Hylton, P. (1993). *Russell, Idealism and the Emergence of Analytic Philosophy.* Oxford: Clarendon Press.

Guy Longworth

ANALYTIC/ SYNTHETIC

An analytic truth is a statement (or proposition) that is true solely by virtue of the meaning of its component words (or concepts). A synthetic truth on the other hand is a truth determined at least in part by features of the world outside of the language system. Almost as well known as the distinction is W. V. O. Quine's description of its use by empiricists as a 'dogma'. The reverberations of Quine's criticism are still felt today.

See also: Generative Semantics; Holism; Logical Positivism; Sense Data; Truth Value
Key Thinkers: Carnap, Rudolf; Kant, Immanuel; Quine, W. V. O.

The contrast between analytically true and synthetically true statements is, on the face of it, an intuitive one, easily conveyed by either definition (as above) or example:

(1) 'All bachelors are unmarried' (analytically true).
(2) 'Bachelors have a higher average disposable income than spinsters' (synthetically true).

The terms 'analytic' and 'synthetic' as they apply to true judgements were coined by Immanuel Kant (1781). But his actual definition, that a true judgement is analytic if its predicate concept is contained within its subject concept and is synthetic otherwise, is now usually treated as having at most historical interest. Some philosophers argue that statements are analytically true if understanding them requires acknowledgement of their truth. Others define the distinction in two stages: first, as it applies to either a belief, proposition, statement, or sentence, and second, as it applies, deriving from this, to some or all other members of this group. For example, if an analytically true proposition is a proposition true solely by virtue of the content of its component concepts, then an analytically true statement would be a statement that expresses an analytically true proposition.

In the twentieth century the analytic/synthetic distinction has been both important and controversial, particularly because of the weight placed on it by logical positivists, and Quine's insistence that it could not bear that weight. Whether or not Quine is right, there may be uses for the distinction in linguistics that are also compatible with his position.

Logical positivists such as Rudolf Carnap had an ambitious goal: to construct a language suited to the needs of science. Anyone with an understanding of this language would be able to extract empirical conditions from any sentence of it used to express a claim. Any properly scientific claim could thus be made to wear its confirmation conditions on its sleeve, so to speak, making it straightforwardly susceptible to empirical confirmation or refutation.

Quine argued that the reason logical positivism* struggled to achieve this goal of a scientific language was its reliance on an unworkable distinction between analytical and synthetic sentences. Synthetic sentences were supposed to include basic-level observation sentences such as 'There is redness to the left of my visual field' as well as higher-level theoretical sentences such as 'Photons have wave-particle duality', with many levels in between. Higher-level synthetic sentences had to mean the same as (that is, be analytically equivalent to) complex basic-level observation sentences, since the latter expressed the former's empirical commitments. Logical positivists needed all synthetic sentences to reduce to complex basic-level observation sentences by the repeated application of definitions of theoretical terms such as 'photon'. Quine thought that the analytic definitions needed to bridge the gap between the more theoretical, higher-level synthetic claims and the basic-level observation sentences were simply not available.

The problem, Quine said, was a lack of adequate guidance on how to distinguish analytic from synthetic claims in practice. Kant's account of the distinction, with its talk of concepts being 'contained in' other concepts, is too metaphorical to be helpful here. Similarly, to say that analytic truths are truths of meaning, or truths by definition, leaves us needing a way of distinguishing truths of meaning from deeply held convictions. Deferring to a dictionary merely passes the buck up to dictionary writers. To fall back on the thought that truths are analytic just in case they are logical truths, as Carnap himself did, is to forget that many supposedly analytic sentences, including (1) above, are non-logically true. Perhaps, Quine conjectures, analytic truths are supposed to be stipulations, true by linguistic convention. Against this he claims that we lack criteria for deciding whether a particular assertion should be classified as true by convention rather than as an empirical conjecture. Is the assertion that photons have wave-particle duality a stipulative truth about the word 'photon' or a substantial empirical assertion? No pre-established glossary for the vocabulary of physics exists that is uncommitted to any particular empirical outlook.

For all that has been said so far, logical positivists could cling to the thought that the analytic sentences are simply those that link theoretical sentences to their confirmation conditions, plus those that enable this link to be derived. It is up to us to identify those links. No one ever claimed this would be easy. Quine's final objection to this faith has, rightly or wrongly, probably been the most influential. He observes that evidence for or against a particular clause in some scientific theory can, in principle, come from anywhere. Evidence for a particular claim in syntax, for example, may presuppose a particular morphology; evidence for this morphology may depend in turn on an analogy with a theory of colour vision tied to specific assumptions about photons; and so on. Given this evidential holism, stating the confirmation conditions for higher-level theoretical claims would require making impossibly detailed and disjunctive reference to all of science. Developing and applying a language that would allow these statements to be formulated, if possible at all, would be no easier than doing science as it is done already.

Interest in and scepticism towards the analytic/synthetic distinction thus grew out of a concern for how scientific methodology might be optimised. But the distinction is also central to a popular conception of what sets philosophy apart from other disciplines and also to an approach to semantics conceived as a part of psychology.

Many philosophers follow Socrates in conceiving of their role as being to analyse concepts. There are more or less sophisticated implementations of this thought, but a typical illustration is the giving of necessary and sufficient conditions that approximately match, or perhaps improve on, those for the proper application of the word

'know'. One motive for this conception of their role is that philosophers realise they are not scientists. What they provide must therefore complement rather than compete with scientific knowledge. Another is immodest: they aim to understand the world at an *a priori* level, that is, at a level impervious to the contingency of experience.

If Quine is right, this model of philosophy may be in trouble. According to him, there are no analytic truths in any interesting sense. Some supporters of the model insist they are not interested in the analysis of scientific concepts. But they need to defend an interest in the analyses they offer. After all, 'folk' ways of thinking are often inferior to scientific ones. Good analyses of concepts such as 'causation' or 'knowledge', if Quine is right, may be susceptible to improvement as science develops. Advances in the cognitive sciences, for example, have shaped our understanding of what knowledge is. Whereas 'Knowledge must be conscious to the knower' would once have been regarded as analytic; it is now commonly regarded as not even true, let alone analytically true. Disputes over the status of analytic truths have, then, broadened out into a split between those who see the philosophy of *x* and the science of *x* as distinct in both subject matter and methodology, and those who see only continuity.

A very different approach to analytic truth emerges from within linguistics itself. It may be that to call a sentence analytically true is merely to give voice to an accidental feature of our language faculty. Certain apparently analytic entailments, such as that killing requires causing to die,

13

may be grounded in the semantic features of our concepts and/or lexical items (see generative semantics*). This approach to semantics has a chequered history, in part because of the difficulty of distinguishing deeply-held beliefs about something from semantic features – the same problem Quine drew attention to in a different guise. That said, appealing to the notion of analyticity in this context would not commit one to logical positivism*. Discovering semantic features could be interesting for what it tells us about the structure and development of the human mind, not because of any help it offers in investigating the world outside the mind.

The intuitive distinction between the analytic and the synthetic has been drawn on by philosophers of science in an attempt to understand how science might be improved, and by other philosophers to explain how what they are doing complements science. Interest in analyticity has also emerged out of the mentalist approach favoured by some semanticists. The challenge facing all who invoke the notion of analyticity is to ascertain how to distinguish in practice between something's being analytically true and its being profoundly but synthetically true.

Primary sources

Carnap, R. (1928). *Der logische Aufbau der Welt*. Berlin-Schlachtensee: Weltkreis-Verlag.

Kant, I. (1781/1933). *A Critique of Pure Reason*, trans. N. Kemp Smith. Second edition. London: Macmillan.

Quine, W. V. O. (1951). 'Two dogmas of empiricism'. *Philosophical Review* 60: 20–43.

Further reading

Boghossian, P. (1996). 'Analyticity reconsidered'. *Noûs* 30(3): 360–91.

Jackendoff, R. (1990). *Semantic Structures*. Cambridge MA: MIT Press.

Jackson, F. (2000). *From Metaphysics to Ethics: a Defence of Conceptual Analysis*. Oxford: Oxford University Press.

Alex Barber

ARTIFICIAL INTELLIGENCE

The ability of machines to think for themselves. More generally the science dedicated to exploring and developing the ability of technology – most commonly in the form of a software program – to think and/or act rationally or similarly to human capability. As it relates to linguistics, the flourishing field of artificial intelligence aims to develop systems that can understand, process, and even generate language as well as a human can.

See also: Generative Semantics; Intentionality; Logic; Speech Act Theory
Key Thinkers: Chomsky, Noam; Montague, Richard; Russell, Bertrand; Searle, John

The study of language often leads to questions over what defines intelligence, as exhibited via language competence and performance. Artificial intelligence (AI) provides us with precious opportunities to apply what we know about language toward useful and often valuable purposes, whether to serve as a proof of concept, to innovate, or to fulfil a specific need. The roots of AI extend to the origins of computers and even logic*. From its foundations in the works of René Descartes and Blaise Pascal, through the nineteenth-century innovations of Charles Babbage and Ada Lovelace, AI flourished in the twentieth century, directly paralleling advancements in both linguistics and computer science, through Bertrand Russell's formal logic, the Turing test, and contributions by such innovators as Joseph Weizenbaum and Hans Kamp, to name a few. Not without its share of criticism, AI has resulted in many practical applications for everyday life, including speech recognition systems, machine translation software, and information retrieval systems.

Humans are capable of many tasks, with language being among the most complex. Language allows us to communicate abstract thoughts through an infinite combination of words and meanings. With this in mind, it is not surprising that Alan Turing designed his now-famous Turing test around language. The Turing test is a way to judge the intelligence of an AI system. It involves a human subject, who carries on a conversation with two entities, one being a human and the other a computer. If the subject cannot distinguish between the human and the computer, the computer is said to have passed the test. The best-known counterpoint to the Turing test is John Searle's Chinese Room argument. We begin this scenario with a computer that has been programmed to return a particular set of Chinese characters as a result of applying a set of rules to another set of Chinese characters received as input. To a Chinese speaker who is interacting with the computer, it would seem that the computer understands Chinese. However, if we replace the computer with a human who does not know Chinese but has been trained to apply rules from a book against Chinese language input to arrive at Chinese language output, we would never say that the human knows Chinese. That is, the simple act of applying predetermined rules (as a computer does during a Turing test) does not constitute thinking, nor does it represent consciousness. Nevertheless, variations of this approach are commonly used to evaluate AI systems against a standard of human ability.

In order to process language as well as a human, an AI system must have the ability both to understand and to generate language. Its means of accomplishing this may differ from human mental processes, but the effect should be equivalent. At a high level, natural language understanding in an AI system entails accepting language input (whether through speech recognition or optical character recognition), analysing it (through parsing and semantic interpretation), and disambiguating the message (at the lexical, syntactic, semantic and pragmatic levels, calling upon outside knowledge of the world, as needed). Likewise, natural language generation requires that the AI system determine a reasonable response, organise its structure, form comprehensible and natural-sounding sentences, and output them as written text or synthesised speech. AI forms an extension of traditional computer science, with linguistic AI being commonly categorised as computational linguistics or natural language processing. These disciplines call upon generative grammar and linguistics in order to apply what we know about language to technology that may be capable of natural language understanding and generation. Linguists involved in AI maintain a keen interest in advancements within the general field of linguistics, as their goal is to equip computers with a comparable sense of the linguistic knowledge and ability we humans innately have, such as grammaticality, phrase structure, government and binding and so on.

Critics of AI argue that computers are incapable of achieving the level of cognitive ability that humans exhibit. To this point, Searle made a distinction between strong AI and weak AI. Strong AI describes a system that is able to reason and perform as well as – or better than – a human. A strong AI system is conscious of itself and operates beyond a strict adherence to pre-programmed rules and algorithms. Most AI systems, however, are better classified as weak AI, capable of only a limited range of skills and lacking in the ability to 'think' as a human does. Hubert Dreyfus, one of the most outspoken critics of AI, states that computers simply cannot accomplish the complex tasks typically associated with strong AI. For example, an AI system can never learn to love, no matter how it is programmed. System design is rarely flawless and the mere prospect of developing a fully capable AI program is downright intractable. Difficulties that face AI systems encompass the variation and creativity inherent in language, such as differences in grammaticality across dialects and a heavy use of metaphor*, with the prevailing constraint that a system should func-

tion as economically and as efficiently as possible. Statistical AI systems offer promising alternatives within natural language processing, incorporating probability theory, Bayesian networks, Markov models, and neural networks. The most effective examples of language AI, in fact, are hybrid models, combining linguistic knowledge with statistical methodologies.

Just as AI draws upon developments in the field of linguistics, it presents valuable opportunities for linguists to test their theories in a computational environment. An AI system ultimately demonstrates linguistic performance with its software resources comprising its linguistic competence. Language-based AI has many practical applications in business and leisure. We encounter AI, for example, in business, where it may be used to forecast market conditions, to analyse large amounts of data, and to save time otherwise spent on tedious tasks. In our homes, we see AI in our appliances, in our automobiles, and on our personal computers, and we may even play chess and other complex games against AI systems. Practical uses of AI are all around us, originating in linguistic and AI circles and ultimately being distributed around the world for an abundance of practical applications.

AI represents an application of linguistic knowledge, and it serves as a driving force to learn more, not only about language, but also about human knowledge and the nature of intelligence itself. It encourages us to revisit questions over what defines intelligence, what sets apart human capability, and what we can programme or train a computer to do. Fictional portrayals of AI systems have created rather humourous public misconceptions, from robot uprisings to world domination, but also some ideas for valuable applications of AI, many of which require linguistic AI in particular. In some cases, such as search engines and some speech recognition systems, language-related AI has become a welcome part of daily life. It brings together many of the things we know about language and tests these theories, sometimes even in the form of annual competitions. Such challenges lead to innovative approaches and services that would otherwise be unattainable through mere human effort and ability. There are endless possibilities for practical applications of AI, especially where there is consumer demand, and it is an important area in which businesses, technological innovators, and philosophers of language can work together.

Primary sources

Dreyfus, H. (1972). *What Computers Can't Do: The Limits of Artificial Intelligence*. Cambridge, MA: MIT Press.

Kamp, H. (1981). 'A theory of truth and semantic representation'. In Groenendijk, J. A. G., T. M. V. Janssen and M. B. J. Stokhof (eds), *Formal Methods in the Study of Language*. Vol. 1: 277–322.

Schank, Roger C. (1972). 'Conceptual dependency: a theory of natural language understanding'. *Cognitive Psychology* Vol. 3: 532–631.

Turing, Alan (1950). 'Computing machinery and intelligence'. *Mind* Vol. 59: 433–60.

Wilks, Yorick (1973). 'The Stanford Machine Translation Project'. In R. Rustin (ed.), *Natural Language Processing*. New York: Algorithmics Press. 243–90.

Woods, William A. (1970). 'Transition network grammars for natural language analysis'. *Communications of the ACM* Vol. 13: 591–606.

Further reading

Charniak, Eugene (1993). *Statistical Language Learning*. Cambridge, MA: MIT Press.

Hutchins, W. John and Harold L. Somers (1992). *An Introduction to Machine Translation*. San Diego, CA: Academic Press.

Jurafsky, Daniel and James H. Martin (2000). *Speech and Language Processing*. Upper Saddle River, NJ: Prentice Hall.

Rabiner, Lawrence R. and Biing-Hwang Juang (1993). *Fundamentals of Speech Recognition*. Upper Saddle River, NJ: Prentice Hall.

Russell, Stuart and Peter Norvig (1995). *Artificial Intelligence: A Modern Approach*. Upper Saddle River, NJ: Prentice Hall.

Jennifer A. Baldwin

BEHAVIOURISM

The study of behaviour without appeal to mental states. Behaviourism had a profound effect on linguistics (especially American structuralist linguistics) and philosophy (logical behaviourism), but was effectively displaced by the cognitive science revolution in the 1960s.

See also: Cognitivism; Empiricism/Rationalism; Innateness; Mentalism; Psychoanalysis; Structuralism;

Transformational-Generative
Grammar
Key Thinkers: Bloomfield,
Leonard; Chomsky, Noam;
Hockett, Charles; Quine, W. V. O.;
Ryle, Gilbert; Skinner, B. F.;
Wittgenstein, Ludwig

Behaviourism was the dominant paradigm in psychology for much of the first half of the twentieth century and until the late 1950s, especially in the United States. Despite important differences between different schools of behaviourism, all behaviourists shared the conviction that behaviour was the only legitimate object of investigation in psychology, and that behaviour cannot be explained by appealing to hypothetical internal states, such as consciousness. As such, behaviourism follows in the tradition of British empiricism*.

J. B. Watson is credited as the founding father of behaviourism. In an article that has come to be known as the 'behaviourist manifesto', Watson (1913) set out the main principles of classical behaviourism: psychology is a natural science; the only legitimate object of psychological study is overt behaviour; internal mental states and emotions are not behaviour and cannot be the causes of behaviour; behaviour is environmentally determined; the same principles are applied to the study of both animal and human behaviour, which do not differ qualitatively. In later work, he acknowledged the importance of Ivan Pavlov's work on what came to be known as classical conditioning and incorporated it into the behaviourist agenda. Classical conditioning is a form of associative learning that modifies involuntary behaviour by repeatedly pairing a neutral stimulus (for example, a bell sound that does not naturally elicit a given response) with an unconditioned stimulus (for example, food, which naturally produces a given response such as salivation in dogs). After repeated pairing, the neutral (now conditioned) stimulus becomes associated with the (now conditioned) response: a dog that has undergone this type of training will salivate when hearing a bell sound, even in the absence of food.

Classical behaviourism had a profound effect on American structuralist linguistics, through the work of linguists such as Leonard Bloomfield, and his student Charles Hockett. Bloomfield espoused the behaviourist credo that only behaviour can be the object of scientific study. He advocated for the study of linguistics what Watson had advocated for the study of psychology: that it should be approached as a natural science, with a firm emphasis on empirical data and rigorous description. In his enormously influential *Language* (1933), he provided an account of meaning which adapted the classical conditioning schema to the interpretation of acts of speech. Language provides a secondary stimulus-response mechanism, pairing a stimulus from the speaker with a response from the listener. He illustrated this in the now famous 'Jack and Jill' story, in which Jill experiences hunger (speaker stimulus) and asks Jack to fetch an apple for her (speaker response). Upon hearing the request (hearer stimulus), Jack fetches the apple (hearer response). Although Bloomfield himself admitted the difficulties of such an analysis of meaning, his commitment to behaviourist principles in the study of language guided research in theoretical and applied linguistics up until the cognitive revolution in the late 1950s and early 1960s.

In philosophy and the philosophy of language, behaviourism became known as logical behaviourism. Logical behaviourism, unlike classical behaviourism, did not deny the validity of inquiring into mental states. According to logical behaviourism, however, all meaningful – that is verifiable – statements about mental phenomena are translatable into statements which refer to physical concepts only. For instance, to be angry includes changes in tone of voice, facial expression, gesture and so on. For the logical behaviourist, all these physical properties are not just manifestations of 'anger', but definitions of the concept 'anger'. In other words, logical behaviourists were committed to the notion that mental phenomena can be reduced to behavioural dispositions. Logical behaviourism is mostly linked to the work of Gilbert Ryle, and the later work of Ludwig Wittgenstein, but other philosophers with behaviourist affiliations include Rudolf Carnap and later W. V. O. Quine. The main criticisms levied against logical behaviourism are that several mental states are not reducible to behavioural dispositions (for instance, 'belief' cannot be understood independently of 'desire to verify the belief or act on the belief') and that it has nothing to say about conceptual relations between mental concepts themselves.

By the early 1950s behaviourist psychology had tackled a number of complex behaviours, but language was not one of them. B. F. Skinner undertook to fill this gap in *Verbal Behavior* (1957). In this work, which took more than twenty years to complete, Skinner asserted that verbal behaviour is a complex habit arising as a result of the interaction between a speaker's environment and his/her past learning history. In his research with animals, Skinner had shown how voluntary behaviour could be modified through operant conditioning: a food-deprived ('motivating operation') rat is placed in a cage and a light is turned on (the 'discriminative stimulus') to signal that food can be obtained if the rat performs the appropriate action. The rat may initially perform a number of actions, such as running around the cage, scratching the cage bars, or pressing a lever in the cage. If by performing one of these actions – for instance, pressing the lever ('response') – the rat obtains food ('reinforcer'), this particular behaviour is reinforced. Skinner claimed that the same type of functional scheme accounts for verbal behaviour as well, with only minor modifications. For instance, if you are hungry ('motivating operation'), and your mother is at home ('discriminating stimulus'), you may say 'Give me some food' ('response'). If your mother gives you some food ('reinforcer'), she rewards your verbal behaviour and you are more likely to say 'Give me some food' next time you are hungry and she is in the house.

In a review of *Verbal Behavior* that became more influential than the book itself, Noam Chomsky (1959) launched an all-out attack on Skinner's approach to language as behaviour. He claimed that human behaviour and more specifically language are infinitely more complex than the types of animal behaviour Skinner had previously studied, and thus principles of animal behaviour cannot be applied to verbal behaviour. He showed that many of the concepts Skinner used, such as stimulus, response, and reinforcement, were hopelessly vague and had no explanatory value in accounting for linguistic knowledge. He argued that Skinner's account is also a poor model of language acquisition, since it fails to account for the speed, efficiency and uniformity with which children acquire language. According to Chomsky, the basic facts of language acquisition point to the existence of an innate predisposition to acquire language. This review, along with work carried out in computer science, was instrumental in the 'demise' of behaviourism and in effecting the move from studying behaviour to studying mental processes using a computer metaphor (the cognitive revolution).

A direct response to Chomsky's criticisms never came from Skinner himself. Kenneth MacCorquodale, one of Skinner's former students, published a response (1970) more than ten years after the review appeared, in which he showed that Chomsky had misunderstood several of the points Skinner was making and that a lot of Chomsky's criticisms were not actually criticisms of Skinner's work but of other behaviourist work popular at the time. This response, however, had a very limited impact, partly because a paradigm shift had already taken place and behaviourism had given way to cognitivism*.

Although behaviourism ceased to be in the mainstream of science in the early 1960s, it still survives in some applied settings (for instance in the treatment of autism) and in certain strands of animal learning theory. The study of the mind/brain and their role in explaining behaviour are now at the forefront of scientific investigation, but the legacy of behaviourism has not disappeared completely: behaviourism, for instance, shares with contemporary connectionist approaches to psychology and language the emphasis on associative learning and on the role of experience on learning.

Primary sources

Bloomfield, L. (1933). *Language*. New York: Henry Holt.

Chomsky, N. (1959). 'Review of *Verbal Behavior*'. *Language* 31: 26–58.

MacCorquodale, K. (1970). 'On Chomsky's Review of Skinner's *Verbal Behavior*'. *Journal of the Experimental Analysis of Behavior* 13: 83–99.

Ryle, G. (1949). *The Concept of Mind*. London: Hutchinson.

Skinner, B. F. (1957). *Verbal Behavior*. New York: Appleton-Century-Crofts.

Watson, J. B. (1913). 'Psychology as the Behaviourist Views it'. *Psychological Review* 20: 158–77.

Further reading

Baum, W. M. (2003). *Understanding Behaviorism: Science, Behavior, and Culture*. New York: Harper Collins.

Skinner, B. F. (1953). *Science and Human Behavior*. New York: Macmillan.

Skinner, B. F. (1986). 'The Evolution of Verbal Behavior'. *Journal of the Experimental Analysis of Behavior* 45: 115–22.

Stavroula-Thaleia Kousta

COGNITIVISM

Cognitivism can be defined as the belief that cognition mediates perception, unlike in behaviourism. In this broad sense, cognitivism is synonymous with mentalism*. But while mentalism has found expression in generative grammar, cognitive linguistics was initiated as an alternative to the generative-transformational paradigm, with significant influences from the generative semantics* approach, Gestalt psychology and the psychology of prototypes. Its main earliest proponents were Ronald Langacker, George Lakoff and Len Talmy in the early 1980s, but the approach soon gathered a broad following in Europe and the United States.

See also: Generative Semantics; Mentalism; Metaphor; Prototype; Transformational-Generative Grammar,
Key Thinkers: Sapir, Edward; Whorf, Benjamin Lee

The basic organisations of cognitive linguistics (CL) are semantic-phonological mappings and in this respect CL is like all semiotic approaches to communication. The significant difference is that CL is squarely focused on meaning and rejects any non-semantic component to the grammar (for example, empty categories). Other characteristics that distinguish CL from other non-cognitive approaches to grammar are prototypicality, schematicity, and perspectivism, as well as more generally, the rejection of modularity and consequently the adoption of an encyclopedic semantics, and the belief that cognition is embodied and affords a significant role to metaphoricity and iconicity.

The centrality of meaning in cognitive grammar is one of the main aspects of the generative semantics heritage in cognitive linguistics. Meaning in CL is taken to be fundamental and directly mapped onto phonological structures. This entails the rejection of modularity (the belief that there exist encapsulated modules that process phonological or morphological information without reference to other levels of language) and the adoption of an encyclopedic model of the lexicon, that is a belief that all sorts of encyclopedic information about lexical items are part and parcel of their meaning and correspondingly no systematic distinction can be drawn between lexical (word-related) and encyclopedic knowledge (knowledge about the world). Typically, lexical knowledge is organised in frames, organised complexes of information relating to a given concept.

The centrality of meaning is not merely axiomatic, but informs the entire CL edifice. CL focuses both on lexical meaning and on grammatical meaning. Generative grammar ignored the lexicon, seen as a repository of exceptions, and assumed that grammar was a formal structure, that is one without meaning. Conversely, grammatical structure, according to CL, is the result of a process of schematisation, that is abstraction of constructional meaning. So, in effect, CL claims that all language is meaning, including grammar, and that grammatical meaning is very abstract schematic meaning. Relatedly, CL is also very keen on constructional meaning, that is the fact that some constructions, such as 'X let alone Y' have a meaning that cannot be predicted from the sum of its parts. Significantly, parts of this meaning would traditionally be considered pragmatic (hence reiterating CL's rejection of modularity).

The notion of prototypicality, elaborated by Eleanor Rosch in the 1970s, and originally applied to categories (such as 'bird' or 'furniture'), is also applied to grammatical categories, in a way recalling generative-semanticist John Ross's notion of 'squish'. This means that some verbs, to take a clear example, are better examples of verb than others (for example, action verbs, such as 'kick', which involve the transfer of force from one entity to another, are better examples of verbs than state-verbs, such as 'own').

CL shares with generative semantics the programmatic rejection of the core/periphery distinction. In generative grammar, it is common practice to focus on the regularities of grammar (core), rejecting exceptions to the periphery, where they are accounted for by pragmatic (the waste-basket theory of pragmatics) or other factors. CL denies the validity of this distinction, and seeks to explain all phenomena of language using the same cognitive principles and hence shows a particular interest in the seeming irregular patters found, for example, in constructions. Moreover, CL incorporates pragmatic and functional explanations within its conceptual apparatus, hence rendering a core/periphery distinction impractical. This parallels CL's rejection of modularity, which presupposes that the same principles and mechanisms apply at all levels of language.

Conceptualisation is a central concept in CL. As we have seen, meaning is the object of CL. Meaning can be defined as the 'content' of an idea, concept, and so on, and its construal, that is the way in which the speaker looks at the content, the perspective in which it is seen. For example, the sentences 'Mary kicked the ball' and 'The ball was kicked by Mary' clearly describe the same factual situation (content) but with two different perspectives, one that privileges the active role of Mary and another, the passive construction, that privileges the recipient of the action. The same reasoning applies to 'downhill/uphill', which depends on where the speaker, so to speak, puts him/herself.

Conceptualisation is said to be embodied and to play an active role in the construal of reality. The embodied nature of conceptualisation refers to the fact that many metaphorical expressions are based on common human characteristics. For example, a common metaphor is that UP is GOOD and DOWN is BAD. This is seen to be rooted in the upright stance of the human body and the elevated position of the human head. Thus, far from being based on abstract categories, conceptualisation is based on shared physical characteristics of humans.

The role of language and its categorisation in our perception of reality are a significant philosophical tenet of CL, which rejects the idea that reality is simply mirrored in language and/or mental representations, and instead sees an active role of linguistic categorisation in shaping the way the world is represented linguistically. The embodied nature of conceptualisation extends to these factors as well, with the assumption that knowledge is organised in ways that are influenced by the needs, goals, and cultural assumptions of the speakers.

Other concepts closely associated with CL are mental spaces, which can be defined as a conceptualisation informed by the relevant frames by a given speaker of a given situation, event, and so on. Mental spaces in CL are similar to possible worlds in formal semantics. Mental spaces have been widely used, for example, to explain counterfactuals, but have also been extended to the theory of literature, deixis, and discourse phenomena.

The study of metaphor* has also been a central interest of CL. Most linguistic approaches see metaphorical meaning as a trope – a figure of speech – and would relegate it to the periphery of language. CL conversely argues that most meaning is metaphorical in nature. Metaphors are seen as mappings between two domains; however, the significant difference between CL accounts of metaphors is that CL sees metaphors as grounded in metaphorical schemata of great generality, such as 'argument is war', which underlie such metaphors as 'he shot down my argument' and 'Mary won the debate'. Furthermore, CL sees meaning dynamically expanding from literal meanings to other metaphorical ones. For example, the meaning of the preposition 'over' is literally related to spatial orientation (an object is above another), but that meaning is then extended metaphorically to motion over an object, and eventually to being past the object, and hence to the meaning of finished action ('the

show is over'). Blending is a more recent theory of how mental spaces can interact (blend) and result in a new mental space with emergent features (features which are not present in either of the original spaces in the blend). Blending has been applied to metaphors, especially novel metaphors, and to an increasing variety of phenomena.

It should be stressed that CL shares with some theories of language such as natural phonology and morphology the use of iconicity (the fact that a linguistic form reflects the form of the referent it describes) as an explanatory concept. For example, the comparative and superlative forms of the adjective are often longer than the positive form: 'pretty – prettier – prettiest'. Relatedly, CL has shown since its inception a fondness for visual schematic representations that use iconic means, such as bolded lines to indicate focus, that have considerable weight in the explication of the concepts, at least intuitively and pedagogically. CL has also always shown a very distinct interest in space and its linguistic representation: witness the intensive study of prepositions which has been one of the great contributions of CL to grammatical analysis, and also the conceptualisation of many events as consisting of a figure and a ground, a trajectory or a landmark, for example.

Finally CL asserts that a good theory of language is a theory of language in use. This is mostly a programmatic claim, but recent developments of CL have emphasised the use of corpora* of naturally occurring utterances, analyses of conversational data, and an increased attention toward pragmatic phenomena and sociolinguistic variation at large.

Primary sources

Lakoff, George and Mark Johnson (1980). *Metaphors We Live By*. Chicago: University of Chicago Press.

Langacker, Ronald W. (1987). *Foundations of Cognitive Grammar, Volume I, Theoretical Prerequisites*. Stanford, CA: Stanford University Press.

Langacker, Ronald W. (1991). *Foundations of Cognitive Grammar, Volume II, Descriptive Application*. Stanford, CA: Stanford University Press.

Rosch, Eleanor (1973). 'Natural Categories', *Cognitive Psychology* 4: 328–80.

Talmy, Leonard (2003). *Toward a Cognitive Semantics – Volume 1: Concept Structuring Systems*. Cambridge, MA: MIT Press.

Talmy, Leonard (2003). *Toward a Cognitive Semantics – Volume 2: Typology and Process in Concept Structuring*. Cambridge, MA: MIT Press.

Further reading

Croft, William and D. Alan Cruse (2004). *Cognitive Linguistics*. Cambridge: Cambridge University Press.

Evans, Vyvyan and Melanie Green (2006). *Cognitive Linguistics. An Introduction*. Edinburgh: Edinburgh University Press

Geeraerts, Dirk (ed.) (2006). *Cognitive Linguistics: Basic Readings*. Berlin/New York: Mouton de Gruyter.

Geeraerts, Dirk and Hubert Cuykens (eds) (2007). *The Oxford Handbook of Cognitive Linguistics*. Oxford: Oxford University Press.

Ungerer, Friedrich and Hans-Jörg Schmid (1996). *An Introduction to Cognitive Linguistics*. London: Longman.

Salvatore Attardo

COMPOSITIONALITY

The notion that the meaning of a complex expression is a function of the meanings of its parts. The 'Principle of Compositionality' has played an important role in the work of a large number of philosophers and semanticists including Gottlob Frege, Donald Davidson and Richard Montague.

See also: Conventional Meaning; Language of Thought; Logic; Logical Form; Mentalism; Model Theoretic Semantics; Possible World Semantics; Propositions; Truth Theories
Key Thinkers: Davidson, Donald; Frege, Gottlob; Montague, Richard; Quine, W. V. O.

The Principle of Compositionality is a guiding principle for many semanticists and philosophers, notably Frege, Davidson and Montague. It is sometimes referred to as 'Frege's Principle', although not everyone agrees that the idea originated with him. Frege (1892) states it as follows: 'The meaning of a complex expression is a function of the meanings of its parts and their syntactic mode of combination'.

Perhaps the main reason that the principle is seen as important is the role it plays in explaining the creativity* and systematicity of language. We can explain how we are able to produce and understand an infinite number of utterances if we assume that we know the meanings of individual expressions and how to combine them into larger units.

It follows from this principle that the contribution of an expression, say the lexical item 'red', to a more complex expression should be the same in all cases. The contribution of 'red' should be the same in the noun phrase 'red wool' as in 'red cotton' and in any other noun phrase. W. V. O. Quine (1960) pointed out some problems with this assumption. For example, the contribution of 'red' in 'red apple' is not the same as the contribution of 'pink' in 'pink grapefruit', since a red apple is usually understood to be an apple with (mainly) red skin on the outside while a pink grapefruit is usually understood to be a grapefruit with (mainly) pink flesh on the inside.

Propositional attitude* reports (utterances which contain a statement about an individual's attitude to a proposition) provide a further test for the principle. For example, we can believe all three of the following:

(1) Chris thinks his next-door neighbour is considerate.
(2) Chris thinks the person who reversed into his bicycle is inconsiderate.
(3) Chris's next-door neighbour is the person who reversed into his bicycle.

Despite these problems, most theorists prefer to retain the Principle of Compositionality rather than attempting to develop a new account of the productivity and systematicity of linguistic knowledge.

Primary sources

Frege, G. (1892). 'On sense and meaning'. In Peter Geach and Max Black (eds) (1980), *Translations from the Philosophical Writings of Gottlob Frege*. Oxford: Blackwell, 56–78. First edition 1952.

Quine, W. V. O. (1960). *Word and Object*. Cambridge, MA: MIT Press.

Further reading

Davidson, D. and G. Harman (eds) (1972). *Semantics of Natural Language*. Dordrecht: Reidel.

Dowty, D. R., R. E. Wall. and S. Peters (1981). *Introduction to Montague Semantics*. Dordrecht: Kluwer.

Thomason, R. (ed.) (1974). *Formal Philosophy: Selected Papers of Richard Montague*. New Haven, CT: Yale University Press.

Billy Clark

CONNOTATION/ DENOTATION

Connotation, from the medieval Latin compound verb *con-noto*, refers to an implied or accompanying feature, as the comitative prefix *con* suggests. Denotation etymologically derives from the postclassical Latin compound verb *de-noto* which conveys the idea of singling out an entity by way of distinctive features.

See also: Sense/Reference; Signs and Semiotics
Key Thinkers: Aristotle; Hjelmslev, Louis; Mill, J. S.; Saussure, Ferdinand de

The notion of denotation can be traced back to Aristotle's classification of denominative names (*Categories I*) where he labelled '*paronyma*' (denominative) the names of entities which are morphologically derived from the names of something else, for example '*grammaticus*' ('grammarian') derives from '*gramatica*' ('grammar'). This is tantamount to saying

25

that the abstract name ontologically precedes any morphological variant. This view was spread in the early Middle Ages by St Anselm of Canterbury who introduced the notion of indirectness. On the one side, denominatives point directly to the property ('grammar') and indirectly to the substance ('grammarian'); on the other, denominatives have both meaning (the concept of grammar, *'significatio'*) and reference (the person who is a grammarian, *'appellatio'*). Two hundred years later, in the fourteenth century, William of Ockham tackled the issue of the semantics of adjectives from the opposite perspective and conceived of a distinction between 'absolute' and 'connotative' terms. The former refers either to the names of qualities (*albedinem*, 'whiteness') or of substances (*canis*, 'dog'). The latter refers to both the names of qualities and the names of substances. Along the centuries St Anselm's theory of denotation was progressively abandoned and it was Ockham's version that became prominent in the nineteenth century within the philosophical approach to semantics of John Stuart Mill. It was Mill who first mentioned the dichotomy between connotation and denotation in his *System of Logic* (1843), two labels that he used in a similar way as sense and reference*, or extension and intension. Mill limited Ockham's 'absolute' terms to proper names and to abstract names for attributes ('whiteness').

The meaning of the two terms is closely related to the theoretical framework taken as a perspective, and it varies broadly across theories. In logico-philosophical semantics, denotation corresponds to the bi-directional relationship between a set of entities in the world and the linguistic expressions used to refer to them, whereas reference/extension is viewed as a more specific relationship between one specific entity in the world and the word in a given utterance used to mention it. In a similar vein, connotation is often paired with sense/intension, but while sense encompasses the whole set of properties of an entity, intension refers to the qualities of the entity which are implied in a given utterance. In modern linguistics Saussure offered a clear distinction between the two labels. Stemming from his semiotic dichotomy of the sign, which is conceived of a signifier and a signified, denotation refers to the meaning of a word as is given in a dictionary, the objective semantic content codified by the signifier, whereas connotation refers to any other semantic implications that are part of the speaker's value in a given context.

Primary sources

Lyons, J. (1995). *Linguistics Semantics. An Introduction*. Cambridge: Cambridge University Press.

Further reading

Rigotti, E. and A. Rocci (2006). *Denotation versus Connotation*. In *Encyclopaedia of Language and Linguistics*. Elsevier. 436–44.

Annalisa Baicchi

CONTINUITY

A view arising from the theory that human language is the product of a unique biological and genetically encoded faculty. The theory of continuity suggests that human language must have evolved over time in the same way as other biological and genetically inherited features. Yet there is little hard evidence to suggest that any other animals have a language faculty with similar capabilities. This is sometimes known as the 'continuity paradox': language must have evolved in humans, but there is no surviving evidence that it did. For many thinkers the 'continuity paradox' is simply an unsolved problem that, in the absence of any explanation, needs to be accepted.

See also: Cognitivism; Creativity; Mentalism; Transformational-Generative Grammar; Universal Grammar
Key Thinkers: Chomsky, Noam; Hockett, Charles

The theory of continuity holds that the human language faculty must have evolved gradually over time, rather than appearing fully formed as a single mutation and that it must be possible to identify the 'continuity' in the evolutionary development of language in humans. Attempts to prove that language in humans is the result of a long process of evolution by natural selection have usually involved animals. Parrots have been trained to 'talk', while chimpanzees, lacking the physical apparatus necessary for human-like speech, have been taught sign language. One of the problems encountered by such experiments is deciding what constitutes 'language' in a human sense and establishing the criteria against which we should measure the linguistic abilities of animals. The work of Charles Hockett in the 1970s and 1980s is central to this effort to describe the key elements of human language, including for example the use of the vocal-auditory channel, semanticity, arbitrariness, and creativity*. But Hockett and others continually changed their minds about what features should be on the list, and the issue of what constitutes human language has since been recognised as a diversion.

One problem for proponents of continuity theory is that they often presuppose that evolution takes place in a linear and hierarchical way, from the most 'primitive' life forms, to the most 'sophisticated', namely humans. However, this view of evolution fails to take account of the fact that while many animals, including humans and chimpanzees, may share a common ancestor, they are not necessarily directly related. In other words, human language may have evolved after the human and chimpanzee 'branches' of an evolutionary tree had split apart. In that case there is no reason why a chimpanzee should ever show human language capabilities. Most scientists now believe that they never will.

Noam Chomsky has often expressed scepticism about the idea that the language faculty evolved in the same way as other biological features, but the lack of evidence for continuity does not mean it is false. As Stephen Pinker argues in *The Language Instinct* (1994), the trunk of an elephant is a feature unique to that creature, but biologists do not spend time testing other animals to see if they are able to use their noses in the same way as an elephant uses its trunk. Viewing human language as a unique adaptation, just as an elephant's trunk is unique, does not preclude evolutionary continuity. Advances in genetics may in the end show how humans came to have language when other animals do not. But in the mean time it is not unreasonable to assume that, as Pinker says, 'There were plenty of organisms with intermediate language abilities, but they are all dead' (1994: 346).

Primary sources

Aitchison, Jean (1989). *The Language Instinct: An Introduction to Psycholinguistics*. London: Unwin Hyman.

Sebeok, T. (ed.) (1968). *Animal Communication: Techniques and Study Results of Research*. Bloomington: Indiana University Press.

Pinker, Steven (1994). *The Language Instinct: The New Science of Language and Mind*. Harmondsworth: Penguin.

Further reading

Uriagereka, Juan. 'The Evolution of Language', in *Seed* (http://seedmagazine.com), 25 September 2007. http://seedmagazine.com/news/2007/09/the_evolution_of_language.php?page=1 (accessed on 30 January 2008).

Christopher Routledge

CONVENTIONAL MEANING

The fact that a sequence of sounds expresses a certain meaning in virtue of a tacit agreement among speakers at a certain time and place, rather than because of any necessary link between the sounds and the meaning thereby expressed. The stored meaning of expressions in the lexicon is an example of conventional meaning. Conventional meaning must be learnt, as it cannot be inferred based on principles of rationality. The distinction between conventional meaning (what an expression means) and speaker's meaning (what a speaker means by using a particular expression) is sometimes used to draw the line between semantics and pragmatics.

See also: Nonnatural Meaning; Signs and Semiotics
Key Thinkers: Aristotle; Grice, H. P.; Lewis, David; Plato; Saussure, Ferdinand de; Strawson, P. F.

The question of whether the origin of linguistic meaning lies with natural necessity or human convention is raised in Plato's *Cratylus*, where Socrates expresses the view that linguistic meaning is a matter of habit, a view echoed in Aristotle's *De Interpretatione*. In contemporary linguistics the conventionality of linguistic meaning is acknowledged in Ferdinand de Saussure's arbitrary association of signifier and signified, which engenders the possibility for this association to shift and change across languages and over time.

More recently, H. P. Grice explained linguistic meaning as a type of nonnatural meaning*. Contrary to other types of signs which are symptomatic of particular states of affairs and thus express natural meaning, the meaning of a linguistic sign is dependent on how speakers use it to bring about particular effects in an audience. Such use is in turn more or less constrained by the customary use of the sign by speakers in a community, that is by its conventional meaning. According to Grice, 'the conventional meaning of the words used' is part of the input to the derivation of conversational implicatures (1967/1989: 31). Nonnatural meaning thus encompasses both conventional (language-dependent) and intentional (speaker-dependent) aspects of meaning.

The continuity between conventional and intentional aspects of meaning is the topic of David Lewis's book *Convention* (1969), where he investigates the rational bases for conventions, explaining these as solutions to co-ordination problems. Context plays an important role in sustaining the transition from nonce meaning to conventional, or coded, meaning. The related notions of conventionalisation and standardisation have been proposed to account for the gradual decontextualisation of recurring meanings of linguistic expressions, such that these meanings eventually become part of an expression's conventional meaning.

Primary sources

Lewis, David (1969). *Convention: A Philosophical Study*. Cambridge, MA: Harvard University Press.
Strawson, Peter (1964). 'Intention and convention in speech acts'. *Philosophical Review* 73, 439–60.

Further reading

Bach, Kent (1998). 'Standardisation revisited'. In A. Kasher (ed.), *Pragmatics: Critical Concepts*. Vol. IV. London: Routledge. 712–22.
Grice, H. P. (1967). 'Logic and Conversation'. William James Lectures, Harvard University typescript. Reprinted in

Grice, H. P. (1989), *Studies in the Way of Words*. Cambridge, MA: Harvard University Press. 22–40.
Morgan, Jerry (1978). 'Two types of convention in indirect speech acts'. In P. Cole (ed.), *Syntax and Semantics*, vol. 9: *Pragmatics*. New York: Academic Press. 261–80.
Traugott, Elizabeth (1999). 'The role of pragmatics in semantic change'. In J. Verschueren (ed.), *Pragmatics in 1998*. Antwerp: International Pragmatics Association. 93–102.

Marina Terkourafi

CONVERSATION ANALYSIS

The systematic study of all aspects of talk in social interaction. The findings of this important discipline, started by Harvey Sacks in the mid-1960s, are significant to all social sciences.

See also: (Critical) Discourse Analysis; Speech Act Theory
Key Thinkers: Austin, J. L.; Grice, H. P.; Sacks, Harvey; Searle, John

According to Anthony Liddicoat, conversation analysis (CA) – also known as ethnomethodology – originated in the work of Harold Garnfikel, an ethnomethodologist whose research in the 1960s centred on how members of a certain community conduct and understand social actions and interactions Liddicoat (2007: 2). These ideas were developed by Sacks who determined that conversation is an organised activity that has a systematic structure. Ironically, Sack's claim was proposed in the mid-1960s, during the heyday of the Chomskyan paradigm, which regarded 'talk' as being unfit as a source of linguistic data because it is riddled with irregularities and flaws. However, Sacks and his collaborators, Emanuel Schegloff and Gail Jefferson, proved that conversation is an orderly, collaborative activity characterised by consistent principles that define what linguistic forms interlocutors use to open and close their contributions, how they repair and rephrase their talk, and when they take the floor during the course of a conversation. In addition to these, CA also investigates the role of proxemics, or inter-personal distance and body language, in communication. The principles of CA have significant implications for a number of disciplines that include linguistics, social psychology and communication, to name a few. It is therefore useful to summarise some of the areas in which CA has proved useful or enlightening.

Since CA investigates the sequential nature of conversation, analysts have studied the systematically recurring linguistic units that open these conversations. The majority of these studies have focused on telephone conversations because of the limitations resulting from the absence of physical clues such as body language, facial expressions and eye gaze. Schegloff has investigated opening sequences in telephone conversations (1979, 1986) and concluded that they are characterised by a predictable sequence in which the answerer of the telephone call speaks first, saying 'hello'. Since making a call is considered to be a summons that requires a response, the answerer is expected to acknowledge that a connection has been established. This opening is followed by making an identification and exchanging greetings.

This pattern recurred in the majority of the telephone calls analysed by Schegloff. However, variations occurred as a result of a number of reasons, including the setting of the call. If the call is made to a workplace, for instance, the answerer would start by giving the name of the organisation and not the personal name. Although face-to-face conversations are characterised by similar features, there are a few differences. These result from the fact that interlocutors can see each other, which would influence the identification part of the opening sequence.

Members of a speech community also need to be aware of the way in which conversations are closed, or concluded. Since talk in social interactions is a collaborative process, it is important to ensure that a conversation is not ended in an abrupt manner that would deprive any of the participants of the right to contribute. It has been observed that participants use certain expressions that signal the end of the conversation, the most common among which is 'goodbye' or one of its synonyms. However, a closing sequence cannot just be introduced at any juncture of the conversation to signal its conclusion. Before terminating a verbal interaction, a pre-closing sequence alerting the participants to the nearness of the conversation end has to be introduced. This is meant to ensure participants are given the opportunity to make whatever contributions they deem necessary. Schegloff and Sacks define a pre-closing sequence as a turn after the production of which every participant 'declines at least one opportunity to continue talking' (1973: 214). Expressions that could function as pre-closing sequences include 'alright', 'right', and 'okay' and they are usually marked by falling intonation. If none of the speakers introduces a new topic, the pre-sequence will be followed by a closing sequence that would mark the conclusion of the conversation. However, if a new topic is introduced, the conversation will continue unless one of the participants is unable to proceed because of time constraint or some other reason.

Another phenomenon characteristic of conversations is 'sequence pairs'. These are conversation contributions by different speakers that are sequentially placed next to each other. Schegloff and Sacks (1973) proposed the term to refer to sequences such as greeting-greeting and question-answer. Since conversation is a collaborative social act to which participants are expected to contribute, a question should be answered and a greeting reciprocated. The failure to do so would be considered an act of non-compliance and a violation of social etiquette. Guy Cook (1989) classifies responses to adjacency pairs into 'preferred' and 'dispreferred'. According to his framework, agreeing with an assessment is the preferred sequence, while disagreeing with it is dispreferred. As for responses to questions, giving the expected answer is the preferred response, while giving an unexpected answer is the dispreferred response. Cook adds that a dispreferred response is usually explicitly justified or non-verbally marked. Although the two parts of an adjacency pair occur next to each other,

which reflects the turn-taking mechanism of conversation, this may sometimes be altered for a certain communicative purpose. If an interlocutor, for instance, needs more information before he/she answers a question, this would result in the interruption of the two elements of the adjacency pair. Cook gives the following example:

A: Did you enjoy the meal? (B: Did you? A: Yes.) B: So did I.

Cook explains that the initial adjacency pair, which is contributor A's first turn and contributor B's second turn, has been interrupted by a second adjacency pair, the one between parentheses. He calls this interrupting element an 'insertion sequence' (1989: 54). It is evident from the example that speaker B needed more information before responding to the question.

Talk in social interaction is a collaborative endeavour in which turn-taking seems to be a highly structured process. Although interruptions and gaps are not uncommon, conversation participants seem to have tacit knowledge of when to 'take the floor' and offer their contribution to the conversation. When asked about what clues they use to start speaking, people often mention pauses and length of contribution as the most reliable clues. Citing several examples, however, Liddicoat argues that neither of these clues are valid markers of a turn's end (2007: 54–6). Sacks et al. (1974) speculate that speakers know when to take the floor because they have tacit knowledge of *turn constructional units*. They define these as linguistic forms that are not identifiable in terms of syntactic structure. A

31

turn constructional unit can be a single word, a phrase, a clause, or a longer stretch of discourse. They add that speakers have knowledge of the pragmatic function of these context-sensitive units, which enables them to identify the end of turns. A variety of other proposals have been offered to explain what clues participants in conversation use to take the floor. These include utilising knowledge of syntactic, semantic and suprasegmental features of conversation, in addition to using visual clues to determine end of turns. Among these is the *paratone*, which Brown and Yule define as a conversational paragraph whose end is marked by a summarising sequence, a significant pause and falling pitch (1983: 101). Another related area of interest is turn allocation, which investigates whether the person holding the floor selects the next speaker, or whether the subsequent speaker self-selects. In their 1974 framework, Sacks et al. state that a speaker holding the floor may:

(a) directly select a subsequent speaker by using a personal name, a pronoun, or asking a question;

(b) indirectly select the next speaker by using gaze and establishing eye contact;

(c) that a speaker holding the floor may not select any one, which leaves it open to participants to self-select.

Despite the tacit knowledge speakers have of turn-taking rules in conversation, gaps and overlaps occur. According to the framework in Sacks et al., silence may take place at a transition relevance place, where any of the participants could claim the floor. This type of silence may also result in an extended lapse in the conversation. Another type of silence, however, occurs at a juncture of the conversation where a specific participant is expected to contribute, for example, to answer a question. This type of silence is considered problematic because it results in an act of non-compliance. Strategies used to repair failure to contribute include repeating the question or changing the topic.

Overlapped speech, on the other hand, may be the result of a participant's misreading of a pause as the end of the speaker's turn and a sign of forfeiting the floor. When that happens, the overlap may persist for some time before one of the participants discontinues. Another possible reason for overlaps in conversation is when, at the end of a speaker's turn, two interlocutors take the floor at the same time. If an overlap occurs at a point that is not a potential juncture for speaker change, it is considered an interruption. O'Grady et al. believe that how overlaps are perceived is culture-specific. Communities that speak the standard North American English varieties, they argue, adhere to a rigid turn-taking mechanism, which results in very few overlaps. The East European Jewish community in New York, however, views overlaps favourably because they reflect the speakers' interest in the conversation. Hence, they call overlaps in which speakers finish one another's sentences 'cooperative overlaps' (2005: 491). Beside cultural differences, other factors that might determine overlaps include the topic, type of conversational interaction and number of participants. In an interview setting, for instance, where only two people are involved, overlaps are rare. On the other hand, if a large number of people are involved in the discussion of a heated topic, overlaps are likely to occur at a high rate.

Unlike written language, in the production of which a significant amount of time is spent on composition and revision, spoken language is planned in the here-and-now. Consequently, conversations are marked by 'repair', a process whereby utterances are modified. Liddicoat states that although repair may target a perceived mistake, people often use repair when they fail to retrieve a specific item from their lexicon, or mental dictionary, in a timely manner (2007: 171). Schegloff et al. (1977) have proposed a taxonomy for the classification of repairs that occur in conversation. Their categorisation takes into account who initiates the repair and who makes it. This yields four types which are: (1) *self-initiated self-repair*, which denotes deficiencies detected and resolved by the speaker; (2) *self-initiated other-repair*, which refers to deficiencies detected by the speaker, but repaired by another; (3) *other-initiated self-repair*, denoting irregularities pointed out by an interlocutor, but repaired by the speaker; and (4) *other-initiated other-repair*, referring to repairs detected and repaired by someone other than the speaker. Typically, Schegloff et al. argue, repairs involving grammatical mistakes are initiated by the speaker, whereas repairs of hearing problems are other-initiated. Citing a variety of examples, the researchers indicate the different junctures of the conversation at which repair occurs.

Because of their unique characteristics as a specific genre of talk, stories have received specific attention from conversation analysts. First, a story requires a fairly extended turn, which may disrupt the orderly turn-taking mechanism of conversation; and, second, in order to maintain coherence and topic continuity, a story has to be introduced at the right juncture in the conversational interaction. Jefferson (1978) proposes two factors that trigger narratives. The first is when a conversation topic reminds a speaker of the events of a certain experience. When that happens, she or he may elect to relate the story; however, the conversation participants have to be alerted by such expressions like 'by the way', or 'incidentally'. According to Jefferson, these serve as disjuncts marking topic transition and providing some kind of a justification for the narrative. Researchers have also asserted the interactive characteristics of story-telling. Contrary to common belief, a story is not a monologue that is delivered by a single speaker. Not only do participants comment on and evaluate the narrative after its delivery, they also frequently ask questions about and make remarks on the story while it is being told. Upon the completion of the narrative, receivers are expected to make some kind of a response. That response may be an evaluation of the story, a comment on its plot, or an expression of empathy. If silence follows the end of a story, that would be regarded as an act of non-compliance.

Deborah Schiffrin has proposed a model for the analysis and interpretation of spoken English that focuses on what she calls local coherence, or coherence between adjacent units in discourse. This, she believes, is accomplished by employing *discourse markers* that speakers use to achieve not only semantic, but also pragmatic goals. Although Schiffrin does not give a concrete definition, her operational definition is that discourse markers are 'sequentially dependent elements which bracket units of talk' (1987: 31). Despite the definition's limitation, which arises from the difficulty of defining speech units, Schiffrin identifies eleven discourse markers: 'oh', 'well', 'and', 'so', 'now', 'then', 'I mean', 'but', 'because', 'y'know' and 'or'. Then she applies these markers to the analysis of authentic conversation explaining how they are used by participants to achieve coherence through accomplishing a variety of communicative goals. Schiffrin (1985) argues that 'well' is the most versatile discourse marker because it does not have inherent semantic or structural attributes. Its meaning, however, derives from the context in which it occurs. Schiffrin distinguished between occurrences of 'well' in adjacency pairs (questions/answers, request/compliance sequences), and occurrences of 'well' which cannot be explained in terms of adjacency pairs.

Examining the distribution of 'well' in answers to wh- questions and yes/no questions, Schiffrin found that 'well' precedes answers to yes/no questions 10 per cent of the time; on the other hand 'well' precedes answers to wh- questions 21 per cent of the time. She attributed this to the fact that yes/no questions delimit the upcoming answer to either an affirmative or a negative response, hence 'well' is not regarded as a coherent marker for answers in these contexts.

Schiffrin also examined the role of 'well' in response to requests. She suggests that in reaction to requests for action, it is more likely for 'well' to be used in responses that indicate non-compliance to requests. In addition to these contexts, Schiffrin investigates other roles of 'well', such as marking requests for clarification, self-repairs and reported speech. Schiffrin emphasises the need for future research that examines the distribution of different markers in different conversational genres. Such research, she asserts, would enable us to understand how coherence is achieved in different types of discourse.

Finally, an issue that is of utmost importance to every conversation analyst is transcription. Since speech is transient, it cannot be studied as it unfolds in real time. Hence, researchers have to tape-record and transcribe it using a variety of conventions whose purpose is to capture all of the conversational aspects discussed above. However, it is not easy to come up with a system of transcription that is neutral and objective. Moreover, a transcription is not a substitute for the conversation. It has been argued that transcription should be modified as researchers listen again to the recording. Although the objective of the transcription is to capture as many features of the conversation as possible, a balance has to be struck between the comprehensibility of the transcription conventions and the accessibility of these conventions to the targeted audience (Liddicoat 2007).

It is widely believed that a transcription should include information about the conversation participants, time and place. Since the anonymity of the participants should be maintained, pseudonyms are usually used. A major issue regarding transcriptions is word representation. Using the conventional orthography has the advantage that it is a system known to the whole literate society. However, since conventional orthography is based on a standard variety of the language, some scholars, for example Duranti (1997), argue that using it would undermine the neutrality and objectivity of the transcription. In addition to the conversation, non-linguistic sounds such as laughter and back channelling forms have to be included. The transcription system also needs to indicate pauses within a contributor's turn. Moreover, a pause between speakers' turns is also significant because its absence is an indication of overlapped conversation, which is significant to the turn-taking mechanism. Suprasegmental features such as stress and intonation have to be transcribed because of their interactional significance. In addition to these features, the transcription should account for overlaps, body language and background noise. Liddicoat asserts that transcripts should be continuously updated, adding that a transcript is 'not an objective account and that it will always be a selective representation of the data itself' (2007: 50). Conversation analysis is an important tool for understanding language in use, but its usefulness to other disciplines, such as anthropology and sociology, is also very significant.

Primary sources

Hutchby, Ian, and Robin Wooffitt (1998). *Conversation Analysis: Principles,* *Practices, and Applications*. Malden, MA: Blackwell Publishing.

Jefferson, G. (1978). 'Sequential Aspects of Storytelling'. In J. Schenkein (ed.), *Studies in the Organization of Conversational Interaction*. New York: Academic. 219–48.

Liddicoat, Anthony (2007). *An Introduction to Conversation Analysis*. London: Continuum.

O'Grady, William, John Archibald, Mark Aronoff and J. Rees-Miller (2005). *Contemporary Linguistics: An Introduction*. Fifth edition. Boston, MA: Bedford/St Martin's.

Sacks, H., E. Schegloff and G. Jefferson (1974). 'A simplest systematics for the organisation of turn-taking for conversation'. *Language* Vol. 50: 696–735.

Schegloff, E. A. (1979). 'Identification and recognition in telephone conversation openings'. In G. Psathas (ed.), *Everyday Language: Studies in Ethnomethodology*. New York: Irvington. 23–78.

Schegloff, E. A. (1986). 'The routine as achievement'. *Human Studies* Vol. 9: 2–3, 111–51.

Schegloff, E. and H. Sacks (1973). 'Opening up closings'. *Semiotica* Vol. 7: 289–327.

Schegloff, E., G. Jefferson and H. Sacks (1977). 'The preference for self-correction in the organization of repair in conversation'. *Language* Vol. 53: 361–82.

Schiffrin, Deborah (1987). *Discourse Markers*. Cambridge: Cambridge University Press.

Further reading

Brown, Gillian, and George Yule (1983). *Discourse Analysis*. Cambridge: Cambridge University Press.

Cook, Guy (1989). *Discourse*. Oxford: Oxford University Press.

Duranti, A. (1997). *Linguistic Anthropology*. Cambridge: Cambridge University Press.

Psathas, George (1995). *Conversation Analysis: The Study of Talk-in-Interaction*. Thousand Oaks, CA: Sage Publications.

Schiffrin, D. (1985). 'Conversational Coherence: The Role of "Well" '. *Language* Vol. 61: 640–67.

Yousif Elhindi

CORPORA

Collections of written texts or spoken utterances representative of a particular language, dialect, population or style. Linguists use corpora to provide real-world context in language analysis and language processing.

See also: Behaviourism, Conversation Analysis, (Critical) Discourse Analysis, Empiricism/Rationalism
Key Thinkers: Firth, J. R.; Sinclair, John

Linguistics calls upon language data to provide evidence to support the existence of particular linguistic phenomena or to challenge theories and algorithms. Linguists may derive such evidence from experience or personal knowledge, or they may refer to a written or recorded set of external data in the form of a corpus. A corpus – from the Latin for 'body', as in 'body of texts' – provides perspective and context for language data. Although modern corpora typically exist as computer databases or files, the idea is far from new. In the mid-twentieth century the empiricist J. R. Firth observed, 'You shall know a word by the company it keeps.' A corpus provides not only such company (technically known as concordance), but also many other linguistic insights. Linguists have numerous pre-existing corpora available to them, or they may choose to assemble their own, such as when they seek to analyse or test criteria or characteristics not adequately represented in existing corpora.

An effective corpus is a representative sample of natural language taken from the population being studied. Linguists must match their needs against the specific criteria of a corpus such that the results of their research and analysis may transfer to the real world what the corpus is meant to reflect. There are a number of characteristics by which corpora vary from one another. For instance, some corpora contain textual data in the form of written words, sentences and punctuation, while others contain speech data in form of utterances, fragments and filled pauses. Another major factor is whether the corpus is raw or annotated. A raw corpus has not been modified from its original form, as in the case of an online book or magazine. By contrast, an annotated corpus has been marked up with tags to identify certain elements, like parts of speech. A corpus may focus on a particular subject area or population, or it may represent a variety of subjects or even genres. Corpora also vary by time period, geographical region and size, and they may even use different languages or dialects. Some corpora are multilingual, containing text or speech in multiple languages. When those different languages express the same content, this is known as a parallel corpus. Existing corpora, available through a number of sources, including the popular Linguistic Data Consortium (LDC), may be available for a fee or free of charge.

Among the first widely-available corpora are those in the the the Brown corpus, named for Brown University, where it was created in the early 1960s. First published as the *Standard Corpus of Present-Day American English* by Henry Kucera and Nelson Francis, it contains 500 written texts and totals more than one million words of running text, averaging over 2,000 words per text. Although it has seen a number of proofreadings and revisions since its creation, the Brown corpus remains an admirable representation of 1961 written American English, spanning a wide range of styles and varieties of prose, including both informative and imaginative prose, such as text from newspapers, novels, non-fiction and academic publications. Kucera and Francis conducted a thorough analysis of the corpus, a landmark in modern corpus linguistics. Another version of the Brown corpus now exists with tagging for parts of speech.

Another important corpus includes texts published by the Associated Press (AP), aptly known as the *North American News Text Corpus*, or more simply the AP corpus. There are actually multiple versions of this corpus. A 1987 version of it contains fifteen million words, and a 1988 version contains thirty-six million. The content came from North American authors, writing news stories in American English for the *Los Angeles Times*, the *Washington Post* and the *New York Times*. A more modern version of the corpus is the *Associated Press World Stream English*, published in 1998 and containing approximately 143 million words. It combines the *North American News Text Corpus* with English-language text written in all parts of the world, usually not in American English. This corpus is marked up in Standard Generalised Markup Language (SGML) to make analysis easier.

Newswire data is also used in the *Wall Street Journal* (WSJ) corpus, which exists in several forms. An early version of it, called CSR-I, contains *Wall Street Journal* news articles read aloud in the early 1990s as part of an effort to support research on large-vocabulary Continuous Speech Recognition (CSR) systems. This was soon revised as CSR-II, containing 78,000 utterances, or seventy-three hours of speech. There are also written text variations of *Wall Street Journal* data, containing thirty million words parsed in a treebank-style (capturing syntactic structure) with part of speech tagging.

Combining both written and spoken text from a wide range of British English sources, the *British National Corpus* (BNC) contains 100 million words and has been updated several times since its birth in 1991. Its massive size is roughly equivalent to 1,000 average paperback books. The written portion of the BNC corpus represents 90 per cent of the total and contains text from British newspapers, periodicals, journals, non-fiction and fiction books, letters and essays. The remaining 10 per cent consists of spoken utterances by British English speakers in the form of informal conversation, business or government meetings and radio shows. Its goal is to represent a cross-section of written and spoken British English, produced by a variety of sources and intended for a mixture of ages and backgrounds, representative of the British population itself. The BNC corpus includes part of speech tagging, as well as built-in identification of its structure, such as headings, paragraphs, and lists.

An important corpus for spoken language data is the SWITCHBOARD corpus, which consists of about 2,430 spontaneous telephone conversations by over 500 diverse native speakers of all major dialects of American English between the ages of twenty and sixty. The conversation topics come from a predetermined list of topics, and the speakers did not already know one another at the time of their recorded conversations. Developed at Texas Instruments in 1991, SWITCH-BOARD contains a total of over 240 hours of data. Unlike the corpora mentioned above, the spoken language within SWITCHBOARD is very natural, not scripted from written text. However, a written version of the corpus does exist, produced later via transcription of the speech data. For each transcription, a time alignment file indicates the beginning time and duration of each word, information that is particularly useful for studying the phonetic characteristics of the speech, as is common in developing and evaluating automatic speech recognition systems. Another advantage of the corpus is that it comes with background information about each speaker along with details surrounding each specific conversation, including the nature of the telephones used.

All of the corpora discussed above are monolingual, representing only the English language. By contrast, the CELEX corpus is multilingual corpus, including not only English, but also German and Dutch. It was developed as a joint effort by the University of Nijmegen, the Institute for Dutch Lexicology in Leiden, the Max Planck Institute for Psycholinguistics in Nijmegen, and the Institute for Perception Research in Eindhoven. This corpus is a database of lexical word forms, with detailed information on orthography (variations in spelling, hyphenation), phonology (phonetic transcriptions, variations in pronunciation, syllable structure, primary stress), morphology (derivational and compositional structure, inflectional paradigms), syntax (word class, word class-specific subcategorisations, argument structures) and word frequency (summed word and lemma counts, based on recent and representative text corpora).

A very popular multilingual corpus is the European Parliament Proceedings Parallel (Europarl) corpus, assembled from 1996 to 2003. Extracted from the proceedings of the European Parliament, it includes parallel text in eleven European languages: Romanic (French, Italian, Spanish and Portuguese), Germanic (English, Dutch, German, Danish and Swedish), Greek and Finnish. It contains roughly twenty million words in 740,000 sentences per language, with each language aligned by sentence or by document. This corpus makes it possible to align 110 language pairs, including languages (particularly Greek and Finnish) that were poorly represented in previous corpora. For this reason, Europarl is frequently used within the field of statistical machine translation to train and evaluate systems to an extent that was previously not possible.

The CALLHOME corpora is a collection of speech data, originally created to support research in large vocabulary conversational speech recognition, which was suffering due to a shortage of speech data for languages other than English. Its creators offered its speakers free telephone calls to their native country in exchange for permission to record their conversations. The result is a series of corpora, arranged by language (English, Spanish, Arabic, German, Mandarins and Japanese), containing unscripted telephone conversations, up to thirty minutes in length and originating in North America. All speakers are native speakers of their respective languages, and many interactions are between family members or close friends. The CALL-HOME corpora were thus named for their collection method.

The corpora discussed here are good examples of the range of corpora available to linguists, who select a corpus based upon their specific needs in analysing data or testing theories or natural language processing (NLP) systems. Data within a corpus may be textual data or speech data, and even speech data may be transcribed such that it, too, exists as text. Text corpora are commonly formatted to identify key elements or structure within the data, and the formatting conventions must be clear to those who use the corpus so that they can properly interpret the data it contains. It is even possible for a single corpus to have multiple instances, each formatted according to a different standard. One such standard is a treebank, where each sentence is annotated as a tree structure based upon its syntactic structure, which itself is often annotated through part of speech tagging. A treebank may represent phrase structure (as in the case of the Penn Treebank) or dependency structure (as in the case of the Prague Dependency Treebank). Another formatting standard, used specifically for bilingual corpora, is a bilingual knowledge bank (BKB), which organises a bilingual corpus into translation units, or aligned 'bitexts'.

Corpora play a supporting role in several fields of research. The most obvious of these is corpus linguistics, which focuses its study of language specifically on corpora and real-world text. To accurately represent language as it is actually used, a corpus must be very large in volume. Corpus linguistics thus relies heavily upon automated methods for conducting proper analysis of data. Technology has given us new analysis techniques that were previously not possible for reasons of sheer quantity of data, particularly when the corpus being studied is annotated with information about the text structure, parts of speech, semantics, and so on. Statistical NLP also uses data from corpora in order to count words and compute word probabilities based on word frequencies within a training corpus, even taking into account such factors as concordance and discourse features. Speech corpora are particularly useful in speech recognition technology, which may involve training software using speech corpora data as well as testing systems against an existing corpora of natural, unscripted speech. It may even play a role in assembling a controlled language to be used for a speech recognition system, identifying the words and phrase structures that regular people may use when interacting with the system. Machine translation (MT) technology also uses corpora for example-based systems working on the assumption that translation involves finding or recalling analogous examples of words and phrases. Corpus-based approaches to MT may be trained using a subset of texts within a particular corpus and then tested against other texts within that same corpus. Finally, corpora are also useful for exploring and interpreting historical documents. For example, researchers working on deciphering an ancient text could use a corpus of texts from the same historical period and geographical location to find clues to better understand the text they are studying.

A key criticism of corpus analysis is that it supports statistical methods that disregard our knowledge of language. Within NLP, systems fall along a spectrum, with purely rule-based approaches at one end and corpus-based (statistical) approaches at the other. Evaluations of competing NLP systems show that hybrid systems, incorporating a combination of language rules and statistical methods, consistently outperform systems that use only one of the two methodologies. Even when a corpus-based (or hybrid) approach is undisputed, a particular corpus itself might not fit the task. A corpus fails its job when it is not an accurate representative sample of the language used by the population of interest. When selecting a corpus or collecting data to build a new corpus, a linguist must identify what type of text a corpus must reflect as well as whether the results of work with the corpus will transfer to the domain of interest. That is, a corpus serves as a powerful tool for linguists, but it cannot wholly substitute for the real world. In general, the larger a corpus, the more useful it is and the more likely it is to capture actual linguistic use. Yet even the largest corpus available is only as useful as the extent to which it reflects the target domain and offers a usable format for analysis. In addition to size, the breadth of a corpus also affects its usefulness and applicability for meaningful research. A valuable corpus for a linguist studying general language use, for example, should contain a variety of text sources, such as newspapers, textbooks, popular writing, fictions and technical material. Another potential drawback specific to speech corpora is that they lack linguistic cues that are otherwise available in a text corpus. Speech corpora include both fragmented, incomplete words and filled pauses, such as 'uh' and 'um'. While these elements reflect how people actually speak, which is crucial for speech recognition systems, they understandably make it harder to work with the data.

The concept of a corpus presents an interesting circular relationship between linguistics and society in general. A corpus captures a subset of real-world language data, while linguists use this data in a format that enables them to study it, to analyse its contents, and to develop and support theories or NLP systems. These NLP systems, developed and tested against theoretically real-world corpora, in turn can help their real-world users to carry out tasks. For example, a speech corpus, like the SWITCHBOARD corpus or CALLHOME corpus discussed above, originates from real-world speech data collected via unscripted telephone conversations. Linguists may use such a corpus to learn about how people communicate over the telephone and thereby develop a speech recognition system that can function properly with practical, real-world speech data. The quality of the final product is a direct reflection of the quality of the speech corpus by which it was trained and evaluated. A poor-quality corpus would result in a speech recognition system that proves to be an inadequate fit for its users' needs. Likewise, a high-quality corpus would result in a speech recognition system that better anticipates the types of utterances its users may give it as input. A corpus aims to reflect real-world language so as to support theories and systems that, too, reflect real-world language.

A single corpus cannot be a perfect fit for every linguistic endeavour, nor can it exhibit all aspects of language use. This is why there are so many existing corpora available to linguists. Nevertheless, linguists often create new corpora tailored to a particular language use scenario, geographical region, demographic group or format. Corpora will continue to play an important role in linguistics and the study of language, and automated methods will improve our ability to collect, format and analyse their data.

Knowing the importance of size, linguists are using technological advancements to make increasingly large corpora to better represent the real world. They also take advantage of statistically-based techniques for automatically deriving probabilities concerning word counts, frequencies and concordance. As long as linguists continue to propose theories, they will need corpora to support them, and as long as they continue to design and build NLP systems, they will need corpora to test them.

Primary sources

Godfrey, John, Edward Holliman and Jane McDaniel (1992). 'SWITCHBOARD: Telephone speech corpus for research and development'. *Proceedings of the IEEE Conference on Acoustics, Speech, and Signal Processing*. San Francisco: IEEE.

Koehn, Philipp (2005). 'Europarl: A Parallel Corpus for Statistical Machine Translation.' *MT Summit 2005*. Unpublished.

Kucera, Henry and Nelson Francis (1967). *Computational Analysis of Present-Day American English*. Providence, RI: Brown University Press.

Marcus, Mitchell, Beatrice Santorini and Mary Ann Marcinkiewicz (1993). 'Building a large annotated corpus of English: the Penn Treebank'. *Computational Linguistics* Vol. 19: 313–30.

Quirk, Randolf (1960). 'Towards a description of English usage'. *Transactions of the Philological Society* 40–61.

Further reading

Biber, Douglas, Susan Conrad and Randi Reppen (1998). *Corpus Linguistics: Investigating Language Structure and Use*. Cambridge: Cambridge University Press.

Edwards, Jane (1993). 'Survey of electronic corpora and related resources for language researchers'. In J. Edwards and M. Lampert (eds), *Talking Data: Transcription and Coding in Discourse Research*. Hillside, NJ: Lawrence Erlbaum Associates.

Morley, Barry (2006). 'WebCorp: a tool for online linguistic information retrieval and analysis'. In A. Renouf and A. Kehoe (eds), *The Changing Face of Corpus Linguistics*. Amsterdam: Rodopi.

Jennifer A. Baldwin

CORRESPONDENCE THEORY

A theory that tries to solve the problem of what constitutes truth as a property of sentences by claiming that there is a relation of correspondence between the meaning of true sentences and the way the world is at a certain place and time.

> *See also*: Language of Thought; Logic; Sense/Reference; Truth Theories; Truth Value
> *Key Thinkers*: Aristotle; Kant, Immanuel; Moore, G. E.; Russell, Bertrand; Tarski, Alfred; Wittgenstein, Ludwig

Correspondence theory is the most prominent of several theories trying to solve the problem of what truth is. It originates in Greek philosophy, specifically in the work of Aristotle, and appears in the medieval period in the work of Thomas Aquinas and William of Ockham. It was later a principle in Immanuel Kant's philosophy, and its contemporary version is mostly influenced by G. E. Moore, Bertrand Russell, Ludwig Wittgenstein and Alfred Tarski. For many people outside philosophy, including linguists and lay-persons, the correspondence solution seems intuitively correct: in our daily lives we have to assume that there is a relation between what people say and the things they talk about. But whether what they say is true or false, we need the concept of truth because without it we would not be able to describe what happens in the world.

One modern way of formulating the correspondence theory solution is to say that a sentence (a proposition) is true iff (if and only if) it corresponds to some fact, or iff it corresponds to some state of affairs. It is not hard to see the problem: in order to appreciate the notion of correspondence one has to grasp the notions of 'sentence', 'fact' and 'state of affairs' respectively. Intuitively we would say that the truth of a sentence has to do with the meaning of the sentence, and this may be differentiated from the state of affairs, which seems to be what is out there, in reality. But can 'sentence meaning' be separated from 'fact'? Some sentences – for example, 'Open the window' – do not express facts, but in general sentences are interpreted as expressing facts of some kind. So, if a sentence meaning conveys true information, what is the difference between the meaning of a sentence and the facts that it conveys? In other words, if 'sentence meaning' and 'fact' are the same thing, how can they not correspond?

Dictionary definitions on the notion of truth usually take up the nature of the relation between language and reality. Some term for the concept of relation seems inescapable and so it is in modern epistemology and philosophy of science. Thus the standard definition of knowledge is 'justified true belief' (Dancy 1985: 23), meaning that there must be a relation between beliefs and what the beliefs are about. If scientific knowledge is to count as trustworthy, it must be true (see Popper 1963: 215–50); there must be an agreement between what science says and how things happen out there.

Kant expressed the correspondence principle in the most transparent way: 'Wahrheit ist die Übereinstimmung der Erkenntnis mit ihrem Gegenstand', 'truth is the correspondence of knowledge with its object' (Kant 1781/1787, 1924/1927: 992), even though he did not consider it a problem, while Tarski offered a technical and rather complicated clarification of the correspondence relation based on predicate logic*. Although it is commonly accepted that some idea of correspondence is a necessary requirement in truth theory*, it is also commonly recognised that the nature of this relation is the source of much controversy.

Primary sources

Kant, Immanuel (1781[A]/1787[B]. Published by Raymund Schmidt 1924/ 1927). *Kritik der reinen Vernunft*. Wiesbaden: VAM-Verlag.
Popper, Karl R. (1963/1989). *Conjectures and Refutations*. Fifth edition. London: Routledge.

Further reading

Dancy, Jonathan (1985). *Contemporary Epistemology*. Oxford: Blackwell.
Tarski, Alfred (1935). 'The concept of truth in formalized language', in *Logic,* *Semantics, Metamathematics*. Indianapolis: Hackett. 152–278.
Wittgenstein, Ludwig (1922). *Tractatus Logico-Philosophicus*. London: Routledge.

Hans Götzsche

CREATIVITY

The ability of the ordinary use of language to be innovative and free from stimulus control. As associated most recently with Noam Chomsky (though with ultimate roots in Cartesian rationalism), it is claimed that this creativity points to the central place of language in the study of human nature.

See also: Behaviourism; Metaphor; Universal Grammar
Key Thinkers: Chomsky, Noam; Descartes, René; Humboldt, Wilhelm von; Skinner, B. F.

In one sense, linguistic creativity has a narrow meaning, referring to the ability of human beings to innovate within the lexico-semantic domain. Speakers, writers and poets can use the elements of their language to draw attention to surprising and interesting aspects of the world through metaphor*, jokes and the like. However, there is another, broader sense of linguistic creativity, most commonly attributed in the modern era to Chomsky, which applies not to the activities of gifted individuals, but rather to the ordinary use of language by everyday speakers. This creativity underlines the fundamental role that language plays in understanding the essential nature of human beings and is often referred to by Chomsky as 'the creative aspect of language use'.

The most general aspect of creativity in this broad sense, and one which connects Chomsky's work to the earlier rationalist traditions of Wilhelm von Humboldt and René Descartes is the observation that human beings can produce (and understand with no sense of novelty) an infinite number of sentences which may be new in their experience or even new in the history of the language. This creativity is thus intimately connected with the 'generative' nature of generative grammar, and forms part of the key motivation for universal grammar*.

As noted in some detail by Chomsky (1959), human language use is also creative in the sense of being free from identifiable stimulus control. It is appropriate to a situation, but it is not caused by it. A traditional behaviourist account of the response 'Dutch' to a painting on the wall would be to say that the speaker was under the stimulus control of the painting's 'Dutchness'. However, as Chomsky observes, a speaker could have just as easily responded 'It's tilted', 'I thought you liked abstracts' or an infinite number of other things.

Chomsky (1966) notes that this freedom from stimulus control was one of the Cartesian arguments for the existence of mind. Machines, once the internal arrangement of the parts and the external conditions are specified, behave in a completely predictable manner (or randomly). However, human linguistic behaviour, like human thought and action more generally, transcends simple 'mechanical'

explanation. Therefore, according to the Cartesians, human linguistic capacities provided evidence for the existence of a second substance 'mind' (as distinct from mere 'body'). Although metaphysical dualism no longer forms part of standard scientific assumptions, these observations regarding linguistic creativity nonetheless do suggest that, in studying language, we are studying one of the foundations on which our humanity rests.

Primary sources

Chomsky, Noam (1959). 'Review of *Verbal Behavior* by B. F. Skinner'. *Language* 35: 26–58.

Chomsky, Noam (1966). *Cartesian Linguistics: A Chapter in the History of Rationalist Thought*. New York: Harper & Row. Reprinted (2002) Christchurch, New Zealand: Cybereditions Corporation.

Geoffrey Poole

DECONSTRUCTION

Deconstruction is an approach to doing philosophy that subverts just about everything mainstream philosophy has stood for through the centuries. It is associated with the name of the controversial Algerian-born French philosopher Jacques Derrida who was strongly influenced by, among others, Friedrich Nietzsche and Martin Heidegger.

See also: Analytic Philosophy; Poststructuralism; Structuralism; Truth Theories
Key Thinkers: Derrida, Jacques

The very mention of the word 'deconstruction' causes jitters among many academic philosophers and calls forth derision from others. It is probably true to say that no other term in philosophy has recently been the target of such tireless tirade and misrepresentation. In common parlance, it is often erroneously and dismissively used as though it were just a fancy word for destruction – thus proving the old adage that one can give a dog a bad name and hang it. When Jacques Derrida first employed the word, scarcely could he have imagined that it would soon be at the epicentre of so much controversy and acrimony. From the 1960s on, when Derrida took the world of philosophy by storm, deconstruction became a catchword among academics across a wide spectrum of disciplines, and his influence is felt in areas as diverse as literary criticism, linguistics, sociology, and even such unlikely disciplines as economics and law.

Both Derrida and the movement he started have understandably been the target of scathing criticism, especially from those scholars who, speaking on behalf of the philosophical 'establishment', rightly sensed a potential threat to the way they went about their routine business. However, to call the approach sceptical or downright nihilistic, or to characterise it as just plain philosophical dilettantism, as some critics have done, is to dismiss it without a fair hearing. To regard deconstruction as a form of textual analysis is to give it a left-handed compliment and, in effect to relegate it to the realm of literary criticism – another way of saying it is anything but philosophical.

There is a grain of truth in the claim that deconstruction engages in textual analysis. But it is important to add that, as Derrida himself once remarked, there is nothing outside the text. What Derrida was trying to press home in his trademark claim was that, contrary to conventional thinking on the matter, the reading of a text does not consist in pitting the text against something that is *essentially* of some other order – say, ideas or intentions in the mind of the speaker/writer or a putative reality 'out there'. Instead, a reading of the text is an extension of that very text. That is to say, no text comes out unaffected by its successive readings. Each new reading of the text adds something to that text and is fully incorporated into the text's 'meaning' so that the meaning of the text – to the extent there is such a thing – may be described as that which is constantly undergoing change, despite the illusory sensation that it is the self-same object that one is dealing with on successive occasions.

So what on earth does Derrida mean by deconstruction and exactly how does it work? It has been remarked that it is easier to 'define' deconstruction by saying what it is not, rather than what it is. In a famous text called 'Letter to a Japanese Friend', Derrida wrote that 'deconstruction is neither an *analysis*, nor a *critique*' and, furthermore, it is 'not a method and cannot be transformed into one'. In fact, as it turns out, the very quest for definitions is antithetical to the spirit of deconstruction. This is so because the idea that meanings can be captured and encapsulated in neat definitions is the very hallmark of philosophy in its traditional sense.

Recall, for instance, Socrates's irritating habit of asking his interlocutors to provide him with a definition of, say, 'piety' (as repeatedly shown in Plato's *Dialogues*). Therefore, to the extent that deconstruction seeks to, as it were, 'call the bluff' of philosophy in respect of its time-honoured pretensions, it is only to be expected that it should stubbornly resist every attempt to enclose it in a neat definition.

The idea that one can define one's terms once and for all rests on the assumption that there are such things as meanings that can remain stable over a period of time and which could be captured and 'imprisoned' in the form of rigorous definitions. Well, among other things, deconstruction is, as we have seen, concerned with reminding us that there are no such stable meanings to begin with, and so the quest for definitions is a wild goose chase. Rather, the meaning of a given text is precisely what is *iterable* – a neologism coined by Derrida, meaning that which comes out different every time one repeats it, as bizarre as this might indeed appear at first blush. It is, to use another of Derrida's coinages, determined by *différance*, an amalgam of deferral and difference.

Derrida maintained throughout that deconstruction is a form of close reading, where all that one needs to mobilise is the text's own internal logic. In other words, texts deconstruct themselves as it were when subjected to relentless close reading. All that a reader needs to do is to press ahead with its own internal logic. That logic, Derrida insisted, is built around the notion of logocentrism, the belief that there are stable meanings out there and that it is the business of the reader to tease it out of specific texts.

The process of unravelling a text's putative meaning begins the moment one notices that the dichotomies that a text's author posits in order to construct his arguments are actually relations of hierarchies, often ingeniously camouflaged in order to be presented as symmetric. In other words, it is invariably the case that, in a dichotomous pair, one side is privileged to the detriment of the other. In his book *Of Grammatology* (1967) Derrida illustrated this by showing how one of the founding dichotomies of linguistics – namely, the one that opposes meaning and the linguistic object (say, the text)–is itself the result of a 'textual prestidigitation' at the hands of Ferdinand de Saussure, the discipline's founding father, who postulated it. Initially presented as a symmetric pair, the distinction between signified and signifier reveals itself, upon closer inspection, to be an hierarchical one. This is because the very stability of that sign relation (the sign being, for Saussure, a relation of bond between a signifier and a signified) is predicated upon there being one side of the relation (namely, the signified) not dependent on the other and thus capable of 'standing alone' – unlike the signifier whose contribution to the sign relation is always that of 'pointing to' the other, namely the signified, conceived of as 'auto-sufficient' in that it is the meaning, period.

Derrida extended his deconstructive analysis to other prized dichotomies of structural linguistics such as speech versus writing. He argued that the linguists' preference for speech to the detriment of writing (the 'wandering outcast of linguistics') is yet another demonstration of discipline's complicity with Western philosophy's trademark logocentrism, which in the case of linguistics takes the form of 'phonocentrism'. Using a very subtle line of reasoning, Derrida maintained that the argument frequently used to bolster up the case of speech as the privileged object of scientific linguistics – its spontaneity and authenticity – crumbles as soon as one realises that it is based on the implicit idea that speech is closer to the speaker's intended meaning than writing is. Aristotle condemned writing for being the imitation of what is already an imitation. This means, Derrida insisted, that speech is always already being conceived of along very much the same lines as writing (namely, the representation of something else), so that the very distinction between speech and writing may be said to be based on an unacknowledged notion of 'archwriting'. Furthermore, the so-called intended meanings are themselves being treated as though they were inscribed in the speaker's mind/brain, ready to be scrutinised any time thanks to what is credited with being the distinguishing feature of writing, its permanence over a period of time.

Using analogous reasoning, Derrida argued that such hallowed dichotomies as nature versus culture, philosophy versus literature, science versus myth, reason and unreason, and so forth – the bedrock of much of Western thought – would not survive deconstructive scrutiny. This has, as he rightly foresaw, devastating implications for the very enterprise of philosophy.

Deconstruction is a constant reminder that reason, when pursued relentlessly and with a rigour it is not used to, will ultimately turn against itself. Derridean philosophy of anti-philosophy has impacted such movements as poststructuralism* and postmodernism. But it is important to register that it has, so to speak, been 'hijacked' by both the political left and the right to serve their own respective agendas.

Primary sources

Culler, Jonathan (1982). *On Deconstruction: Theory and Criticism after Structuralism*. Ithaca, NY: Cornell University Press.

Derrida, Jacques (1967). *Of Grammatology*. Trans. Gayatri Spivak. Baltimore: The Johns Hopkins University Press.

Derrida, Jacques (1991). *A Derrida Reader. Between the Blinds*. Ed. Peggy Kamuf. Hertfordshire: Harvester Wheatsheaf.

Norris, Christopher (1982). *Deconstruction: Theory and Practice*. London: Methuen.

Further reading

Wood, David (ed.) (1992). *Derrida: A Critical Reader*. Oxford: Blackwell.

Kanavillil Rajagopalan

DEDUCTION/ INDUCTION

Deduction is a form of reasoning in which one proceeds from general principles or laws to specific cases. Induction is a form of reasoning in which one arrives at general principles or laws by generalising over specific cases.

47

The status and role of these two forms of reasoning/inference in human thought and language have been much discussed in the history of both philosophy and linguistics. No-one doubts that human beings are capable of both kinds of reasoning, but there has been much debate as to exactly what role they play in establishing human knowledge, including linguistic knowledge. Central to these debates has been the role of inductive generalisations. A simple example of an inductive generalisation is the generalisation that the sun comes up every day. We arrive at such generalisations by observing specific events, such as the sun coming up on a specific day, and then generalising over other events which are thought by the observer to count as instances of the same type of event, for example, the sun coming up on subsequent days.

The eighteenth-century philosopher David Hume distinguished between (a) propositions concerning states of affairs that are certain (such as the proposition that 2 + 2 = 4), and (b) propositions which are unlike such mathematical propositions in that they rely on observed objects and events. The latter sorts of proposition include propositions based on inductive generalisations arising from the perception of those objects and events (such as the proposition that the sun comes up every day). Hume argued that these latter types of proposition are less certain. He claimed that inductive generalisations are not well-founded in logic*: from the fact that the sun has come up on all the preceding days of our lives, it does not follow logically that it will come up tomorrow, or, more generally, that there is a valid general law which states that it comes up every day. A clear example of the uncertain nature of inductive generalisations is the case of the generalisation that all swans are white. From the fact that all swans one has previously observed were white, it does not follow that the next swan one will observe will be white. The discovery of black swans in Australia showed that this particular inductive generalisation, once held to be true, was in fact false.

These features of inductive generalisations make inductive reasoning different in kind from deductive reasoning, since deduction *is* founded in logic: in the syllogism 'All men are mortal; Peter is a man; therefore Peter is mortal', the conclusion that Peter is mortal follows logically as a deduction from the premises. Whether the premises are well-founded is another matter: the argument is logically sound. The deduction in the following argument is equally well-founded: (a) 'All rabbits are carnivores', (b) 'Rupert is a rabbit', therefore (c) 'Rupert is a carnivore'. In stating that inductive generalisations have no basis in logic, one need not deny that such generalisations are well-founded psychologically, and Hume's theory of induction was indeed a psychological theory: he argued that repeated observation of the 'same' event causes us to arrive at inductive generalisations. He took that to be a central feature of human psychology.

Hume's theory of induction was later re-examined in the twentieth century by the philosopher Karl Popper (1963 and elsewhere), who argued that no two (or more) events (say, the observation of a flash of lightning) will ever be exactly the same, and that we therefore need to appeal to the idea of two (or more) events counting as 'the-same-for-us' (or indeed, the same for a member of another species, which may not be quite the same thing as it is for our species). Popper argued that human beings are born with an innate propensity to seek out regularities, and that it is this propensity that underlies our capacity to form inductive generalisations. This is similar, if not identical, to Bertrand Russell's claim that induction is 'incapable of being inferred from experience or from other logical principles' (1946: 647). Popper's claim is not to be confused with the doctrine of innate ideas, associated with the work of, among others, René Descartes in the seventeenth century and Noam Chomsky in the twentieth century.

The propensity to seek out regularities is, arguably, intimately connected with our capacity to form categories, and our capacity to take a specific event on a specific occasion to be a token of a type, in the sense invoked by the twentieth-century American philosopher Charles Saunders Peirce. If one takes, say, a specific flash of lightning to be a token of the type 'flash of lightning', or a specific speech sound token (say, a [t] uttered on a specific occasion) to be a token of the type '[t]', then one's perceptual system is functioning on the basis of categories, and these are said by many to play a central role in human perception, including speech perception. Central to the formation of inductive generalisations and the formation of categories is the notion of similarity: in order to take two events or objects to be instances of the same thing, we need to be able to perceive similarity between those instances. That capacity to perceive similarities may well be innate, and is arguably at the heart of much of human cognition. It appears to underlie our capacity to establish similes and metaphors* which linguists such as George Lakoff take to lie at the heart of human language.

There has been much discussion of the role of deduction and induction in the field of child language acquisition. Chomsky's approach to the child's linguistic development is founded on his linguistic rationalism (otherwise known as linguistic nativism): he postulates innate linguistic knowledge, often referred to as an innate language module or faculty, and also referred to by many as universal grammar*. The child is said by Chomsky to be born with an innate set of universal linguistic principles which are not, by definition, acquired by the child in his/her interaction with the mind-external world. The input (otherwise known as 'the stimulus') to which the child is exposed is said by Chomsky and his followers to be 'impoverished' in certain ways: it is said to be full of hesitations, false starts, utterances of sentences which are never completed, and so on. Chomsky argues that, given the sheer complexity of adult linguistic knowledge, it could not have been acquired on the basis of this 'impoverished' stimulus alone. Put another way, adult linguistic knowledge is underdetermined by the input. This is the poverty of the stimulus argument for an innate linguistic module of mind. Chomsky has also appealed to what he calls the logical problem of language acquisition. The problem is said to be based on the difficulty of arriving at fully-fledged adult linguistic knowledge on the basis of the supposedly impoverished input/stimulus. The problem is said to be a logical one since the child is born in possession of knowledge of the nature of language, in the form of general linguistic principles and a set of parameters, and is said to deduce the properties of the ambient language. An example of a parameter is the position of the verb in sentence structure. The child is said by Chomskyans to deduce the parameter settings in universal grammar, thus yielding the specific language he/she is being exposed to.

Deduction is thus central to Chomsky's vision of child linguistic development. Chomskyans, such as Smith (2004), argue that general learning mechanisms play a very limited role in that development. The capacity for inductive generalisation forms part of our general learning mechanisms: we can form inductive generalisations in any cognitive domain, from knowing about the seasons to knowing what the traffic might be like at a given point in the day. Because Chomskyans do not take the child's linguistic development to constitute a kind of learning, they play down the role of inductive generalisation in child linguistic development. Equally, they play down the role of our capacity for forming analogical generalisations in

the course of that development. Since Chomsky adopts a version of naturalism, in which a postulated biologically-endowed module of mind, on exposure to the input, undergoes biological growth, linguistic development is said not to be something that the child does; rather, it is something that happens to the child. It is important to note that this is an entirely passive conception of the child's linguistic development. The importance of this lies in the fact that rationalists often depict empiricist approaches to child linguistic development as a passive conception of first language acquisition, a depiction that is at odds with much present-day empiricism. Note too that appeal by rationalists to the act of setting parameters and engaging in deduction runs counter to the claim that the acquisition process does not amount to the child actively doing anything to acquire a first language.

Those who oppose Chomskyan rationalism typically emphasise the role of inductive and analogical generalisation in child language acquisition. Examples of such generalisations are child expressions such as 'Three sheeps comed' ('Three sheep came'), in which the irregular plural 'sheep' and the irregular past tense 'came' are regularised. This suggests that the child has arrived at the regular rules for plural and past-tense formation in English via induction based on repeated exposure to regular forms, followed by analogical extension of the inductive rule to irregular nouns and verbs. The emphasis on analogy and induction is central to the work of linguists such as Joan Bybee, who seek to re-establish the importance of usage (performance, in Chomskyan terms) in understanding the nature of linguistic knowledge. Bybee (2001) argues that frequency of occurrence of specific words in language usage plays a major role in the synchronic state of a given language, and in its historical development. She distinguishes between token frequency, which is the extent to which specific word-forms are uttered, and type frequency (see below). She argues that words with high token frequency, such as the past-tense form 'kept' in English, are more resistant than words with lower token frequency (such as the verb 'weep') to the kind of analogical changes that would yield regularised past-tense forms such as 'keeped': lower-token frequency 'weep' is likely to regularise, via analogy, to 'weeped', whereas higher-token frequency 'keep' is much less likely to be regularised, via analogy, to 'keeped'. Type frequency is defined as the frequency of occurrence of a specific pattern, such as the English past-tense '-ed' pattern, which applies to the vast majority of English verbs. High type frequency is said to determine the productivity of a specific pattern. In this case, the '-ed' pattern is highly likely to be applied to novel word formations (such as the past-tense verb form 'googled') and to borrowed verbs (such as 'nuanced'). Type frequency, like token frequency, is based on inductive and analogical inferences.

Some twenty-first-century child language researchers, such as Michael Tomasello, argue that induction plays a central role in child language acquisition. For Tomasello (2001), the child possesses no innate linguistic knowledge at birth. Rather, the child is said to be born into a world in which

he/she must acquire knowledge of a set of social conventions, including linguistic conventions (such as knowing that the subject precedes the verb in English sentences, or knowing that regular plurals of nouns consist of the singular form with a specific kind of suffix). The child can acquire these conventions by observing the conventional word orders used by other human beings in his/her linguistic environment. Crucial to Tomasello's view of child language acquisition is the social, interactive nature of the child's world, in particular the child's coming to attribute intentions to the people that he/she is interacting with, along with the child's ability to have intentions towards those intentions.

Not all inductive reasoning is conscious. While adults and children alike can engage in explicit learning, involving conscious reasoning, there is a form of implicit learning which even very young infants (in the first year of life) can engage in. This kind of learning rests on the human capacity to extract probabilities from speech input, such as probabilities about likely sequences of words and speech sounds. For instance, children in the first year of life have been shown to prefer made-up words which conform to the phonotactic constraints of the language they are being exposed to. By 'phonotactic constraints' is meant the constraints on sequences of sounds in the syllable structure of words. The sequences /pr/, /pl/, /tr/, /kr/, /kl/ are all permissible sequences at the beginning of words in English, but the sequences /pn/, /ps/, /tl/ and many others are not. Infants in the first year of life prefer made-up words which contain the permissible, rather than the non-permissible, sequences. This is because they have the capacity to tune in to the high frequency of the permissible sequences and to extract the phonotactic patterns. Infants are capable of this kind of probabilistic (otherwise known as stochastic) learning without conscious effort. The existence of this kind of unconscious inductive learning has been used by opponents of Chomskyan nativism to show that the stimulus which the child is exposed to is rich in information, which the child can access, rather than impoverished, as claimed by supporters of linguistic nativism.

One of Chomsky's fiercest critics, the British linguist Geoffrey Sampson, adopts an empiricist approach to child language acquisition. Sampson, like Tomasello, and unlike Chomsky, argues that children learn language, and that they do so in the same way as they learn anything else: using general learning mechanisms. The most central part of child language acquisition, for Sampson, is the hypothetico-deductive method: the child is said to come up with hypotheses as to the nature of the language he/she is being exposed to, and then uses the capacity for deduction to deduce testable claims about the structure of that language. These are then said to be tested against the data the child is exposed to. The child can then modify or abandon his/her hypotheses about the structure of that language, and thus come to learn the language. This is the view that the child is 'a little scientist' in his/her attempts at coming to grasp the structure of his/her native language. This emphasis on the hypothetico-deductive method is central to the work of Popper, whose ideas in the philosophy of science form the basis for Sampson's empiricism. Interestingly, Sampson and Chomsky both stress the role of deduction in the child's linguistic development, but for very different reasons, and in different ways. Note that earlier claims by Chomskyans that the child is a little scientist, whose hypotheses are constrained by a postulated innate language acquisition device, run counter to the present-day view of Chomsky that the child's linguistic development is entirely passive.

Appeal to the hypothetico-deductive method in the child's conceptual and linguistic development can be found in current work by Alison Gopnik. She proposes a 'theory theory' of child development: the child is said to be actively constructing theories about the surrounding world, including the ambient language. Gopnik (2001) reports on experiments which seem to show that certain stages in the child's conceptual development, such as the capacity to grasp the idea of a means towards an end, come on stream just ahead of the relevant child's expressions denoting such notions. This work seems to suggest that, for such stages in conceptual development, it is the concept which comes first, followed by an utterance-type for that concept. Gopnik also argues for a version of the Sapir-Whorf hypothesis, according to which aspects of the structure of the ambient language will induce the child to conceptualise certain kinds of events and objects in specific ways. For instance, in a language such as Korean, ellipsis of nouns is much more common than in English. Because of this, a child of fifteen to twenty-one months acquiring Korean monolingually will be delayed in the 'naming explosion' stage, and on categorisation tasks, in comparison with a child of the same age acquiring English monolingually. But these Korean-acquiring infants are advanced on means-ends abilities in comparison with English-acquiring infants of the same age. Gopnik claims that these differences in development are the result of the child using the hypothetico-deductive process to arrive at conclusions about the shape of the ambient language and the nature of the world they inhabit.

Current work by Annette Karmiloff-Smith (1998), who works in the tradition established by Jean Piaget, adopts a version of constructivism with respect to child development. She argues that there is no innate language module, but there may well be innate biases in different cognitive domains (such as the recognition of familiar faces). These biases are said to develop with training on the environment: the child's perceptual input is said to shape those biases into domain-specific cognitive capacities which appear modular in nature (such as the face recognition module). Inductive generalisations play a role in this approach to child development, since the child's initial biases are said to become increasingly richly developed as a result of training on specific sorts of input, where repeated exposure to specific kinds of sensory event results in the forming of inductive generalisations in that domain.

The issue of the respective roles of induction and deduction in the construction of linguistic knowledge remains a central topic of research and debate in contemporary language study.

Primary sources

Bybee, Joan (2001). *Phonology and Language Use*. Cambridge: Cambridge University Press.

Chomsky, Noam (2000). *New Horizons in the Study of Language and Mind*. Cambridge: Cambridge University Press.

Gopnik, Alison (2001). 'Theories, language and culture: Whorf without wincing'. In M. Bowerman and S. Levinson (eds), *Language Acquisition and Conceptual Development*. Cambridge: Cambridge University Press.

Hume, D. (1748). *An Enquiry Concerning Human Understanding*. Reprinted in A. Flew (ed.) (1962), *David Hume On Human Nature and The Understanding*. London: Collier Macmillan.

Karmiloff-Smith, Annette (1998). 'Development itself is the key to understanding developmental disorders'. In *Trends in Cognitive Sciences* 2. Reprinted in M. Tomasello and E. Bates (eds) (2001), *Language Development: The Essential Readings*. Oxford: Blackwell, 331–50.

Popper, Karl R. (1963). *Conjectures and Refutation*. London. Routledge and Kegan Paul.

Russell, Bertrand (1946). *The History of Western Philosophy*. London: Routledge (2004).

Sampson, Geoffrey (1997). *Educating Eve: The 'Language Instinct' Debate'*. London: Cassell.

Sapir, Edward (1921). *Language: An Introduction to the Study of Speech*. New York: Harcourt Brace.

Tomasello, Michael (2001). 'Perceiving intentions and learning words in the second year of life'. In M. Tomasello and

E. Bates (eds), *Language Development: The Essential Readings*. Oxford: Blackwell. 132–58.

Further reading

Pinker, S. (1994). *The Language Instinct*. London: Penguin.

Pullum, G. K. and B. Scholz (2002). 'Empirical assessment of stimulus poverty arguments'. *The Linguistic Review* 19: 9–50.

Sampson, G. (2002). 'Exploring the richness of the stimulus'. *The Linguistic Review* 19: 73–104.

Scholz, B. and G. K. Pullum (2002). 'Searching for arguments to support linguistic nativism'. *The Linguistic Review* 19: 185–223.

Smith, Neil (2004). *Chomsky: Ideas and Ideals*. Second edition. Cambridge: Cambridge University Press.

Philip Carr

DEFINITE DESCRIPTIONS

Denoting phrases that are introduced by the definite article 'the', or by a possessive such as 'my' or 'Sherlock Holmes's'. Bertrand Russell's logical analysis of sentences containing definite descriptions has been highly influential, and highly controversial, throughout the past century.

See also: Analytic Philosophy; Connotation/Denotation; Logic; Logical Form; Names; Ordinary Language Philosophy; Presupposition; Propositions; Sense/Reference

Key Thinkers: Frege, Gottlob; Russell, Bertrand; Strawson, P. F.

In 1905 Bertrand Russell published an article drawing attention to what he saw as some specific and philosophically interesting properties of definite descriptions. Phrases introduced by 'the' appear to indicate not only the existence but also the uniqueness of some entity. In this respect they can be contrasted with indefinite descriptions; 'the leader of the free world' conveys the idea that there is only one such person, while 'a leader of the free world' does not. According to Frege's account of meaning, definite descriptions should be treated as names*, having both a sense and a reference. In opposition to this analysis, Russell draws attention to the problem of definite descriptions that do not have any actual reference in the world; 'a phrase may be denoting, and yet not denote anything' (1905: 471).

Russell discusses this problem in relation to his now-famous example 'the present king of France is bald'. According to Frege's account, this sentence expresses a simple proposition of subject-predicate form. Since the subject fails to refer, the proposition as a whole should fail to have a truth value*; it should be nonsense. Russell argues against this reading on the grounds that 'it is not nonsense, since it is plainly false' (1905: 484). This can be explained, he claims, once we realise that definite descriptions do not operate in the same way as names. In fact, it is not appropriate to discuss their meaning in isolation; the meaning of a definite description can be considered only in relation to the sentence in which it appears. The presence of the definite description ensures that the logical form of the sentence is a complex set of propositions that concern existence and uniqueness as well as baldness. The logical form of 'the present king of France is bald' could be paraphrased as 'there is an entity x such that x is the present king of France, no entity that is not equivalent to x is the present king of France, and x is bald', or more informally 'there is one, and only one, king of France, and he is bald'.

This analysis allowed Russell to explain his conviction that the sentence is false. The simple proposition that a present king of France exists is false. This is sufficient to make the logical form* of the sentence, which is a coordination of this and two other propositions, false also. The analysis also allowed Russell to maintain a classical bivalent logic* for language. If 'the present king of France is bald' is false, then logic dictates that 'the present king of France is not bald' must be true. This is indeed the case if the negation is read as having scope over the whole of the logical form: as Russell paraphrases it, the negative sentence can be read as 'it is false that there is an entity which is now king of France and is bald'. The negative sentence is ambiguous, however. On another reading it can be interpreted as 'there is an entity which is now king of France and is not bald', and on this reading it is as false as its positive equivalent.

Russell's theory is very much a product of his analytic approach to philosophy. It draws attention to what he sees as a discrepancy between the grammatical form of a sentence and its logical form. The implication is that where necessary the messy and imperfect constructions of natural language must be 'translated' into logically correct form before they can provide suitable subject matter for philosophical analysis. This has been the cause of a number of responses to Russell. Perhaps the most significant of these has been that put forward by Peter Strawson in his 1950 article 'On referring'. Coming from a background in ordinary language philosophy* (OLP), Strawson criticises Russell for being obsessed with logic and mathematics, at the expense of attending to the realities of natural language. Russell was overlooking important facts about the ways in which speakers actually use expressions containing definite descriptions; as Strawson puts it, '"mentioning", or "referring", is not something an expression does; it is something that someone can use an expression to do' (1950: 326).

Strawson claims that someone encountering an utterance of 'the present king of France is bald' would not be likely to reply 'that's false', as Russell's account would seem to predict. Rather they would be stuck for a response of any kind, feeling that there was something badly wrong with this statement; the question of whether it is true or false would just not arise. For Strawson, the proposition that there exists a present king of France is not part of the logical form of the statement, but is a presupposition* attached to its use. It is necessary for this presupposition to be fulfilled for the sentence to be either true or false. Hence both 'the present king of France is bald' and 'the present king of France is not bald' must be categorised as neither true nor false. By allowing that some statements can lack a truth value* in certain contexts of use, Strawson was arguing that natural language did not conform to the usual laws of logic; it should be studied and analysed on its own terms. Russell strongly rejected this conclusion, arguing in a response to Strawson that 'common speech' must be modified before it is fit for philosophy. He points out that 'my theory of descriptions was never intended as an analysis of the state of mind of those who utter sentences containing descriptions' (1957: 388).

Keith Donnellan (1966) also criticises Russell for being unable to account for the intentions and purposes with which people actually use definite descriptions in everyday language. He draws attention to a distinction between two different ways in which definite descriptions are used, the referential and the attributive uses. Used referentially, definite descriptions pick out an individual in order to say something about that individual. A person who uses a definite description attributively 'states something about whoever or whatever is the so-and-so' (1966: 285). If someone sees a distinguished-looking man drinking from a martini glass at a party and asks 'Who is the man drinking a martini?', that person is using the definite description referentially. In this case the particular attribute ascribed to the individual is not very important; the speaker would still successfully have referred to the distinguished-looking man even if it turned out that he had only water in his glass. The same definite description, in the same sentence, could also be used attributively. If the chairman of the teetotallers' society is informed that someone is drinking a cocktail at their Christmas party, he might ask 'Who is the man drinking a martini?' in order to establish the identity of the culprit. In this case the attribute ascribed to the individual is all-important. If it turned out that the individual in this case was drinking only water, then there is no possible right answer to the chairman's question. Donnellan also discusses examples of definite descriptions introduced not by 'the', but by possessives: examples such as 'Smith's murderer is insane'. He argues that, for different reasons, neither Russell's nor Strawson's account can adequately handle the distinction between referential and attributive uses of definite descriptions.

Despite criticisms such as these, Russell's theory of definite descriptions has been widely regarded as an exemplary application of analytic philosophy*. It is a measure of the continuing importance of 'On denoting' in the philosophy of language that a special edition of *Mind* was devoted to commemorating the centenary of its publication. At the start of his contribution to this edition, Stephen Schiffer comments that Russell's article not only contributed to defining a new philosophy of language, but also remains the dominant theory of definite descriptions in the present day.

Primary sources

Donnellan, Keith (1966). 'Reference and definite descriptions'. *Philosophical Review* 75: 281–304.

Frege, Gottlob (1892). 'On sense and meaning'. In Peter Geach and Max

Black (eds) (1980), *Translations from the Philosophical Writings of Gottlob Frege*. Oxford: Blackwell. (First edition, 1952.) 56–78.

Russell, Bertrand (1905). 'On denoting'. *Mind* 14: 479–99.

Russell, Bertrand (1957). 'Mr. Strawson on referring'. *Mind* 66: 385–9.

Strawson, P.F. (1950). 'On referring'. *Mind* 59: 320–44.

Further reading

Bezuidenhout, A. and M. Reimer (eds) (2004). *Descriptions: Semantic and Pragmatic Perspectives*. Oxford: Oxford University Press.

Devitt, Michael and Kim Sterelny (1999). *Language and Reality*. Second edition. Cambridge, MA: MIT Press. Chapter 3.

Evans, Gareth (1982). *The Varieties of Reference*. Oxford: Oxford University Press.

Ostertag, G. (1998). *Definite Descriptions: A Reader*. Cambridge, MA: MIT Press.

Schiffer, Stephen (2005). 'Russell's theory of definite descriptions'. *Mind* 114: 1135–83.

Siobhan Chapman

DESCRIPTIVISM

Primarily a synchronic method of linguistic analysis in which the structure and variation of written and spoken language are portrayed dispassionately and non-judgementally. Advocates of descriptivism, borrowing from methodology employed by linguists in the nineteenth century, furthered the development of linguistics as a science and focused on cataloguing and characterising – not judging or criticising – language produced within a particular speech community.

See also: Langue/Parole; Structuralism; Transformational-Generative Grammar
Key Thinkers: Bloomfield, Leonard; Boas, Franz; Brugmann, Karl; Chomsky, Noam; Halliday, M. A. K.; Hockett, Charles; Labov, William; Pike, Kenneth; Rask, Rasmus; Sapir, Edward; Saussure, Ferdinand de

Descriptivism became an important trend in linguistics after 1900. Its theories and principles support an open attitude toward language and linguistic study. It is opposed to prescriptivism, the term most often used to refer to a linguistic school of thought in which individuals seek to promote one particular variety of a language, formulate its rules, and enforce adherence to those rules. Descriptive linguists strive to present a picture of language as complete as possible as it actually exists at a specific point in time and place; they first describe observable facts about a particular spoken and written language and note generalisations about that information. They then draw conclusions about that language and tie their conclusions to an analysis of human language in general.

Nineteenth-century European linguists such as Karl Brugmann and Rasmus Rask moved the study of language away from 'fanciful' notions of philosophy or folklore to a more disciplined analysis of written language. Although these scholars concentrated on diachronic studies of

European languages, their systematic, scientific approach appealed to early twentieth-century linguists such as Franz Boas, Edward Sapir and Ferdinand de Saussure, who refined the methodology and used it to present synchronic analyses of various languages, including those of North American Indian tribes. Descriptivism is especially associated with Leonard Bloomfield, Charles Hockett, William Labov and Kenneth Pike, who established procedures for examining phonology, morphology, syntax and semantics, and who insisted that linguists eliminate value judgements from their studies and avoid social, cultural and moral grandstanding. They believed that linguists should observe actual speech in linguistic communities, form hypotheses about common trends in language and interrelationships between various parts of language, and test their hypotheses.

The heyday of descriptivism spanned the years 1930 to 1960. Afterwards, an increasing number of linguists found the approach too limiting. For example, in the 1960s Noam Chomsky and supporters of transformational-generative linguistics expressed the view that scholars should investigate speakers' unconscious awareness and knowledge of their language's abstract system of rules. In the 1970s M. A. K. Halliday and other sociolinguists asserted that language could not be studied and explained without examining the structure of the society in which it is spoken. Regardless of reservations or criticisms, the openness, inclusiveness and rigour of descriptivism continue to provoke and inform linguistic debate into the twenty-first century.

Primary sources

Bloomfield, Leonard (1933). *Language*. New York: Henry Holt.
Hockett, Charles Francis (1958). *A Course in Modern Linguistics*. New York: Macmillan.

Further reading

Harris, Zellig (1951). *Methods in Structural Linguistics*. Chicago: University of Chicago Press.
Hudson, R. A. (1980). *Sociolinguistics*. Cambridge: Cambridge University Press.
Newmeyer, Frederick J. (1996). *Generative Linguistics*. London: Routledge.
Pedersen, Holger (1931). *Linguistic Science in the Nineteenth Century: Methods and Results*. Trans. John Webster Spargo. Cambridge, MA: Harvard University Press.

David V. Witkosky

(CRITICAL) DISCOURSE ANALYSIS

A term applied to a broad and heterogeneous range of approaches to language which share a family resemblance in their focus on the linguistic characteristics, organisational patterns and communicative functions in context of naturally-occurring text, be it spoken or written (or signed). It has been argued that the centre of gravity of linguistic study has shifted over the past thirty years from the sentence to the text, that is, from syntax to discourse; this shift reflects an increasing acceptance that linguistics should be concerned with describing and explaining language in use.

See also: Conversation Analysis; Corpora; Implicature; Integrationism; Langue/Parole; Politeness; Relevance Theory; Systemic-Functional Grammar; Speech Act Theory
Key Thinkers: Austin, J. L.; Bakhtin, Mikhail; Cameron, Deborah; Grice, H. P.; Halliday, M. A. K; Labov, William; Sacks, Harvey; Sinclair, John; Tannen, Deborah

Discourse analysis is often defined as the analysis of language beyond the sentence. This is over-simple, but it has the merit of making clear how it differs from traditional linguistics centred around syntax, since the sentence is accepted as the maximum domain within which syntactic structures operate. A further crucial difference is that, whereas theoretical linguistics has, since Ferdinand de Saussure, insisted on the autonomy of linguistics and attempted to isolate it from other fields by strictly circumscribing its domain, discourse analysis is strongly oriented towards interdisciplinarity. It makes contact, and partly overlaps, with a wide spectrum of other social sciences including social and cognitive psychology, sociology, ethnography, anthropology, pedagogy and communication studies. In turn, it has been applied in those other fields (and in some cases it has then lost almost all characteristics that relate it to linguistics as a discipline). A core feature of 'linguistic' discourse analysis is that the language itself

remains a central focus. One consequence of this openness to other disciplines, however, is that it is sometimes difficult to trace the limits of what is and is not included in discourse analysis.

This indeterminacy is compounded by the inherently multifaceted nature of discourse, which can be approached at a micro level, such as exploring how each utterance in turn relates to the next in an interaction, at a macro level, for example investigating the discourse of medicine from the perspective of its role as a form of regulative control within a society, or anything in between. It is reflected in the number of terms which can be seen as alternative labels (although many of the practitioners would stress the differences): discourse studies, text analysis, text linguistics, register analysis, genre analysis and so on. It is also reflected in uncertainty over the boundaries between pragmatics and discourse analysis, and over whether approaches such as speech act theory* or conversation analysis* come under the umbrella of discourse analysis, or are compatible but separate fields of inquiry (the plurality of views can be seen simply by typing 'discourse analysis' into an Internet search engine such as Google and opening the first five or six links in the list). It is therefore perhaps best to think of discourse analysis less as a unified approach and more as a predisposition on the part of the linguist to aim to relate language forms to their contexts of use. What is striking is that this predisposition has come to dominate linguistic inquiry in a way that would have seemed unlikely in the early days when the structural linguistics of Bloomfield, Chomsky and others was exerting its hegemony.

The first use of the term 'discourse analysis' is generally ascribed to Zellig Harris in a 1952 paper. However, his paper did not set an agenda that discourse analysis has followed since. Although he focused on structure above the sentence, his aim was to extend existing methods for analysing sentence structures, based purely on distribution with no recourse to meaning, to the analysis of texts. A pioneer whose contribution is recognised as more relevant is T. F. Mitchell who, in a 1957 article, identified functional stages in interactions between buyers and sellers in a particular cultural context. This study had certain key features that came to be characteristic of much discourse analysis: it analysed naturally-occurring text; it worked at text level; it explored how discourse is organised to carry out the communicative purposes of the interactants, particularly by highlighting the ways in which each stage served different functions but all contributed to the achievement of the interactants' goals; it demonstrated that such interactions are not randomly recreated each time but follow conventions that are accepted as appropriate by, and reflect the norms of behaviour of, members of that culture; and it identified linguistic signals that distinguished each stage of the interaction.

One of the most significant starting points in the study of language beyond the sentence was the publication of Michael Halliday and Ruqaiya Hasan's 1976 book on cohesion. This explored the non-structural cohesive links which play a central part in tying sentences together into a text ('non-structural' in the sense that they cannot be adequately described in terms of clause structures such as subject-verb-object). These include conjuncts (for example, 'However'), reference items (for example 'These' at the start of the present sentence referring back to 'links' in the preceding sentence), and repetition (for example, the phrase 'language beyond the sentence' above is repeated from an earlier paragraph to signal the continuity of topic). Halliday and Hasan's definition of 'text' (1976: 2) marked a conscious departure from the concerns of structural linguistics: 'A text is best regarded as a semantic unit: a unit not of form but of meaning.'

Although much work was done from the late 1960s on that laid the foundations for discourse analysis, the first explicit introduction to the field was Malcolm Coulthard's 1977 book, which was soon followed by other ground-breaking volumes by Beaugrande and Dressler (1981), Brown and Yule (1983) and Stubbs (1983). There are naturally areas of overlap, but the differences between these four books reflect some of the most important directions in which discourse analysis developed. For Coulthard, whose treatment was inspired by the findings of an earlier study that he and John Sinclair had carried out into the classroom language of teachers and pupils, 'discourse' essentially refers to spoken interaction: he draws on work in speech act theory* and other areas of pragmatics, and in conversation analysis*, as well as work by Hymes (1974) and others on the ethnography of speaking, and by Labov (1972) and others on sociolinguistics. Coulthard is particularly interested in the structure of exchanges (multi-part stretches of conversation that form functional units, such as question-answer-acknowledgement), and the ways in which utterances constrain what can follow them, and provide the context in which the following utterances make sense. Beaugrande and Dressler, on the other hand, focus on the general characteristics of texts, with more attention to written text. They outline seven 'standards of textuality' which distinguish texts from non-texts. They argue that, to be accepted as a text, a stretch of discourse must have qualities such as cohesion (largely in Halliday and Hasan's sense), coherence (recognisable unity of content) and situationality (recognisable appropriacy to the communicative situation). Brown and Yule establish a distinction between text-as-product and discourse-as-process: that is, they see 'text' as the record of a process of communication, while 'discourse' is the process itself. This leads them to place emphasis on the psycholinguistic processing aspects of discourse: the ways in which producers organise their messages so as to guide receivers to the intended meaning, and receivers use their background knowledge and powers of inference to construct meaning. Finally, as the subtitle of his book ('the sociolinguistic analysis of natural language') indicates, Stubbs is concerned with the ways in which discourse can only be fully analysed if it is situated in its sociocultural context. Like Coulthard, he explores speech acts and exchange structure, but he also highlights the ethnographic dimension, and devotes much space to methodological issues of collecting, transcribing and analysing data. Such issues are generally of little relevance to theoretical linguists, who rely on intuition; but they are crucial for discourse analysts, for whom data is the starting point of inquiry.

Between them, the four books thus cover 'text'-oriented aspects of speech (how utterances function in relation to each other) and writing (what makes a text hang together as a text), 'process'-oriented aspects (how producers and receivers construct meaning collaboratively) and 'context'-oriented aspects (how discourse reflects and constructs social contexts of use). These four lines of inquiry, sometimes pursued separately but often combined in the same study, were to provide rich ground for discourse analysis over the following decades.

At around the same time as these volumes were appearing, further impetus for the focus on discourse came from applied linguistics and more specifically, from the teaching of English for Specific Purposes (ESP), which expanded dramatically from the 1980s on. Teachers trying to help their students cope with, for example, writing academic articles in English, soon realised that it was not enough to teach them to produce grammatically correct sentences. They needed to be shown how to write texts in the ways that were conventionally accepted in their field. This involved, among many other things, knowing how to organise their text following accepted patterns, such as the IMRAD (introduction, methods, results and discussion) format of scientific research articles, and how to deploy language choices appropriately in different stages of the text – for example, in an academic paper, using tense in the literature review to show the degree of centrality of cited work to their own research, or using modality* to adjust the strength of claims in the discussion section. Since traditional grammar did not cover such topics, many ESP teachers became discourse analysts in order to work out what their students needed to know: they were enthusiastic consumers of the growing research in the field, and they applied it and fed their insights back into the discipline, enriching and extending it. Probably the best-known example of the ESP discourse analysis tradition is John Swales's 1990 book *Genre Analysis*, based on research going back to the late 1970s, but this is only one representative of the huge body of work arising from the educational needs of learners of English.

At the same period, the educational context in Australia inspired a slightly different kind of discourse analysis, also under the label 'genre analysis'. Jim Martin and his colleagues (for example, in Martin 1985/1989) applied systemic-functional grammar* in investigating the genres that pupils and students are required to master in their mother tongue. Their work has a very strong sociocultural orientation: Martin's definition of genre is that it is 'a staged, goal-oriented, purposeful activity in which speakers engage as members of our culture . . . Culture seen in these terms can be defined as a set of generically interpretable activities' (1985: 25). Education is in essence the process of helping children to extend the range of genres in which they can operate

successfully and in order for this process to be implemented effectively, the genres need to be analysed and described in a way that simultaneously uncovers the functions that language serves in a particular genre and shows the place of that genre in relation to other genres in the culture.

The stages (or, in Swales's terms, the moves) of a genre are identified in terms of their function in achieving the overall communicative aim. The more delicate description of the language choices in the stages then involves register analysis. A register is seen as a variety of language associated with particular communicative contexts which members of a culture recognise as recurring in accepted patterns: for example, classroom interactions, school textbooks, recipes, news broadcasts, research articles and so on. All registers use the same language system (for example, research articles and recipes in English are recognisably in the same language), but the probabilities of occurrence of particular configurations of grammatical and lexical choices from the system vary from register to register. To take a simple example, recipes (in the instruction stage) have a markedly high number of imperatives of verbs of action ('mix', 'add', and so on); research articles, on the other hand, have many fewer imperatives, and the verbs in these cases are from a small conventional set referring to mental processes ('see', 'consider', and so on). Martin and Rose (2003) is an accessible introduction to this view of genre and register.

By the mid-1980s, discourse analysis had already developed much of its all-encompassing nature. It was certainly losing overall coherence through the proliferation of often-conflicting methodologies and assumptions about language, society and the main goals of the analysis, but at the same time it was gaining strength through the sheer range of topics that could be covered and through the increasing sophistication of the analytical methods on offer. A sense of the diversity can be gained by inspecting the spectrum of areas covered in surveys of discourse analysis such as those edited by van Dijk (1985) and by Schiffrin et al. (2003). The diversity can also be seen by comparing publications such as (to take just two examples fairly randomly) Georgakopoulou and Goutsos (1997), which keeps to a firmly text-linguistic approach and highlights especially the linguistic and organisational differences between narrative and non-narrative discourse, and Wetherell et al. (2001), a reader designed to introduce discourse analysis to students of the social sciences and oriented strongly towards ethnographic and socio-cultural issues. The discipline is also served by an increasingly wide selection of journals including *Discourse Studies*, *Discourse and Society*, *Text & Talk* and others.

One of the more recent manifestations of discourse analysis that is worth special mention has been in the form of critical discourse analysis (CDA), as developed by scholars such as Norman Fairclough (1995), Teun van Dijk and Ruth Wodak. This starts from the basic constructionist assumption in most discourse analysis that discourse inherently functions to construct and reproduce social identity and norms (that is, discourse does not simply reflect existing external 'facts', it plays a central role in constructing the world as we see it). However, CDA goes further in focusing especially on the role of discourse in constructing and reproducing social inequalities as embodied, for example, in racial and sexual discrimination. Certain forms of discourse are available to those with power, while other forms of discourse construct the users as (relatively) powerless. To take a simple example, each time someone fills in a tax return, providing the information required in the format specified, they are accepting and thereby reaffirming the authority of the institution controlling their behaviour. This seems completely natural, and most people do not take a resistant attitude, whatever their feelings about paying tax. The discourse embodied in tax forms and the like has become so naturalised that we no longer notice the implications, in terms of reinforcing the unequal distribution of power, of doing as we are told – that is, of playing our assigned roles in a discourse event. The set of naturalised assumptions about the 'state of things' with which language users work, and which are reflected in the language they use, are seen as making up the users' ideology. The more inequality is built into one's ideology – that is, the less obvious it is – the more difficult it is to resist or even to question. CDA practitioners set themselves the task of using various forms of analysis to bring to light the ideological assumptions underlying any discourse, particularly those which embody dominant forces in the society.

As the above outline makes clear, it is difficult in the scope of this article to provide a straightforward overview of what discourse analysis is. The lack of a clearly-defined domain has been the focus of much criticism over the years, together with the complaint (however elegantly expressed) that discourse analysis is not 'real linguistics' but simply impressionistic commentary. It is certainly true that the centrality of theoretically-grounded analysis of language is sometimes overlooked: Antaki et al. (2002) is both a useful summary of the problems and a reminder that they need to be avoided. However, the achievements of discourse analysis have proved its robustness: they have shown that it is as rigorous as other social sciences in its study of language in its contexts of use, and that this can provide uniquely valuable insights into how we conduct our lives through language.

Primary sources

Beaugrande, Robert de and Wolfgang Dressler (1981). *Introduction to Text Linguistics*. London: Longman.

Brown, Gillian and George Yule (1983). *Discourse Analysis*. Cambridge: Cambridge University Press.

Coulthard, Malcolm (1977). *An Introduction to Discourse Analysis*. London: Longman. Second edition 1985.

Fairclough, Norman (1995). *Critical Discourse Analysis*. Harlow: Longman.

Georgakopoulou, Alexandra and Dionysis Goutsos (1997). *Discourse Analysis: An introduction*. Edinburgh: Edinburgh University Press.

Halliday, Michael A. K. and Ruqaiya Hasan (1976). *Cohesion in English*. London: Longman.

Martin, J. R. (1985). *Factual Writing: Exploring and Challenging Social Reality*. Geelong, Australia: Deakin University Press. Republished by Oxford University Press 1989.

Schiffrin, Deborah, Deborah Tannen and Heidi E. Hamilton (2003). *The Handbook of Discourse Analysis*. Oxford: Blackwell.

Stubbs, Michael (1983). *Discourse Analysis: The Sociolinguistic Analysis of Natural Language*. Oxford: Basil Blackwell.

Swales, John (1990). *Genre Analysis: English in Academic and Research Settings*. Cambridge: Cambridge University Press.

Van Dijk, Teun A. (ed.) (1985). *Handbook of Discourse Analysis* (four volumes). London: Academic Press.

Wetherell, Margaret, Stephanie Taylor and Simeon J. Yates (2001). *Discourse Theory and Practice: A Reader*. London: Sage.

Further reading

Antaki, Charles, Michael Billig, Derek Edwards and Jonathan Potter (2002). 'Discourse analysis means doing analysis: a critique of six analytic shortcomings'. *Discourse Analysis Online* 2, http://www.shu.ac.uk/daol/articles/open/2002/002/antaki2002002-paper.html (accessed 11 October 2007).

Harris, Zellig (1952). 'Discourse analysis'. *Language* 28: 1–30.

Hymes, Dell (1974). 'Ways of speaking'. In R. Baumann and J. Sherzer (eds) *Explorations in the Ethnography of Speaking*. Cambridge: Cambridge University Press. 433–52.

Labov, William (1972). *Sociolinguistic Patterns*. Philadelphia: University of Pennsylvania Press.

Martin, J. R. and David Rose (2003). *Working with Discourse: Meaning*

Beyond the Clause. London and New York: Continuum.

Mitchell, T. F. (1957). 'The language of buying and selling in Cyrenaica'. *Hesperis* 44: 31–71.

Geoff Thompson

DISTINCTIVE FEATURES

The smallest units of linguistic structure, from which larger units are built, sometimes seen as the attributes by which phonemes* can differ. The idea is fundamental in phonology, where many generalisations are standardly stated in terms of features.

See also: Generative Phonology; Phoneme; Optimality Theory
Key Thinkers: Chomsky, Noam; Jakobson, Roman; Trubetzkoy, N. S.

One of the few areas of phonological consensus is that segments are composed of features. Features play crucial phonological roles, being used (1) to express how segments contrast with each other and (2) what groups of segments ('natural classes') formally have in common, (3) to model what changes in phonological processes in generative phonology*, and (4) in the formulation of constraints in optimality theory*. The Prague Linguistic Circle provided the first detailed expression of the ideas behind feature theory, and relevant ideas occur in American structuralist work. Roman Jakobson, seen as the father of distinctive feature theory, developed these ideas to propose what became, through further reworking by Noam Chomsky and Morris Halle, the standard model.

Although the notions were implicit in earlier phonetic description, Nikolai Trubetzkoy (1939) focused attention on phonology's subsegmental level. Trubetzkoy described 'oppositions' between phonemes, invoking the idea that phonemes are characterised by the contrasts they exhibit in languages. American structuralists also spoke of phonemes' features, principally to oppose the distinctive and non-distinctive properties of languages' indivisible phonemes. Jakobson revised these largely language-specific notions and sought a small language-universal set of features, which exist independently of the segments that they compose.

Trubetzkoy focused on distinctive oppositions – those which signal phonological contrast. These could be privative (a marked property is either present or absent), equipollent (both members are of equal status) or gradual (with several gradations of one property). All Jakobson's features were arguably equipollent, with two values, each characterising a definite property (for example, tense/lax, nasal/oral). Jakobson's work (some collaborative, clearly expressed in Jakobson, Fant and Halle 1952) based features primarily on segments' acoustic properties. Chomsky and Halle (1968) redefined features using principally articulatory definitions, and used them in phonological rules, setting the scene for standard generative phonology. They reinforced features' binary nature, using plus and minus values (for example, [+back], [−nasal]) in underlying representations and virtually all rules.

Phonologists have since refined the set of features, or sought structure in their organisation (to account for group behaviour in processes). Features are now linkable to multiple segments, and sometimes reinterpreted as exclusively privative (and given different names, such as 'autosegments', 'components' or 'elements'). Theory is fundamental in phonology: certain currents now push for a less categorical notion of feature, but these smallest linguistic units are in no danger of being split further.

Primary sources

Chomsky, Noam and Morris Halle (1968). *The Sound Pattern of English*. New York: Harper and Row.
Jakobson, Roman, Gunnar Fant and Morris Halle (1952). *Preliminaries to Speech Analysis*. Cambridge, MA: MIT.
Trubetzkoy, N. S. (1939). *Grundzüge der Phonologie*. Baltaxe. Trans. *Principles of Phonology*, Berkeley: University of California Press, 1969.

Further reading

Anderson, Stephen (1985). *Phonology in the Twentieth Century*. Chicago: University of Chicago Press.

Patrick Honeybone

EMIC/ETIC

Terms coined by Kenneth Pike, from (phon)emic and (phon)etic respectively, to refer to two complementary ways of analysing behavioural data. Emic refers to categorising behaviour from the perspective of the insider in ways that are meaningful to the people producing that behaviour, while etic refers to categorising behaviour from the perspective of an outsider in ways that are applicable to different systems and can be used to compare them. Since the 1950s the terms have gained currency in the humanities and social sciences, especially in the fields of anthropology and cross-cultural psychology.

See also: Phoneme
Key Thinkers: Pike, Kenneth; Sapir, Edward

The emic/etic distinction is part of Pike's theory of tagmemics, according to which verbal and nonverbal aspects of behaviour are inseparable and must be studied in tandem, for the significance of the one frequently can only be discovered through reference to the other. Pike saw the compartmentalisation of levels of analysis prevailing in linguistics as producing only etic analyses, or what is worse, disguising emic categories as etic – for example, as when asking the natives for judgements of sameness/difference necessitating recourse to meaning, while explicitly rejecting meaning as a category external to the linguistic system. By proposing the emic/etic distinction, inspired by Edward Sapir, Pike aimed to increase awareness of the pitfalls of projecting one's own emic categories onto an alien system, and to emphasise the need to keep apart the two perspectives, of the native speaker and of the analyst.

Pike did not, however, perceive a rigid dichotomy between these two perspectives. Rather he recognised a progression from emic to etic, once emic units discovered via analysis of one language are applied to analysis of another. To the extent that they are relevant to the latter, these units constitute part of an etic inventory that is no longer internal to any single language. The International Phonetic Alphabet is an example of such an inventory, while the phonologies of individual languages correspond to the emic systems from which the former is abstracted.

An inventory of etic units is created by the analyst prior to the analysis of the particular language to which it is applied. Etic units correspond to raw observational data, often measurable by instrumental means. Since they do not combine into a system of meaningful contrasts, they are pre-structural. Conversely, emic units result when the raw data are interpreted by natives, though they are not necessarily consciously known (named) by them. They are thus structural and valid for only one language. Combining emic and etic perspectives yields 'a kind of "tri-dimensional understanding" of human behaviour instead of a "flat" etic one' (Pike 1954: 12).

Primary sources

Pike, Kenneth (1954). *Language in Relation to a Unified Theory of the Structure of Human Behaviour*. Glendale, CA: Summer Institute of Linguistics.

Further reading

Headland, Thomas, Kenneth Pike and Marvin Harris (eds) (1990). *Emics and Etics: The Insider/Outsider Debate*. Frontiers of Anthropology. Vol. 7. London: Sage.

Jahoda, Gustav (1977). 'In pursuit of the emic-etic distinction: can we ever capture it?'. In Y. H. Poortinga (ed.), *Basic Problems in Cross-Cultural Psychology*. Amsterdam: Swets & Zeitlinger. 55–63.

Marina Terkourafi

EMPIRICISM/ RATIONALISM

Put simply, empiricism is the view that all knowledge derives from experience; rationalism is a contrasting view in which knowledge comes from reasoning. In epistemology, the branch of philosophy concerning theories of knowledge, empiricism and rationalism are types of position that have been taken about the sources of knowledge, in particular in discussions about what is required for a state to count as knowledge. In psychology and its philosophy, empiricism and rationalism concern the sources of psychological states and capacities that may include, but are not confined to, states of knowledge.

See also: Analytic/Synthetic; Behaviourism; Deduction/Induction; Holism; Innateness; Linguistic Relativity; Logical Positivism; Mentalism; Universal Grammar
Key Thinkers: Berkeley, George; Chomsky, Noam; Descartes, René; Frege, Gottlob; Hume, David; Locke, John

In a general sense, a position is a form of empiricism insofar as it holds that knowledge (or other psychological states and capacities, indicated henceforth: (etc.)) about some particular subject matter, S, derives from experience of that subject matter; and a position is a form of rationalism insofar as it holds that knowledge (etc.) about some particular subject matter, *S*, derives from the use of reason or, more generally, from our rational nature(s). Traditionally, these positions, and disputes among their proponents, have concerned knowledge (etc.) about mind-independent subject matters, about how the world is independent of particular views that we might take about it.

In the twentieth century a central debate between empiricists and rationalists concerned our knowledge of mathematics. Gottlob Frege attempted to show, first, that our knowledge of mathematics is substantive knowledge – knowledge of an independent subject-matter and, second, that mathematics derives from logic* so that our knowledge of mathematics can be seen to derive from the use of (pure) reason. Frege's empiricist predecessors, like J. S. Mill, had attempted to treat mathematical knowledge as deriving from experience. In the face of Frege's critique of that move, his empiricist successors, like A. J. Ayer, attempted to treat mathematical knowledge as derivative from knowledge of meaning and so (they argued) not really a substantive form of knowledge. This debate in turn raised questions about the status of our knowledge of language: is this knowledge derived from reason (more generally, an aspect of our natures as rational beings), or is it rather a form of experiential knowledge?

With respect to the study of language, major disputes between forms of empiricism and rationalism have focused upon our knowledge of meaning (although issues surrounding the structure of language and the possibility of a perfect language – a language designed perfectly to reflect the structure of reason – have also been of some importance). Thus, the empiricist David Hume argued that *ideas* – that is concepts, including the meanings of words – must derive ultimately from *impressions* – experiential input. On the basis of this constraint, Hume argued that we can have no idea corresponding with genuine causation – that is, no idea whose content outstrips our experience of one type of occurrence regular following another type. Similarly, in the twentieth century, logical positivists like Ayer argued that, in order for a sentence to be meaningful, it must be possible to *verify* (or *falsify*) it – to determine whether it is true or false on the basis of experience. Opponents of the logical positivists argued in turn that this *Verification Principle* was not itself verifiable by appeal to experience. Some of these opponents took themselves to be pushing for an empiricism that was even more extreme than that of the positivists: they would argue that this shows that the Verification Principle is itself meaningless and that we need to construct a different form of empiricism. Other opponents argued that knowledge of some very general claims must derive from the use of reason; the latter form of opposition may reasonably be viewed as a form of rationalism.

Three major traditional points of dispute between empiricists and rationalists centre on the following three characteristic rationalist theses: (1) knowledge of a particular subject matter is underwritten by intuition (or rational insight) and deductive reasoning, rather than by experience of that subject matter; (2) knowledge of a particular subject matter is innate (very roughly, determined by nature rather than, for example, by the particular course of experience); and (3) the concepts or ideas that constitute our abilities to think about a particular subject matter are innate. Rationalists about knowledge (etc.) about a particular subject matter characteristically endorse at least one of (1)–(3) with respect to that subject matter. Empiricists about knowledge (etc.) of a particular subject matter characteristically reject (1)–(3) with respect to that subject matter. Since epistemological forms of empiricism and rationalism concern the justification or warrant required for a state to count as knowledge, and not the sources of psychological states and capacities in general, it is possible to adopt psychological forms of each type of position without also adopting epistemological forms. For instance, one might hold that a particular belief is innate – and so be a psychological rationalist with respect to the belief – and also hold that in order to be justified or warranted the innate belief must be supplied with experiential support – and so be an epistemological empiricist with respect to the belief. Alternatively, one might hold that a particular belief is only acquired on the basis of experience, but that the justification or warrant for the belief derives from reason. In that case, one would be a psychological empiricist and an epistemological rationalist.

Two points are worth noting about the approximate account of the two types of position, both pertaining to

its lack of specificity. First, articulating the precise content of a form of empiricism is dependent upon further specification of the notion of experience employed in the approximate account. For instance, one form of empiricism holds that knowledge (etc.) about a particular subject matter derives solely from sense experience of that subject matter – visual, auditory or tactile experience – and not from other forms of experience – introspective experience or religious revelation. Further specification of that form of empiricism would be dependent upon further specification of the boundaries of sensory experience. Correlatively, articulating the precise content of a form of rationalism is dependent upon further specification of the extent of reason or our rational nature(s). Whether a particular form of rationalism is in dispute with a particular form of empiricism depends upon the details of such further specification. In particular, it depends upon whether the type(s) of experience to which appeal is made in characterising the particular form of empiricism includes, or excludes, the outputs of the type(s) of reason, or our rational nature(s) to which appeal is made in characterising the particular form of rationalism.

Second, someone who holds that there are sources of knowledge in addition to experience and reason, or our rational nature(s), might reject empiricism (or rationalism) about a subject matter without endorsing rationalism (or empiricism) about that subject matter. For instance, that person might hold that knowledge about some subject matters depends upon aspects of our non-rational nature(s) that are not sense-perceptual; or that it depends upon non-sensory experience.

There are other dimensions along which particular forms of empiricism or rationalism might vary. But we can see already that classifying a position as a form of empiricism or rationalism is quite unrevealing. And we can also see that there is no such thing as *the* dispute between empiricism and rationalism; rather, there are – or could be – various disputes each taking place between particular forms of each broad type of position.

Finally, we can see that care is required in classifying individual thinkers as empiricists or rationalists, for careless adherence to such a broad scheme of classification can serve to disguise differences between particular members of one of the groups and similarities between members of the different groups. René Descartes, Benedictus de Spinoza and Gottfried Leibniz are often aligned as paradigmatic rationalists, the so-called Continental Rationalists. They are often seen in opposition to John Locke, George Berkeley and David Hume, the so-called British Empiricists, who are often treated as paradigmatic empiricists. However, it is important to look beyond that preliminary classification in coming to a proper appreciation of the works of those important thinkers.

Where a dispute arises between a particular form of empiricism and a particular form of rationalism, the dispute characteristically takes the following general form. The rationalists characteristically offers two types of consideration in favour of their position. The first type of consideration – sometimes known as a 'poverty of the stimulus' or 'poverty of evidence' consideration – is that our knowledge (etc.) about the target subject matter could not have been acquired through, for example, sense experience, so that empiricism is ruled out. The second type of consideration is an account of how the rationalists' favoured source – reason or our rational nature(s) – could have underwritten our acquisition of knowledge (etc.) of the subject matter. For instance, a rationalist about our knowledge of ethics might attempt to account for our knowledge about what we ought to do in a particular case by appeal to our possession of innate knowledge of general ethical principles from which our knowledge about particular cases is derived.

In response to the first type of consideration, empiricists will attempt to argue that experiential resources suffice to explain the knowledge that we in fact possess. Empiricists will develop their response either by attempting to provide an account of how the knowledge (etc.) could have been acquired on the basis of experience, or by arguing that we do not in fact possess the knowledge that rationalists claim we do. For instance, an empiricist about our knowledge of mathematics might attempt to argue that this knowledge is supported by induction from our experiences of groups of objects. And an empiricist about our putative knowledge of ethics might claim that we do not really have such knowledge but only various feelings about particular courses of action. Since such disputes typically concern knowledge (etc.) about a particular mind-independent subject matter, the empiricist might attempt to argue that we have the knowledge that the rationalist claims we do, but that it is knowledge about the operations of our own minds, or relations among our concepts or ideas, rather than about mind-independent reality.

In response to the second type of consideration, the empiricist will attack the rationalist account of how we come to have the knowledge (etc.) that rationalists claim we possess. For instance, the empiricist might follow Locke in attempting to argue that the claim that a piece of knowledge (etc.) is innate is either false or consistent with empiricism. If the rationalist claims that a piece of knowledge (etc.) is innate only if it is possessed by everyone at birth, then the empiricist will point to the absence of that piece of knowledge (etc.) in the very young or the dysfunctional. Alternatively, if the rationalist opts for looser requirements on innateness by counting a piece of knowledge (etc.) as innate if we are born with a capacity to acquire it, then the empiricist will also be willing to accept that all knowledge is innate in that very thin sense. As Locke puts it:

> If the capacity of knowing, be the natural impression contended for, all the truths a man ever comes to know, will, by this account, be every one of them, innate; and this great point will amount to no more, but only an improper way of speaking; which whilst it pretends to assert the contrary, says nothing different from those, who deny innate principles. For nobody, I think, ever denied, that the mind was capable of knowing several truths. (Locke, 1690: book I, chapter II, section 5, p. 61)

The most prominent contemporary defender of a form of rationalism is Noam Chomsky. Chomsky, together with numerous co-workers in linguistics, psychology and philosophy, has used 'poverty of stimulus' considerations in support of the thesis that human knowledge of natural language has a significant innate component. And Chomsky, again together with co-workers in a variety of disciplines, has developed an increasingly detailed account of the development of our knowledge of particular natural languages – for example, particular dialects of English or particular Bantu languages – that makes appeal to innate structures and capacities.

Of course, Chomsky accepts that experience plays some role in the acquisition of knowledge of language, since it would otherwise be a mystery that children typically acquire knowledge of language that enables them to communicate with those whose speech they experienced during acquisition. But he holds that the role of experience is primarily to select from amongst the child's innate repertoire the bits that will be operative in the competence that they come to employ.

Chomsky's form of rationalism has been subjected to both sides of the standard empiricist critique. First, versions of Locke's objection have been pressed, according to which Chomsky's appeal to innate psychological states or capacities either fails to distinguish his position from empiricism or is easily falsified. Because Chomsky aims to provide a detailed, predictive account of the course of acquisition of particular languages, his position appears to avoid the second horn of Locke's dilemma by going beyond the bland claim that we are predisposed to acquire language. And because he provides an account according to which our initial state of knowledge is shaped by experience in the course of normal development, his account avoids falsification by the fact that small children and subjects of abnormal development lack ordinary knowledge of language.

However, important questions remain concerning the precise content of the claim that a basic component of human linguistic capacity or state is innate. And the fact that many theorists who align themselves with either empiricism or rationalism – including Chomsky – agree that both innate and experiential factors play a role in shaping knowledge of language tends to undermine the utility of their classification as empiricists or rationalists. Second, empiricists have attempted to provide accounts of language acquisition that make more limited appeals to innate psychological states and capacities. Some empiricist approaches agree with the rationalist assessment of what the child acquires and attempt to provide accounts of how the child might acquire it more or less solely on the basis of experience. Other empiricist approaches involve an attempt to show that the child acquires less than the rationalist has claimed, so that the task of accounting for their acquisition is made easier for the empiricist. Thus far, no empiricist account has been provided that has anything approaching the depth, detail and coverage of rationalist accounts.

Chomsky's form of rationalism appears to differ in certain respects from some more traditional forms of rationalism. That should not be surprising now that we have recognised the variety of possible rationalist positions. But some of the apparent differences are especially striking and have been taken by some thinkers to undermine Chomsky's classification as a rationalist, or the bearing of his work on the standing of more traditional forms of rationalism.

First, although Chomsky talks of *knowledge* of language, it is not clear that he thinks of this knowledge as the sort of propositional knowledge – knowledge that such-and-such – that is of concern to epistemologists. Some philosophers have thought that the knowledge is really knowledge-how – that is, practical knowledge – like knowledge how to ride a bicycle. Although Chomsky rejects that interpretation, it remains an open question whether he is right to do so. And Chomsky admits other reasons for thinking that the sort of knowledge in question differs from the sort that concerns epistemologists. For instance, he does not think that knowledge of language is justified or warranted and he does not think that we are typically conscious of possessing it; he thinks of it as *tacit* knowledge. Moreover, some of these reasons might also be grounds for thinking that knowledge of language is not really a psychological state, so undermining Chomsky's classification even as a psychological rationalist.

Second, Chomsky does not think that knowledge of language is knowledge about a mind-independent subject matter. Rather, on Chomsky's view, facts about an individual's language are constituted by facts about the individual's psychology, in particular facts about their knowledge of the language. If he were right about this, then it would form another difference between knowledge of language and ordinary propositional knowledge. Third, although Chomsky thinks that knowledge of language is determined as a part of human nature, he does not appear to think that it is determined as a part of our *rational* nature(s). See also the entry on universal grammar*. For a readable introduction to some considerations that support Chomsky's position, see Pinker (1994).

To sum up, let's return to the earlier twentieth-century debate concerning the tenability of empiricist restrictions on the possible meanings of sentences. Recall that the logical positivists argued that meaningfulness coincides with the possibility of verification (or falsification) on the basis of experience. The empiricist position here was that there could be nothing in our knowledge of language, including our knowledge of meaning, that was not put there by experience. Chomsky's work casts doubt on that view. For if Chomsky is right, then our knowledge of language is shaped as much by our biology as by our experience. Moreover, Chomsky's work makes plain that views about possible limits to our knowledge must engage with (experience-based) work in the sciences concerned with human nature or constitution. Hence, even those who seek a more empiricist view about our acquisition of knowledge of language typically seek to support that view by appeal to work in those sciences. Needless to say, the various disputes in this area are far from being resolved.

Primary sources

Berkeley, G. (1975). *Philosophical Works, Including the Works on Vision*. Ed. M. R. Ayers, Everyman edition. London: J. M. Dent.

Chomsky, N. (1988). *Language and Problems of Knowledge*. Cambridge, MA: MIT Press.

Descartes, R. (1641/1984). *Meditations on First Philosophy*. In *The Philosophical Writings of Descartes*, vol. 2. Trans. J. Cottingham, R. Stoothoff and D. Murdoch. Cambridge: Cambridge University Press.

Hume, D. (1748/1999). *An Enquiry Concerning Human Understanding*. Ed. T. L. Beauchamp. Oxford: Oxford University Press.

Leibniz, G. (c. 1704). *New Essays on Human Understanding*. In G. H. R. Parkinson (ed.) (1973), *Leibniz: Philosophical Writings*. Trans. M. Morris and G. H. R. Parkinson London: J. M. Dent and Sons.

Locke, J. (1690/1997). *An Essay on Human Understanding*. Ed R. Woolhouse. London: Penguin Books.

Further reading

Carruthers, P. (1992). *Human Knowledge and Human Nature*. Oxford: Oxford University Press.

Cottingham, J. (1984). *Rationalism*. London: Paladin Books.

Kenny, A. (ed.) (1986). *Rationalism, Empiricism and Idealism*. Oxford: Oxford University Press.

Loeb, L. (1981). *From Descartes to Hume: Continental Metaphysics and the Development of Modern Philosophy*. Ithaca, NY: Cornell University Press.

Pinker, S. (1994). *The Language Instinct*. London: Penguin Books.

Spinoza, B. de (1677/1985). *The Ethics*. In *The Collected Works of Spinoza*, vol. 1.

Ed. and trans. E. Curley. Princeton, NJ: Princeton University Press.

Stich, S. (ed.) (1975). *Innate Ideas*. Berkeley, CA: California University Press.

Guy Longworth

FEMINISM

Feminism is a hotly contested term but it can broadly be described as a range of social movements and theories that have discrimination on the basis of gender as their key concern. Feminist linguistics explores the interrelationship between language and gender.

> *See also*: Conversation Analysis; Deconstruction; (Critical) Discourse Analysis; Political Correctness; Poststructuralism
> *Key Thinkers*: Cameron, Deborah; Tannen, Deborah

Feminist linguistics, or 'language and gender' as the field is more widely known, emerged in the context of the second feminist movement of the 1960s and 1970s. Linguists of the time who were also feminists started to ask what part language played in the widespread discrimination against women. This early work found a focal point in Robin Lakoff's 1975 book *Language and Woman's Place*. The author argued that men and women spoke differently and that those differences were evidence of male domination: women were described as less confident speakers, for instance, who

were silenced and interrupted by men. Another influential study of the area is Pamela's Fishman's 1978 analysis of the home conversations of American couples: she found that women did a lot of the interactional 'shitwork' – as she termed it – that is mundane but sustains relationships, in the same way that they do other mundane work that sustains the family, such as housework.

Some of the researchers of the time did not only argue that male dominance led to gender differences in speech but to female deficiencies. The 'deficit approach' as an extension of the 'dominance approach' was carried over from an earlier period where men were seen as 'default human beings' and everything that deviates from the male norm was seen as deficient. Thus speaking like a woman was not only seen as feminine but, at the same time, as deviating from 'normal' – that is male – speech. It is one of the lasting achievements of this early work to identify the 'double bind' in which women as speakers found themselves: if they talked 'like a lady', they were considered less than a full human being; if they talked like a man, they were considered insufficiently feminine.

By the 1980s the political climate had changed and while the students of these pioneers were still interested in researching the way men and women spoke differently, they were no longer ready to see those differences as an expression of female subjugation and male dominance. Feminism had turned into a social movement that was more focused on celebrating female difference. Consequently the 'dominance' and 'deficit' approaches of the 1960s and 1970s started to be replaced by the 'difference approach'. The key exponent of this approach is best-selling linguist Deborah Tannen. In books such as *That's Not What I Mean* (1986) and *You Just Don't Understand!* (1990), she argues that communication between men and women could best be understood through applying the framework of intercultural communication – for example, the way people who grew up in different parts of the world may sometimes create communication difficulties – but men and women, she argues, have communication difficulties because they operate with different values. Men are apparently driven by competition and women by cooperation. These different values are expressed in different communicative styles, which lead to misunderstandings and fights between the sexes. Representatives of the difference approach were keen to stress that while men and women had different communicative styles, these were equally valid.

By the late 1980s language and gender had changed from an almost esoteric interest of some female linguists to become a thriving research field which was institutionally based in university departments and curricula. However, this high level of research activity also had a surprising side-effect that led to a complete conceptual rethinking of the field: as more and more researchers tested the various claims about female and male speech empirically, differences no longer appeared as clear-cut as they had seemed to exponents of both the dominance and the difference approach. For instance, there was empirical evidence that women talked more than men and equally solid evidence that men talked more than women. At the same time, the universalist underpinnings of the feminist movement started to be questioned by women of colour, the queer movement and others who did not see themselves represented in the stereotypical straight white middle-class US–American woman who seemed to have been taken to represent the prototypical female experience up until then. Both the 'dominance approach' and the 'difference approach' came in for substantial criticism on a number of grounds, particularly for treating 'men' and 'women' as homogeneous categories; for a lack of attention to context; for an unsophisticated understanding of power relations; and for insensitivity to ethnic, racial, social, cultural and linguistic diversity.

As a result, poststructuralist approaches to language and gender started to emerge. Deborah Cameron's book *Feminism and Linguistic Theory* (1985) is often considered a foundational text for this new approach. Poststructuralism* does not start from the assumption that men and women speak differently – it does not even start from the assumption that men and women naturally exist as meaningful categories. Rather it is language that calls the (gendered) identity of speakers into existence. Gender is thus no longer treated as a given but the linguistic concern is now with the way in which gendered subjectivities are constituted in language. Once the question 'how do men and women talk differently?' had become obsolete, feminist linguistics was in a position to focus on new questions.

One such new question is related to the construction of gendered identities in interaction. Such studies have shown that gender is not some form of static identity but changes from context to context: in some contexts gender may not matter at all, in others we may highlight or downplay certain aspects of our gender identities.

Another new question that has been particularly taken up by scholars working in (critical) discourse analysis* centres around the representation of particular types of femininity or masculinity in the media. Media discourses have a central influence on many facets of identity in contemporary societies from gendered risk-taking to gendered parenting. There have also been inquiries into the ways in which gender structures access to linguistic resources. For instance, immigrant women often find it more difficult to learn the majority language as they may have less access to the public spaces where it is taught and used. In other contexts, girls may find it easier to access foreign language learning because it may be discursively constructed as a 'girlie' thing to do while boys are discouraged from language learning because of these very associations.

What all these questions and approaches have in common is that they do not treat gender as given and static but as emergent in context and as being comprised of a range of performances, some of which may be more hegemonic than others. Gender thus turned from a noun into a verb. Language and gender today has a place in probably every sociolinguistics undergraduate class in the world. Despite being highly relevant in areas

such as applied linguistics, feminism and language and gender are only slowly finding their way into language education (Pavlenko et al. 2001). Irrespective of the approach, it is a key characteristic of most feminist linguistics that it is committed to a political cause, namely emancipation in various forms. Since the inception of the field, feminist linguists have not only aimed at describing linguistic practices. They have also been committed in various degrees to engagement with 'the real world' and to challenging practices that disadvantage groups of speakers.

Primary sources

Cameron, Deborah (1992). *Feminism and Linguistic Theory*. London: Macmillan. First edition 1985.

Fishman, Pamela (1978). 'What do couples talk about when they're alone?'. In Douglas Butturff and Edmund L. Epstein (eds), *Women's Language and Style*. Akron, OH: L&S Books. 11–22.

Lakoff, Robin (1975). *Language and Woman's Place*. New York: Harper and Row. (A revised and expanded edition with commentaries by contemporary feminist linguists was edited by Mary Bucholtz and published by Oxford University Press in 2004.)

Tannen, Deborah (1986). *That's Not What I Meant! How Conversational Style Makes or Breaks Relationships*. New York: Ballantine Books.

Tannen, Deborah (1990). *You Just Don't Understand: Women and Men in Conversation*. New York: Ballantine Books.

Further reading

Pavlenko, Aneta, Adrian Blackledge, Ingrid Piller and Marya Teutsch-Dwyer (eds) (2001). *Multilingualism,*

Second Language Learning, and Gender. Berlin and New York: Mouton de Gruyter.

Ingrid Piller

GENERATIVE PHONOLOGY

A branch of generative grammar that aims to establish a set of rules, principles or constraints capable of producing the surface phonetic forms of a language and of modelling the internalised linguistic knowledge of the native speaker. Generative phonology was a central idea in linguistic research throughout the 1960s and although it has undergone reforms and changes in subsequent decades, it continues to be the dominant framework for many developments in phonological theory.

See also: Adequacy; Distinctive Features; Optimality Theory; Transformational-Generative Grammar; Universal Grammar
Key Thinkers: Bloomfield, Leonard; Chomsky, Noam; Jakobson, Roman; Trubetzkoy, N. S.

Generative phonology originated with the work of Noam Chomsky and Morris Halle at the Massachusetts Institute of Technology (MIT) in the late 1950s. It built on N. S. Trubetzkoy's idea of phonemic oppositions and Roman Jakobson's later work on distinctive features*. More specifically it drew on the general aspiration of generative grammar to stipulate a set of rules capable of producing all

and only the surface forms of a natural language, focusing on its speech sounds. As with any such set of rules, the measure of its success was the adequacy* with which it was consistent with underlying linguistic knowledge, known as universal grammar*.

Chomsky and Halle's book *The Sound Pattern of English* (1968), known as 'SPE', is widely regarded as the defining text of generative phonology. In it they attempted to specify the phonological rules underlying the speech sounds of native English speakers. SPE established the standard framework for this type of theory. That framework is as follows: that there are abstract rules determining the actual acoustic output of speech; that the rules apply sequentially to produce a series of derivations resulting in an abstract representation of the phonetic representation; that the phonetics consists of a series of segments that could be exhaustively defined in terms of sets of binary features; that the rules are strictly ordered.

By the 1970s SPE had become a benchmark against which most other work in phonology was measured. But critics began to find problems with some of its basic assumptions. For instance, SPE's focus on abstract rules, rather than detailed phonetic analysis, and the formal complexity of many of its proposals, became stumbling blocks for many linguists. These criticisms led to developments such as 'Natural Generative Phonology', which attempted to establish rules that were more psychologically plausible than the abstractions of SPE. Later work on optimality theory* did away with rigid sequential derivation in favour of an algorithm for selecting surface forms from a set of possible alternatives.

In the twenty-first century, phonology might appear to have moved some way from the rigid model imposed in SPE. Nevertheless the formal and principled approach of generative phonology and the wider generative project remains an important foundation for much work in the field.

Primary sources

Chomsky, Noam (1964). *Current Issues in Linguistic Theory*. The Hague: Mouton.

Chomsky, Noam and Morris Halle (1968). *The Sound Pattern of English*. New York: Harper and Row.

Halle, Morris (1962). 'Phonology in Generative Grammar'. *Word* 18, 54–72.

Prince, Alan and Paul Smolensky (1993/2004). *Optimality Theory: Constraint Interaction in Grammar*. Rutgers University and University of Colorado at Boulder. Oxford: Blackwell.

Further reading

Carr, Philip (1993). *Phonology*. Houndmills: Macmillan Press.

Kenstowicz, M. and C. Kisseberth (1986). *Generative Phonology: Description and Theory*. New York: Academic Press.

Christopher Routledge and Siobhan Chapman

GENERATIVE SEMANTICS

An approach to the treatment of semantics within transformational-generative grammar* popular between the second half of the 1960s and the 1970s. It opposed the approach dubbed 'interpretive semantics' favoured by Noam Chomsky and others. Among its major proponents were George and Robin Lakoff, Paul Postal, John (Haj) Ross, and James McCawley. Generative semantics is credited for bringing attention to meaning in linguistics and for ushering in interest in pragmatics, cognitive linguistics and some aspects of sociolinguistics.

See also: Cognitivism; Prototype; Transformational-Generative Grammar
Key Thinkers: Austin, J. L.; Chomsky, Noam; Grice, H. P.; Searle, John

Chomsky's standard theory (1965) postulates the presence of formal rules which generate syntactic sentence skeletons which are then filled by lexical insertion rules to create deep structures. These are then turned by transformations into questions, passives and so on. According to Chomsky, transformations do not affect meaning. Chomsky and many of his collaborators took the position that lexical semantics had to take place after deep structures had been generated, relegating the role of lexical semantics to the interpretation of structures that had already been generated, just like phonology (hence the name given to this position: interpretive semantics). The generative semanticists took a different position, that lexical insertion had to happen both in the deep structure and after some transformations, but most significantly that transformations affected meaning, hence the name 'generative semantics'.

The debate between the two camps was fierce and highly technical, revolving, for example, on the correct decomposition of the verb 'kill' in 'cause to become not alive'. The details are beyond an introductory account (but see Harris 1993) but the result of the controversy was that the generative semanticists, while essentially correct, did not present a cohesive research programme and moved on to other fields, including gender research (Robin Lakoff), pragmatics (Georgia Green), cognitive linguistics (George Lakoff, Ronald Langacker), or developed other theories of syntax (Paul Postal, James McCawley).

In general, generative semantics is to be credited with the attention to meaning that characterised the fields of pragmatics and cognitive linguistics in the last quarter of the twentieth century and the first decade of the twenty-first. In particular, generative semantics' interest in broad data, often resulting in odd, whimsical or arcane examples, led to an interest in notions that defied the rigid categorisation of transformational grammar, such as Ross's 'squish', Lotfi Zadeh's 'fuzzy logic', and Eleanor Rosch's 'prototypicality', which are at the core of cognitive linguistics. Generative semantics was also instrumental in bringing J. L. Austin's, H. P. Grice's and John Searle's ideas to the forefront of linguistic theory and contributing significantly to the creation of the discipline of pragmatics.

Generative semantics can then be seen as the precursor of many of the most significant contemporary approaches to the study of linguistic meaning and as having brought about a significant shift in paradigm toward the study of meaning and its relations to social interaction.

Primary sources

Harris, Randy Allen (1993). *The Linguistics Wars*. New York and Oxford: Oxford University Press.

Further reading

Chomsky, Noam (1965). *Aspects of the Theory of Syntax*. Cambridge, MA: MIT Press.
Rosch, Eleanor (1975). 'Cognitive representations of semantic categories'. *Journal of Experimental Psychology: General* 104: 192–233.
Ross, John Robert (Haj) (1973). 'Nouniness'. In Paul Kiparsky, John Robert Ross, James D. McCawley and Osamu Fujimura (eds), *Three Dimensions of Linguistic Theory*. Tokyo: TEC Corporation. 137–257.
Zadeh L. A. (1965). 'Fuzzy sets'. *Information and Control* 8: 338–53.

Salvatore Attardo

GLOSSEMATICS

A structuralist approach to the study of language that attempts to establish a formal and abstract theory of language equivalent to the exactness of theories in the natural sciences by setting up a formal system of description based on a elementary unit called a 'glosseme'. The theory was developed in the 1930s by the Danish scholar Louis Hjelmslev in collaboration with Hans Jørgen Uldall and is the most prestigious outcome of the works of the 'Copenhagen Linguistic Circle'. Any list of linguistic theories mentions glossematics, but apart from accounts of the phonematic systems of some dialects, the theory has not been adopted by many linguists.

See also: Logical Positivism; Phoneme; Signs and Semiotics; Structuralism
Key Thinkers: Hjelmslev, Louis; Greimas, Algirdas; Jakobson, Roman; Saussure, Ferdinand de

The point of departure in glossematics consists in a few axiomatic claims: language is one of the semiotic systems employed by humans to think and communicate, the linguistic system is an immanent, self-contained, structure that should be described without any 'metaphysical' or 'psychological' claims, and the formal system of glossematics is the adequate tool for that. The theory is a hierarchically-ordered set of terms conceiving 'function' (in a non-mathematical sense) as the key-concept on which the other terms are elaborated. Basically it denotes dependence relations between other entities, called 'functives'. According to the intrinsic logic of glossematics, it presents a complicated nomenclature of 'functions' and 'functives', the most important of which are the terms 'constant', a 'functive whose presence is a necessary condition for the presence' of another 'functive', and 'variable' which is a 'not necessary' condition. The apparatus is utilised on both sides of the linguistics sign, 'expression' and 'content', implying that minimal units of the same nature, 'glossemes', can be found both in the 'expression form' and the 'content form'. Form as a concept should be conceived of as a synonym for structure, and it is opposed to 'sub-stance', which may best be understood as unformed matter.

The most fundamental work in glossematics was written in Danish (Omkring sprogteoriens grundlæggelse (English translation: Prolegomena to a Theory of Language (1953)) and it is significant that in Paul L. Garvin's review of the translation by Francis J. Whitfield, he says that 'The Prolegomena are probably among the most unreadable books in linguistics'. Partly due to this and partly due to the fact that, apart from writings in Danish, the bulk of Hjelmslev's works was written in French, the details of the theory are a challenge for the non-initiated, and although the intellectual achievements of glossematics are widely acknowledged, the approach has had little impact on empirical studies. Its most prominent status is as an inspiration for linguists and as a beacon of scholarly rigour.

Primary sources

Garvin, Paul L. (1954). 'Review of Prolegomena to a Theory of Language'. American Anthropologist, vol. 56, no. 5, part 1: 925–6.
Hjelmslev, Louis (1943). Omkring sprogteoriens grundlæggelse. Copenhagen: University of Copenhagen. Reprinted Akademisk Forlag 1966. Trans. Francis J. Whitfield (1953), Prolegomena to a Theory of Language. Baltimore: Waverly Press.
Hjelmslev, Louis (1975). Résumé of a Theory of Language. Copenhagen: Nordisk Sprog-og Kulturforlag.

Further reading

Hjelmslev, Louis (1928). Principes de grammaire générale. Copenhagen: Høst and Søn. Reprinted Copenhagen: Munksgaard, 1968.

Hjelmslev, Louis (1932). *Etudes baltiques.* Copenhagen: Levin & Munksgaard.

Hjelmslev, Louis and Hans Jørgen Uldall (1957). *Outline of Glossematics.* Copenhagen: Nordisk Sprog-og Kulturforlag.

Hans Götzsche

HOLISM

Holism about meaning, or semantic holism, is the idea that there are no independent units of meaning smaller than the entire representational system, that is, the language. While some have happily embraced semantic holism, others have claimed that its allegedly unpalatable consequences undermine otherwise seemingly attractive theories in the philosophy of language or psychology.

See also: Analytic/Synthetic; Descriptivism; Indeterminacy
Key Thinkers: Dummett, Michael; Fodor, Jerry; Quine, W. V. O.

'Holism' has several different meanings, according to what is being said to be holistic (as opposed to 'atomistic'). Some other forms of holism will be mentioned here, but the focus is on semantic holism, which is a pivotal idea in the philosophy of language.

Semantic holism itself has both a linguistic and a mentalistic guise. The linguistic form holds that what one word in a language means depends on what all the other words mean. For example, perhaps 'giraffe' depends for its meaning on the meaning of 'neck' and 'long', the second of which itself depends for its meaning on 'space', and so on until the meanings of all words are seen to belong to an interconnected web. The mentalist form holds that the content of concepts (the components of propositions*) depends on that of all other concepts in the thinker's repertoire. The pros and cons of semantic holism are usually unaffected by which form it takes. A word's meaning is, after all, given by the concept it expresses. Early discussions of holism tended to be framed linguistically. Latterly it has been framed in terms of the content of the language of thought*.

Most arguments for semantic holism have a two-premise pattern. The first premise is that some property other than meaning is holistic. The second is that semantic facts are grounded in this other property. Meaning therefore inherits the holism of the other property. The three instances of this form of argument presented below centre on evidence, on translation, and on psychological explanation respectively.

Holism about evidence ('confirmation holism') is the thesis that whether some empirical discovery confirms a given proposition depends on the confirmation status of a good number of other propositions, and ultimately of every other proposition. Science stands or falls as a whole, since it consists of mutually supporting theses, not evidentially isolated ones. If we accept this, and also hold (more contentiously) that the meaning of a sentence is constituted by its confirmation conditions, semantic holism results. Tying meaning to confirmation conditions can have different motives. Logical positivists, for example, wished to streamline science by making this link. Others think that if a sentence is independent in principle to confirmation or disconfirmation, then it would never be rationally assertible and its meaning could never be learnt.

Translation holism is the thesis that how we translate one word can depend on how we translate any other word in the same language. Consider how we might complete the translation from Old English of the following Saxon law:

> (1) No man shall kill *hwyđer* except in the presence of two or three witnesses; and then he shall keep his skin for four days.

Clearly we need to know something about what skinned creature it might have been impermissible (in the culture of the utterer) to kill save in the presence of witnesses. But we know that this is what we need to figure out only because we have already translated the other words in the sentence. Semantic holism follows if we add the further assumption that the meaning of a word is constituted by its translatability. This further claim is not entirely implausible. After all, communicability is a fundamental aspect of word meaning, and depends on our translating (or interpreting) one another's words.

Holism about psychological explanation ('cognitive holism') is best approached by example. Suppose we explain why someone walked towards their kitchen by saying that they desired food. This only explains their behaviour if we assume they think that there is food in their kitchen, that its door is not locked, that no assassin lies

waiting in the cupboard, and so on. Ultimately, it seems, an agent's acts emerge out of a whole sea of rationally coherent propositional attitudes* and related mental states. According to cognitive holists, this deeper truth is disguised by the way we highlight just one propositional attitude in our ordinary explanatory practices. To get from this alleged truth to semantic holism (of the mentalistic kind in this case) we must make a further assumption: that a mental state's content is grounded in the state's explanatory potential. Since this potential is holistic, mental content is holistic.

Having sketched three popular arguments for semantic holism, let us turn to objections, not to the arguments, but to semantic holism itself. If successful, these objections can tell us more about meaning than that it is non-holistic. They also show that, for each of the three arguments just considered, either the underlying property is not holistic after all, or that meaning is not constituted out of confirmation conditions, translatability or other such aspects.

One common objection to semantic holism is that to understand any word or concept one would have to instantaneously understand every word in the language, or every concept in an entire repertoire. Even if this is not impossible, it certainly seems not to be how we do achieve semantic competence. One response is to insist that children acquire concepts one by one, but these morph, becoming gradually distinct and more sophisticated concepts, reflecting the beliefs they acquire on the way to adulthood. A more radical strategy is to accept that we do indeed acquire concepts *en masse*, but to express this more plausibly as the view that we become proper subjects for the attribution of propositional attitudes in a kind of *Gestalt* event.

A different objection centres on the commitment of holists to a fine-grained conception of meaning. The nature of a person's concept is read off from the sum of beliefs that person has involving that concept, since a belief is just a linking of one concept to other concepts. A change in belief could change the concept's identity. Ultimately, a single discrepancy in beliefs held would mean that two people had no concepts in common. This is, to say the least, counterintuitive: we could neither understand, learn from, nor disagree with one another, or with our previous selves after we have changed our minds, for that matter. Semantic holists try to reply by saying that while, strictly speaking, we have no concepts in common, our concepts are similar enough to allow understanding, learning, disagreement and so on.

Finally, some commentators think that holism is incompatible with compositionality. The meaning of a phrase like 'pet fish' ought to be a function of the meanings of 'pet' and 'fish'. But if semantic holism is correct, the meaning of 'pet fish' ought to be associated with that of 'golden', even though there is nothing in the meaning of either 'pet' or 'fish' to predict this association. A possible response, here, is to insist that semantic holism applies only to simple phrases or concepts; the meaning of complex phrases or concepts is determined by compositionality*.

Semantic holists respond in kind by pointing out problems with the atomistic alternatives. These latter usually identify the meaning of a word or mental representation with a causal relation of some kind. It has proven immensely difficult to get straight on what kind of causal relation could work. The debate here often collapses into that between descriptivist theories of reference (popular with holists) and direct theories of reference (popular with atomists).

Even so, it is a simplification to treat the debate as a choice between semantic holism and semantic atomism. There is an intermediate position – semantic molecularism – and a hybrid position, either of which may evade the difficulties faced by the purer views. In semantic molecularism a word or concept's meaning is from its connection to some proper subset of the other words or concepts in the language or conceptual system, rather than being either independent from all these connections or dependent on all of them. The difficulty here, as critics have pointed out, is how to distinguish between ancillary connections and constitutive connections.

The hybrid position involves adopting an atomistic theory for some purposes and a holistic theory for others. For example, 'two factor' theories of mental content say that, for purposes of cognitive explanation, a holistic account is better, while an atomistic theory is better suited to the purpose of understanding the conditions under which a belief is true. Each hybrid theory needs to be evaluated on its merits, but a general problem attaches to the strategy: how to fuse the two elements of the theory.

Holism about meaning is distinct from other forms of holism but it is common to argue for semantic holism from holism of these other kinds by making a constitutive assumption about semantic facts. Equally, the alleged incoherence of semantic holism has led others to go in the other direction and reject these constitutive assumptions. Nevertheless, arguments about holism touch on many other areas of the study of meaning.

Primary sources

Block, N. (1986). 'Advertisement for a semantics for psychology'. In P. A. French (ed.), *Midwest Studies in Philosophy, vol. X*. Minneapolis: University of Minnesota Press. 615–78.

Davidson, D. (1975). 'Thought and talk'. In S. Guttenplan (ed.), *Mind and Language*. Oxford: Oxford University Press.

Devitt, M. (1996). *Coming to Our Senses*. Cambridge: Cambridge University Press.

Dummett, M. (1976). 'What is a Theory of Meaning?' In G. Evans and J. Mcdowell (eds), *Truth and Meaning: Essays in Semantics*. Oxford: Clarendon Press. 67–137.

Dummett, M. (1991). *The Logical Basis of Metaphysics*. Cambridge, MA: Harvard University Press.

Fodor, J. (1981). 'The present status of the innateness controversy'. In J. Fodor, *Representations*. Brighton: Harvester.

Fodor, J. and E. Lepore (1991). *Holism: A Shopper's Guide*. Cambridge, MA: Blackwell.

Quine, W. V. (1960). *Word and Object*. Cambridge, MA: MIT Press.

Further reading

Fodor, J. A. and E. Lepore (1993). *Holism: A Consumer Update*. Amsterdam: Rodopi.

Alex Barber

IDEATIONAL THEORIES

Ideationalists hold that the meaning of words is inherited from the meaning of mental entities (ideas or concepts) rather than the other way around. Two classic statements of ideationalism have had an enduring influence, the first by John Locke and the second by H. P. Grice.

See also: Nonnatural Meaning; Private Language
Key Thinkers: Grice, H. P.; Locke, John; Putnam, Hilary; Wittgenstein, Ludwig

Locke sought to answer the question: '[How can] the thoughts of men's minds be conveyed from one to another?' (1706/1997: III.1.2). Having a thought, according to him, was a matter of having 'ideas' – roughly, perceptual and abstract concepts – in one's mind. The existence and content of an idea was supposed to be private, that is, directly accessible only to its possessor. Language allows this privacy to be overcome so that knowledge can be pooled. Words 'stand as marks for the ideas within [the speaker's] own mind, whereby they might be made known to others'. That is to say, spoken words have a proxy content that is inherited from the speaker's ideas and, with luck, appropriately decoded by the hearer.

Locke treated the principle of ideationalism as obvious, and focused instead on confusions that arise when we ignore how imperfect a vehicle for ideas language can be. The first influential criticism of ideationalism did not emerge until two centuries later when Ludwig Wittgenstein criticised the notion of a private bearer of content – a Lockean idea. On one reading of his private language* argument, Wittgenstein is suggesting that Lockean ideas could never be held mistakenly, and hence that it is also meaningless to talk of their being held correctly. If content is a matter of correctness conditions, Lockean thoughts lack content and so cannot be the source of our words' content.

Ideationalists need not be wedded to Locke's specific model of human psychology. Grice, for example, argued in 1957 that utterances inherit their meaning from the peculiar intentions with which they are performed. If an utterance 'Snow is cold' means that snow is cold, it does so because it was intended to cause the hearer to believe that snow is cold, and to do so through the hearer's recognising this very intention. Nothing here commits Grice to Lockean ideas. In a second major potential problem for ideationalism, Hilary Putnam in 1975 developed a famous thought experiment involving 'Twin Earth' to argue against the view, then prevalent, that a word's content depends entirely on the internal mental states of the person uttering it. Our intuitions appear to show that the content of an utterance of 'water' or 'gold' can depend in part on factors outside the utterer's skull, such as the physical composition of the colourless liquid in local lakes or the opinions of experts.

Grice could embrace Putnam's conclusion by allowing that the intentions from which our utterances inherit their content are not internal mental states but external ones. That is, perhaps the content of our intentions is itself subject to extra-cranial influence, which is hence passed on to the content of utterances. To make this move would, however, undermine the classification of Grice as an ideationalist. Ideationalists insist that words inherit their meaning from mental states. To allow that external factors, including characteristics of the linguistic community, can influence the content of our mental states is to allow that the inheritance relation may also run in the other direction.

These reflections suggest that ideationalism is a tendency rather than a specific thesis. It is difficult to deny that the meaning of linguistic expressions and our utterances of them depends in some way on language users having mental states. But how that dependency is spelled out, and whether the dependency ever runs in the other direction, are questions whose answer is as yet unsettled.

Primary sources

Grice, H. P. (1957). 'Meaning'. *Philosophical Review* 66: 377–88.

Putnam, H. (1975). 'The Meaning of "Meaning"'. In Gunderson, K. (ed.), *Minnesota Studies in the Philosophy of Science VII: Language, Mind, and Knowledge*. Minnesota: University of Minnesota Press.

Locke, J. (1706/1975). *An Essay Concerning Human Understanding*. Ed. P. Nidditch. Oxford: Clarendon Press.

Further reading

Davis, Wayne A. (2006). *Nondescriptive Meaning and Reference: An Ideational Semantics*. New York: Oxford University Press.

Alex Barber

IMPLICATURE

When a sincere performance of a speech act takes place in a certain context of utterance, what is conveyed by the performance, under the circumstances, beyond what is then being literally said by it, is an implicature of it.

See also: Nonnatural Meaning;
Relevance Theory
Key Thinkers: Grice, H. P.

'I meant what I said, and I said what I meant', said an elephant called Horton in *Horton Hatches the Egg*, a book for children by an author and illustrator called Theodore Seuss Geisel, otherwise known as Dr Seuss. What Horton said about himself makes sense, because what Horton meant is not necessarily what Horton said. Generally speaking, when a person performs a speech act in some context of utterance, a full report of what the person did under the circumstances will have to include an answer to the question, 'What was conveyed by the utterance made by the speaker under the circumstances?' It is a major insight into the nature of language use that the required report is dividable into two separate parts: one, reporting what was said, and an additional one, reporting what was conveyed beyond what was said.

Interesting examples abound of speech acts that convey more than what they say, but much less so systematic depictions of what is conveyed but not said by a certain speech act in a certain context of utterance and systematic understanding of how a speech act conveys what it does not say. The Homeric expression 'not the weakest of the Achaeans was it that had smitten [Hector]' has been usually taken to convey, when uttered by the author of *The Iliad* (15.1) about Ajas, that Ajas was rather the strongest of the Achaeans. The usage of such expressions of understatement was marked in early rhetorical studies as 'litotes' (Hoffmann 1987), but the theoretical *problem of delineation* and *problem of derivation* of what is conveyed but not said remained open until the second half of the twentieth century.

It was the philosopher H. P. Grice who made the first crucial contributions to a theory of implicature that purports to delineate whatever is conveyed beyond what is said when a certain speech act is sincerely performed in a certain context of utterance and to show how to derive what is conveyed but not said from the speech act and its context of utterance. Grice's major ideas were made public during the 1960s, first in a 1961 paper on the causal theory of perception, and then in the 1967 Harvard University William James lectures, parts of which were distributed and published in various forms, and then in a revised version. They appeared in full in Grice (1989), which includes also related 'Prolegomena' and 'Retrospective epilogue'.

Grice's theory is about contexts of utterance that involve a speaker, a speech act, which includes a sentence or other expressions, and a hearer. Such a context of utterance is one in which the speaker performs a speech act intending to have some communicative effect on the hearer. Grice's theory introduces two major ideas about communicative, 'conversational' contexts of utterance. Roughly speaking, the first idea is that speech acts performed in conversational contexts of utterance are governed by certain principles and maxims of conversation; the second idea is that what is conveyed but not said is what follows from the speaker's observing those maxims and what follows from the speaker's seemingly flouting those maxims. It is clear that such ideas can serve in solving the delineation problem of what is conveyed but not said. It will become clear in the sequel that the same ideas are of much significance in an attempt to solve the derivation problem as well. We turn now to a brief presentation of these two ideas.

Speech acts that are performed in conversational contexts of utterance are governed, according to Grice's theory, first and foremost, by what Grice labelled the Cooperative Principle:

(CP) Make your conversational contribution such as is required, at the stage at which it occurs, by the accepted purpose or direction of the talk exchange in which you are engaged.

The fundamental (CP) gives rise to supermaxims and maxims of conversation, classified by Grice into four groups, 'echoing Kant', entitled in terms of the categories of Quality, Quantity, Relation and Manner:

(Quantity maxims)
(1) Make your contribution as informative as is required (for the current purposes of the exchange).
(2) Do not make your contribution more informative than is required.

(Quality supermaxim)
Try to make your contribution one that is true.

(Quality maxims)
(1) Do not say what you believe to be false.
(2) Do not say that for which you lack adequate evidence.

(Relation maxim)
Be relevant.

(Manner supermaxim)
Be perspicuous.

(Manner maxims)
(1) Avoid obscurity of expression.
(2) Avoid ambiguity.
(3) Be brief (avoid unnecessary prolixity).
(4) Be orderly.

'and one might need others'. (Grice 1989: 27)

Grice's Cooperative Principle and supermaxims and maxims apply to conversations in different ways. The following distinctions are crucial for a proper understanding of Grice's theory. For the sake of brevity, we will use the term 'the norms' for the Cooperative Principle, supermaxims and maxims.

Conversational implicatures by simple observation of the norms versus. conversational implicatures by dramatic observation of the norms
Given an ordinary context of utterance, one often, or even usually, assumes that the speakers who participate in the conversation observe the

87

norms. Conversational implicature by simple observation of the norms is implicature that follows from the assumption that the norms have been observed, under the given circumstances, in which there is no indication – real or apparent – to the contrary. If a speaker says, in an ordinary context of utterance, 'It is raining here', we assume the person is observing the norms, in particular Quality supermaxim and maxim 1, given no indication to the contrary. A conversational implicature by simple observation would be that the speaker believes, at that context of utterance, that it is raining there. This explains the so-called Moore's Paradox, which emerges when a persons says: 'It is raining here, but I don't believe it is' or a similar expression. The conversational implicature that follows from the first part of the assertion contradicts what is said in the second part of the same assertion.

Conversational implicatures by simple observation abound and are of much significance in ordinary interaction. More interesting however, at least from a theoretical point of view, are conversational implicatures that are drawn in contexts of utterance in which the norms are actually observed though there are seeming indications to the contrary. When a speaker answers the question, 'Have you read the present top best-selling book', by saying, 'I saw the movie', the speakers apparently flouts the Cooperative Principle, because strictly speaking the reaction is not an answer. The question is of the form called 'yes'/'no'-question and the speaker's reaction does not seem to be the required one, because it includes neither a 'yes' nor a 'no'.

However, as every fluent speaker of the language knows, the speech act of saying 'I saw the movie' under such circumstances counts as an appropriate reaction to the posed question, being cooperative and informative, though in an indirect and implicit way. First, assuming the speaker does observe the norms, we understand the speaker as holding that the movie is sufficiently similar to the book, to the extent that a person who is acquainted with the movie can be regarded as a person acquainted with the book. Notice that such an understanding rests on the assumption that in reacting the way the speaker did, the speaker observed the Relation maxim and reacted in a relevant way. Secondly, assuming the speaker observed Quantity maxim 1 and Quality maxim 1, we have a possible explanation for the speaker not answering the posed question in the affirmative. Hence, by assuming the speaker observed the norms, we reach the conversational implicature that the speaker had not read the book. Here the question arises: If the speaker had not read the book, why didn't the speaker admit it and simply answer 'No'? The response would be in terms of two insights we gain by trying to apply the norms to the conversation under discussion. Notice, first, that the answer 'No' would have been less cooperative and less informative than the reaction 'I saw the movie'. The latter helps the person who posed the question to make the next step in the conversation, pursuing the goal he tried to reach, had the answer been 'Yes'. If acquaintance with the movie is enough, the conversation will go on as planned for that stage of it. Moreover, by assuming the speaker observed

Quantity maxim 2, we draw the conversational implicature that the speaker believes that, for the sake of the present conversation, it is sufficient to point out the fact that he had seen the movie, conveying but not admitting that the speaker had not read the book.

The distinction between conversational implicature by simple derivation from the norms and conversational implicature by what Grice called 'dramatic' derivation from the norms will have to be manifest in each attempted improvements on Grice's theory.

Particularised conversational implicatures versus generalised conversational implicatures
Our discussion of the conversational implicatures that can be drawn from a speech act of saying 'I saw the movie' applied to the particular context of utterance, in which that speech act served as a response to a particular question about the speaker, 'Have you read the present top best-selling book?'. We can easily imagine contexts of utterance in which the same speech act appears, even in reference to the same movie, made by the same speaker, where none of the above-mentioned conversational implicatures can be drawn. Hence, those conversational implicatures are called 'particularised' ones.

However, not all conversational implicatures are particularised. If a speaker uses the expression 'most' in an ordinary speech act, a conversational implicature is going to be usually drawn in terms of 'not all'. Thus, for example, an ordinary usage of 'Most of my colleagues read fiction' would conversationally implicate that

not all of my colleagues read fiction. Such a conversational implicature is called 'generalised'.

Conversational implicatures versus conventional implicatures
An implicature in general is what is conveyed by a performance of a speech act beyond what is said when the speech act is performed. According to Grice's theory, it is possible to convey by a performance of a speech act what is beyond what is said independently of the norms of conversation which produce conversational implicature. There is a class of implicatures Grice called 'conventional implicatures', which do not rest on the norms of conversation but rather on conventions that govern the use of certain expressions. Consider an ordinary use of 'but', such as 'What they did was legally permissible, but ethically wrong'. On the level of what is said, one may replace 'but' with 'and' without changing the propositional significance of the assertion and its truth-value. However, the use of 'but' conveys that there is some significant contrast between the two parts of the assertion. The significance of the contrast varies, but not its conveyed appearance.

Grice himself thought the nature of conventional implicatures should be better explained before 'any free use of it, for explanatory purposes'. Some scholars have tried to reduce all conventional implicatures to other phenomena of language use, such as conversational implicature, presupposition* or what is said. Related theoretical debates are still ongoing.

Grice's theory lends itself to three types of study, related to the following theoretical problems. First, what is the nature of the norms and what justifies each of the maxims? Second, do speakers usually observe the norms of conversation? Third, what alternative theories of language use would serve as improvements upon Grice's theory, explaining the facts better and more broadly?

The first attempt to show the foundation of Grice's system of norms, disregarding debatable details, was Kasher (1976), further developed in what appears as an appendix in Kasher (ed.) (1998). The major idea of the explanation is that speech activity is ideally rational, that is, it acts according to the Rationality Principle:

(R) Given a desired end, one is to choose that action which most effectively, and at least cost, attains that end, everything else being equal.

When the best means at one's disposal are the verbal ones, then one follows (R) by performing a certain speech act. It is not difficult to explain the 'most effectively' requirement of (R) when a desired end is given, but it is much more difficult to elucidate the 'at least cost' requirement. A simple reading of Grice's norms shows what he took to be some of the costs, such as verbal effort, related to number of words uttered and the time it takes to voice them and similar attributes of speech. Other 'at least cost' parameters include inaccuracies (avoided by expressions of the Henry James style) and hurt feelings (avoided by using politeness manifestations). Kasher (1976) includes arguments against (CP) and arguments that show that supermaxims and maxims are derivable from (R) without any resort to (CP).

To move to our second question, several types of empirical studies of Grice's theory should be mentioned. One type includes surveys of linguistic behaviour that result in apparent counter-examples, such as people regularly making vague comments or references in conversation. Such examples can, however, be shown to be compatible with and even explained by Grice's theory, where the 'at least cost' part of (R) involves yet another parameter, such as commitment or guilt on grounds of being shown to be mistaken, which should be minimised.

Empirical studies of other types are related to different theoretical ways of explaining data about what is conveyed but not said (Bezuidenhout and Morris, in Noveck and Sperber 2006), to the psychological processes of computing conversational implicatures (Chierchia et al., in Noveck and Sperber 2006), to the operation of implicature production devices in the brain (Kasher et al. 1999), and to child acquisition of such devices (Noveck, in Noveck and Sperber 2006). Such studies are related to the issue of modularity (in the sense of Fodor 1983), where much remains to be studied.

Finally, let us consider three theories of implicature that have been developed in the footsteps of Grice's theory. The first two have been labeled 'neo-Gricean'. All of them have fundamental principles of the above-mentioned form 'most effectively and at least cost'.

Laurence Horn suggested (see Horn 1984 and 2004) a replacement of Grice's maxims by two principles:

(1) The Q-Principle (where Q stands for quantity): make your contribution sufficient; say as much as you can, given the R-principle.

(2) The R-principle (where R stands for relation): make your contribution necessary; say no more than you must, given the Q-principle.

The Q-principle gives rise to Horn scales, such as <good, excellent>. A sincere speech act that portrays a thesis as a good one has a Q-implicature that the thesis is not an excellent one.

Stephen Levinson (2000) suggested an additional fundamental principle of a different nature. The M-principle for the speaker (where M stands for manner): do not use a marked expression without reason. A marked expression indicates an unusual situation, while an unmarked expression indicates a usual one. A sincere speech act that describes a certain action as 'not unreasonable' has an M-implicature that the action is not perfectly reasonable.

Relevance theory*, as developed by Sperber and Wilson (see Sperber and Wilson 1987 and Wilson and Sperber 2004) and their followers, rests on their principle of relevance, according to which human cognition is ideally geared to maximising relevance. Here a major shift from Grice's theory is manifest. Whereas Grice was interested in rational speech activity, relevance theory is about cognitive effects and processes. According to relevance theory, relevance is a function of cognitive effects, which should be maximised, and of processing efforts, which should be minimised. Relevance theory was one of the dominant ideas in pragmatics in the 1980s and early 1990s.

Primary sources

Fodor, Jerry (1983). *The Modularity of Mind*. Cambridge, MA: MIT Press.

Grice, H. P. (1989). *Studies in the Way of Words*. Cambridge, MA: Harvard University Press.

Hoffmann, Maria E. (1987). *Negatio Contrarii: A Study of Latin Litotes*. Assen: Van Gorcum.

Horn, Laurence R. (1984). 'Toward a new taxonomy for pragmatic inference: Q-based and R-based implicature'. In D. Schiffrin (ed.), *Meaning, Form and Use in Context: Linguistic Applications*. Washington, DC: Georgetown University Press. 11–42.

Horn, Laurence R. (2004). 'Implicature'. In Laurence R. Horn and Gregory Ward (eds) (2004). 3–28.

Horn, Laurence R. and Gregory Ward (eds) (2004). *The Handbook of Pragmatics*. Oxford: Blackwell.

Kasher, Asa (1976). 'Conversational maxims and rationality'. In Asa Kasher (ed.), *Language in Focus: Foundations, Methods and Systems*. Dordrecht: Reidel. 197–216. Republished with an appendix, 'Gricean inference revisited', in Kasher (ed.) (1998), vol. IV: 181–214.

Kasher, Asa, Gila Batori, Nahum Soroker, David Graves and Eran Zaidel (1999). 'Effects of right- and left hemisphere damage on understanding conversational implicatures'. *Brain and Language* 68: 566–90.

Levinson, Stephen C. (2000). *Presumptive Meanings: The Theory of Generalized Conversational Implicature*. Cambridge, MA: MIT Press.

Noveck, Ira A. and Dan Sperber (eds) (2006). *Experimental Pragmatics*. Basingstoke: Palgrave Macmillan.

Sperber, Dan and Deirdre Wilson (1987). *Relevance: Communication and Cognition*. Oxford: Blackwell.

Wilson, Deirdre and Dan Sperber (2004). 'Relevance theory'. In Laurence R. Horn and Gregory Ward (eds), The *Handbook of Pragmatics*. Oxford: Blackwell. 607–32.

Further reading

Carston, Robyn (2004). 'Relevance theory and the saying/implicating distinction'. In Laurence R. Horn and Gregory Ward (eds), The *Handbook of Pragmatics* Oxford: Blackwell. 633–56.

Davis, Wayne A. (1998). *Implicature: Intention, Convention, and Principle in the Failure of Gricean Theory*. Cambridge: Cambridge University Press.

Gazdar, Gerald (1979). *Pragmatics: Implicature, Presupposition and Logical Form*. London: Academic Press.

Grandy, Richard E. and Richard Warner (eds) (1986). *Philosophical Grounds of Rationality*. Oxford: Clarendon Press. (See, in particular, 'Paul Grice: a view of his work' by the editors and the reply by Grice.)

Kasher, Asa (ed.) (1998). *Pragmatics: Critical Concepts*. Six volumes. London: Routledge. (See in particular vol. IV which includes seventeen classical papers on implicature.)

Asa Kasher

INDETERMINACY

'Indeterminacy' in a linguistic context has various interpretations, but in most senses it is taken to refer to the idea that linguists cannot make definite pronouncements about the meanings of expressions and utterances precisely because there are no meanings about which to be definite. Meaning does not exist as an autonomous entity but only in observable behaviours within a language community. Writers starting from quite diverse sets of initial assumptions have found themselves advocating this sceptical and, to many thinkers, counterintuitive thesis.

See also: Behaviourism; Holism
Key Thinkers: Kripke, Saul; Quine, W. V. O.; Wittgenstein, Ludwig

Indeterminacy in linguistics is most commonly associated with W. V. O. Quine's 1960 discussion of translation. Quine alleged that translation is indeterminate because words themselves do not have meaning; all that linguists can do is observe patterns of behaviour in relation to particular language use. Quine's 'meaning scepticism' finds an echo in a puzzle raised by Saul Kripke. Kripke's puzzle purports to show that we do not follow any determinate meaning-rule in applying a word in novel circumstances.

In his 1960 discussion Quine is not offering practical advice but scrutinising the notion of meaning. For this reason he asks us to imagine we are what he calls 'radical translators', developing a 'translation manual' – in other words, a recipe for going from sentences in some entirely unfamiliar language to sentences of our own language. To develop this manual we may use only a narrow range of clues. In particular we may not rely on the two languages having a common origin and we certainly may not use a dictionary. The only evidence we may use is behavioural: dispositions on the part of native speakers to assent or dissent in varying circumstances to utterances of sentences of their language. Quine limits himself to this evidence on the grounds that sentence meanings, in so far as there are such things (and he ends up doubting there are), must be *constituted* by translatability on these terms. Allowing other evidence would be presupposing rather than coming to understand the nature of a sentence's meaning. Indeterminacy of translation is the thesis that, in the context of radical translation, there will always be at least two acceptable but incompatible translation manuals available.

Quine gives an example. Suppose that, as a rabbit scurries by, a native speaker utters the one-word sentence, 'Gavagai'. You guess it means 'Lo, a rabbit'. Tests on future occasions using assent and dissent to this same sentence bear out your hypothesis. Before adopting this as 'the' correct translation, however, you must rule out alternatives. But this cannot be done. For example, why not take 'Gavagai' to mean 'Lo, undetached part of a rabbit'? In those few contexts where the difference between this and your translation shows up, Quine holds that it will be possible to tweak other parts of the manual to accommodate the discrepancy. Imagine you point to one part of a rabbit, then another part of the same rabbit, and solicit assent or dissent from 'This gavagai is the same as that gavagai' – or rather, 'Shiz gavagai sumo shaz gavagai', as it may be. Native-speaker assent here will not automatically rule out the alternative translation manual. We could take 'sumo' to translate as 'is

part of the same whole as' rather than 'is the same as'; the alternative manual would then correctly predict assent. Quine is confident that, after complementary juggling of different clauses, alternative but equivalent translation manuals will always be available. Translation, he insists, is a matter of fitting a complete manual to all the sentences of the other language (see holism*); Quine treats as myth the view that successful translating is a matter of revealing the one true meaning of individual words and sentences.

Some critics have argued that it will always be possible to isolate at most one translation scheme compatible with assent/dissent patterns. There is certainly more room for manoeuvre with Quine's 'Gavagai' example than he initially realised. In 1970 Quine expressed regret at the focus on this particular example. He tried to show, quite generally, how his controversial *indeterminacy* thesis follows from a widely accepted *underdetermination* thesis. According to this, empirical evidence rarely forces any particular scientific theory upon us. His inference from underdetermination of theory to indeterminacy of translation has failed to convince the majority of commentators. Other critics have questioned whether indeterminacy of translation, even if correct, generates trouble for the notion of meaning. Most target the behaviourism* built into his statement of the evidence available to a radical translator.

Kripke's 1982 indeterminacy puzzle is inspired by his reading of Wittgenstein's *Philosophical Investigations* (1953). To set up the puzzle, Kripke uses, for illustrative purposes, the expression '+' ; or, in spoken English, 'added to'. Suppose you are asked 'What is 68 + 57?' Suppose further that this is a question you have never before had occasion to address (there will always be some such question). You answer with confidence: '125'. You are assuming that the expression '+' refers here to what it has always referred to, namely, the plus-function. But a sceptic challenges you: 'How do you know that '+' has always referred to the plus function?' Perhaps it has always referred to the quus (pronounced 'qwus') function, shown in Figure 1.

$$x \text{ quus } y = \begin{cases} 5 \text{ if } x = 68 \text{ and } y = 57 \\ \\ x \text{ plus } y \text{ otherwise} \end{cases}$$

Figure 1

The only way you could ascertain which of the two functions '+' referred to earlier is to apply the expression in the context of figuring out the sum of fifty-seven and sixty-eight. But by hypothesis you could not have done this.

Kripke's imagined sceptic has thus far claimed to establish only that you do not at present *know* whether earlier uses of '+' referred to plus rather than quus; and hence that you do not *know* if the correct answer to the present question is '125' rather than 'five'. This is bad enough. But the sceptic also denies the possibility of knowing whether you meant plus by '+'in the past, and so mean plus now. It is not a matter of ignorance as to which you mean: there is simply no fact of the matter as to which you meant in the past, or which you mean now.

The puzzle can be generalised in various ways. First, it extends to expressions other than '+'. Suppose you ask yourself, right now, 'Is this a book I am reading?' Your answer depends on what you mean by 'book'. Perhaps 'book' refers now, as in the past, to quooks, defined in Figure 2.

The conclusion we are invited to accept is that whenever we come to apply a familiar word in a novel context, there is nothing in virtue of which our application is correct or incorrect, since nothing in previous uses determines that the word means one thing rather than another. Moreover, since every context of a word being used was novel once, the puzzle applies to every use of any word. Finally, the puzzle is not just about communication. It applies even when we silently ask ourselves a question, so it is a puzzle about thought itself, not just about the exchange of thoughts through spoken language.

$$x \text{ is a quook} \begin{cases} \text{true if } x \text{ is a book not called } \textit{Key Ideas in Linguistics and} \\ \textit{the Philosophy of Language}; \\ \\ \text{false otherwise.} \end{cases}$$

Figure 2

The *quus* and *quook* readings cannot be dismissed on the grounds that 'quus' and 'quook' are defined in terms of the more familiar 'plus' and 'book', and are hence less simple. After all, it is equally possible to define the latter in terms of the former. Nor does it help to observe that, since we are disposed to reply '125' rather than 'five', we must mean plus rather than quus. If what we mean by a word is a product of how we are disposed to apply it, it would be impossible ever to make an erroneous application and that would be absurd. Kripke himself tentatively offers what he calls a sceptical solution. This seeks to understand the role of meaning-statements within discursive practice without allowing that they assert anything true or false. Rather, they show something about the statement-maker's willingness to use a term like '+' or 'book' in a particular way. Few have embraced Kripke's solution, but there is no consensus over where his sceptical argument breaks down.

Quine's and Kripke's discussions both threaten the widespread assumption that words and sentences have a particular meaning. A more recent literature (albeit on a very old topic) also calls semantic determinacy into question. Suppose I were to ask you 'Have you had breakfast?'. Am I asking you whether you have had breakfast *ever*, or just whether you have had breakfast *this morning*? It is tempting to appeal to the context. But after setting aside formal indexicals ('I', 'here', 'tomorrow', and so on), context's contribution to utterance meaning is difficult to systematise, even for 'Have you had breakfast?'. To say that its contribution is impossible to systematise would be to say that there is no determinate function from sentences and contexts of utterance onto propositions*. This apparent indeterminacy lies at the heart of the question of how we ought to distinguish between words' contribution to an utterance's meaning (broadly, semantics) and the utterance context's contribution (broadly, pragmatics). See Recanati (2004) and Cappelen and Lepore and (2005) for opposing views.

We have seen that challenges to determinate meaning can take different forms. The interest attaching to these challenges often lies not in the scepticism they generate about meaning but in the resources developed to meet them, and the clarity that emerges from reflecting on the assumptions that give rise to them.

Primary sources

Cappelen, H. and E. Lepore (2005). *Insensitive Semantics*. Oxford: Blackwell.

Kripke, S. (1982). *Wittgenstein on Rules and Private Language*. Oxford: Blackwell.

Quine, W. V. O. (1960). *Word and Object*. Cambridge, MA: MIT Press. Chapter 2.

Quine, W. V. O. (1970). 'On the reasons for indeterminacy of translation'. *Journal of Philosophy*, 67: 178–83.

Recanati, F. (2004). *Literal Meaning*. Cambridge: Cambridge University Press.

Wittgenstein, L. (1953). *Philosophical Investigations*. Oxford: Blackwell.

Further reading

Miller, A. (1998). *Philosophy of Language*. London: UCL Press. Chapters 4–6.

Alex Barber

INNATENESS

The claim that some aspects of linguistic competence are genetically specified rather than learnt through experience. This claim has been driving research in generative linguistics and language acquisition since the late 1950s.

See also:
Acceptability/Grammaticality;
Continuity; Mentalism;
Transformational-Generative
Grammar; Universal Grammar
Key Thinkers: Chomsky, Noam;
Descartes, René; Plato

Noam Chomsky has proposed that humans possess domain- and species-specific knowledge of the structure of possible languages, which enables human young to acquire language with speed, efficiency and uniformity. This view can be traced back to Cartesian cognitivism and Platonic philosophy. Opponents claim that language acquisition is innately constrained but only by mechanisms that underlie general cognitive ability. In other words, it is currently uncontroversial that language acquisition is innately constrained; what is the object of heated debate is exactly what is innate.

The argument that has most forcefully been used in support of the linguistic innateness position is that the stimulus argument, in which children learn language by experience, is seriously flawed (Chomsky 1980: 34). For example, since language is a complex system, it could only be acquired through experience if negative evidence was available. Children only ever have access to positive evidence (information about grammatical sentences), yet they successfully acquire language.

From this basis one has to conclude that humans are genetically hardwired for language: children are born equipped with a universal grammar* (Chomsky 1981), containing information about linguistic universals enabling them to form hypotheses about the structure of the language they are learning. The proposed existence of a critical period for language (typical language acquisition is not possible after a certain age) and studies of deaf children who spontaneously develop sign language have been used as further evidence in support of linguistic nativism.

Opponents of the Chomskyan view claim that the richness of the data available to children is vastly underestimated; the stimulus argument fails only given the generative definition of what language is. One of the strongest challenges to nativism comes from Connectionist psychology (Elman et al. 1996) where artificial neural networks have been trained to reproduce linguistic behaviours such as recursion, previously thought to be possible only through innate pre-programming. Research on innateness has spurred research with animals and in genetics. In 2001 Cecilia Lai and colleagues suggested that a mutation in the FOXP2 gene is causally involved in language disorders. Despite widespread enthusiasm in the popular press about the 'language gene', the exact role of FOXP2 in relation to language development is far from clear.

Although the innateness question is still unresolved, interdisciplinary research that straddles the gap between linguistics, anthropology, artificial intelligence, genetics and neuroscience has opened up novel, exciting ways in which the question can be addressed.

Primary sources

Chomsky, N. (1965). *Aspects of the Theory of Syntax*. Cambridge, MA: MIT Press.

Chomsky N. (1980). *Rules and Representations*. Oxford: Blackwell.

Chomsky, N. (1981). *Lectures on Government and Binding: The Pisa Lectures*. Holland: Foris Publications.

Further reading

Elman, J. L., E. A. Bates, M. H. Johnson, A. Karmiloff-Smith, D. Parisi and K. Plunkett (1996). *Rethinking Innateness: A Connectionist Perspective on Development*. Cambridge, MA: MIT Press.

Hauser, M. D., N. Chomsky and W. T. Fitch (2002). 'The faculty of language: What is it, who has it, and how did it evolve?' *Science* 298: 1569–79.

Lai, C. S. L., S. E. Fisher, J. A. Hurst, F. Vargha-Khadem and A. P. Monaco (2001). 'A forkhead-domain gene is mutated in severe speech and language'. *Nature* 413: 519–23.

Stavroula-Thaleia Kousta

INTEGRATIONISM

An approach to linguistics which is radically opposed to the assumptions on which much of mainstream linguistics has been based since the time of Ferdinand de Saussure, and insists that language must be seen as action embedded in context. Integrationists challenge what they characterise as 'segregational' linguistics, which treats language as an autonomous object of study separate from non-linguistic aspects of communication, and argue forcefully that the attempt to decontextualise language leads to a profound distortion.

See also: Acceptability/ Grammaticality; Conversation Analysis; Creativity; (Critical) Discourse Analysis; Indeterminacy; Systemic-Functional Grammar; Structuralism; Transformational-Generative Grammar
Key Thinkers: Chomsky, Noam; Firth, J. R.; Halliday, M. A. K.; Malinowski, Bronislaw; Saussure, Ferdinand de

The dominant tradition in Western linguistics over the twentieth century and into the twenty-first century has insisted on the autonomy of linguistics as a science. This has meant defining and delimiting the subject in such a way that language can be investigated in isolation from other phenomena which might be thought to impinge on it. It is accepted that areas of contact with the non-linguistic world may be worth exploring, through sociolinguistics, speech act theory*, semantics, discourse analysis* and so on; but these are all seen as in some way less 'pure' extensions from the investigation of the essential linguistic core, which is autonomous syntax. Integrationism, which grew from a series of books published by Roy Harris from 1980 on, rejects this stance completely. Following Harris's lead, integrationists have set out to demolish what they see as the suspect foundations on which the linguistic edifice has been constructed. There have been integrational studies of areas such as fictional dialogue, irony, legal arguments and so on, but the primary aim has been to force mainstream linguists to at least question, if not revise, many assumptions that they have taken for granted.

The integrationist critique highlights three key interrelated problems with the linguistic tradition founded on Saussure's work. The first is what Harris in his 1981 book terms the myth of 'telementation'. This is the image (introduced in a famous diagram in Saussure 1916/1922 of two heads with arrows passing between them representing ideas being transferred) of language as serving to convey the thoughts of the speaker into the mind of the hearer. The ideas are assumed to be transferred undistorted, fully comprehensible and fully comprehended. Integrationists argue that, even when mainstream linguists claim publicly not to work with this model of communication, their practice indicates that they do. A fundamental flaw in the model is that there is in fact no way of knowing to what extent, or even whether, the meanings understood by the hearer are those intended by the speaker. It also restricts 'meaning' to 'ideation', thus ignoring interpersonal or other aspects of meaning (compare systemic-functional grammar*, where these other types of meaning are fully integrated in the model). Experience shows that the telementation model does not correspond to reality: very often hearers do not understand everything that they hear, and are content to cope with degrees of vagueness,

obscurity and ambiguity* in order to maintain the smooth flow of communication. Speakers are often unconcerned with avoiding these apparent hindrances, secure in the knowledge that the hearer will, all things being equal, collaborate in making enough sense of the utterances for communication to take place satisfactorily. A valid integrationist model of linguistic behaviour cannot relegate this to 'performance factors' which do not affect the underlying 'competence': it is a key distinguishing feature of communication which must be taken into account.

The second point on which integrationists take issue with the mainstream is the determinacy of the linguistic sign. If, as in the telementation model, ideas were transferred undistorted, this would have to rely on signs (words) having determinate meanings which are known to, and accepted by, both interactants. But, as Harris and others have stressed, if this were the case, lawyers would be completely unnecessary, since much of their work involves negotiating over the precise application of laws to individual cases – that is, exactly what the law 'means' in a particular context. This seems odd, since legal language is designed to be as exact and determinate as possible. If indeterminacy* occurs here, it is even more likely to be inherent in everyday uses of language. For integrationists, interactants are engaged in a constant process of making sense of communication in particular contexts. They can draw on their experience of previous situations which they perceive as similar, but these perceptions of similarity are not dependent on some kind of communally held 'dictionary' which is the final arbiter – they are the result of general problem-solving abilities applied (unconsciously and instantaneously, because of years of practice) to seeing what function utterances need to serve in context in order to be an appropriate contribution to the communicative event. Signs are inherently indeterminate, and are only rendered determinate (to whatever degree is judged necessary by the interactants) in particular contexts. Taking this to the next level, segregationist approaches are underpinned by the view that a language is a fixed code, so that sentences can be deemed unequivocally to be 'grammatical' (part of the code) or 'ungrammatical' (not part of the code). However, for the integrationist this is an equally untenable distortion: this could only be true of a grammar held in the mind of the 'ideal speaker-hearer in a homogeneous speech community' – an imaginary entity that does not, and cannot, exist.

The third point of contention involves a claim which seems counterintuitive, but which follows logically from the points above: 'language' exists but 'languages' do not. Speakers do, of course, find it useful to refer to 'languages' such as English and French, but the integrationist sees that as a convenient fiction which is unnecessary and misleading as a basis for linguistics. 'A language' implies determinate signs and a fixed code which are, at least potentially, shared by all speakers of that language. But who decides which parts of 'English' belong to the code and which do not? Some linguists would attempt to get round this question by arguing that there is a fixed core that is recognised and accepted by all (educated) speakers (as represented by the linguist him/herself), and around this is a periphery of variation in forms, including the usages of individuals or groups (such as dialects), which have an uncertain relationship to the code but which can be left to sociolinguists and other scholars with 'fringe' interests to deal with. Integrationists would see this as merely ducking the issue (and, in the process, taking an sweepingly arrogant view of society). For them, language is in a state of constant flux, geographically and historically but also moment-by-moment as speakers negotiate and create meaning in context; and generalisations about the characteristics of a particular 'language' will necessarily exclude the variability that is fundamental to the way that language operates.

A charge that has been levelled against integrationism is that its robust attacks on mainstream linguistics have not been balanced by any clear programme or methodology to replace current practices. Michael Toolan counters this by arguing that such a complaint 'reflects a way of thinking deeply committed to the prevailing post-Saussurean cognitivist-mechanistic paradigm' and that the term integrational linguistics 'names a principle rather than a method' (1996: 23). He notes that much of the work in ethnography, conversation analysis* and discourse analysis is in practice congruent with integrationism, and the way forward will probably involve adapting methods from those approaches. A more theoretical counter-attack from a 'segregationist' position (though they would reject the label) can be found in Borsley and Newmeyer (1997) who insist that mainstream linguistics does not in fact work with a telemention model. This paper, and the response in Toolan (1998), give a flavour of the debate. It is hard to judge how far the integrationist critique has altered the course of linguistics as its proponents would wish. An increasing number of approaches have independently arrived, by different routes, at rather similar conclusions, and key aspects of the integrationist position (such as the indeterminacy of the sign) have themselves become mainstream, though generally under different labels. Integrationism can claim to have contributed to weakening the hegemony of a particular view of linguistics, but there is as yet little sign that it has brought about its demise.

Primary sources

Davis, Hayley G. and Talbot. J. Taylor (eds) (1990). *Redefining Linguistics*. London: Routledge.

Harris, Roy (1981). *The Language Myth*. London: Duckworth.

Harris, Roy (1998). *Introduction to Integrational Linguistics*. Oxford: Pergamon.

Harris, Roy and George Wolf (1998). *Integrational Linguistics: A First Reader*. Oxford: Pergamon.

Toolan, Michael (1996). *Total Speech: An Integrational Linguistic Approach to Language*. Durham/London: Duke University Press.

Wolf, George and Nigel Love (eds) (1997). *Linguistics Inside Out: Roy Harris and His Critics*. Amsterdam/Philadelphia: John Benjamins.

Further reading

Borsley, Robert and Frederick, J. Newmeyer (1997). 'The Language Muddle: Roy Harris and Generative Grammar'. In G. Wolf and N. Love (eds), *Linguistics Inside Out*. Amsterdam. Philadelphia: John Benjamins. 42–64.

Saussure, Ferdinand de (1922/1983). *Course in General Linguistics*. Second edition. Trans. Roy Harris. London: Duckworth.

Toolan, Michael (1998). 'A few words on telemention'. In R. Harris and G. Wolf (eds), *Integrational Linguistics*. Oxford: Pergamon. 68–82.

Geoff Thompson

INTENTIONALITY

Directedness or aboutness; the property of mental states whereby they are about, or directed towards, states of affairs in the world, typically expressed in language through such 'intentional verbs' as 'believe', 'desire', 'know', and 'intend'. Intentionality is an important concept in both philosophy of mind and ethical theory as a way of recognising responsibility towards other beings, and in distinguishing humans and other higher animals from computers.

See also: Artificial Intelligence; Nonnatural Meaning; Phenomenology; Speech Act Theory
Key Thinkers: Husserl, Edmund; Searle, John

Intentionality is an important concept in both continental and analytic philosophy. It was introduced by the German philosopher Franz Brentano, and developed by his pupil Edmund Husserl, for whom it is one of the foundational and essential concepts of phenomenology. Intentionality is also recognised as Husserl's most important influence on the analytic tradition of philosophy, in which it is especially associated with the speech act theory* of John Searle.

The term 'intentionality' was first used in its modern sense by Brentano in his *Psychology from an Empirical Standpoint* (1973, first published 1874), although the idea is ultimately derived from Aristotle's concept of 'mental inexistence', the notion that when one thinks of an object, one has an object 'in mind', but the object in mind does not 'exist' in the same way that the object in the world exists. According to Brentano (1973: 88), 'every mental phenomenon is characterised by . . . the intentional (or mental) inexistence of an object, and what we might call . . . reference to a content, direction toward an object, . . . or immanent objectivity'. Brentano's purpose here is to distinguish the mental from the physical, and in turn to define the mental and to characterise mental states. According to Brentano, all mental phenomena are intentional; indeed, that something is intentional defines it as a mental phenomenon. This is what has become known as an 'irreducibility thesis': the mental cannot be reduced to the physical.

Brentano's biggest influence was on Husserl, who in his *Ideas* (1913) extends the concept of intentionality to all experiences of thought, feeling or will: intentionality and phenomenal experience are for Husserl inextricably linked. In a celebrated pastiche of René Descartes' description of the experience of looking around his room, Husserl describes the experience of perceiving a sheet of white paper in a dim light, to draw a distinction between perceptual experience and something perceived. The concrete experience of the paper appearing from a particular angle, with lack of clarity because of the light, is a conscious experience, and description of that experience is phenomenological description, as opposed to a scientific description of something perceived. A description of consciousness and a description of phenomenal experience are for Husserl one and the same thing: 'the basic character of intentionality [is] the property of being a "consciousness of something"' (Husserl 1931: 120). Moreover, 'the pregnant meaning of the expression *cogito*' (as in Descartes' *cogito ergo sum*, 'I think therefore I am'), is 'I have consciousness of something', or 'I perform an act of consciousness' (Husserl 1931: 118). Thus for Husserl the Cartesian *cogito* is also an intentional act, and Descartes is unwittingly the true father of intentionality.

More recently, intentionality has become of interest to philosophers working in the analytic tradition. In his 'Minds, Brains and Programs' (1980), John Searle demonstrates that a programmed digital computer cannot have cognitive states such as understanding. He does this through a famously elegant thought experiment called the 'Chinese Room'. Searle imagines himself locked in a room and given a batch of Chinese writing. He is then given a second batch of Chinese writing, with a set of rules (in English) correlating the second batch with the first. Finally, he is given a third batch of Chinese writing, with instructions, again in English, for correlating elements of the third batch with the first two batches. Unknown to Searle, who understands no Chinese, the people giving him the batches of Chinese writing call the first a 'script', the second a 'story', and the third 'questions'. Eventually Searle becomes so good at following the instructions for manipulating the symbols that, from the point of view of someone outside the room, his answers to questions are indistinguishable from those of a native Chinese speaker. However, we remember that Searle still understands no Chinese. Unlike the native Chinese speaker, Searle in his room is merely manipulating symbols. This shows that although a computer might in theory be programmed with the sum total of all information there is to be had about the world, this would not mean that the computer understood the world. Understanding is an intentional phenomenon, along with perceiving, acting and learning. Computers merely manipulate symbols, and hence are incapable of being attributed with these intentional phenomena.

Searle elaborates this position in two subsequent essays, 'What is an Intentional State?' (1982) and *Intentionality: An Essay in the Philosophy of Mind* (1983), which connect intentional states with speech acts. According to Searle, 'intentional states represent objects and states of affairs in exactly the same sense that speech acts represent objects and states of affairs' (1982: 260). This is not to say that intentionality is essentially linguistic: on the contrary, 'language is derived from intentionality, and not

conversely' (ibid.). Nevertheless, the speech-acts distinction between propositional content and illocutionary force has a parallel in intentional states, where it is expressed as a distinction between representative content and psychological mode. For example, a sentence containing a speech-act verb, such as 'I predict that you will leave the room', can be analysed into its illocutionary force of predicting, and its propositional content *that you will leave the room*. A sentence containing an intentional verb, meanwhile, such as 'I believe that you will leave the room', can be analysed into its psychological mode of belief, and its representative content *that you will leave the room*. Further, just as there is a range of 'fits' of speech acts – they may be true or false, obeyed or disobeyed, kept or broken, for example, depending on whether the acts are assertive, directive, commissive and so on – so there is a range of 'fits' of intentional sentences. Beliefs are true or false, while intentions are complied with or not complied with, and desires are fulfilled or unfulfilled. Moreover, an intentional state is a sincerity condition of its type of speech act; 'the performance of the speech act is *eo ipso* an expression of the corresponding intentional state' (Searle 1982: 263), so that it sounds odd to assert, for example, 'Congratulations on winning the prize, but I am not glad you won the prize'. And finally, speech acts and intentional states are linked by 'conditions of satisfaction' or 'conditions of success'. Just as a statement is satisfied if and only if it is true, a promise is satisfied if and only if it is kept, and so on, so a belief is satisfied if and only if it is true, a desire is satisfied if and only if it is fulfilled, and so on. In short, intentional states, like linguistic entities, are not things, but representations – they have logical properties, not ontological ones.

The concept of intentionality continues to be of relevance today, since it is recognised as essential to the ascription of consciousness to beings. The question of how intentionality is produced, and what the criteria are for having a mental state, is therefore important to computer scientists and philosophers of cognitive science. Daniel Dennett (1987, 1993), for example, takes a contrary view to Searle, being prepared to ascribe intentionality to computers and to various animals if they manifest what is perceived to be intentional behaviour.

Primary sources

Brentano, Franz (1973). *Psychology from an Empirical Standpoint*. Trans. A. C. Rancurello, D. B. Terrell and L. L. McAlister. London: Routledge.

Dennett, Daniel C. (1987). *The Intentional Stance*. Cambridge, MA and London: MIT Press.

Dennett, Daniel C. (1993). *Consciousness Explained*. London: Penguin.

Husserl, Edmund (1931). *Ideas: General Introduction to Pure Phenomenology*. Trans. W. R. Boyce Gibson. London: Allen & Unwin.

Searle, John R. (1980). 'Minds, brains, and programs'. *The Behavioral and Brain Sciences* 3: 417–57.

Searle, John R. (1982). 'What is an intentional state?'. In H. L. Dreyfus with H. Hall (ed.), *Husserl, Intentionality, and Cognitive Science*. Cambridge, MA and London: MIT Press.

Searle, John R. (1983). *Intentionality: An Essay in the Philosophy of Mind*. Cambridge: Cambridge University Press.

Further reading

Dreyfus, Hubert L. (1992). *What Computers Can't Do: A Critique of Artificial Reason*. Cambridge, MA and London: MIT Press.

Harney, Maurita J. (1984). *Intentionality, Sense and the Mind*. The Hague: Nijhoff.

Karl Simms

INTUITION

Speakers' introspective judgements about aspects of their language. A source of evidence for theories of language and cognition which has been used extensively in recent decades, particularly under the influence of Noam Chomsky.

See also: Acceptability/ Grammaticality; Adequacy; Corpora; Creativity; Empiricism/Rationalism; Innateness; Mentalism; Transformational-Generative Grammar; Universal Grammar
Key Thinkers: Austin, J. L.; Chomsky, Noam; Greenberg, Joseph; Katz, J. J.; Sinclair, John

Informant intuitions about language have been a major source of data for linguists since the work of Chomsky was first published in the late 1950s. Chomsky argued that there was clear evidence that speakers share systematic intuitions about their languages and that these should be used as data in studying language. Chomsky's work led to major changes in linguistics and in psychology (often referred to as 'the Chomskyan revolution') and a large amount of work in these disciplines is now based on data from intuitions.

Chomsky's work changed linguistics in several ways. He introduced a new way of thinking about what was the object of study (mental grammars) and also about the methods to be used in studying it. Before Chomsky's work, the most common methods used by linguists were 'discovery procedures', which were techniques for 'discovering' facts about the language being studied. Chomsky argued that these techniques must be based on a number of factors, including intuition, and also that speakers' intuitions provide evidence for the existence of an internalised language system which should be the object of study for linguistics. He suggested that the best method for studying the system was to explore the intuitions. One famous data set discussed by Chomsky concerns the examples in (1) and (2):

(1) (a) John is easy to please.
    (b) It is easy to please John.
(2) (a) John is eager to please.
    (b) It is eager to please John.

Chomsky pointed out that (2b) is not a possible way of expressing the same thing as is expressed by (2a) (it is a possible utterance, of course, but only if we take 'it' to refer to a particular entity capable of being eager to please someone). There is no logical reason why (2b) could not be a way of saying the same thing as (2a) by analogy with the pattern in (1a) and (1b), but this is not possible in English. Speakers have

consistent intuitions about this and so this constitutes good data about their underlying system of linguistic knowledge. A large amount of work in linguistics and psychology has been based on evidence from intuitions like this.

From the outset, there was considerable discussion of issues associated with the use of intuitions as data. Chomsky himself pointed out that not all intuitions are as clear, or as clearly shared, as the intuitions about examples like (1)–(2), and he suggested that theories should be based as much as possible on the clearer cases. Other linguists have questioned the usefulness of intuitions at all, arguing that it is better to look at naturally-occurring data, such as data gathered in a corpus. Chomsky has always rejected this view, pointing out what he sees as serious problems with such naturally-occurring data. One problem is that there is an element of luck in whether a corpus will provide relevant examples. Related to this is the fact that a corpus cannot provide negative evidence; it cannot show us what is not possible in a language. We cannot, for example, use corpus data to find out that sequences like 'It is eager to please John' (with the same reading as (2a)) or 'Which student did Sylvia tell the teacher who taught to go home' are not possible in English.

But the reasons why these are not possible are important if we aim to understand the nature of our language system. Another reason is that Chomsky sees the object of study as an internalised system, which he originally termed 'competence' (Chomsky 1965) and distinguished from language in actual usage, which he termed 'performance'. A large number of irrelevant factors affect performance, for example interruptions, reformulations, the physical and mental state of the speaker. Any corpus shows many examples of 'ungrammatical' utterances involving overlap, false starts, hesitation, repetition, reformulation, unfinished utterances and so on. Chomsky argued that what we should do is look for sophisticated ways of finding data which reveal facts about the underlying system of competence. The best data, he argued, come from the intuitions of speakers.

What are the intuitions exactly? They are often referred to as 'grammaticality judgements' but this is slightly misleading, particularly if we take seriously the distinction between 'grammaticality' and 'acceptability'. Chomsky argues that mental grammars are systems of 'tacit' knowledge: speakers know that (2b) does not work like (1b) but they cannot explain why. There are also a number of well-known examples which speakers reject but which are nevertheless considered to be grammatical, and vice versa. Strictly speaking, then, speakers cannot be relied on to make judgements about 'grammaticality' but only about 'acceptability', that is about whether particular examples 'sound OK' or whether they can imagine hearing or saying them.

This means that intuitions are quite far removed from the system of grammar which is the object of study. Chomsky (1980: 189–92) acknowledged this remoteness, making an analogy with the study of thermonuclear reactions inside the sun. We cannot set up a laboratory inside the sun and observe directly what is happening there. But we can observe light and heat coming from the sun and make inferences about what must be causing what we observe. Similarly, we cannot look directly at the competence of speakers but we can make inferences based on their intuitions about particular examples.

Birdsong (1989) and Schütze (1996) considered methodological issues with the use of intuitions, and used the term 'metalinguistic performance' to describe what speakers are doing when they make these judgements. This term makes clearer what the judgements are and highlights the fact that this approach is using performance data to explore competence.

One major issue which all researchers need to address is that the intuitions of speakers vary. While most speakers will agree on (1)–(2) above, a large number of examples are judged differently by different speakers. One source for the variation in judgements is that all speakers have slightly different language backgrounds and experiences resulting not just in 'dialectal' variation (variation based on where the speaker lives or has lived) but also 'idiolectal' variation reflecting the speaker's individual linguistic history. While there is significant agreement about examples like (1)–(2), there would be variation in responses to (3)–(4):

(3) He and Sylvia will go.
(4) All of the staff are pleased to work here.

In fact, Chomsky has suggested that language is 'an *individual* phenomenon' and that 'no two individuals share exactly the same language' (1988: 36).

Given this variation, linguists need to make idealisations about the language they are studying. They need either to abstract away from the variation and imagine a group of speakers who do share a language, or to focus on describing the competence of just one speaker. In practice, for many linguists, the object of study is their own mental grammar. But even individual speakers do not always make the same judgements about particular examples. So linguists need to be careful not to accept too readily the judgements of informants. A number of studies have compared actual recorded usage of speakers with what they report about themselves and found significant differences.

Schütze (1996) makes a number of suggestions to help address these difficulties. He suggests that it is legitimate to continue to use intuitions as data but suggests that certain 'precautions' should be followed and that linguists should aim to develop other techniques, in particular experimental work. As well as a number of specific suggestions about materials and the procedure of gathering intuitions, one of the main precautions urged by Schütze is that subjects who provide intuitions should never themselves be linguists since there is a risk that their training will interfere with their judgements.

Chomsky has been resolute in rejecting alternative kinds of data, suggesting for example that gathering corpus data is unlikely to lead to significant insights. Other linguists suggest that intuitions are unreliable and that 'naturally-occurring' corpus data should be used instead. Others, like Schütze, envisage research carrying on using a range of kinds of data. For methodologically eclectic linguists, the range of possible sources of data includes elicitation (engaging speakers in conversations which are likely to elicit utterances of the forms being considered), interviews, questionnaires, experiments and corpora.

Primary sources

Chomsky, N. (1965). *Aspects of the Theory of Syntax*. Cambridge, MA: MIT Press.

Schütze, C. T. (1996). *The Empirical Base of Linguistics: Grammaticality Judgements and Linguistic Methodology*. Chicago: Chicago University Press.

Further reading

Birdsong, D. (1989). *Metalinguistic Performance and Interlinguistic Competence*. New York: Springer-Verlag.

Chomsky, N. (1957). *Syntactic Structures*. The Hague: Mouton.

Chomsky, N. (1980). *Rules and Representations*. Oxford: Basil Blackwell.

Chomsky, N. (1988). *Language and Problems of Knowledge: The Managua Lectures*. Cambridge, MA: MIT Press.

Billy Clark

LANGUAGE GAMES

The idea that language use can be compared to a game, where conversational participants are the players and the goal of their conversation can be reached if they perform certain types of moves within the context of publicly-known rules. The philosophical outline was most famously provided by Ludwig Wittgenstein and further developed by a number of researchers in logic*, linguistics, artificial intelligence* and computation.

See also: Artificial Intelligence; Implicature; Speech Act Theory
Key Thinkers: Grice, H. P.; Lewis, David; Wittgenstein, Ludwig

The use of games as paradigms for dialectical situations involving a questioner and an answerer goes back to Aristotle. The idea that all conversation can be understood in terms of a language game, however, is commonly ascribed to Ludwig Wittgenstein who utilises the term to refer to the complex of a particular language and the actions in which it is anchored. In *Philosophical Investigations*, Wittgenstein strives to understand how we acquire the meanings of words. He notes that simply knowing how to name a concept is not sufficient for us to be able to use the word in a conversation; we must also know about the conventions or rules governing its use. In this sense, language can be compared to a game of chess; if we were to teach someone how to play chess, it would not be sufficient to give them the names of the chess figures, we would also have to explain to them how the figures can move on the chess board. Depending on the context, the use of a word or a sentence that exists in the language – a move – can be viewed as more or less appropriate; non-existing language elements are not moves at all.

Jakko Hintikka further extends Wittgenstein's notion in his framework of game-theoretical semantics, an account closely related to Paul Lorenzen's dialogue games (Lorenzen 1955, Lorenzen and Lorenz 1978). In this approach, semantic games between a verifier (the player who is trying to prove that the statement is true) and a falsifier (proving that the statement is false) are used to evaluate logical formulas in a negation normal form. For example, a formula in which the outmost component is an existential quantifier would be interpreted as a game in which the verifier has the first move, selecting a witness to the truth of the formula. The verifier thus substitutes a variable with a proper name referring to an entity which substantiates the property or relation contained in the formula. Similarly, the presence of a disjunction prompts a verifier's move in that she chooses which disjunct she will support. Universal quantifier and conjunction, on the other hand, are moves appointed to the falsifier. A player is said to have a winning strategy (a proof) if she can win disregarding the choices of the opposing player. The semantic game can become more complex if we impose imperfect knowledge on the players, for example by making them 'forget' some of their earlier moves (imperfect recall). Hintikka's game-theoretical semantics has received important applications in logic and on fragments of natural language.

Other recent developments in the field of language and games have primarily been based on research in game theory. Classical game theory describes the behaviour of interacting rational agents who take into account their knowledge of each other's preferences;

it makes use of tools employed by utility and decision theory. Evolutionary game theory includes a description of the changes in players' strategies as they dynamically adapt to their environment.

Various lines of research have been based on the idea that language can be compared to a coordination game (Lewis 1969; Parikh 2001), in accordance with H. P. Grice's view of a conversation as an interaction between rational agents with a shared goal. In a coordination game, players' 'payoffs' are aligned – that is, unlike in other sorts of games examined in the context of game theory, the players do not have opposing interests. Based on their prior beliefs and preferences, the agents would interact in a way that leads them to a good decision as to which actions to perform (problem-solving games) or, in a special case of problem solving, which propositions to consider to be true (inquiries). The shared knowledge of the purpose of the game helps them to code and interpret meaning efficiently and successfully. For example, in David Lewis's signalling games, a signalling system (in fact, a language) evolves between a sender and a receiver if the receiver reacts appropriately to the sender's signal by choosing an action that matches the state of the world. The speaker and the receiver can be compared to two people travelling in a boat; the role of the sender is to signal possible danger ahead; and the role of the receiver is to steer the boat accordingly. A signalling system will evolve if the interaction results in success above chance level, depending on the strategy the agents employ.

For example, in Prashant Parikh's game-theoretic model of communication (an extensive cooperative game with partial information), the hearer disambiguates a speaker's utterance by reasoning about its alternatives and by taking into account the cost associated with producing (and processing) complex expressions.

According to other accounts, a conversation can more appropriately be described as a game of opposing interests (a zero-sum game) or a bargaining (mixed-motive) game, in which the interests of the players are only partially aligned (Merin 1994). According to Arthur Merin's Algebra of Elementary Social Acts, the general purpose of the game is to establish the content of the conversational common ground. The players must have strictly opposing preferences regarding the adoption of the proposition under discussion, since otherwise there would be no point debating it. The communicating agents also have different bargaining powers in the game, expressed by the dominance parameter. Different states of the game – actually, different types of dialogue acts (claim, concession, denial and retraction) – are characterised as sets of values for the dominance parameter, as well as the actor role, initiator role and preference with respect to the proposition under discussion.

As observed in a number of studies, game-theoretical approaches to communication offer the possibility to account for the construction of form-meaning pairs in terms of solution concepts. A well-known solution concept is the Nash Equilibrium – a profile with the players' best response to the choices of other players, all of whom are trying to maximise their payoff. Dekker and Van Rooy (2000) propose to use Nash Equilibria to characterise winning candidates in two-dimensional optimality theory, an extension of optimality theory* employed on the semantics-pragmatics interface. Under the two-dimensional optimality theoretic interpretation, a form-meaning pair is optimal if it satisfies both the speaker's and the hearer's communicative goals, originally expressed by the Gricean maxims and later subsumed under the Q- and R-principle (Horn 1984). The principles capture the intuition that the speaker's and the hearer's attempt to minimise communicative effort leads to opposing preferences (for the speaker, to say as little as possible; for the hearer, to maximise the information value of the message). If the speaker acted only on the basis of her own preferences, our language would consist only of expressions involving low articulatory effort with a high degree of homonymy. A division of the pragmatic labour results in the use of unmarked forms in unmarked situations and marked forms in marked situations.

Other recent accounts of pragmatic phenomena in which the authors make use of game-theoretical results concern indirect speech acts and underspecification, credibility, question-answer pairs and grounding (Benz, Jaeger and van Rooij 2005). The game jargon has also been utilised in computational analyses of dialogue, where dialogue acts are characterised as 'moves' appropriate for different game types. Here, the idea of a language game serves as a loose metaphor rather than as a vehicle for precise formalisation.

Primary sources

Benz, A., G. Jaeger and R. Van Rooij (2005). *Game Theory and Pragmatics*. Basingstoke: Palgrave Macmillan.

Hintikka, J. (1973). *Logic, Language Games and Information: Kantian Themes in the Philosophy of Logic*. Oxford: Clarendon Press.

Lewis, D. (1969). *Convention*. Cambridge, MA: Harvard University Press.

Merin, A. (1994). *Algebra of Elementary Social Acts*. In Tshatzidis, S. (ed), *Foundations of Speech Act Theory*. London: Routledge.

Parikh, P. (2001). *The Use of Language*. Stanford, CA: CSLI Publications.

Wittgenstein, L. (1958). *Philosophical Investigations*. Trans. G. E. M. Anscombe. Oxford: Blackwell.

Further reading

Dekker, P. and R. Van Rooy (2000). 'Bidirectional optimality theory: an application of game theory'. *Journal of Semantics* 17: 217–42.

Horn, L. R. (1984). 'Towards a new taxonomy for pragmatic inference: Q-based and R-based implicatures. In D. Schiffrin (ed.), *Meaning, Form, and Use in Context*. Washington: Georgetown University Press. 11–42.

Lorenzen P. (1955). *Einführung in die operative Logik und Mathematik*. Berlin: Springer.

Lorenzen, P. and K. Lorenz (1978). *Dialogische Logik*. Darmstadt: Wissenschaftliche Buchgesellschaft.

Osborne, M. J. and A. Rubinstein (1994). *A Course in Game Theory*. Cambridge, MA: MIT Press.

Marie Nilsenová

LANGUAGE OF THOUGHT

The Language of Thought Hypothesis is the hypothesis that thinking and thought are conducted in a mental language ('mentalese') that is innate, distinct from all natural languages, universal among all thinking beings, and physically realised in the brain. The language of thought is an important concept in the attempt to find a cognitive and neurological explanation for language and consciousness.

See also: Innateness; Intentionality; Mentalism; Private Language; Propositional Attitudes; Propositions; Universal Grammar
Key Thinkers: Chomsky, Noam; Fodor, Jerry

The Language of Thought Hypothesis (LOTH) was first postulated by Jerry Fodor in 1975. According to this hypothesis, thought and thinking are done in a mental language, 'mentalese'. It is a bold hypothesis insofar as this language is held to be innate, distinct from all natural languages, and physically realised in the brain. LOTH is derived from work on 'propositional attitudes'*, which are described by sentences of the form 'Mary believes that pigs might fly'. The general form of such sentences is '*S As* that P', where *S* is the subject who holds the attitude, *A* is an 'attitudinal' verb such as 'believe', 'desire', 'hope', 'intend' and *P* is any sentence. It may be seen that 'attitudinal' verbs coincide with what elsewhere in the philosophy of mind are called 'intentional' verbs: there is a sense, there-fore, in which LOTH is an alternative to the theory of intentionality*.

LOTH is predicated on a number of theses. The first is so-called 'representational realism', or the holding of a Representational Theory of Mind (RTM). According to this theory, there is a unique, distinct, dedicated psychological relation for each propo-sitional attitude, and each thought incorporating an attitudinal verb is a token of this mental type. Thinking is thoughts joined up – in other words, causal sequences of tokenings of this mental representation of the attitude, be it belief, desire, or whatever. It fol-lows that there is a strong rationalist bias in LOTH: thinking is defined as rational thought, the ratiocinative process consisting of thoughts in causal sequence.

The second LOTH thesis is that these mental representations belong to a representational or symbolic system that is itself language-like. This is the part of the hypothesis that is most closely influenced by Noam Chomsky: roughly speaking, this sym-bolic system (often called 'mentalese') corresponds to what Chomsky calls 'competence' or 'deep structure'. Mentalese has its own grammar, and one which is, moreover, universal. LOTH, despite being concerned with propositional attitudes rather than propositional content, is thus situated in the tradition of linguistic thought stretching back to Port-Royal logic*, which sees the purpose of language as being predicative, that is to make propositional statements about the world which are demonstrably true or false. LOTH is incompatible with the 'meaning is use' tradition of linguistic philosophy promulgated by Ludwig

Wittgenstein and developed by such philosophers of language as J. L. Austin, H. P. Grice and John Searle. Indeed, Fodor (1975: 55–97) explicitly argues, *contra* Wittgenstein, that a private language* is not impossible, but necessary, and that mentalese is just that private language.

A third LOTH thesis is that the language of thought is distinct – that is, it is not identical to any spoken language. This is again a strengthening of a Chomskian position: in LOTH, an attempt is made not only at grammatical (syntactic) transformations from deep structure to surface structure, but also at semantic (representational) transformations from mentalese to spoken language.

Fourth, LOTH is a nativist or innatist hypothesis: the language of thought is held to be universal in humans, and to be genetically determined. LOTH is therefore also an empirical hypothesis: it is believed that the language of thought can be discovered as a material reality, as can the biological mechanism that generates it. While this is a development of Chomsky's theory, again it is more radical: for Chomsky, language is uniquely human, whereas for LOTH, it is at least partly possessed by all species which have cognitive processes. And while Chomsky holds that a being needs a language acquisition device in order to learn language, LOTH holds that a being needs a language in order to learn a language – and that language is mentalese. The language of thought is the hypothesis used to explain how it is that certain animals, and pre-linguistic infant children, can be seen to be thinking, even though they have no spoken language

capacity. Innateness is necessary to the hypothesis in order to guard against an infinite regress: if mentalese is innate, then there is no need to postulate a language that a being would need in order to learn a language in order to learn a language, and so on, since mentalese is not learned.

As well as being a nativist thesis, LOTH is also a naturalist one. It attempts to answer the 'hard question' of consciousness, which in Fodor's own words is, 'How could anything material have conscious states?' (1991: 285). LOTH answers this question by collapsing mind into brain: contrary, for example, to psychoanalysis*, it has no need of psychic processes.

According to LOTH, propositional thought cannot be accounted for exclusively through mental images, but requires a syntax that combines sentences. It follows that, finally, LOTH is predicated on a theory of 'semantic completeness'; in other words, any predicate that has meaning in any spoken language is also expressible in the language of thought.

It is the second LOTH thesis – that mental representations belong to a language-like representational or symbolic system, mentalese – which is the most original feature of the hypothesis, and also the most contentious. LOTH holds that each propositional attitude (belief, desire and so on) is a function in the mathematical or computational sense. LOTH is often characterised as a species of 'functionalist materialism'. According to this view, that a being should have a propositional attitude is enabled (some would say, caused) by physical properties of that being, especially neurological properties. These physical properties realise mental representations through performing computational operations, expressed as functions, on them. Moreover, each function is specific to a certain attitude: belief is expressed through a belief-function, desire through a desire-function and so on. Thus the general form of the language of thought, '*S As* that P' may be read as '*S* performs a computational operation on *P*'. According to this view, subjects do not directly believe that, for example, it is raining, but rather believe the proposition 'it is raining' to be true.

This computational theory of language and mind implies that a computer could be constructed with propositional attitudes, and that conversely, a certain kind of computer could serve as a model of the human mind-brain. This once again pits LOTH against speech act theorists such as Searle, who in his Chinese Room thought experiment sought to demonstrate that a digital computer could not have intentionality*. Searle's answer to the question of what intentionality 'is' was that it is not a thing, but a logical property. LOTH's answer to the same question, on the other hand, is that intentionality is reducible to a specific computational operation. In this view, 'intentionality' becomes a misnomer: propositional attitudes are propositional functions of mental processes. Interactions between thoughts and concepts are merely computations, and 'meaning' is merely the internal interaction of thought with concept.

As an empirical, naturalistic theory of how the mind works, LOTH, despite the controversy it continues to generate, is an important hypothesis in cognitive psychology and neuroscience. It is especially important as a conceptual tool in attempts to make the findings of cognitive science accord with folk psychology (people's commonsensical beliefs about other people's propositional attitudes), as seen, for example, in the work of Daniel Dennett.

Primary sources

Carruthers, Peter (1996). *Language, Thought and Consciousness: An Essay in Philosophical Psychology*. Cambridge: Cambridge University Press.

Dennett, Daniel C. (1987). 'Reflections: the language of thought reconsidered'. In *The Intentional Stance*. Cambridge, MA and London: MIT Press, 227–35.

Fodor, Jerry A. (1975). *The Language of Thought*. Hassocks: Harvester.

Fodor, Jerry A. (1987). *Psychosemantics: The Problem of Meaning in the Philosophy of Mind*. Cambridge, MA and London: MIT Press.

Fodor, Jerry A. (1990). *A Theory of Content and Other Essays*. Cambridge, MA and London: MIT Press.

Fodor, Jerry A. (1991). 'Replies'. In B. Loewer and G. Rey (eds), *Meaning in Mind: Fodor and his Critics*. Oxford: Blackwell. 255–319.

Further reading

Cain, M. J. (2002). *Fodor: Language, Mind and Philosophy*. Cambridge: Polity.

Loewer, Barry, and Georges Rey (eds) (1991). *Meaning in Mind: Fodor and his Critics*. Oxford: Blackwell.

Karl Simms

LANGUE/PAROLE

Referring to two aspects of language examined by Ferdinand de Saussure at the beginning of the twentieth century, *langue* denotes a system of internalised, shared rules governing a national language's vocabulary, grammar, and sound system; *parole* designates actual oral and written communication by a member or members of a particular speech community. Saussure's understanding of the nature of language and his belief that scholarship should focus on investigating the abstract systematic principles of language instead of researching etymologies and language philosophy led to a revolution in the field of linguistics.

See also: Phoneme; Signs and Semiotics; Structuralism; Transformational-Generative Grammar
Key Thinkers: Bakhtin, Mikhail; Barthes, Roland; Bloomfield, Leonard; Boas, Franz; Chomsky, Noam; Jakobson, Roman; Pike, Kenneth; Sapir, Edward; Saussure, Ferdinand de

The discussion concerning *langue* and *parole* was first suggested by Ferdinand de Saussure and popularised in his *Cours de Linguistique Générale* (*Course in General Linguistics*), a series of Saussure's university lectures collected by his students and published posthumously in 1916. Abandoning the mindset, goals and objectives of historical linguistics, Saussure advocated a synchronic examination of language. Not interested in studying a particular language or the linguistic habits of any one member of a given speech community, Saussure sought to examine language in general and to identify the systems or rules and conventions according to which language functions. Saussure's views on language influenced linguistics during the twentieth century, and his imprint can be found in theoretical works discussing phonetics, phonology, morphology, syntax, pragmatics and especially semantics. Indeed, the distinction between *langue* and *parole* forms an important part of the theoretical basis of structuralism*.

A popular lecturer at the University of Geneva, Saussure suggested ideas and concepts that fascinated his students, yet he did not personally write an authoritative guide to his views. Two colleagues of his, Charles Bally and Albert Sechehaye, collected and edited student notes from three occasions during 1906–11 when he delivered his lectures, publishing the assembled remarks under the title *Cours de Linguistique Générale* in 1916. In the 1990s newly-edited versions of student notes based on Saussure's lectures, along with translations into English, appeared. At the beginning of the twenty-first century, there is still disagreement about a number of Saussure's statements, and problems surrounding the fragmented nature of some of the student notes have not been fully resolved.

Through *Cours de Linguistique Générale*, Saussure's views concerning language and the study of language were introduced to scholars throughout the world. Saussure rejected the nineteenth-century notion that linguistics should be primarily historical and comparative, and disagreed vigorously with the idea that substantial effort should be made to identify, codify and promote the standard form of any national language; he felt it was more worthwhile to focus attention on describing language as it exists at a given point in time, and believed that this activity could be conducted in an impartial manner.

For Saussure, three aspects of language could be potential objects of consideration in linguistic study, and he used the French words *langage*, *langue* and *parole* to designate these aspects. *Langage* refers to the anatomical ability and psychological need or urge of humans to create a system of linguistic signs for expressing ideas. *Langue* represents a system of rules, usages, meanings and structures that are products of the human ability to create language and are shared by members of a specific speech community. *Parole* is often equated with speech. It is the concrete realisation of a collectively-internalised system and also reflects the personality, creativity and physiological capabilities of an individual speaker.

Overall Saussure paid little attention to *langage*, considering it the subject matter of other fields of inquiry, and he regarded *parole* as too idiosyncratic. Instead, he believed that linguistics should study *langue* in order to gain a picture of the comprehensive, complex, ordered assemblage of sounds, words and syntactical units. Making use of a concept suggested in the writings of the French sociologist and philosopher Émile Durkheim, Saussure viewed language as a social fact. According to Saussure, language is acquired through the socialisation process; it is not created through a speaker's ingenuity or experimentation. Moreover, he felt that an individual's potential influence on language is minimal. An individual might create a memorable turn of phrase, but that person is unable to affect the overall structure or sound system of a given language. Finally, speakers can manipulate language in minor ways, but language imposes its rules, order and possibilities on all speakers without exception.

As part of their intuitive knowledge of *langue*, members of a speech community share possession and comprehension of a body of signs (*signes*). According to Saussure, a sign consists of two components: a signifier (*signifiant*) and a signified (*signifié*). Linguistic signs can encompass words, units of grammar, and expressions. The signifier is a sound or series of sounds, and the signified is the meaning that the sounds represent. Saussure was careful to note that signs are actually linked to clusters of meanings or associations and not to specific things. For example, the word 'house' does not refer to a specific object in the world but rather to a concept involving images and associations that speakers have in mind when they say or write the word. Furthermore, the connection between the series of sounds and the cluster of images and emotions is arbitrary. The words 'girl', 'Mädchen', and 'niña' might all refer to a female child, but there is no direct connection between the sounds of each word and the meaning. Even so, speakers form a strong connection in their minds between sounds and meaning.

Saussure stated that *langage*, the psychological and physiological faculty to produce meaningful language, does not manifest itself solely in the creation of individual sounds, words or units of meaning, and he stressed that *parole*, individual communication within a speech community, does not take on the form of a string of unrelated utterances. *Langage* becomes a reality in *langue* – and ultimately in *parole* – through the rules governing the use and organisation of signs. These linguistic conventions are expressed in the form of syntagmatic and paradigmatic rules, two types of systems that enable language to convey messages by organising and sequencing the building blocks of sound and meaning. Syntagmatic relationships refer to the limitations governing sequences of sounds, parts of words, and complete words offered by a given national language to create meaning. Paradigmatic relationships concern the existence of words of similar meaning or grammatical form that can substitute for each other in a given context.

Saussure's views concerning *langue* and *parole*, as well as his understanding of the purpose and goals of linguistics, have exerted immense influence on linguists in Europe and North America. Leonard Bloomfield, Franz Boas and Edward Sapir adopted Saussure's method of objective, synchronic language study as the basis for their descriptive analyses of various North American Indian languages. Bloomfield also incorporated elements of Saussure's innovative teachings into his writings, most notably *Language* (1933). Roman Jakobson and other members of the Prague School of Linguistics were inspired by Saussure as they investigated sound systems and developed theories of phonetics and phonology. On occasion, agreement or disagreement with Saussure's beliefs can be traced back to an individual's political and philosophical leanings. The Marxist linguist Mikhail Bakhtin disapproved of Saussure's efforts to distinguish individual production of language (*parole*) from collective knowledge and linguistic awareness (*langue*), a division that, to Bakhtin's way of thinking, isolates an individual from society; he was much more in favour of a theory of language that portrays speech as dependent on, and a product of, a specific social context. Stimulated by Saussure's discussion of the sign and its two components – the signified and the signifier – Roland Barthes investigated the contrast between the message of our speech and its form and articulation, and Kenneth Pike advanced his system of tagmemics, a type of grammatical analysis developed in the 1950s. Noam Chomsky, too, responded to Saussure's ideas when he transformed Saussure's concepts of *langage*, *langue* and *parole* into 'language capacity', 'competence' and 'performance', and achieved a new understanding of the Saussurean concepts. Twenty-first-century linguists remain attracted to Saussure's concept of the dual nature of language and to his theory of meaning.

Primary sources

Saussure, Ferdinand de (1996). *Premier Cours de Linguistique Générale (1907): d'après les cahiers d'Albert Riedlinger.* French ed. Eisuke Komatsu. English ed. and trans. George Wolf. Oxford: Pergamon.

Saussure, Ferdinand de (1997). *Deuxième Cours de Linguistique Générale (1908–1909): d'après les cahiers d'Albert*

Riedlinger et Charles Patois. French ed. Eisuke Komatsu. English ed. and trans. George Wolf. Oxford: Pergamon.

Saussure, Ferdinand de (1993). *Troisième Cours de Linguistique Générale (1910–1911): d'après les cahiers d'Émile Constantin*. French ed. Eisuke Komatsu. English ed. and trans. Roy Harris. Oxford: Pergamon.

Saussure, Ferdinand de (1966). *Course in General Linguistics. Cours de Linguistique Générale*. Trans. Wade Baskin. New York: McGraw-Hill. First French edition 1916.

Further reading

Chomsky, Noam (1964). *Current Issues in Linguistic Theory*. The Hague: Mouton.

Harris, Roy (1987). *Reading Saussure: A Critical Commentary on the 'Cours de Linguistique Générale'*. London: Duckworth.

Harris, Roy (2004). *Saussure and His Interpreters*. Edinburgh: Edinburgh University Press.

Koerner, E. F. K. (1973). *Ferdinand de Saussure: The Origin and Development of His Linguistic Thought in Western Studies of Language*. Amsterdam: Benjamins.

Sanders, Carol (ed.) (2004). *The Cambridge Companion to Saussure*. Cambridge: Cambridge University Press.

David V. Witkosky

LINGUISTIC RELATIVITY

The idea central to the Sapir-Whorf hypothesis, which states that the limits of the native speaker's language are the limits of his/her world. In theories of linguistic relativity, the vocabulary and linguistic structure of one's native language limits or influences one's *Weltanschauung* or world view.

See also: Feminism; Political Correctness; Structuralism
Key Thinkers: Humboldt, Wilhelm von; Peirce, C. S.; Sapir, Edward; Saussure, Ferdinand de; Whorf, Benjamin Lee

The idea that the native language colours the speaker's world view has been in the forefront of linguistic science since the time of Wilhelm von Humboldt, and has found advocates and critics from various disciplines. The American philosopher Charles Sanders Peirce postulated that the symbolic universe could only make sense through language, which he defined as semiotic, a system of signs. Ferdinand de Saussure, in the *Cours de Linguistique Générale*, stated that: 'No ideas are established in advance, and nothing is distinct, before the introduction of linguistic structure' (1916: 155). However, the notion of linguistic relativity has largely become associated with Benjamin Lee Whorf, who along with Edward Sapir, his linguistic mentor at Yale University, used modern linguistic concepts to advocate the position that language limits, or at least influences, the way a speech community conceives of its world view and reality.

Part of the groundwork for this hypothesis was laid by Whorf's work as a fire insurance investigator. During his career, he had the opportunity to analyse many reports as to why fires broke out in factories. He found that workers would use extreme caution when around 'full' drums of gasoline. Just as one would expect, workers were careful not to smoke around 'full' drums. Yet, these same workers when around 'empty' drums of gasoline would often toss lit cigarettes nearby. This caused a violent explosion because an 'empty' drum (unknown to the smoker) still contained volatile gasoline vapour; an 'empty' drum was really much more of a threat than a 'full' one. Using these data, Whorf concluded that the meanings of certain words had an effect on a person's behaviour.

It was the research of both Sapir and Whorf into the grammatical systems of many American Indian languages, however, that proved to have the greatest impact on this hypothesis. By predicating their insights into the interrelationships of language and culture on what they had learned from the structures of these so-called 'exotic' languages, the basic idea of language shaping the perceptions of its speakers and providing for them a vehicle so that their experiences and emotions can be placed in significant categories, was given scientific underpinnings. Generally, Sapir is credited with giving the problem of establishing the link between language and culture its initial formulation, continuing in the tradition of Johann Gottfried Herder and Humboldt. Whorf is honoured as the one who took this idea and developed it into a *bona fide* hypothesis. Hence, the resultant supposition is commonly given the designation the 'Whorfian hypothesis'. Pointing to Sapir's pre-eminent stature as a linguist, some writers prefer the appellation the 'Sapir-Whorf hypoth-esis'. When viewed in terms of output, one could counter that a more appropriate label would be the 'Whorf-Sapir hypothesis'.

A rather interesting development in this debate over giving credit where credit is due has been the attempt to disassociate Sapir from the hypothesis entirely. Desirous of preventing the image of the great *maestro* Sapir from being tarnished by the taint of controversy, some, most notably Alfred L. Kroeber, have claimed that Edward Sapir's views were not really pro-Whorfian. This viewpoint is not borne out by an examination of Sapir's own writings. For example, as one can plainly see in the following passage, there can be no doubt that Sapir's position was fundamentally one that equated language with culture and thinking. In Sapir's words:

> Language is a guide to 'social reality' . . . it powerfully conditions all our thinking about social problems and processes. Human beings do not live in the objective world alone, nor alone in the world of social activity as ordinarily understood, but are very much at the mercy of the particular language which has become the medium of expression for their society. It is quite an illusion to imagine that one adjusts to reality essentially without the use of language and specific problems of communication or reflection . . . No two languages are ever sufficiently similar to be considered as representing the same social reality . . . We see and hear and otherwise experience very largely as we do because the language habits of our community predispose certain choices of interpretation. (1929: 209)

There are really two different yet related versions of the Whorfian hypothesis, which is understandable when one considers that Whorf did all of his professional writing in the rather short period between 1925 and 1941. His ideas, quite naturally, were continuously developing. The strong version of the hypothesis, which is called linguistic determinism, holds that language determines thinking, or as Stuart Chase writes in the foreword to Whorf's collected works: 'All higher levels of thinking are dependent on language' (in Carroll 1956: vi). This position is most difficult to defend primarily because translation between one language and another is possible, and 'thinking' can take place without language at all, as evidenced by fine art.

Mirroring Sapir's thoughts as mentioned above, Whorf notes in his 1940 article 'Science and Linguistic':

> We dissect nature along lines laid down by our native languages ... We cut nature up, organize it into concepts, and ascribe significances as we do, largely because we are parties to an agreement to organize it in this way – an agreement that holds throughout our speech community and is codified in the patterns of our language. (In Carroll 1956: 213)

The milder version of the Whorfian hypothesis is labelled 'linguistic relativity'. This states that our native language *influences* our thoughts or perceptions. In fact, it was Whorf who coined the phrase 'linguistic relativity'. In the article 'Linguistics as an Exact Science', Whorf commented:

what I have called the 'linguistic relativity principle', which means, in informal terms, that users of markedly different grammars are pointed by their grammars toward different types of observations and different evaluations of externally similar acts of observation, and hence are not equivalent as observers but must arrive at somewhat different views of the world. (In Carroll 1956: 221)

Perhaps the most incontrovertible piece of evidence in favour of linguistic relativity comes from the realm of numbers and numerals. There are languages, such as Hottentot, also known as Nama, which only have words for the numerals for 'one' and 'two' and a word roughly translatable as 'many' for three or more. A few languages have no numerals whatsoever and their speakers are consequently unable to undertake even basic arithmetic.

In Whorf's undated manuscript 'A Linguistic Consideration of Thinking in Primitive Communities', it is shown that the problem of 'thinking' by so-called 'primitive' peoples is 'approachable through linguistics' (in Carroll 1956: 65). Further, as linguists have come to fully appreciate only fairly recently, Whorf maintained that 'linguistics is essentially the quest of MEANING' (in Carroll 1956: 73). Example after example is given of things which are relatively easy to say in Hopi but awkward or clumsy to say in such Standard-Average-European (SAE) languages as English, Spanish and German. The term SAE was of Whorf's own invention.

In the classic 'An American Indian Model of the Universe', Whorf argues that since there is neither an explicit nor an implicit reference to time in the Hopi language and thus no tenses for its verbs, according to the Hopi view of the world 'time disappears and space is altered' (in Carroll 1956: 58). Whorf's basic contention is that Hopi metaphysics, which underlies its cognition, is different from our own. In other words, the Hopi calibrate the world differently because their language defines experience differently for them.

As more information has surfaced about Hopi, some of Whorf's specific grammatical points have not withstood the test of time. Although most linguists today dismiss many of Whorf's claims, it should be pointed out that Whorf's basic idea of linguistic relativity – that the structure and vocabulary of one's mother tongue influences one's world view – although not proven to be correct, also has not been proven to be wrong.

Primary sources

Carroll, John B. (ed.) (1956). *Language, Thought and Reality: Selected Writings of Benjamin Lee Whorf*. Cambridge, MA: MIT Press.
Mandelbaum, David G. (ed.) (1949). *Selected Writings of Edward Sapir in Language, Culture, and Personality*. Berkeley: University of California Press.
Sapir, Edward (1929). 'The status of linguistics as a science'. *Language* 5: 207–14.

Further reading

Saussure, Ferdinand de (1916/1966). *Course in General Linguistics (Cours de Linguistique Générale)*. Trans. Wade Baskin. New York: McGraw-Hill.

Alan S. Kaye

LINGUISTIC VARIABLE

A descriptive unit defined as a category of two or more linguistic alternatives co-varying with one another in one of three ways: in a categorical way (the variation always occurs given certain circumstances); in a quasi-predictable or probabilistic way (in line, for example, with another linguistic variable or a social variable); or in an apparently unpredictable, random way ('free variation'). The central idea is that there are 'multiple ways of saying the same thing', though debate continues as to whether two different linguistic structures are ever exactly equivalent in function and/or meaning, and about the extent to which individual language users are able to exercise conscious choice over which alternative to select from the range available.

See also: Acceptability/ Grammaticality; Conversation Analysis; Corpora; (Critical) Discourse Analysis; Descriptivism; Emic/Etic; Empiricism/Rationalism; Intuition; Speech Act Theory; Type/Token
Key Thinkers: Cameron, Deborah; Halliday, M. A. K.; Pike, Kenneth; Labov, William; Milroy, Lesley; Sapir, Edward

Variables operate at all levels of linguistic structure. Grammatical variables capture some aspect of optionality in the occurrence of morphological or syntactic forms. For instance, the use of double modal constructions like 'might could' (+ main verb) is not obligatory in those varieties of English which permit it. The study of lexical variables, traditionally the province of nineteenth-and twentieth-century dialect geographers, involves examination of alternative words or phrases for the same object or concept in a language's different dialects or sociolects. Discourse variables, such as tag questions and the focus marker 'like', are more difficult to handle given that it is not always clear that utterances in which they occur can necessarily be viewed as functionally equivalent to those in which they could occur but do not. Problems involving incomplete synonymy of syntactic structures, discourse variables and lexical variables tend not to arise with phonological variables, as the equivalence of two alternative pronunciations is generally unambiguous. For example the use of [ω] rather than [w] in the word 'which' indicates a difference in two individuals' geographical and/or social origins, rather than a difference in the word's meaning.

Knowing that there are different ways of expressing the 'same thing' is almost certainly an intrinsic component of untrained native speakers' knowledge of their language(s). Awareness of the variable's utility as a means of formally accounting for linguistic alternations is apparent in the Sanskrit grammar of Pānini (seventh to fourth centuries BC) which contains variable rules allowing for differing outputs. The notion is implicit in the historical linguistics and dialectology of more recent centuries, for example in the work of William Jones on genetic affiliations between Indo-European languages, and it forms a central element of the theoretical machinery of variationist sociolinguistics, enabling quantitative analysis of language data.

Primary sources

Watt, Dominic (2007). 'Variation and the variable'. In C. Llamas, P. Stockwell and L. Mullany (eds), *The Routledge Companion to Sociolinguistics*. London: Routledge. 3–11.

Wolfram, Walt (1991). 'The linguistic variable: fact and fantasy'. *American Speech*. Vol. 66:1, 22–32.

Further reading

Cornips, Leonie and Corrigan, Karen (eds) (2005). *Syntax and Variation: Reconciling the Biological and the Social*. Amsterdam: John Benjamins.

Guy, Gregory (1997). 'Competence, performance and the generative grammar of variation'. In F. Hinskens, R. van Hout and L. Wetzels (eds), *Variation, Change and Phonological Theory*. Amsterdam: John Benjamins. 125–43.

Dominic Watt

LOGIC

Logic is the study of argument. Logic is central to philosophy, linguistics and many other fields.

> See also: Logical Form; Port-Royal Logic; Truth Value
> Key Thinkers: Aristotle; Frege, Gottlob; Russell, Bertrand

An argument is an attempt to persuade using reasoning. Arguments are composed of statements. As standard, each statement has a truth value*: it is either true or false, but not both. Normally, an argument has at least one premise and exactly one main conclusion. The main conclusion of an argument is the statement it ultimately aims to support. The premises are the statements that are meant to support the conclusion. An inference is a step in reasoning.

Logic is primarily concerned with deductive arguments. These aim to be valid. An argument is valid if and only if the truth of the premises would guarantee the truth of the conclusion. If it is consistent to assert an argument's premises and deny its conclusion, the argument is invalid. The validity or invalidity of an argument does not depend on the actual truth values of its parts: it depends on their possible truth values. As Figure 3 shows, four permutations of truth-values are possible.

The only permutation of truth values that debars an argument from being valid is 3. This is because valid inferences are truth-preserving: if the inference from a given set of premises to a given conclusion is valid, then if the premises are all true, the conclusion must also be true. (Embodying 1, 2 or 4 does not make an argument valid, but nor does it disqualify the argument from

being valid.) To appreciate that it is possible, rather than actual, truth values that matter to validity, consider the following arguments embodying 2 and 4:

Argument 2*

P1 All US presidents are communists.
P2 George W. Bush is a US president.
C George W. Bush is a communist.

Argument 4*

P1 All US presidents before 2007 were male.
P2 Eugene McCarthy was a US president before 2007.
C So, Eugene McCarthy was male.

In 2*, P1 is false and C is false. However, if we assume, for the purposes of testing for validity, that P1 and P2 are both true, then we cannot deny C without being committed to a contradiction. So, the argument is valid: if its premises were all true, then its conclusion would be true. In 4*, P2 is false. If the premises of 4* were all true, then the conclusion would have to be true as well, on pain of contradiction. So again we have a valid argument.

1	3
All the premises are true. The conclusion is true.	All the premises are true. The conclusion is false.
2	4
At least one premise is false. The conclusion is false.	At least one premise is false. The conclusion is true.

Figure 3

To assess an argument for validity by informal means, first suppose that all its premises are true. Then ask whether, under this supposition, the conclusion must also, on pain of contradiction, be considered true as well. If so, the argument is valid. If not, it is invalid. Consider the following argument:

Argument T

P1 If the war in Iraq was a war for oil, then it was an unjust war.
P2 The war in Iraq was not a war for oil.
C The war in Iraq was not an unjust war.

Suppose, for the test, that P1 and P2 of Argument T are both true. Would this then guarantee that C is true? No. P1 does not assert that the only way in which the war could have been unjust is by being a war for oil. Nothing in the content of the premises rules out that the war was unjust by virtue of some other factor, so the conclusion does not follow.

Aristotle founded the discipline of logic. He defines a proposition as 'a statement denying or affirming something of something' (*Prior Analytics*, 24ᵃ). Propositions* are of subject-predicate form, where a subject term picks something out and a predicate term says something about it. Aristotle uses letters to serve as term variables, that is, to stand proxy for any terms whatever. For example, 'If *A* predicated of every *B*, *B* every *C*, *A* be predicated of every *C*' (*Prior Analytics*, 26ᵃ) depicts a valid argument form. Here is an instance of that form:

Argument F
Every human is mortal.
Every philosopher is human.
So, every philosopher is mortal.

By using term variables, Aristotle is able to discuss the logical forms of various arguments in abstraction from the general terms (for example, 'human', 'mortal', 'philosopher') those arguments employ in natural language. Formal logic goes beyond the informal method of testing for validity. The formal logician codifies deductive reasoning to help distinguish valid argument forms from invalid ones. Aristotle is a formal logician in our sense: the term variables he uses enable him to discern various patterns of inference valid by virtue of their structures. As well as being a term logic, Aristotle's logic is syllogistic. A syllogism is an argument with two premises and a conclusion, in which both premises and the conclusion are general sentences. The sorts of general sentence Aristotle is concerned with are what he calls 'universal' and 'particular' sentences (*De Interpretatione*, 17ᵃ–17ᵇ): sentences that use expressions equivalent to 'all', 'some' and 'no'. The following types of general sentence can feature in a syllogism:

Every *A* is *B*. (Universal affirmative)
No *A* is *B*. (Universal negative)
Some *A* is *B*. (Particular affirmative)
Some *A* is not *B*. (Particular negative).

The Stoics were also ancient pioneers of logic. Chrysippus (c. 280–c. 207 BC) was the most important Stoic logician. He regarded as valid such forms as 'If the first, then the second; but the first; therefore the second' and 'If the first, then the second; but not the second; therefore not the first' (see Kneale and Kneale 1962: 162–3). 'The first' and 'the second' here are place-markers for complete 'assertibles'. Assertibles are the meanings of declarative sentences (see Bobzien 2003). Stoic logic is a type of propositional (or 'sentential') logic. The Stoics put what are now called the 'logical operators' of propositional logic at the centre of their investigations. Their English equivalents are 'If . . . then . . .', '. . . or . . .', '. . . and . . . ' and 'It is not the case that. . .'. These operators are used to form complex statements: that is, statements with other statements as parts.

In symbolic logic, artificial, 'formal' languages are constructed and employed, in contrast with the mixture of artificial symbols and natural language used by earlier formal logicians. Symbolic logic in this sense developed with the work of Gottlob Frege and of Bertrand Russell and A. N. Whitehead, following earlier nineteenth-century innovations. Frege's work is of unparalleled influence and importance.

Among Frege's most valuable contributions to logic were the inventions of modern predicate logic (also known as 'quantificational logic' and 'predicate calculus') and the first formal system, both originally included in his *Begriffsschrift* (1879). While Frege's notation is obsolete, contemporary logic is built upon his predicate logic and his systematisation of the notion of proof.

A formal language consists of a lexicon (a set of symbols) and a syntax (a set of rules for using the symbols). Logicians distinguish between the 'logical' and the 'non-logical' vocabulary of the lexicon. Let us consider a language of propositional logic, called 'PL' (after Tomassi 1999). The lexicon of PL consists of:

i. The sentence letters: 'P', 'Q', 'R', and so on, which symbolise atomic sentences – that is sentences with no other sentences as parts.

ii. The propositional operators: '~', '&', 'v', '→', '↔', at least roughly equivalent to 'it is not the case that . . .', '. . . and . . .', '. . . or . . .', 'If . . . then . . .', and '. . . if and only if . . .'.

iii. The parentheses: '(' and ')', used as a type of punctuation.

A PL formula is any string of symbols from the lexicon of PL. A well-formed formula (WFF) of PL is a formula constructed in observance of the following formation rules:

1. Every sentence letter is a WFF.
2. Prefixing a WFF with '~' gives a WFF.
3. For any WFFs containing A B, putting them either side of '&' or 'v' or '→' or '↔' and putting parentheses round the resulting formula gives a WFF.
4. Nothing else is a WFF.

The propositional operators are the logical vocabulary of PL. In propositional logic, the quantifiers 'some', 'all' and 'no' (and equivalent expressions) are not treated as logical vocabulary. Thus, not every valid argument is propositionally valid. For example, the validity of a valid syllogism, like Argument F above, depends on expressions other than the propositional operators.

After Aristotle and Frege, predicate logic treats these quantifiers as logical vocabulary. A language of predicate logic both retains and supplements the logical and non-logical vocabulary of a language of propositional logic. Let us specify such a language of predicate logic called 'QL' (for 'Quantificational Logic') broadly after Tomassi (1999). The lexicon of QL consists of the lexicon of PL (that is, i–iii above) plus:

iv. Individual constants: '*a*', '*b*', '*c*', and so on. These are lower-case letters from the beginning of the alphabet, used to symbolise proper names (such as 'Socrates', 'London').

v. Predicate letters: '*F*', '*R*', and so on, used to symbolise predicative expressions (such as '. . . is a man', '. . . loves . . .').

vi. The quantifiers '∃' (the existential quantifier, for 'some') and '∀' (the universal quantifier, for 'all').

vii. Individual variables: '*x*', '*y*', '*z*', and so on.

viii. The identity sign: '='.

ix. The brackets: '[', ']', which are another form of punctuation.

Though formation rules are specifiable for QL, let us instead note two features of QL. First, its logical vocabulary includes the logical operators of PL plus the quantifiers, the individual variables and the identity sign. Second, the non-logical vocabulary of QL, specifically the individual constants and the predicate letters, allows us to formalise, at a sub-sentential level, sentences that do not contain any propositional operators. Both points can be illustrated using a valid argument that is neither propositionally nor syllogistically valid:

Argument A

Socrates is a philosopher.
Therefore, someone is a philosopher.

To translate 'Socrates is a philosopher' into propositional logic, we assign a sentence letter, such as 'P' to the sentence. Since 'Someone is a philosopher' is a different sentence, we assign it a different sentence letter, such as 'Q'. With these assignments, Argument A comes out as:

Argument A*

Premise P
Conclusion Q

The problem with this is that no logical form is revealed, since there are no logical operators in play. So, A* cannot be an instance of a valid logical form of PL and cannot capture the intuitive validity we assign to A. Predicate logic solves this problem. Logical form within atomic sentences is revealed. The way A is dealt with in QL is as follows.

First, we specify a domain of quantification, **D**. This is the set of entities we are quantifying over. Then we specify the meanings of the non-logical vocabulary we are going to use in translating from English to QL. So, we can begin to translate Argument A by specifying the following.

D{human beings}

a Socrates
F . . . is a philosopher

We can now translate the premise of Argument A as:

Fa

We read this as '*a* is *F*'. By convention, we put a predicate letter before a name to which it applies.

The existential quantifier '∃' and the universal quantifier '∀' are used, with the individual variables, to express 'some' and 'all'. Thus, we can translate the conclusion of Argument A as follows:

$$\exists x[Fx]$$

We read this as 'There is an *x* that *x* is *F*', or 'For some *x*, *x* is *F*'. ('*x*' is an individual variable.) So, the translation of Argument A is:

Argument A**

Premise *Fa*
Conclusion ∃*x*[*Fx*]

The validity of A** (and thus of A) is formally demonstrable in predicate logic. (For example, the argument can be proven by using an inference rule called 'Existential Introduction'.) Modern predicate logic has greatly superior expressive power to its predecessors: it captures all the logical form they could capture and logical form that eluded them. This is a legacy from Frege (see Noonan 2001, ch. 2).

Frege also presented the first formal systems of propositional and predicate logic. Minimally, a formal system consists of a formal language plus a method of proof. The latter is a procedure for demonstrating the validity of valid arguments in a formal language. In working with this idea of a formal system, contemporary logicians follow Frege.

The sort of logic normally studied on an introductory course is first-order classical logic. A system of quantifica-tional logic is first-order when it quantifies over individuals but not over properties. 'Higher-order' systems quantify over properties. Such systems include predicate variables among their vocabulary. The bearing of the first-order/higher-order distinction cannot be explored here.

The term 'classical' in 'classical logic' does not refer to the ancient world, but to some basic features shared by all classical systems. These include, among others, adoption of the principle of bivalence (see the entry on truth value*) and an account of logical consequence according to which a given conclusion follows from a given set of premises if and only if the negation of the conclusion is inconsistent with the premises. Non-classical logic is obtainable by extending or revising classical logic.

What is it to extend classical logic? A system of logic *S** is an extension of a system of logic *S* if *S** supplements the language and derivational appara-tus of *S*. By supplementing the lan-guage of *S*, we mean keeping all the symbols and formation rules of *S* and adding further symbols and formation rules. The inference rules of *S** will also supplement those of *S*. Thus, every *S*-argument will be *S**-valid, but not every *S**-valid argument will be *S*-valid. But why extend classical logic? The usual motive is that classi-cal logic does not capture enough validity. For example, classical logic provides us with no formal means of counting as valid such inferences as:

Argument H

It is necessary that Socrates is human.
Therefore, it is not impossible that Socrates is human.

125

Supplementing the vocabulary and rules of inference of a classical system with logical operators standing for 'It is necessary that' and/or 'It is possible that', enables the development of systems of modal logic. A formal system S is said to 'under-generate' relative to natural language if there are valid arguments of natural language that are not S-valid. Modal logicians hold that, in failing formally to account for the validity of such arguments as H, classical logic under-generates.

What is it to revise classical logic and why do so? A system of logic S^* is a revision of a classical system of logic S if and only if S^* discards one or more of the inference rules of S. A formal system is said to 'over-generate' if there are arguments that ought to be considered invalid but which come out as valid within the system. Some logicians object to the classical account of logical consequence on the basis that it results in over-generation. This objection sometimes stems, as in the case of intuitionist logic, from rejection of a principle of classical semantics (see the entry on truth value). If there are classically valid arguments which ought not to be considered valid at all, then at least one of the inference rules of classical logic must be rejected or restricted.

Revisions to classical logic include intuitionist, relevant, fuzzy and dialethic logics. The relevant logician, for example, notes a seemingly odd feature of classical validity: that from contradictory premises any conclusion whatever can validly be inferred. Read (1995: 55) gives the following example:

Ernest is brave and Ernest is not brave. So Ernest is a mountaineer.

The premise here is a contradiction, so it cannot be true. So, we cannot be in a situation in which the premise is true and the conclusion false. Thus we have a classically valid argument. Logicians in the field hold that arguments like Read's example show that the classical account of validity over-generates.

Linguists and philosophers of language investigate the relationship between logic and natural language, asking, for example, about the relationship between logical and grammatical form and the extent to which semantic theory for natural language can be modelled on the formal semantics for logic. Logic is also interesting for linguists because the syntax of a formal language is finitely specifiable by reference to a set of recursive formation rules (for example, the PL formation rules set out above). An analogous set of rules for a natural language would be explanatory with respect to a speaker's capacity to form sentences never previously encountered.

Analytic philosophy* of language, inaugurated by Frege and Russell, has logic at its heart, and some of the foundational works of modern symbolic logic were its impetus. In linguistics, formal semanticists and contemporary syntactic theorists use logic in their analyses of natural language. A solid grounding in logic goes a long way for the student of linguistics or the philosophy of language.

Primary sources

Aristotle. *De Interpretatione*. Trans. J. L. Ackrill. In Jonathan Barnes (ed.)

(1984), *The Complete Works of Aristotle*, vol. 1. Princeton: Princeton University Press. 25–38.

Aristotle. *Prior Analytics*. Trans. A. J. Jenkinson. In Jonathan Barnes (ed.) (1984), *The Complete Works of Aristotle*, vol. 1. Princeton: Princeton University Press. 39–113.

Frege, Gottlob. *Begriffsschrift* (1879/1967). Trans. Stefan Bauer-Mengelberg. In Jean van Heijenoort (ed.) (1967), *From Frege to Gödel: A Sourcebook in Modern Mathematical Logic, 1879–1931*. Cambridge, MA: Harvard University Press. 5–82.

Further reading

Allwood, Jens, Lars-Gunnar Andersson and Östen Dahl (1977). *Logic in Linguistics*. Cambridge: Cambridge University Press.

Bobzien, Susanne (2003). 'Stoic logic'. In Brad Inwood (ed.), *Cambridge Companion to the Stoics*. New York: Cambridge University Press. 85–123.

Noonan, Harold W. (2001). *Frege: A Critical Introduction*. Cambridge: Polity.

Kneale, William and Martha Kneale (1962). *The Development of Logic*. Oxford: Clarendon.

Read, Stephen (1995). *Thinking about Logic*. Oxford: Oxford University Press.

Tomassi, Paul (1999). *Logic*. London: Routledge.

Stephen McLeod

LOGICAL FORM

On one central conception, the logical form of a sentence consists in those of its structural features which clarify why it logically entails other sentences that it entails and why it is entailed by other sentences that logically entail it. Questions about logical form are important to the characterisation of logic and to its relationship with natural language.

See also: Definite Descriptions; Logic; Logical Positivism
Key Thinkers: Aristotle; Chomsky, Noam; Russell, Bertrand

Bertrand Russell aimed to put a conception of logical form at the centre of the practice of philosophy. Logical form in this sense is distinct from the notion called 'LF' by linguists after Noam Chomsky. The investigation of logical form begins with the inquiry into deductive reasoning initiated by ancient logicians. For example, Aristotle noted that any argument that is an instance of the pattern below is deductively valid:

Some As are Bs.
All Bs are Cs.
So, some As are Cs.

Statements themselves have logical forms: 'Some philosophers are logicians' is an instance of the pattern 'Some As are Bs'.

With the development of modern symbolic logic*, a view arose that grammatical form can be misleading as to logical form. For example, on Russell's account, sentences that use definite descriptions* have logical features not evident at the level of surface syntax. In 'The present King of France is bald', none of the words is a logical operator. Russell claims, however, that the sentence is to be analysed as employing covert logical operators.

127

On one view, logical form is construed as relative to a formal language. A sentence in a natural language then has a certain logical form in virtue of its being translatable into an instance of a given sort of formula in the formal language. Alternatively, logical form can be conceived as already present in natural language itself, independently of a given formal language's attempts to represent it. On this second conception, a sentence's logical form is not a matter of it having a certain relation to some construction in a formal language. Rather, the aim of the formal language is to capture intrinsic structural features of sentences of natural language. A related question concerns whether logical form is distinct from, or instead a level of, grammatical form (see Bach 2002).

A central criticism concerns how any division of the vocabulary of a natural language into logical and non-logical terms is to be justified (see Jackson 2006). That is, which words in a natural language are logical operators and which are not? Scepticism about logical form may start from the claim that there is no entirely non-arbitrary answer to this question.

Primary sources

Russell, Bertrand (1914). 'Logic as the essence of philosophy'. In *Our Knowledge of the External World*. Chicago: Open Court. 33–59.

Further reading

Bach, Kent (2002). 'Language, logic, and form'. In Dale Jacquette (ed.), *A Companion to Philosophical Logic*. Oxford: Blackwell. 51–72.

Jackson, Brendan (2006). 'Logical form: classical conception and recent challenges'. *Philosophy Compass* 1/3, 303–316, 10.1111/j.1747–9991.2006.00017.x.

Stephen McLeod

LOGICAL POSITIVISM

A movement in twentieth-century philosophy whose adherents argued that philosophically legitimate discussion must be limited to statements that could be assigned a determinate truth value*. Logical positivism triggered some important debates about the nature of meaning and the appropriate methods and terminologies for the analysis of language.

See also: Analytic Philosophy; Analytic/Synthetic; Deduction/Induction; Empiricism/Rationalism; Logic; Truth Value
Key Thinkers: Ayer, A. J.; Carnap, Rudolf; Russell, Bertrand

Logical positivism was practised in various forms in Europe and the USA in the early and mid-twentieth century, but it is most closely associated with the work of the Vienna Circle. This was a group of philosophers led by Moritz Schlick and including Rudolf Carnap, Otto Neurath and Friedrich Waismann who held meetings at the University of Vienna during the 1920s and 1930s. They were committed to establishing a rigorously scientific mode of philosophical inquiry where positive, or empirically justified, knowledge was expressed in logically coherent language. Members of the Vienna Circle published a number of monographs and journal articles in German, but their ideas were disseminated more widely, and in particular became available to an English-speaking audience, when A. J. Ayer published *Language, Truth and Logic* in 1936, after a attending a number of meetings of the Circle on an extended visit to Vienna.

Logical positivism was not primarily concerned with the analysis of natural language; in fact Carnap and others were openly dismissive of everyday usage. They saw it as imprecise and illogical; its statements were in need of translation into a logically acceptable form before they could be the subject of serious discussion. Rather, the impact of logical positivism on language study was due largely to its criterion of meaningfulness. To be counted as meaningful and therefore admitted into philosophical discussion, a statement must be capable of being classified as either true or false. Analytic statements, a class taken by the logical positivists to include the statements of mathematics and logic*, were meaningful because they were true by virtue of their own internal properties. Synthetic statements could be admitted as meaningful if they were capable of being subjected to an identifiable process of verification: that is, if it was possible to establish what sort of empirical evidence a statement could be evaluated against in order to establish whether it was true or false. All other statements – synthetic statements that were not amenable to verification – were simply meaningless. This class included the statements of meta-

physics, of aesthetics and, most controversially of all, of ethics and religion.

Logical positivism was beset with various problems, for instance to do with the reliability of empirical evidence and the method of induction* on which it depended, and was gradually modified or abandoned. However, its influence has continued to be felt in the philosophy of language and subsequently in linguistics, largely because of the alternative ideas about meaning that its critics suggested. For instance, W. V. O. Quine advocated holism* in an account of meaning, rather than expecting each statement in a language to be justified by an independent process of verification. J. L. Austin argued that 'true' and 'false' were not the only philosophically interesting labels that could be applied to uses of language, a position that led to his development of speech act theory*. This in turn has had a significant impact on how meaning is discussed in present-day linguistics.

Primary sources

Ayer, A. J. (1946). *Language Truth and Logic*. Second edition. Harmondsworth: Pelican (1971). First edition London 1936.

Ayer, A. J. (ed.) (1959). *Logical Positivism*. Glencoe, IL: The Free Press.

Carnap, Rudolf (1932). 'The elimination of metaphysics through logical analysis of language'. In A. J. Ayer (1959), *Logical Positivism*. Glencoe, IL: The Free Press. 60–81.

Schlick, Moritz (1930). 'The turning point in philosophy'. In A. J. Ayer (ed.) (1959) *Logical Positiviism*. Glencoe, IL: The Free Press. 53–9.

Further reading

Gower, Barry (ed.) (1987). *Logical Positivism in Perspective*. London: Croom Helm.

Stadler, Friedrich (ed.) (1993). *Scientific Philosophy: Origins and Developments*. Dordrecht: Kluwer Academic Publishers.

Siobhan Chapman

MENTALISM

A notion that can be applied to any linguistic theory that deals with the relationship between language and the mind. It explores the relationship between language, thought and reality, and describes the internal language devices which explain the creativity in language acquisition and the processes involved in thinking, speaking and understanding.

> *See also*: Artificial Intelligence; Behaviourism; Cognitivism; Innateness; Language of Thought; Linguistic Relativity
> *Key Thinkers*: Bloomfield, Leonard; Chomsky, Noam; Descartes, René; Sapir, Edward; Skinner, B. F.; Whorf, Benjamin Lee

Mentalism dates back to the emergence of scientific psychology in the early twentieth century. It has been in constant rivalry with behaviourism* ever since John B. Watson's (1919) reaction to the mentalist methods of introspection and descriptions of feelings and thoughts. Whereas for mentalists the main concern is the question of whether the mind is accessible for introspection, behaviourists base their investigations on objectively observable data. Behaviourists see language acquisition as a conditioning process, while mentalists propagate an inborn device according to which language is acquired systematically.

The first mentalists were psychologists such as Edward Thorndike and Edward Bradford Titchener, whose aim was to study the mind scientifically using methods of association and introspection. Their objects of inquiry were 'mental facts', and they were convinced that by replacing speculation with experimentation, the mind could be analysed into the components from which complex thoughts are constructed.

Another kind of mentalist linguistic theory is rooted in the study of Native American languages. Edward Sapir (1921) and Benjamin Lee Whorf (1956) claimed that every language has its own descriptive categories through which the world is seen. Language shapes thought and is not just an expression of thought; thus it is evidence of how people think.

Mentalism was revived and developed by Noam Chomsky (1965, 1968), based on René Descartes' rationalism, as a reaction to Leonard Bloomfield's structuralistic approach and B. F. Skinner's radical behaviourism. In contrast to these theories, which concentrated on observable surface structures, Chomsky postulated an underlying deep structure as well as an innate language acquisition device that enables human beings to develop their linguistic competence.

Cognitive linguistics investigates the mental processes involved in the acquisition and use of language and of knowledge in general. It is closely linked to cognitive psychology and to artificial intelligence*, which tries to make machines carry out tasks requiring intelligence and in doing so examines how humans perform such tasks.

The theory that mental states and processes are independent of but can explain behaviour has had its impact on linguistics and related fields throughout the twentieth century. Although criticised heavily by the behaviourists, it remains a concept to be considered in any approach to language and its applications.

Primary sources

Chomsky, Noam (1965). *Aspects of the Theory of Syntax*. Cambridge, MA: MIT Press.
Whorf, Benjamin L. (1956). *Language, Thought, Reality: Selected Papers*. Ed. John B. Carroll. New York: Wiley.

Further reading

Chomsky, Noam (1968). *Language and Mind*. New York: Harcourt, Brace and World.
Sapir, Edward (1921). *Language: An Introduction to the Study of Speech*. New York: Harcourt, Brace and World.
Watson, John B. (1919). *Psychology from the Standpoint of a Behaviorist*. Philadelphia: Lippincott.

Jürg Strässler

METAPHOR

A figure of speech in which a term that is usually associated with a certain entity is used to describe another, as in 'the dawn of history'. In their seminal work *Metaphors We Live By*, George Lakoff and Mark Johnson (1980) affirm that metaphors are deeply ingrained in our thoughts, actions and everyday language.

See also: Ideational Theory; Linguistic Relativity; Possible World Semantics; Signs and Semiotics
Key Thinkers: Derrida, Jacques; Saussure, Ferdinand de; Whorf, Benjamin; Wittgenstein, Ludwig

Lakoff and Johnson (1980) state that, contrary to common belief, a metaphor is not a rhetorical device employed to embellish literary language. They argue that metaphors constitute the foundation of our conceptual system and influence our thoughts, actions and communication. In addition to their description and classification of metaphors, Lakoff and Johnson discuss their significance in both philosophy and linguistics. Zoltán Kövecses (2002) proposes a detailed framework of cognitive metaphors and their role in linguistics, literary analysis, ethics and politics. In his (2005) publication, Kövecses focuses on the diversification of metaphors as a result of cultural differences. He explores the correlations between metaphoric and cultural variations. Murray Knowles and Rosamund Moon (2006) give a comprehensive account of how metaphors pervade a diverse number of disciplines, including semantics, literature, religion, cinema and music.

Criticising philosophers and linguists for their failure to appreciate the significant role metaphors play in our perception and communication, Lakoff and Johnson (1980) point out numerous everyday expressions that

131

are metaphoric in nature. These expressions include such conceptual metaphors like ARGUMENT AS WAR (Lakoff and Johnson use small capitals to denote conceptual metaphors and differentiate them from metaphoric expressions). To support their hypothesis they provide a multitude of expressions associated with this and other metaphorical concepts. These include our speaking about 'argument' as if it were 'war' when we use such expressions as 'attacking or defending a position', 'winning or losing an argument', or talking about claims as being 'indefensible'. Another conceptual metaphor is TIME AS MONEY, which generates a number of expressions that include 'saving', 'wasting' or 'investing' time.

In addition to this type, which they regard as complex and call 'structural metaphors' because 'one concept is metaphorically structured in terms of another' (1980: 14), Lakoff and Johnson identify a number of simple types of metaphors, including orientational and ontological metaphors. The majority of the morphemes belonging to the former type are related to spatial orientation. They speculate that these metaphors may have resulted from our cultural and physical experience. The most commonly used of these is the up-down metaphor. In Western culture 'up' is associated with positive concepts like 'happiness' and 'health', whereas 'down' is related to negative ones such as 'sadness' and 'illness'. This gives rise to such metaphoric expressions as 'high spirits', 'feeling up', 'falling ill' and 'being depressed'. Ontological metaphors, on the other hand, include diverse expressions most of which refer to

nonphysical entities as physical ones. Examples include the quantification of abstract entities, like speaking about someone as having 'a lot of patience', or describing the world as being 'filled with intolerance'. The most prominent type of ontological metaphors, according to Lakoff and Johnson, is personification, which is giving a nonhuman entity a human quality or attribute. This is evident in expressions like talking about inflation 'eating up' someone's savings, or a disease 'catching up' with somebody.

Another figure of speech that is metaphoric in nature is metonymy, which is employing an entity or feature to make reference to another. Examples of this include making reference to restaurant clients by the meals they order, for example 'The chicken lasagna left a big tip', or 'The beef burrito spilled his drink'. A major category of metonyms, according to Lakoff and Johnson's framework, involves using THE PART AS A WHOLE. This phenomenon, which has traditionally been called synecdoche, is exemplified by expressions such as 'wheels' to make reference to 'cars', or 'fresh blood' as a reference to 'new people' in a work-place setting. Lakoff and Johnson refute the claim that metonyms are purely referential in nature when compared with metaphors. They argue that the 'part' used to make the reference would usually have a vital role in determining the significance of the utterance.

In *Philosophy in the Flesh*, Lakoff and Johnson argue that 'the banishment of metaphor from the realm of truth explains why metaphor has traditionally been left to rhetoric and literary analysis' (1999: 120). Challenging this – among other – Western philosophical principles, they assert metaphors form the basis of conceptualisation. Without them, therefore, the discussion of science, morality or philosophy would not be possible. Even a universal concept like 'time' is metaphorically anchored because it is perceived of, and spoken about, metaphorically, not temporally. Citing examples from English, they discuss a number of expressions related to the various aspects of 'time'. Some of these are metaphoric expressions that indicate the passage of 'time' as 'approaching', 'arriving', 'running' and 'flying'. This metaphorisation of time, they believe, is culturally specific as reflected in different languages. In English, for instance, we 'look forward' to future events and regard past ones as being 'behind us' whereas in Aymara, a language spoken in the Chilean Andes, the future is 'behind'. In this culture, the metaphorisation of future events as being behind indicates the unforeseeable nature of such events (1999: 141).

Lakoff and Johnson's pioneering research on metaphor sparked interest in the field and paved the way for a multitude of subsequent publications. Reiterating the basic principles of their framework, Kövecses (2002) argues that the formula proposed to explain conceptual metaphors, which states that a target domain is understood in terms of a source domain, is insufficient. Using expressions such as 'someone is starved for love' or 'hungry for affection', he argues that the traditional explanation of such figures of speech, which are based on the conceptual metaphor LOVE AS A NUTRIENT, has been that the target domain 'food', a physical entity, is understood in terms of the source domain 'love', a nonphysical entity. Such a simplistic view of the relationship between the source and target domains, Kövecses argues, is not sufficient to explain the various metaphorical expressions based on the complex relationship between the two domains. He argues that the intricate mappings between 'love' and 'nutrient', and our ability to highlight different aspects of them enable us to use metaphors like 'love' as 'food', 'the desire for love' as 'hunger', and 'consequences of love' as 'effects of nourishment'. These complex mappings, Kövecses argues, enable speakers to highlight specific source-target relationships that would make it possible for them to express subtle meanings (2002: 79–92).

Since its inception as an independent, vital discipline, metaphor theory has seen a number of developments. One of these is the universality of metaphors and their variation in different cultures. Although Lakoff and Johnson (1999) alluded to this aspect of metaphors, Kövecses (2005) is credited with its development. Kövecses predicates the potential universality of many conceptual metaphors on the similarity of human physiological and conceptual experiences. Anger in humans, for instance, results in many physiological changes, including an increase in body temperature and blood pressure. Kövecses believes this accounts for diverse cultures utilising figures of speech based on the PRESSURISED CONTAINER conceptual metaphor. English metaphoric expressions like 'boiling blood', 'simmering

133

down' and 'blowing one's top', for example, have parallels in languages as diverse as Chinese, Japanese, Hungarian, Wolof, Zulu and Polish (2005: 39). However, Kövecses adds, there are a number of variations in metaphoric expressions within the same culture and between different ones. He attributes this variation to regional, social and experiential differences.

Other developments in metaphor theory include work on metaphor and the brain, acquisition of metaphors by children, and nonverbal metaphors. Despite the inconclusiveness of the evidence, research suggests that metaphors are processed by the right hemisphere of the brain. This hypothesis is consistent with lateralisation studies that characterise the left hemisphere as being specialised in holistic types of processing that are creative and nonliteral. Knowles and Moon cite research showing that patients who had right-hemisphere aphasia found it difficult to process metaphors (2006: 62). Since figurative competence is acquired relatively late, it has been determined that children acquire metaphoric processing between the ages of ten and twelve. Finally, nonverbal metaphors in cinema, music and pictorial representation have also been areas of interest.

Primary sources

Knowles, Murray and Rosamund Moon (2006). *Introducing Metaphor*. New York: Routledge.
Kövecses, Zoltán (2002). *Metaphor: A Practical Introduction*. Oxford: Oxford University Press.
Kövecses, Zoltán (2005). *Metaphor in Culture: Universality and Variation*.

Cambridge: Cambridge University Press.
Lakoff, George and Mark Johnson (1980). *Metaphors We Live By*. Chicago: University of Chicago Press.
Lakoff, George and Mark Johnson (1999). *Philosophy in the Flesh: The Embodied Mind and its Challenge to Western Thought*. New York: Basic Books.

Further reading

Aitchison, J. (2002). *Words in the Mind: An Introduction to the Mental Lexicon*. Oxford: Blackwell.
Cameron, L. and G. Low (eds) (1999). *Researching and Applying Metaphor*. Cambridge: Cambridge University Press.
Kövecses, Z. (2000). *Metaphor and Emotion: Language, Culture and Body in Human Feeling*. Cambridge: Cambridge University Press.
Lakoff, George and M. Turner (1989). *More Than Cool Reason: A Field Guide to Poetic Metaphor*. Chicago: University of Chicago Press.
Whorf, B. L. (1956). *Language, Thought and Reality*. Cambridge, MA: MIT Press.

Yousif Elhindi

MINIMALISM

A cover term for ideas related to the Minimalist Program, an approach to the study of the human language faculty chiefly associated with Noam Chomsky. It is driven by a radical conceptual and technical parsimony and explores the possibility that the design of the human computational system for language optimally satisfies constraints imposed only by the need to service a sensori-motor interface (PF) and a conceptual-intentional interface (LF).

See also: Adequacy; Logical Form; Transformational-Generative Grammar; Universal Grammar
Key Thinkers: Chomsky, Noam

The Minimalist Program, the successor framework to Noam Chomsky's Government-Binding Theory, was initially articulated in the book of the same name (Chomsky 1995) which brought together several earlier papers with some new material. It was expanded upon principally in Chomsky (2000, 2001, 2004, 2005). The leading idea, often called by Chomsky the 'strong minimalist thesis', is that language is a 'perfect solution' to the problems imposed by virtual conceptual necessity. In other words, there are certain inescapable constraints on the computational system of the human language faculty. If it is to relate sound and meaning, the computational system must interface with at least a sensory-motor system (Phonetic Form/PF) and a semantic/conceptual-intentional system (Logical Form/LF). The strong minimalist thesis hypothesises that the only constraints are those imposed by these interfaces, and that computational system satisfies these constraints in an optimal fashion.

As with previous radical changes in framework developed by Chomsky, questions of simplicity, and ultimately the logical problem of language acquisition, were central. By the early 1990s there was within Government-Binding Theory a sense that explanations were

approaching the same order of magnitude of complexity as the phenomena themselves. Similar concerns motivated the transition from the Revised Extended Standard Theory to Government-Binding Theory in the late 1970s. Additionally, various principles began to emerge which had a 'least effort' flavour, or were computationally more simple: namely local metrics for determining the domain of certain syntactic effects. As a result of considerations such as these, the strong minimalist thesis began to emerge in the mid-1990s.

Not surprisingly, this thesis has far reaching implications for every aspect of the computational system, and much of the organisation and technology of Government-Binding Theory has undergone revision. If PF and LF are the only linguistic levels with any significance (being the only two seemingly mandated by virtual conceptual necessity, though see below), then other linguistic levels, such as D-structure and S-structure, must be eliminated. Linguistic principles stated in terms of these levels must be reformulated.

Structure-building has also undergone radical revision, returning to a version of generalised transformations from Chomsky's early work in the 1950s. Rather than building up syntactic objects in a top-down fashion through recursive phrase-structure rules, the so-called Merge operation builds structure from the bottom up, combining two syntactic objects of arbitrary complexity: that is, individual lexical items or larger, previously created syntactic objects. Consistent with the goal of appealing only to virtual conceptually necessary mechanisms, it is claimed that Merge 'comes for free', insofar as language is undeniably hierarchically recursive.

As language is hypothesised to be an 'optimal' solution to the conditions imposed by the two interfaces, questions of 'economy', both of representation and derivation, have taken on a new prominence. Economy of representation prohibits 'superfluous' symbols. This entails that the interface levels of PF and LF may only be composed of symbols which are interpretable at that interface. This is the principle of Full Interpretation. Features uninterpretable at a given interface must be eliminated prior to that interface. The syntactic computation therefore becomes principally driven by the need to eliminate these uninterpretable features. Economy of representation also entails the principle of Inclusiveness, which states that the computational system may not itself introduce any symbols into the derivation. As a result many mechanisms in previous Chomskyian frameworks, such as traces, binding-theoretic indices and the like, do not exist. Syntactic principles which make reference to them must be eliminated or reformulated. Economy of derivation stipulates that the syntactic derivation itself proceed in an optimal fashion.

In another radical change from previous Chomskyan approaches, the Minimalist Program claims that structure-building and structure-changing are essentially the same operation. Movement is simply an instance of Merge where the object merged at the root comes from *inside* the existing syntactic object rather than from outside; Chomsky usually distinguishes *Internal Merge* (Move) from *External Merge*. As Chomsky notes, this view of structure-changing entails the copy theory of movement. The two elements of the chain have to be identical, rather than one being an inclusiveness-violating 'trace', because Merge cannot change what it operates on. What would traditionally be referred to as the head and the tail of the chain can still be distinguished, however, by examining the context in which the copies appear.

Insofar as it is features, rather than lexical items themselves, that are relevant to the PF and LF interfaces, these become the focus of the syntactic derivation within the Minimalist Program. As alluded to above, a distinction is made between *interpretable* and *uninterpretable* features. Certain features are plausibly interpretable at LF, though only on certain elements. Consider 'agreement features', such as person, number and gender (usually referred to as phi-features). Whether a given Noun Phrase (NP) is singular or plural, second-person or third-person, affects the way in which the item is interpreted. However, although person and number features can appear on functional categories such as Tense (reflected ultimately in subject-verb agreement), they seem not to have the same interpretive implications for Tense at LF. Thus the phi-features on NPs are an instance of 'interpretable' features at LF, while phi-features on Tense are uninterpretable at LF and must be eliminated.

In the earliest minimalist literature of the early-mid 1990s, movement or Internal Merge was the mechanism by which uninterpretable syntactic features were eliminated. However, in the early 2000s these operations became separated. The feature-checking operation is Agree. It consists of a probe, a syntactic element which has an uninterpretable feature (say, phi-features on Tense), and a goal, an element which has an interpretable version of this feature (say, an NP). The Agree-relation deletes the uninterpretable feature of the probe and provides a 'value' for morphological purposes based on the appropriate feature of the goal. This recreates the traditional claim that it is tensed verbs that agree with their subjects, not vice versa. Displacement itself is triggered by an *edge feature* (often also referred to as an EPP feature) which particular functional categories possess and which can act as a probe. Edge features further underline the essential identity of Merge and Move within the Minimalist Program, as it is also the edge feature of a lexical item which permits it to be merged with another syntactic object (its complement).

One of the most important minimalist developments relating to structure-building and changing concerns the concept of the *phase*, first introduced in Chomsky (2001). In a bid to reduce computational complexity, Chomsky suggested that derivations were inspected for legitimacy at particular key points; specifically, after the Merge of a *phase head*: vP (the light verb sister to VP which is implicated in transitivity) or CP.

Chomsky (2004) notes that even the *levels* of PF and LF can be eliminated under the assumption that spell-out and interpretation take place cyclically, at the level of the phase. When a phase is completed, the operation Transfer hands the syntactic object over to the sensory-motor interface and the conceptual-intentional interface, preserving a strong version of the strict cycle. On this view, the difference between overt and covert movement lies in whether an element is displaced before or after deciding to spell out the phase.

Cyclic spell-out and interpretation entails a Phase Impenetrability Condition. Since material within a phase has already been spelled out and interpreted, it is no longer accessible to the syntactic computation. However, so as not to completely rule out successive-cyclic movement in any form, it is hypothesised that material at the edge of a phase (a specifier or adjunct of a phase head) and the phase head itself are accessible to further operations.

Potentially one of the most interesting things about the minimalist Program, as noted by Chomsky (2004), is its contribution to the longstanding question of adequacy*. The highest level of adequacy, explanatory adequacy, is attained when there is a general theory of grammars that provides the basis for selecting the most descriptively adequate grammar from a selection of possible grammars. However, explanatory adequacy may be just description at a higher level, to the extent that the general theory of grammars merely incorporates whatever features the most descriptively adequate grammars happen to possess. Minimalism allows one to go beyond explanatory adequacy, in theory at least. Not only can the general theory of grammars select the most descriptively adequate grammar, but if language truly is a 'perfect' solution given the constraints imposed, then we can explain why a minimalist grammar ends up being the most descriptively adequate.

Primary sources

Chomsky, Noam (1995). *The Minimalist Program*. London: MIT Press.

Chomsky, Noam (2000). 'Minimalist inquiries: the framework'. In R. Martin, D. Michales and J. Uriagereka (eds), *Step by Step: Essays on Minimalism in Honor of Howard Lasnik*. Cambridge, MA: MIT Press. 89–155.

Chomsky, Noam (2001). 'Derivation by phase'. In M. Kenstowicz (ed.), *Ken Hale: A Life in Language*. Cambridge, MA: MIT Press. 1–52.

Chomsky, Noam (2004). 'Beyond explanatory adequacy'. In A. Belletti (ed.), *Structures and Beyond – The Cartography of Syntactic Structure*, vol. 3. Oxford: Oxford University Press. 104–131.

Chomsky, Noam (2005). 'Three factors in language design'. *Linguistic Inquiry* 36.1: 1–22.

Further reading

Hornstein, Norbert, Jairo Nunes and Kleanthes K. Grohmann (2005). *Understanding Minimalism*. Cambridge: Cambridge University Press.

Boškovic, Željiko and Howard Lasnik (2007). *Minimalist Syntax: The Essential Readings*. Oxford: Blackwell Publishing.

Geoffrey Poole

MODALITY

The expression of the speaker's attitude concerning the truth of a proposition or the realisability of a proposition by some agent. The former is usually called epistemic modality and the latter, deontic modality. In formal semantics and modal logic, modality concerns the possibility or necessity of the predication and its negation.

See also: Speech Act Theory; Politeness; Propositions
Key Thinkers: Aristotle; Austin, J. L.; Searle, John

A proposition such as 'They go home at this hour' can be communicated with different attitudes marking its modality. There are two basic types: (1) epistemic modality, which is about the truth of the proposition, such as guessing ('They may have gone home at this hour') and (2) deontic modality, which is about the realisability of the proposition by some agent, such as granting permission ('They may go home at this hour'). Closely related to deontic modality is dynamic modality which expresses ability (or inability) to put the assertion into practice independently of the judgement or will of the speaker, such as 'They can go home; they still have the return tickets'. Often held as part of epistemic modality is evidentiality – that is the warrant the speaker has for the assertion, such as in 'The show seems to be a success – whereby the speaker relies on some evidence, for example, applause heard, rather than subjective judgement.

Epistemic modality is also called proposition-modality, or speaker-oriented modality. Deontic modality is also known as event-modality since it is about the realisability of the state of affairs expressed in the proposition. In some recent literature, deontic modality is also described as agent-oriented modality because it characterises how some agent will carry out the proposition.

Modality is expressed lexically or grammatically or a combination of both. Lexical expressions include adverbs such as 'possibly', 'maybe', 'probably', 'presumably', 'supposedly', for example. Grammatical expressions make use of the modal verbs 'can', 'may', 'must', 'shall', 'will'. In a number of languages, the morphology of the verbal predicate also indicates modality, hence the traditional term mood, such as statement, question, imperative. Note that the illocutionary force of a statement may generate modality, such as 'This room is a bit dark' can be interpreted as a request to switch on the light, or a question like 'Have we finished?' may mean an invitation to leave.

Primary sources

Palmer, F. R. (2001). *Mood and Modality*. Second edition. Cambridge: Cambridge University Press.

Von Wright, G. H. (1951). *An Essay in Modal Logic*. Amsterdam: North-Holland.

Further reading

Hoye, Leo (1997). *Adverbs and Modality in English*. London and New York: Longman.

Palmer, F. R. (1990). *Modality and the English Modals*. Second edition. London and New York: Longman.

Bybee, J. L., R. D. Perkins and W. Pagliuca (1994). *The Evolution of Grammar: Tense, Aspect and Modality in the Languages of the World*. Chicago: University of Chicago Press.

Bybee, J. L. and S. Fleischman (eds) (1995). *Modality in Grammar and Discourse*. Amsterdam and Philadelphia: Benjamins.

Lyons, J. (1977). *Semantics*. Two vols. Cambridge: Cambridge University Press.

Agustinus Gianto

MODEL-THEORETIC SEMANTICS

One of the mainstream approaches to the study of meaning in natural languages. Model theory is a branch of mathematical logic concerning the description of the semantics of artificial languages. A model-theoretic approach to the semantics of natural languages was first put forward by the Polish logician Alfred Tarski in 1935. Following the Tarskian tradition, current model-theoretic approaches in linguistics usually embrace a truth-conditional theory of semantics. Model-theoretic semantics provides a mathematically rigorous and elegant way of describing and explaining extremely intricate semantic phenomena.

See also: Analytic Philosophy; Compositionality; Logic; Logical Form
Key Thinkers: Frege, Gottlob; Montague, Richard; Tarski, Alfred

The most influential application of model theory to natural language semantics can be found in the work of the American logician and philosopher of language Richard Montague. Analytic philosophers advocated the systematic study of formal, idealised languages as a means of better understanding slippery notions like entailment (logical consequence) and contradiction. They also believed that by approaching such semantic phenomena through the analysis of artificial languages, one could avoid the ambiguities, vagueness and paradoxes that are frequently found in natural languages.

Montague was of the same opinion. He famously held the view that natural languages are not fundamentally different from formal languages and that, consequently, the same approach can be employed fruitfully in their study (Montague 1970). Thus Montague extended the mathematical techniques that were traditionally used in the semantics of formal languages to the study of meaning in natural languages.

One such technique was model theory. Model theory was used by logicians to provide a precise specification of the truthconditions of sentences in artificial languages. Starting with Tarski's seminal essay 'The Concept of Truth in Formalized Languages' (1935), the concept of truth has played a fundamental role in the semantics of formal languages. Tarski suggested that describing the interpretation of a given sentence in a formal language involved giving, in a metalanguage previously understood, a precise specification of the conditions under which that sentence is true. Montague's model-theoretic semantics for natural language is truth-conditional, as it provides a theory of truth for a fragment of English. (Partee (1975, 1996, 1997) provides a comprehensive overview of the main ideas and historical development of Montagovian model-theoretic semantics, and its influence in linguistic semantics.)

Central to the model-theoretic approach to semantics is the notion of 'truth with respect to a model'. In other words, the specification of the truth conditions of sentences in a language is not provided in a vacuum, but rather relative to an abstract mathematical model of some state of affairs in the world, which we could think of informally as a 'snapshot' of reality. The construction of idealised models of certain aspects of reality is a common practice in many scientific contexts, as these can provide the basis for successful explanations of difficult phenomena in the natural sciences.

Model-theoretic semantics provides interpretations for sentences in a language by first specifying the entities that exist in the state of affairs in the world being modelled. Thus models can be very complex and they can comprise abstract as well as real entities. For example, models usually contain two special abstract entities referred to as True (or 1) and False (or 0), the truth values, which are often assumed to be the semantic values of true and false sentences, respectively. Models are, in effect, idealised representations of what sentences in a language can be about. It is important to point out, however, that logical models of natural language are not meant to capture our knowledge of language, and therefore should not be construed epistemologically.

Having specified the ontology of the model, the task of a model-theoretic semantics is to assign interpretations to the basic expressions of the object language by associating them with entities in the model. Of course, different expressions may denote, or refer to, different kinds of things in the model. For example, a proper name such as 'Mary' denotes a member of the set of individuals in the model, whereas the adjective 'clever' is taken to denote a subset of that set, namely the set of individuals in the model who are clever. A sentence like 'Mary is clever' is assigned a truth value*: true if the sentence is actually true – that is, if Mary is in fact a member of the set of clever individuals in the model – or false otherwise. As we can see, models have internal structure. In order to have a systematic way of describing these distinctions, models are often structured into different domains according to the types of things that each domain comprises. For example, the three expressions mentioned above denote members of different domains in the model: respectively the domain of individuals, the domain of sets of individuals and the domain of truth values.

A set of recursive syntactic rules defining the class of well formed sentences of the language must be provided, together with a precise specification of how the various basic expressions can be combined syntactically to yield complex expressions. For each of these syntactic rules, there is a corresponding semantic rule which determines the interpretation of the complex expressions on the basis of the interpretation of their parts, in accordance with the principle of compositionality* of meaning (sometimes also referred to as 'Frege's Principle'). Ultimately, a model-theoretic semantics must explicitly define the condi-

tions that must be obtained for sentences in the object language to be true relative to the model under consideration. Bach (1989), Cann (1993), Dowty, Wall and Peters (1981) and Gamut (1991) provide excellent introductions to model-theoretic semantics as it is currently practised in linguistics.

Perhaps the most important advantage of the notion of 'truth with respect to a model' is that it allows us to define, in a rigorous and formally precise way, key semantic properties of natural language sentences like validity and contradictoriness, as well as important meaning relations that exist between them such as entailment or logical equivalence. Equipped with this notion, we can quantify over the class of possible models and say, for example, that a sentence S1 entails a sentence S2 just in case every model in which S1 is true is a model in which S2 is true as well; or that any two sentences S1 and S2 of our object language are logically equivalent just in case S1 is true in exactly the same models in which S2 is true and in no others; or that a sentence S1 is contradictory just in case it is false with respect to every possible model. A correct understanding of these properties and relations is at the heart of any scientific theory of natural language semantics.

An issue that causes disagreement between different theories of model-theoretic semantics is the syntax-semantics interface. For example, some theories postulate a separate level of linguistic representation mediating between natural language syntax and model-theoretic semantics. This additional level of representation, which is derived from other linguistic levels by transformational operations in the syntax, is called logical form* (May 1985). On the other hand, the strict compositionality constraint between form and meaning built into Montague's original theory precludes the need for such an additional level of syntactic representation.

Model-theoretic semantics can provide interpretations for (semantic representations of) linguistic expressions in a way that accurately captures our pre-theoretical semantic judgements of such expressions. It is currently the focus of a great deal of research in linguistics, but much of this research also unifies and expands various other disciplines, such as philosophy, cognitive science, artificial intelligence*, and theoretical computer science. Work in model-theoretic semantics has made significant contributions to our understanding of truth and meaning in natural languages, for example in areas as diverse as tense and aspect, generics, negation, and plurality.

Primary sources

May, Robert (1985). *Logical Form: Its Structure and Derivation*. Cambridge, MA: MIT Press.

Montague, Richard (1970). 'Universal grammar'. *Theoria* 36: 373–98.

Partee, Barbara H. (1975). 'Montague grammar and transformational grammar'. *Linguistic Inquiry* 6: 203–300.

Partee, Barbara H. (1996). 'The development of formal semantics in linguistic theory'. In S. Lappin (ed.), *The Handbook of Contemporary Semantic Theory*. Oxford: Blackwell Publishing. 11–38.

Partee, Barbara H. (with Herman L. W. Hendriks) (1997). 'Montague grammar.' In J. van Benthem and A. ter Meulen (eds), *Handbook of Logic and Language*. Amsterdam and Cambridge, MA: Elsevier and MIT Press. 5–91.

Tarski, A. (1935). 'The concept of truth in formalized languages'. In J. Corcoran (ed.) (1983), *Logic, Semantics, Metamathematics*. Indianapolis, IN: Hackett Publishing. 152–278.

Further reading

Bach, Emmon (1989). *Informal Lectures on Formal Semantics*. Albany: SUNY Press.

Cann, Ronnie (1993). *Formal Semantics: An Introduction*. Cambridge: Cambridge University Press.

Dowty, David R., R. E. Wall and S. Peters (1981). *Introduction to Montague Semantics*. Dordrecht: D. Reidel Publishing.

Gamut, L. T. F. (1991). *Logic, Language and Meaning (Volume 2): Intensional Logic and Logical Grammar*. Chicago: University of Chicago Press.

Iván García Álvarez

NAMES

In philosophy the term has been used sometimes to describe any word or phrase that can refer, and sometimes in the more restricted sense of a word that uniquely identifies an individual. In linguistics, names or proper nouns are recognised as a separate class of linguistic signs, distinct from common nouns. The field of name studies, or onomastics, is increasingly moving from language-internal criteria to contextual ones.

See also: Definite Descriptions; Sense/Reference; Use/Mention

Key Thinkers: Frege, Gottlob; Kripke, Saul; Mill, J. S.; Russell, Bertrand; Searle, John

The nature of names has exercised philosophers of language for a very long time. The best known early treatise is probably Plato's *Cratylus* Dialogue which centres around the question of whether names have an intrinsic relation to their referent or are as arbitrary as other linguistic signs. The discussion of names in modern philosophy was initiated by John Stuart Mill (1867), who distinguished between 'connotative' names, such as 'The father of Socrates', which refer to an individual by means of describing that individual, and 'non-connotative' names, such as 'Sophroniscus', which simply refer. In contrast, Gottlob Frege (1892) argued that all names, including personal names, have both a reference and a sense. According to Bertrand Russell (1919), personal names can be used to refer directly to an individual who is immediately present, but in most instances are used as 'abbreviated descriptions'. There are various problems for Russell's account, including the fact that, since different speakers may identify an individual by means of different descriptions, the meaning of a name would seem to vary depending on who is using it. In one attempt to address this problem, John Searle (1958) developed his 'cluster theory' account. In perhaps the most influential philosophical discussion of names since Russell, Saul Kripke (1972) argued that names are 'rigid designators' that succeed in referring to individuals

because of a chain of communication established within a community of speakers.

In linguistics, unique reference is usually taken to be the key distinction between names and common nouns. However, this distinction is not as clear-cut as it may seem. First, some common nouns such as 'sun' or 'hell' have unique reference but they are not considered names. Second, the referents of many names have certain things in common: all referents of the name 'Mary', for instance, are female, born to English-speaking parents (or they are learners of English as a second language who are using an English name in addition to their native one), and, given that most personal names are subject to fashion, one may even make an educated guess about the age of many Marys.

The syntactic criterion that distinguishes proper nouns from common nouns in English is the absence of a determiner. However, not all common nouns can take the full range of determiners: 'a music', for example, is not a possible expression in English. The non-translatability of names has been put forward as another distinction criterion. However, counter-examples are easy to find such as German 'Schwarzwald', which becomes 'Black Forest' in English.

Thus, it is obvious that proper and common nouns form a gradient, with prototypical cases at either end and many fuzzy ones in between. Ultimately, the intention and perception of language users is the only way to distinguish between common nouns and proper nouns. However, this distinction is no longer systematic and

143

inherent in language but a matter of naming practices in context.

There can be no doubt that the relationship between a name and its referent has more psychological reality for language users than that pertaining between any other linguistic signs and their referents. Modern linguistics and onomastics, however, have tended to dismiss this widely held assumption as 'primitive' or 'superstitious'. This stance has led to an ever-widening chasm between limited academic interest in names and naming and widespread popular interest. In the philosophy of language, the relationship between names and their referents remains an enduring focus of interest.

Primary sources

Frege, Gottlob (1892). 'On sense and meaning'. In Peter Geach and Max Black (eds) (1980), *Translations from the Philosophical Writings of Gottlob Frege*. Oxford: Blackwell. 56–78. First Edition 1952.

Kripke, Saul (1972). 'Naming and necessity'. In D. Davidson and G. Hartman (eds), *Semantics of Natural Language*. Dordrecht: Reidel.

Mill, J. S. (1867). *A System of Logic*. London: Longman. Chapter 2.

Russell, Bertrand (1919). *Introduction to Mathematical Philosophy*. London: George Allen and Unwin.

Searle, John (1958). 'Proper names'. *Mind* 67: 166–73.

Further reading

Evans, Gareth (1982). *The Varieties of Reference*. Oxford: Oxford University Press.

Ingrid Piller and Siobhan Chapman

NONNATURAL MEANING

A type of meaning, which includes linguistic meaning, in which there is no necessary link between a sign and what it represents. In his influential account of nonnatural meaning, H. P. Grice emphasised the importance of a speaker's intentions and a hearer's recognition of these intentions.

See also: Conventional Meaning; Implicature; Intentionality; Signs and Semiotics; Use/Mention
Key Thinkers: Grice, H. P.; Peirce, C. S.; Saussure, Ferdinand de; Searle, John; Strawson, P. F.

The idea that linguistic meaning can be distinguished from natural meaning is long standing. It can be traced back to classical philosophy, and in more recent times can be found in Peirce's account of words as 'symbols' and in Saussure's discussion of the arbitrary nature of the sign. However, Grice's short article 'meaning' attempted a more precise characterisation.

Grice draws attention to two different ways in which the verb 'mean' is used, exemplified by 'Those spots mean measles' and 'Those three rings on the bell (of the bus) mean that the bus is full'. The first case involves natural meaning; the spots simply are a symptom of the disease. In the second case, there is no necessary connection between the three rings and the meaning, but rather someone (the bus conductor) meant something by the rings; we can say that the rings mean 'The bus is full'. Unlike in the case of natural meaning, the rings are not a guarantee of the truth of this statement; the bus conductor may be mistaken or deliberately trying to deceive. Grice labelled this second type of meaning 'nonnatural meaning', for which he coined the abbreviation 'meaning$_{nn}$'. Linguistic meaning is a type of meaning$_{nn}$.

For Grice, meaning$_{nn}$ is determined by a speaker's intention to communicate something, and by a hearer's recognition of that intention. If A is a speaker and x an utterance, then '"A meant$_{nn}$ something by x" is roughly equivalent to "A intended the utterance of x to produce some effect in an audience by means of the recognition of this intention"' (1957: 385). Grice raises but does not fully develop the idea that linguistic meaning ('what x means$_{nn}$') may itself be determined by speakers' intentions, and hence that conventional meaning is to be defined in terms of psychology. He also hints that what speakers intend to communicate in specific contexts may sometimes go beyond what their words actually mean$_{nn}$.

'Meaning' has largely been favourably received by philosophers and linguists alike, although some have put forward criticisms that suggest flaws in Grice's theory (Strawson 1964; Searle 1969; Schiffer 1972). 'Meaning' also introduced Grice's interest in the distinction between what our words mean and what we mean by using our words, which he explored further in his work on conversational implicature*.

Primary sources

Grice, Paul (1957). 'Meaning'. *The Philosophical Review* 66: 377–88.
Schiffer, Stephen (1972). *Meaning*. Oxford: Clarendon Press.

Searle, John (1969). *Speech Acts*. Cambridge: Cambridge University Press.
Strawson, P. F. (1964). 'Intention and convention in speech acts'. *The Philosophical Review* 73: 439–60.

Further reading

Avramides, Anita (1989). *Meaning and Mind*. Cambridge, MA: MIT Press.
Chapman, Siobhan (2005). *Paul Grice: Philosopher and Linguist*. Basingstoke: Palgrave.

Siobhan Chapman

OPTIMALITY THEORY

A framework in theoretical linguistics used to formalise analyses in phonology, and less frequently other areas of linguistics. Its core is the assumption that linguistic generalisations should be described using a set of violable constraints on surface representations which are ranked in terms of their importance.

See also: Generative Phonology; Universal Grammar
Key Thinkers: Chomsky, Noam

Optimality theory (OT) took centre stage in theoretical linguistics during the 1990s. Its basic tenets were both familiar and revolutionary and this has doubtless contributed to its success. It developed ideas long present in linguistics, but gave them new characteristics, considerably changing the understanding of the grammar. Despite some influence from neural networks, OT was essentially

145

conceived as a development of generative phonology*, so it maintains the basic competence/performance distinction, and that between underlying and surface levels of representation, although these are reinterpreted. One central OT assumption is that only constraints should be used to characterise linguistic generalisations. There are no substantive rules or transformations. A set of potential surface forms ('candidates') are evaluated by the grammar and one is chosen as the optimal candidate (the 'output') because it violates a language's constraints in the least bad way. This is possible thanks to another key characteristic: all constraints are violable, and languages rank them in order of importance, so it is worse to violate a high-ranked constraint than a low-ranked one. As the standard assumption is that the set of constraints (known as CON) is universal, language learners must work out how constraints are ranked in the languages they acquire.

OT provided linguists with new ways to work and new theoretical problems to crack, although some have rejected it as fundamentally misguided. It was introduced by Alan Prince and Paul Smolensky and has been developed by many others, most notably John McCarthy. OT was created with phonological problems in mind, and is still most popular among phonologists, but is also used in syntax and other areas. After early presentations in 1991, Prince and Smolensky distributed the manuscript *Optimality Theory: Constraint Interaction in Generative Grammar* in 1993. Although not published until 2004, this was highly influential, setting out the OT approach (along with work by McCarthy and Prince).

OT analyses are formulated in a 'tableau', exemplified below (see Table 1) for German Final Obstruent Devoicing (FOD) in its standard description: syllable-final voiced obstruents are devoiced, as in *Bund* [bʊnd] 'federation' (a contentious but standard assumption here is that [d] in German is specified for [voice], while [t] is unspecified). The tableau's top row shows the input (the underlying representation), and then the constraints, in ranked order from left to right. The first column shows the set of candidates, one of which is chosen as the output (indicated by a pointing finger). The other columns show constraint violations, each receiving one asterisk. The 'fatal' violation (which rules candidates out) is indicated by an exclamation mark. There are two basic types of constraint: markedness and faithfulness constraints. Markedness constraints penalise candidates which contain marked structures: the analysis of FOD uses *FINALOBSTRUENT/VOICE (*FOV), which dictates that final obstruents may not be specified for [voice]. Faithfulness is a crucial innovation of OT: markedness constraints can exert pressure for an output to differ from its input, but faithfulness constraints do the opposite, requiring identity between input and output. Individual constraints regulate particular aspects of faithfulness: IDENT() that the value of [voice] be the same in input and output, and MAX requires everything in the input to have some correspondent in the output, ruling out deletion.

/bʊnd/	*FOV	Max	Ident(voice)
bʊnd	!*		
☞bʊnt			*
bʊn		!*	
bʊ		!**	

Table 1

Fully faithful [bʊnd] is rejected because it violates high-ranked *FOV. An unlimited number of candidates are in fact produced (by the function Gen,which simultaneously performs every possible process on the input to derive the candidates). In practice, only a few 'reasonable' candidates are considered in analyses (outlandish candidates are assumed to be ruled out by high-ranked faithfulness constraints). The candidates include [bund], which satisfies *FOV, with no voicing in its final obstruent. [bund] violates Ident(), but is still the output because other candidates violate higher-ranked constraints. The other two candidates do not violate *FOV, as they have no final obstruent (having undergone deletion), but they do violate Max, also ranked above Ident(). This ranking is shown by the unbroken line between Max and Ident(). The broken line between *FOV and Max shows that their mutual ranking is irrelevant here. The above ranking is specific to languages with FOD. In English, with no FOD, the constraint *FOV must be ranked below Ident().

It is worth noting that the right candidate would still be selected if the input were /bʊnd/. In fact, in some cases, the precise nature of the input is indistinct: thus it does not matter whether or not stops are aspirated underlyingly in English, as these segments do not contrast and, assuming that aspiration is enforced by a high-ranked Aspiration constraint ('initial stops must be aspirated'), then [pɪk] could be derived from either [pɪk] or [pʰɪk]. Which of these is the underlying form is simply not an important (or relevant) question. This characteristic is known as the Richness of the Base, and has some theoretical benefits. In the German case, however, alternations (such as *Bund~Bundes* [bʊnd]~[bʊndəs] 'federation'~'federation-GENITIVE') show that the underlying segment must be voiced.

OT analyses can often be linked to pre- or non-OT work by implementing as a violable constraint what such work sees as a universal principle. This has likely contributed to OT's success because it expresses what phonologists have wanted to be able to say: certain principles often play a role in the phonology of languages, but not always. For example, the Obligatory Contour Principle (OCP) was introduced in the 1970s to forbid adjacent identical aspects of structure, such as adjacent high tones or specifications for place. By the late 1980s, it had been shown that the OCP is not absolute, but is best understood as a tendency in languages, elevated to the level of an inviolable principle in some. This is exactly what OT predicts, and OT thus allows phonologists to formalise tendencies.

Theoretical development in OT has largely involved either work on the types of constraints allowed, driven by attempts to find new, better ways to express linguistic generalisations, or work on additions to the basic theoretical machinery, often to remedy perceived shortcomings in the model, such as its inability to account for opacity. The former includes work on 'positional faithfulness', which preferentially preserves input specifications in strong positions, such as the onset. FOD can also fit into a positional faithfulness model: a positional IDENTONSET(voice) can require that the value of [voice] be the same in input and output in onsets, and conflict with a general *OBSTRUENT/ VOICE, which requires that no obstruent be specified for [voice]. This achieves the same result, but also opens up new 'positional' analytical options.

Opponents of OT often argue that its central tenets are mistaken. Critics have claimed that the status of inputs is problematic. The Richness of the Base has been criticised on both psycholinguistic and theoretical grounds (much previous theoretical success was due to the ability to specify the characteristics of underlying forms). The fact that OT has largely led its practitioners to abandon work on phonological representation (especially at the segmental level) has been condemned. The contents of CON have also proved controversial. As we have seen, the constraints needed to analyse simple FOD are subject to debate: there is not necessarily one straightforward way to analyse any phenomenon, because there is no clear theory of CON. Some see this as an opportunity for debate, others as a problem: how can we know which constraints exist? A more fundamental criticism questions whether we really should formalise all tendencies as cognitive constraints on surface forms. Should 'ease of articulation' (formalised in OT as LAZY) be seen as the same kind of thing as constraints on the faithfulness of features?

Despite such criticism, OT has a firm place in theoretical linguistics, as the framework for most analysis and debate in phonology, and considerable work in other areas of linguistics. It provides a novel set of principles to guide analysis and has allowed new answers to old problems. For those who follow its direction, it has focused work on the status of constraints and moved attention away from representations and underlying levels. The framework for constraint interaction has also been adopted by linguists who reject generative assumptions. Its influence is felt widely in linguistic theory.

Primary sources

Prince, Alan and Paul Smolensky (1993/2004). *Optimality Theory: Constraint Interaction in Grammar*. Rutgers University and University of Colorado at Boulder. Oxford: Blackwell.

McCarthy, John and Alan Prince (1993). *Prosodic Morphology: Constraint Interaction and Satisfaction*. University of Massachusetts, Amherst and Rutgers University.

McCarthy, John and Alan Prince (1995). 'Faithfulness and reduplicative identity'. In Jill Beckman, Laura Walsh Dickey and Suzanne Urbanczyk (eds), *University of Massachusetts Occasional Papers in Linguistics* 18: 249–384.

Further reading

McCarthy, John (2002). *A Thematic Guide to Optimality Theory*. Cambridge: Cambridge University Press.

Patrick Honeybone

ORDINARY LANGUAGE PHILOSOPHY

Ordinary language philosophy (OLP) is the name given to a philosophical movement that developed in England during the years between the two World Wars and enjoyed its heyday in the late 1940s through the early 1960s. Its adherents saw ordinary, everyday language as the starting point for their philosophical inquiries. Through the central ideas of its leading figures such as J. L. Austin and Ludwig Wittgenstein, OLP continues to echo in a wide variety of disciplines.

See also: Analytic Philosophy; Implicature; Speech Act Theory; Truth Theories
Key Thinkers: Austin, J. L.; Derrida, Jacques; Grice, H. P.; Russell, Bertrand; Ryle, Gilbert; Searle, John; Strawson, P. F.; Wittgenstein, Ludwig

Ordinary language philosophy is also variously referred to as Oxford philosophy or linguistic philosophy, but these terms should not taken as accurately descriptive. It is true that Oxford University served as its principal *locus*, with key Oxford philosophers such as Gilbert Ryle, P. F. Strawson and J. L. Austin contributing to its development. But it is often pointed out that many of the ideas of the later Wittgenstein also had an impact on the movement, and John Wisdom, associated like Wittgenstein with the University of Cambridge, is generally considered a sympathiser of OLP. Furthermore it is not true that there was anything approaching a consensus among the philosophers of Oxford regarding the main ideas of the movement; it is arguable that the group did not even constitute a movement or a school in any real sense. At best they shared some common attitudes concerning the nature of language and ways of doing philosophy. To use a term attributable to Wittgenstein, the farthest one may go in characterising the group is to say that there was a 'family resemblance' among the positions assumed by many of its members.

The term 'linguistic philosophy' is more to the point. These philosophers put language at the centre of their inquiry. This was in sharp contrast with the customary practice of regarding it as merely (and, in the views of some, lamentably) a *tertium quid* (third element) between René Descartes' *res extensa* (extended matter or material reality) and *res cogitans* (thinking substance or, simply, the mind). In this sense, linguistic philosophy marked a major departure from the long tradition of analytic philosophy, of which it is nevertheless an offshoot. However, even here, one cannot point to any consensus. John Searle, of the University of California at Berkeley, probably the most famous of Austin's followers, has categorically denied being a linguistic philosopher, claiming to be only a philosopher of language.

The term 'ordinary language philosophy' captures an important element that distinguishes the movement from the work of earlier philosophers, particularly those inspired by logical positivism* or what may contrastively be referred to as 'ideal language philosophy'. Bertrand Russell, for one, was openly scornful of ordinary language which he thought was full of ambiguity* and vagueness and hence inadequate for the philosophers' purposes. Unlike many of their contemporaries and predecessors who believed in first positing a logically perfect language and then lamenting how our ordinary, everyday language pales in comparison with it, ordinary language philosophers insisted on examining ordinary, everyday language at its face value.

In stark contrast with the apologists of ideal language, Wittgenstein argued in his *Philosophical Investigations* (1953) that ordinary language was perfectly in order as it stood, and that many of the puzzles that professional philosophers and linguists encountered and sought to resolve were actually the result of an inadequate understanding of the subtleties of ordinary, everyday language. In his essay 'Systematically Misleading Expressions', Ryle (1932) made a strong case for a careful analysis of ordinary language expressions as a way of doing philosophy, or rather, as a way of 'dissolving' many of the problems that crop up in philosophy,

arguing that such an approach would clarify matters by blocking misuses of language. In other words, most of philosophy, on careful inspection, would boil down to straightforward linguistic analysis.

J. L. Austin, one of the principal exponents of ordinary language philosophy, used to quip that if one wants to embark on a career in philosophy one had better equip oneself with a good dictionary. His point was that our ordinary, everyday language, unlike its ideal or formal counterpart, was fashioned into its present form by generations of speakers. In that long process, the language has been invested with most, if not all, of the distinctions that its speakers felt necessary. Not that the ordinary language cannot be improved or further distinctions introduced into it to suit fresh needs. Ordinary language may not provide us with the last word on philosophical problems, but it should certainly be the starting point of all philosophical inquiry.

The philosophical importance of conferring pride of place upon ordinary language can hardly be overestimated. In a way it debunked the very enterprise of philosophy or at least a traditional way of going about doing philosophy. The image of the prototypical philosopher is best captured by the famous statue called 'The Thinker' by the French sculptor Auguste Rodin. Lost in meditation, the philosopher is completely out of touch with the work-a-day world. Introspection is his preferred *modus operandi* and solitude his self-imposed ambience. This is perfectly in tune with philosophy's proverbial disdain for language in the everyday sense of the word. Gottfried

Wilhelm Leibniz, the German philosopher, is famously said to have exclaimed that if God Almighty were one day to descend upon the earth, He would certainly address us ordinary mortals in the language of mathematics – it was inconceivable for the philosopher that an all-perfect God would have recourse to any language other than the all-perfect language of mathematics.

Traditionally, philosophy is concerned with conceptual analysis. It is not primarily concerned with words. Words are believed to embody concepts at best. For the most part, traditional philosophers distrusted words, judging them misleading representations of the concepts behind them. Recall the Socratic practice, illustrated in several of Plato's *Dialogues*, of insisting that his interlocutor provide a definition of, say, piety, instead of pointing to examples of pious persons. The moral is that true understanding comes from pure conceptual analysis which is what a definition is all about. In Socrates' view, examples give the false impression that one has got to grips with the concepts behind them.

Austin's attitude to this time-honoured practice among philosophers was eloquently expressed in a paper entitled 'Are there any *a priori* concepts?', originally presented in 1939 before the Aristotelian Society. In it Austin surprised his audience by arguing that he had no idea of what that question meant because he did not know what concepts were to begin with. So the question of concepts being *a priori* or *a posteriori* simply did not arise. On this question and on many others, Austin was an Aristotelian to the hilt. True to the austere tradition of sober empiricism, the hallmark of British thought, he preferred to start his philosophical inquiry with the tangibles – to start from the concrete (words) and work his way towards the general or the abstract, rather than the other way around. And he was in no hurry to finish that job. He believed that philosophy demanded a great deal of painstaking spadework. He once said that the sentence 'Neither a be-all nor an end-all be' could make an excellent motto for philosophy.

Another essay by Austin, 'A Plea for Excuses', is widely regarded as a prime example of OLP at work. By carefully teasing out the different uses of the word 'excuse' (which exculpates the doer of an action), Austin distinguishes it from 'justification' (which, by contrast, 'absolves', as it were, the action itself of any imputation of wrong-doing). This essay also highlights what may be seen as yet another hallmark of OLP – deflecting the focus from the naming of an act (along with the hypostatisation that it invariably involves) to the more mundane doing of the act or, simply put, the action itself. This idea found its full expression in *How to Do Things with Words* (1962a), undoubtedly Austin's most famous work. Before proceeding any further, it is important to comment on the title of the book, originally presented as a series of twelve lectures presented at the University of Harvard in 1955 under the title 'Words and Deeds' and published posthumously. It has been suggested that Austin chose that title somewhat lightheartedly after Dale Carnegie's bestselling *How to Win Friends and Influence People*. In fact, many an

Austin reader has a rather difficult time coming to terms with what is best described as his blithe irreverence for the sober, lofty style that one typically associates with philosophy, and his use of a thoroughly colloquial style. But it is important to realise that Austin is making an important philosophical point here (Rajagopalan 2000a).

In *How to Do Things with Words* Austin argued that a sentence such as 'The cat is on the mat', which has long been seen as a declarative (or, 'constative' as he calls it) and hence capable of being judged true or false, is actually a 'performative'* which cannot be judged true or false but only happy or otherwise, depending on the circumstances in which it is uttered or 'performed'. Thus was launched the idea that speaking a language is performing a series of acts. This seminal idea has inspired a number of scholars from a number of diverse disciplines including linguistics, psychology, anthropology, sociology, and even such unlikely fields as economics.

A discussion of Austin's legacy would be incomplete without a mention of his book *Sense and Sensibilia* (1962b) (the echo of Jane Austen's celebrated novel is unmistakable here). Austin takes on the fashionable approach to the analysis of perception in terms of sense data* and proceeds to deconstruct the so-called 'argument from illusion'. For instance, he says, the right answer to the question as to what it is that you actually see, posed apropos of a church camouflaged so as to look like a barn, is precisely what that description says, namely, 'a church camouflaged so as to look like a barn' and not, as the traditionally

expected answer would have it, 'a barn'. Austin thus challenges what may be described as a mainstay of Platonic realism, namely, the idea that epistemology can only play second fiddle to ontology or, to put it more simply, what there is can by no means be affected by what one comes to know about it.

The performative view of language thus has important things to say in respect of what has, from time immemorial, been the philosopher's Holy Grail: the concept of truth. P. F. Strawson advanced what is referred to as the 'performative theory of truth' according to which truth is not something to be approached solely with the tools of the trade available in philosophy in its conventional sense, but something invariably mediated by language. Truth claims, in other words, take precedence over truth *ipsis*. To call something true is to perform the speech act of endorsing it or giving it one's stamp of approval.

Historians of philosophy often treat OLP as a chapter in the unfinished book of analytic philosophy but the point is debatable. Both the later Wittgenstein and Austin produced immense challenges to what was the established dogma in philosophy. Perhaps the best proof of the radical nature of their philosophical positions is the publication in 1959 of a book by Ernest Gellner entitled *Words and Things: An Examination of, and an Attack on, Linguistic Philosophy*. The book even carried a laudatory preface by Bertrand Russell in which he lamented that his former pupil Wittgenstein seemed to have taken a holiday from serious intellectual activity, meaning thereby that he considered

OLP at best a diversion from philosophy proper and at worst an aberration. But the very fact that the book became a major sensation immediately after it was published speaks volumes for the popularity of OLP at that time and the threat it represented to mainstream philosophy. No doubt Gellner's book did quite some damage to OLP, though once the heat of the moment had died down, many scholars were of the opinion that the book threw very little light on substantive issues, instead contenting itself with mud-slinging and vituperative rhetoric.

Perhaps the real damage to OLP was done not by die-hard detractors like Gellner, but by those responsible for clever appropriations of the heritage of some of its principal figures, notably Wittgenstein and Austin. We have already seen how Bertrand Russell, a towering figure in British philosophy who personally supervised Wittgenstein's earlier work *Tratactatus Logico-Philosophicus* (Wittgenstein 1922/1961), simply brushed aside his later work, *Philosophical Investigations* (Wittgenstein 1953/1968), dismissing it as at best frivolous. This furnished the vital clue to many succeeding generations to stay with the earlier Wittgenstein and to summarily dismiss the later Wittgenstein.

With Austin, the philosophical establishment adopted a different tactic. After his untimely death in 1960, his mantle was widely considered to have fallen on John Searle who had studied at Oxford in the early 1950s and who therefore knew him personally. In 1969 Searle published his book *Speech Acts: An Essay in the Philosophy of Language* which was an instant success in linguistics, where he was widely acclaimed as Austin's intellectual legatee. The book was welcomed by many as genuinely Austinian in spirit and an improvement upon Austin's own *How to Do Things with Words*, which had left many readers perplexed and unsure of just what Austin had in mind. What many readers of Searle's book failed to take serious notice of was something Searle had declared right in the subtitle of his book: *An Essay in the Philosophy of Language*. The philosophy of language casts a much wider net than linguistic philosophy, which is one way of philosophically looking at language but not the only one. In fact, in work since then, Searle has evinced little sympathy for many of the trademark positions assumed by linguistic philosophers, notably Austin himself (Rajagopalan 2000b).

It has been argued that Searle reinterpreted Austin and put his ideas back on the beaten track of traditional analytic philosophy. In the process, many of the potentially subversive elements in Austin's thought were either downplayed or simply ignored. Without doubt this made Austin a household name in disciplines such as linguistics, but many critics have complained that the Austin appropriated by Searle is a far cry from the Austin who so vigorously and implacably defended linguistic philosophy.

Be that as it may, the later Wittgenstein and Austin have had a considerable influence elsewhere in academia, and continue to do so. Wittgenstein's influence on contemporary linguistic thought is undeniable. His insistence on the normative character of language has profound implications for contemporary emphasis on ethics and politics in relation to language. Note that Wittgenstein's position is in stark contrast with the position assumed in much of linguistics where the belief has been that a grammar must ideally be descriptive rather than prescriptive. Another area that has been influenced by Wittgenstein's thought is cognitive science. The theory of prototypes* – a model of graded categorisation that eschews the classic, Aristotelian distinction between essences and accidents – is a direct spin-off from Wittgenstein's notion of 'family resemblance'. The idea that class membership does not have to be a matter of all or nothing, but can be a matter of more or less, has important consequences for how different societies categorise entities in the work-a-day world (Rosch and Lloyd 1978; Lakoff 1987).

Austin's influence on contemporary thought is less often acknowledged, thanks to the widespread tendency to credit it to Searle instead. Jacques Derrida has made no secret of the enormous influence of Austin's thinking on his own. He even became involved in a protracted exchange with Searle over the legacy of Austin. An unlikely area of inquiry taken by storm in the 1980s, thanks to the influence of OLP, was economics. In 1985 Deirdre (then, Donald) Mac-Closkey published a book in which she argued that economists are closer to poets and story-tellers than they think, and that their claims are mistakenly taken to be constative, whereas they are just as performative as any other. Perhaps a most significant testimony to the vitality of linguistic philosophy in general and Austin's heritage in particular is

Judith Butler's notions of 'performativity' and 'performance' (Butler 1997), both inspired by Austin's 'performative utterance'. Building on Austin's insights, Butler argues that gender is not a matter of what one is (constative), but rather what one does (performative). While OLP is often associated with a specific time and place, its influence goes much wider than linguistics and the philosophy of language thanks to the ongoing work of scholars in other disciplines who find inspiration in its central tenets.

Primary sources

Austin, J. L. (1939). 'Are there *a priori* concepts?'. In J. L. Austin (1961), *Philosophical Papers*. London: Oxford University Press. 32–54.

Austin, J. L. (1956). 'A plea for excuses'. In C. Lyas (ed.) (1971), *Philosophy and Linguistics*. London: Macmillan Press. 79–101. Originally published in the *Proceedings of the Aristotelian Society*. 1956–7. Reprinted in J. L. Austin (1961), *Philosophical Papers*. London: Oxford University Press. 175–204.

Austin, J. L. (1961). *Philosophical Papers*. London: Oxford University Press.

Austin, J. L. (1962a). *How to Do Things with Words*. Oxford: Clarendon Press.

Austin, J. L. (1962b). *Sense and Sensibilia*. Oxford: Clarendon Press.

Gellner, Ernest (1959). *Words and Things: An Examination of, and an Attack on, Linguistic Philosophy*. London: Victor Gollancz.

Ryle, Gilbert (1932). 'Systematically misleading expressions'. In Richard Rorty (ed.) (1967), *The Linguistic Turn*. Chicago: University of Chicago Press.

Searle, J. R. (1969). *Speech Acts: An Essay in the Philosophy of Language*. Cambridge: Cambridge University Press.

Wittgenstein, Ludwig (1922/1961). *Tractatus Logico-Philosophicus*. London: Routledge and Kegan Paul.

Wittgenstein, Ludwig (1953/1968). *Philosophical Investigations*. Oxford: Basil Blackwell.

Further reading

Butler, Judith (1997). *Excitable Speech: A Politics of the Performative*. New York: Routledge.

Hacking, Ian (1975). *Why Does Language Matter to Philosophy?* Cambridge: Cambridge University Press.

Lakoff, George (1987). *Women, Fire and Dangerous Things: What Categories Reveal about the Mind*. Chicago: University of Chicago Press.

McCloskey, Deirdre (1985). *The Applied Theory of Price*. Second edition. New York: Macmillan.

Rajagopalan, Kanavillil (2000a). 'Austin's humorous style of philosophical discourse in light of Schrempp's interpretation of Oring's "incongruity theory" of humor'. *Humor: An International Journal of Humor Research* 13 (3): 287–311.

Rajagopalan, Kanavillil (2000b). 'On Searle [on Austin] on language'. *Language and Communication* 20 (4): 347–91.

Rajagopalan, Kanavillil (2004a). 'John Langshaw Austin'. In Philipp Strazny (ed.) (2004), *Encyclopedia of Linguistics*. New York: Fitzroy Dearborn. 98–100.

Rajagopalan, Kanavillil (2004b). 'John Searle'. In Philipp Strazny (ed.) (2004), *Encyclopedia of Linguistics*. New York: Fitzroy Dearborn. 936–8.

Rosch, Eleanor and Barbara B. Lloyd (eds) (1978). *Cognition and Categorization*. Hillsdale, NJ: Lawrence Erlbaum Associates.

Kanavillil Rajagopalan

PERFORMATIVE

A description of utterances, sentences and speech acts the use of which is meant to create facts in addition to the fact of one of them having been used. Often, the appearance of 'hereby' marks the performative nature of the expression, as in 'Master Little John is hereby created Sheriff of Nottingham' (*Robin Hood*).

See also: Speech Act Theory
Key Thinkers: Austin, J. L.; Searle, John

For a long period, philosophers of language and logicians of natural language were interested in sentences the utterance of which in appropriate contexts expresses propositions that are either true or false, for example, 'Shakespeare is the author of *Romeo and Juliet*' or 'All ravens are white'. It was always clear that not all sentences are of that type, for example English sentences in the interrogative or the imperative. It was J. L. Austin (1961) who drew attention to sentences of a seemingly different type that are quite commonly used, the 'performatives'.

The leading intuition underlying the distinction between propositional utterances and performative ones is that in the former case the story of the utterance, as commonly intended, conveyed and understood, is that of presenting a given fact about the state of affairs, while in the latter case the story involves some additional element that creates a new fact. Thus sincerely saying 'The door is open' is describing what the speaker takes to be a fact about the door, under the circumstances of utterance, while sincerely saying 'I promise to return the book' is creating a commitment on the part of the speaker to return the book. The commitment is created by the linguistic institution of promising. According to the rules that constitute and regulate that institution, uttering a sentence of the form 'I promise to do this and that' counts as undertaking a commitment to do this and that.

Promising is a linguistic institution. Appointing is a non-linguistic institution, according to the rules of which an utterance of 'I hereby appoint you deputy sheriff', under appropriate circumstances, counts as creating you a deputy sheriff. What is common to both linguistic and non-linguistic institutions is that they determine felicity conditions for creating new facts, such as a certain person having a certain commitment or serving in a certain capacity, which are institutional facts.

The question whether a performative utterance is an utterance of an assertion has been debated. Searle (1989) answers it in the negative, while Bach and Harnish (1992) argue that such an utterance is primarily assertoric.

According to the debatable Performative Hypothesis developed within generative semantics*, the deep structure of every sentence, including indicative ones, includes a prefix of the form 'I + (performative) verb'. Hence, every utterance is made within the framework of some institution.

Primary sources

Austin, J. L. (1961) 'Performative Utterances'. In J. O. Urmson and G. J. Warnock (eds), *J. L. Austin, Philosophical Papers*. Oxford: Clarendon Press. 233–52.

Bach K. and R. M. Harnish (1992). 'How performatives really work'. *Linguistics and Philosophy* 15: 93–110.
Searle, John (1989). 'How performatives work'. *Linguistics and Philosophy* 12: 535–58.

Asa Kasher

PHONEME

A term generally understood in the British and American structuralist traditions to refer to a fundamental abstract linguistic unit physically realised by multiple context-dependent, phonetically similar speech sounds, and possessing the capacity to change meaning but bearing no semantic properties of its own. Several definitions of the term exist, and disagreement persists over when and by whom it was first used.

See also: Distinctive Features; Emic/Etic; Generative Phonology; Optimality Theory; Poststructuralism; Type/Token
Key Thinkers: Bloomfield, Leonard; Firth, J. R.; Hockett, Charles; Jakobson, Roman; Jones, Daniel; Martinet, André; Pike, Kenneth; Saussure, Ferdinand de; Trubetzkoy, N. S.; Whorf, Benjamin Lee

Daniel Jones (1967) characterises phonemes as 'small families of sounds, each family consisting of an important sound of the language together with other related sounds which, so to speak, "represent" it in particular sequences or under particular conditions of length or stress or intonation' (p. 7). These family members are known as *allophones* (derived from the Greek for 'other sound') following Benjamin Lee Whorf's first use of the term in the early 1930s.

A language's phonemes stand in relationships of contrast with one another in that commutation (switching) of one phoneme for another in a given phonological frame through the creation of a 'minimal pair' (for example, substituting /p/ for /b/ in 'big' to produce 'pig') brings about a change in the words meaning. Phonemes are therefore said to be in 'parallel distribution'. Their allophones, which are contextually determined, are said to be in 'complementary distribution'.

In *The History and Meaning of the Term 'Phoneme'* (1957), Jones attributes the simultaneous 'discovery' of the phoneme to the late nineteenth and early twentieth-century linguists Baudouin de Courtenay and Henry Sweet, although elsewhere (Jones 1967) he cites J. R. Firth's contention that the term 'phoneme' as distinct from 'phone' (that is, an actual speech sound) was coined in 1879 by Nikolaj Kruszewski, one of Baudouin de Courtenay's students. Jones points to various kinds of evidence indicating that all spoken language users have intuitions about phonemic units, and cites the development of alphabetic writing systems as a good example of evidence of the 'natural sense' in which native speakers consider sounds to 'have a kind of sameness', even when their phonetic forms differ from each other.

Although the phoneme was superseded in the 1980s by non-linear models of phonological representation, its existence still appears to be taken as self-evident by researchers in domains outside theoretical phonology, for instance in the study of first and second language acquisition, speech and hearing disorders and remediation, speech technology, psycholinguistics and psychology more generally. The phoneme is also argued to be a structural element of signed languages.

Primary works

Jones, Daniel (1957). *The History and Meaning of the Term 'Phoneme'*. London: International Phonetic Association.

Jones, Daniel (1967). *The Phoneme: Its Nature and Use*. Third edition. London: W. Heffer & Sons.

Swadesh, Morris (1934). 'The phonemic principle', *Language* Vol. 10: 117–29.

Further reading

Anderson, Stephen R. (1985). *Phonology in the Twentieth Century: Theories of Rules and Theories of Representations*. Chicago: University of Chicago Press.

Goldsmith, John (ed.) (1996). *The Handbook of Phonological Theory*. Oxford: Blackwell.

Dominic Watt

POLITENESS

The formulation of linguistic utterances in such a way that they contribute to good social relationships between participants in an exchange. Since their inception in the 1970s, politeness studies have developed into one of the most active research areas in pragmatics and sociolinguistics, with several studies focusing on the realisation of politeness in different cultures.

See also: Implicature; Speech Act Theory; Conversation Analysis
Key Thinkers: Grice, H. P.; Searle, John

The importance of politeness as a factor motivating particular turns of phrase was acknowledged early on by linguists such as Charles Bally and Otto Jespersen. Later, it was also acknowledged by H. P. Grice (1967) and John Searle (1975), who associated it with departures from rational efficiency and with indirectness, respectively. However, it was not until the 1970s with Robin Lakoff's work on the rules of politeness (1973) and, most notably, the publication of Penelope Brown and Stephen Levinson's essay 'Politeness: Universals in Language Usage' (1978) that the integration of politeness into existing theoretical frameworks became a serious theoretical concern. A major contribution of Brown and Levinson lay in proposing the notion of face, inspired by Ervine Goffman's work on ritual aspects of everyday exchanges, as the unifying principle underlying the expression of politeness through language.

Brown and Levinson distinguish two aspects of face: positive face refers to the desire to be liked and approved of, while negative face corresponds to the wish for privacy and freedom from imposition. The two aspects of face may thus be viewed as pulling in opposite directions, with positive face promoting sociability and contact with others (as signalled, for example, through, the use of endearment terms and in-group language), and negative face satisfied through avoidance of contact (as signalled through 'for example, questioning and hedging). These two aspects of face allow for a four-way classification of speech acts into acts that inherently threaten the speaker's or the hearer's positive or negative face. Prior to performing an act x that inherently threatens face, known as a face threatening act or FTA, the speaker assesses the weightiness of the threat using the formula $Wx=D(S,H)+P(H,S)+Rx$. In this formula, $D(S,H)$ stands for the distance between the speaker and the hearer, a symmetric measure of familiarity or similarity between them; $P(H,S)$ is the power of the hearer over the speaker, an asymmetric measure of the amount of control the hearer can exercise over the speaker; and Rx is the ranking, or seriousness, of the imposition entailed by x in the culture in question. The sum of these three sociological values guides the speaker's choice among five strategies for the realisation of FTAs, ranging from 'Bald on record' (Wx is negligible), to 'Don't do the FTA' (Wx is very high) (see Figure 4). The bulk of Brown and Levinson's essay is dedicated to cataloguing the linguistic expressions that may realise the first four strategies (since the last one results in silence), which they illustrate with examples from English, Tamil (a Dravidian language) and Tzeltal (a Mayan language).

It is hard to overestimate the impact of Brown and Levinson's model to field of politeness studies. Integrating politeness with anthropological notions such as face, as well as the theoretical frameworks of implicature*

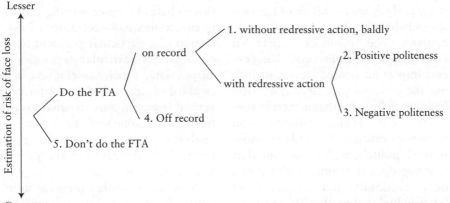

Figure 4 Strategies for performing FTAs (Brown and Levinson 1987: 60)

and Speech Act Theory*, their work has been instrumental in shaping our thinking about how human dyadic relationships are reflected in, and constituted through, language. Moreover, their comprehensive analysis of fieldwork data has inspired a multitude of articles and books exploring politeness phenomena in a variety of languages and cultures, often using the data collection method of Discourse Completion Tests (DCTs). Nevertheless, these works have also produced criticisms and refinements of Brown and Levinson's model. Some of the most important ones concern the definition of face and prioritising of negative over positive aspects; their focus on face threatening acts to the exclusion of face enhancing/boosting acts; the definitions and adequacy of the three sociological variables and their assumed independence; the association of politeness with degree of indirectness; the nature and content of politeness implicatures; the (inscrutable) role of silence in their model; the little attention paid to the role of the audience and surrounding social conventions (an aspect of 'discernment') with concomitant over-emphasising of individual rationality (also termed 'volition'); and the universal applicability of their claims.

More recently, and in tandem with the challenging of Gricean and Searlean accounts of meaning as not flexible enough to account for the ongoing co-construction of meaning by participants in interaction, a new set of concerns focusing on social theoretic aspects of politeness and favouring a more holistic approach to politeness phenomena have emerged. Responding to a paradigm shift within politeness studies, recent studies distinguish between first-order politeness (Politeness1), corresponding to participants' own definitions and perceptions of politeness in interaction, and second-order politeness (Politeness2), corresponding to the technical definition of politeness by researchers, building on, for example, anthropological notions such as face. Although researchers do not necessarily agree on which of the two should be the focus of scholarly analysis, the distinction between Politeness1 and Politeness2 has several important consequences, including the possibility of finer gradation between behaviour that is merely adequate (now termed 'politic'), and behaviour that goes beyond that (now termed 'polite'), with behaviour that is inappropriate falling at either end of a continuum that ranges from 'over-polite' to 'impolite.' In this way, the question of the scope of a theory of politeness is also raised, with impoliteness/rudeness increasingly attracting scholarly attention.

At the level of methodology, the focus has shifted from isolated utterances to longer chunks of discourse, which are often analysed using conversation-analytic tools. Rather than aiming at providing an inventory of devices, either lexical or structural, by which politeness is expressed, as in earlier studies, emphasis is now placed on the utterance situation as a whole, including the addressee's reception of the speaker's utterance, prosodic aspects, and any paralinguistic cues available. The use of recorded conversational data is paramount in this respect. Further to the qualitative analysis of these data, the value of their quantitative analysis is also increasingly acknowledged. Such quantitative analysis presupposes the availability of large conversational corpora*, in which regularities of usage (or norms) may be investigated. While the existence of such norms, and hence their value as analytic tools, have been brought into question, quantitative analysis of conversational corpora may hold the key to

this debate. In other words, the frequent, contextually-conditioned association of a particular perlocutionary effect with a particular expression in corpus data, if such association can be established, provides an empirically verifiable baseline as to what constitutes the 'unmarked' case, and an analyst-independent vantage point from which to locate and analyse various cases as 'marked'.

Politeness is neither inherent in linguistic forms in isolation from their context of utterance (it is not a matter of structure), nor does it reside (wholly) in the speaker's intention, independently of its recognition by the hearer (it is not a matter of agency). Rather, politeness may be viewed as the mutual constitution of face by participants in an exchange, which is greatly facilitated by their partaking of similar societal norms – what may be described in terms drawing on Bourdieu as their having developed 'homologous habitus'. Approaches to politeness have thus increasingly turned to social-theoretic notions, such as habitus and communities of practice, to analyse the contribution of language in constructing, maintaining and endangering good social relationships.

Primary sources

Brown, Penelope and Stephen Levinson (1978). 'Politeness: universals in language usage'. In Goody, E. (ed.), *Questions and Politeness: Strategies in Social Interaction*. Cambridge: Cambridge University Press. 56–324. Reprinted as Brown, Penelope and Stephen Levinson, (1987) *Politeness: Some Universals in Language Usage*. Cambridge: Cambridge University Press.

Lakoff, Robin (1973). 'The logic of politeness; or minding your p's and qs'. In *Papers from the Ninth Regional Meeting of the Chicago Linguistic Society*. Chicago: Chicago Linguistic Society. 292–305.

Leech, Geoffrey (1983). *Principles of Pragmatics*. London: Longman.

Further reading

Bousfield, Derek and Miriam Locher (eds) (2007). *Impoliteness in Language*. Berlin: Mouton de Gruyter.

Eelen, Gino (2001). *A Critique of Politeness Theories*. Manchester: St Jerome.

Grice, Herbert Paul (1967). 'Logic and conversation'. William James Lectures, Harvard University typescript. In P. Cole and J. Morgan (eds) (1975), *Syntax and Semantics. Vol. III: Speech Acts*. New York: Academic Press. 41–58. Reprinted in Grice, H. P. (1989), *Studies in the Way of Words*. Cambridge, MA: Harvard University Press. 22–40.

Kerbrat-Orecchioni, Catherine (2005). 'La Politesse dans le discours en interaction'. In C. Kerbrat-Orecchioni. *Le Discours en Interaction*. Paris: Colin. 187–284.

Searle, John (1975). 'Indirect speech acts'. In P. Cole and J. Morgan (eds.), *syntax and Semantics. Vol. III: Speech Acts*. New York: Academic Press. 59–82.

Terkourafi, Marina (2005). 'Beyond the micro-level in politeness research', *Journal of Politeness Research* Vol. 1:2, 237–62.

Watts, Richard (2003). *Politeness*. Cambridge: Cambridge University Press.

Watts, Richard, Sachiko Ide and Konrad Ehlich (eds) (2005). *Politeness in Language*. Second edition. Berlin: Mouton de Gruyter.

Marina Terkourafi

POLITICAL CORRECTNESS

In its most general sense the term 'political correctness' refers to an individual's or group's conscious avoidance of linguistic terms associated principally with race, ethnicity, nationality, gender, religious belief system and sexual orientation that are perceived to be pejorative or at any rate to have the potential to cause offence to others. A more specialised sense refers to an uncritical adherence to and advocacy of a particular political credo, such as Marxism.

> *See also*: Conversation Analysis; (Critical) Discourse Analysis; Feminism; Metaphor; Names; Politeness
> *Key Thinkers*: Cameron, Deborah; Milroy, Lesley; Tannen, Deborah; Whorf, Benjamin Lee

The term 'political correctness' originated on American campuses among New Left activists in the 1960s and 1970s, when it was used primarily in connection with feminist criticisms of perceived sexism in language. Nowadays the term is used mainly by critics of proposed linguistic and social reforms and is therefore almost exclusively pejorative. Opponents of political correctness claim that is is overly concerned with trivial linguistic prescriptivism. Those on the other side of the debate draw on a form of 'weak Whorfianism' to claim that language influences perception, therefore that linguistic change is a necessary precursor to changing social attitudes.

While practically all language users observe the conventions prohibiting the public use of taboo forms, the degree of sanction attached to individual words or phrases in the social domains mentioned above is highly fluid, such that terms considered acceptable at a particular place or time may quickly become stigmatised if they are considered insufficiently politically correct or 'PC' by one or more politically or economically influential groups. Awareness of the often serious consequences of deliberately or accidentally flouting the conventions of politically correct language have strongly influenced linguistic habits at almost all levels of society in English-speaking countries, perhaps most particularly in the United States, where a high degree of sensitivity to certain terms perceived to betray racist attitudes has resulted in the sacking of several high-profile public figures. For example, the use of the word 'coon' by American radio talk-show host Dave Lenihan in an item about US Secretary of State Condoleezza Rice broadcast in 2006 was apparently accidental (he claims to have intended to say 'coup'), while the previous year Las Vegas TV weatherman Rob Blair's alleged use of the same form, supposedly substituted for 'King' in the phrase 'Martin Luther King Junior Day', could plausibly have resulted from an anticipatory speech error. Both Lenihan and Blair were nonetheless dismissed from their posts almost immediately. In 1999 vociferous objections to the contextually valid use in a private meeting of the word 'niggardly' by David Howard, an aide to the mayor of Washington DC, led to Howard's resignation.

Political correctness is tightly bound to censorship, and to other forms of legislation seeking to proscribe the public use of 'offensive' language. Since 2000 extensions to existing linguistic legislation have been made in the United Kingdom, for example, ostensibly in the interests of protecting religious minorities from persecution in the aftermath of the events of 11 September 2001. The Racial and Religious Hatred Act 2006 specifies that it will be an offence to incite (or 'stir up') hatred against a person on the grounds of his or her religion, by prohibiting 'threatening words' and 'the display of any written material which is threatening' if the intention by so doing is to stir up religious hatred.

Resistance to the introduction of such measures takes several forms. Key among these are the holding up of PC language to public ridicule, for example James Finn Garner's series of 'politically correct stories', and the appropriation (and thereby subversion) of 'non-PC' terms such as 'queen' and 'nigger' by the gay and the black communities, respectively.

Primary works

Cameron, Deborah (1995). *Verbal Hygiene*. London: Routledge.

Dunant, Sarah (1995). *The War of the Words: The Political Correctness Debate*. London: Virago.

Further reading

Fairclough, Norman (2003). 'Political correctness: the politics of culture and language'. *Discourse and Society* Vol. 14:1, 17–28.

Holborow, Marnie (1999). *The Politics of English*. London: Sage.

Dominic Watt

PORT-ROYAL LOGIC

Colloquial name for *La Logique ou l'Art de Penser* (*Logic or the Art of Thinking*) written by Antoine Arnauld and Pierre Nicole but published anonymously in 1662 (the fifth edition was published in 1683). The *Logic* elaborated a traditional syllogistic logic wedded to a Cartesian epistemology and metaphysics. The work also contains many insights in natural language syntax that were not surpassed until the work of Noam Chomsky in the mid-twentieth century.

> *See also*: Analytic/Synthetic;
> Empiricism/Rationalism; Logic;
> Propositional Attitudes;
> Transformational-Generative
> Grammar
> *Key Thinkers*: Aristotle; Arnauld,
> Antoine; Chomsky, Noam;
> Descartes, René; Frege, Gottlob;
> Russell, Bertrand

With its companion, *Grammaire Générale et Raisonnée de Port-Royal* (published by Arnauld and Claude Lancelot in 1660), the *Logic* seeks to show that the new Cartesian philosophy of *ideas* provides a general account of judgement and reasoning and a sound basis for a demarcation of 'good' and 'bad' arguments. It further provides many detailed analyses of how linguistic 'surface forms' systematically mismatch the complex combination of ideas they express.

Following Aristotle, the *Logic* categorises judgements in terms of quantity and quality, and adopts the standard syllogistic forms with modifications from the scholastic studies. Propositions* are understood to be complexes formed by acts of will (judgement) that combine a subject idea with a predicate idea, with the verb carrying affirmative force; a negative judgement is the converse, where the predicate is separated from the subject. The *Logic* falls prey here to not being able to distinguish a proposition from an attitude towards it. The reasoning, however, brings into relief the 'unity problem' that was to bedevil Bertrand Russell.

The *Logic* also distinguishes between explicating and determining subordinate propositions (relative clauses). For example, 'The invisible God created the visible universe' can be analysed as 'The God who is invisible created the universe which is visible', where the first relative clause explicates its subject, and the second further determines its subject. This development was perhaps the first formal account of the analytic/synthetic* distinction.

The *Logic* fell into neglect after the rise of modern function-argument logic and the prevailing behaviourism* empiricism* in the first part of the twentieth century. In the mid-1960s, however, Chomsky argued that the Port-Royal approach was the high point of a Cartesian first 'cognitive revolution', in its search for underlying mental structures behind the surface of language. Although Chomsky's historical remarks have been broadly misconstrued, they did stimulate fresh interest in Port-Royal and both the *Logic* and *Grammar* are now recognised as the forerunners of much that is characteristic in modern linguistic analysis.

Primary sources

Arnauld, A. and P. Nicole (1996). *Logic or the Art of Thinking*. Trans. and ed. J. V. Buroker. Cambridge: Cambridge University Press.

Arnauld, A. and C. Lancelot (1975). *General and Rational Grammar The Port-Royal Grammar*. Trans. and ed. J. Rieux and B. E. Rollin. The Hague: Mouton.

Further reading

Chomsky, N. (1966). *Cartesian Linguistics*. New York: Harper and Row.

John Collins

POSSIBLE WORLD SEMANTICS

A theory of formal and natural language semantics that assumes truth-conditions to be the meaning of linguistic expressions and sentences, and claims that the truth value* of particular sentences relative either to the actual world or to one or more of the other possible worlds is what makes any unique sentence true or false, thereby establishing its meaning. The idea goes back to Gottfried Wilhelm Leibniz and has been elaborated by Rudolf Carnap, but the main figures of the modern version, especially associated with modal logic, were Saul Kripke and David Lewis. Possible world semantics was, to some extent, utilised by Richard Montague.

See also: Connotation/Denotation; Correspondence Theory; Definite Descriptions; Logic; Modality; Names; Sense/Reference

Key Thinkers: Carnap, Rudolf; Kripke, Saul; Leibniz, Gottfried Wilhelm; Lewis, David; Montague, Richard

From a common-sense point of view the idea of possible worlds may seem at odds with normal intuitions since one may think the world is what it is; what it might have been instead is just a matter of speculation. But Leibniz saw the world as a manifestation of God's will and in God's mind there are an infinite number of possible worlds, from which God has chosen this one. Since God is both benevolent and omnipotent He has chosen the best of all the possible worlds. When taking up the idea in a modern context, the first kind of concern is what is understood by the concept 'possible world' if it is not the notion proposed by Leibniz. It may most easily be captured in the perspective of the choices we make as human beings. Consider the sentence:

(1) John bought a red car yesterday

Whoever John is, he chose to buy a car and he chose the colour red. Reconstructing the situation in retrospect we know that he (i) might have chosen not to buy a car and, if anyhow he did buy a car, he (ii) might have chosen another colour. Had he chosen otherwise, the world would also have been otherwise in the respect that John might have no car or a car with another colour. We can also, in retrospect, construe the situation in which John made his choices and imagine the scenarios that were going through his mind at the car dealer: (i) car versus . no car, and (ii) red versus other colours. Each scenario represents a minor difference in the way the world may look depending on the choices made by John; in the history of the universe it may seem insignificant what John chose to do, but in the context of what linguistic expressions – and especially sentences – mean, it may be crucial. Taking (1) as an ordinary life utterance, it is expected to have an inherent meaning more or less evident to the interlocutors engaged in a conversation, and in modern philosophical semantics this is supposed to be established by its truth value, that is, whether it is true or false according to its truth conditions. This in turn is the way the world looks like in the circumstances surrounding John's buying a car or not.

So far one might accept the claim that the meaning of sentences has to do with the relation between the words uttered and the world, but there are two problems here. One is that it may not be evident how the meaning of sentences is identical with the question of whether they are true or false. Intuitively one may think that in order to decide the truth value (relative to a specific state of affairs) of a sentence, one has to understand it, and to understand it is to know its meaning. But, it is claimed, to know its meaning is to know its truth value based on its truth conditions, which it follows is the same thing as its meaning. There seems to be a kind of circularity predicament as an immanent part of truth-value semantics, and this is one of the problems possible world semantics tries to solve. A further complication is the following question: if meaning is truth conditions – that is, there is a kind of correspondence between a sentence and the

world – what then is the meaning of a false sentence? Can a *lack* of correspondence be the meaning of a sentence? Possible world semantics may not have a clear answer to this.

Another problem is the question about the relation between words and the world, in that we may ask: what world? It seems evident that we can talk directly about things in our environment because we can observe them while talking. In general we also feel fairly sure that our environment is relatively stable: for instance, that when we get up in the morning, our home will look the way it looked when we went to bed. We may realise that the building may have burned down over night, but only as a hypothetical possibility. Philosophers have spent much time debating the fact that we think we know, and can talk about, things we do not observe while talking, and basically we cannot be totally sure that we do know. The fact that we nevertheless maintain that we actually do know is based on our experience and the belief that our experience is reliable. Therefore one of our linguistic skills – affiliated with our mental faculty and our memory – is the ability of displacement, namely that we can talk about things that are not present, or even things we have never experienced anything about, like Napoleon, the far side of the moon or Jack the Ripper. This, too, is one of the issues for possible world semantics. In the special and technical framework of formal logic, possible world semantics will also comprise a kind of modal logic, the modality* of which is so-called alethic modality, which deals with propositions expressing what is possible versus what is necessary.

The modern notion of possible world semantics has its roots in Carnap's *Meaning and Necessity* (1947) in which, as opposed to his earlier work, he engaged in semantic questions, adjusting Gottlob Frege's basic notions of *Sinn* ('sense') and *Bedeutung* ('meaning') in order to make them work in his system of modal logic. In the general modern version of possible world semantics – in which the term 'possible world' had its technical meaning coined by Kripke in a paper in 1959 – it works as a way of clarifying the meaning of either normal declarative sentences or sentences containing the words 'possible' and 'necessary' (or some of the morphological derivations of them) or containing epistemic modals (verbs in the past tense expressing counterfactuals or unsubstantiated information). Consider the sentence below:

(2) The present queen of Denmark was crowned queen in 1972.

This proposition is true in the actual world because her father the king died that year. This is a normal declarative sentence and its truth value is a matter of contingency, that is, it may be either true or false, and one has to check the evidence in order to decide what the facts are. One also has to do so when listening to (3) in order to conclude that it is a false contingent proposition:

(3) The present queen of Denmark has an older brother.

A possible world semantics will tackle these details by saying that (2) is true at the actual world, as mentioned, while (3) is false at the actual world,

and, accordingly, contingent propositions are true at some possible worlds and false at some other possible worlds. Obviously things might have gone otherwise, and (4)

(4) The present queen of Denmark was crowned queen in 1971.

might have been true if only her father the king had not lived the last few days of his life. Therefore (4) is a proposition that is possibly true – that is, in possible world semantics it is true in some (at least one) possible worlds. In contrast, (5) is an impossible proposition:

(5) The present queen of Denmark is a man.

This is true in no possible world and is therefore false by necessity, while (6)

(6) The present queen of Denmark is a woman.

is a proposition that is true by necessity – that is, it is true at all possible worlds. When using the word 'possibly', one is able to set up an explicit hypothetical scenario:

(7) The queen of Denmark is *possibly* meeting the American president this moment.

and the same job can be done with an epistemic modal:

(8) The queen of Denmark *might* be meeting the American president this moment.

Both (7) and (8) may be true in some possible worlds and false in others, but the trouble with such sentences is the fact that their truth value is not given by the meanings (reference of the subject and extension of the predicate) of their parts, as is the case with the previously mentioned subject-predicate sentences. Hence (7) and (8) cannot be used as truth-functional conjuncts in the same way. This other kind of logic may be expressed in a formal and symbolised language (so-called alethic formal logic) using special logical operators. Thus in (9)

(9) $\Box p$ = 'it is necessary that p'

the symbol $\Box$ is an operator signifying the necessity of the content of the proposition 'p'. If p is supposed to be (6) 'The present queen of Denmark is a woman' then p is true – that is, (6) is true at all possible worlds. However, if p is, for instance, (5) 'The present queen of Denmark is a man' and somebody claims that

(10) $\Diamond p$ = 'it is possible that p'

using $\Diamond$ as a possibility operator, then (10) is false by necessity because the sentence p is true in no possible world. By combinations of these operators and connectors from traditional logic, one is able to construct larger formal systems (languages) with compound propositions. Using the letters w, v, u as variables for possible worlds, one may state the propositions:

(11) 'the 'Big Bang' initiated the universe' and 'the universe will expand forever'

putting them together in

(12) 'if the "Big Bang" initiated the universe [antecedent] then it will expand forever [consequent]'

and adding the alethic expression 'it is possible that' as a prefix. This can be formalised, first, as

(13) $p \rightarrow q$

where p is the antecedent and q the consequent in (12) and, second, as

(14) $\Diamond(p \rightarrow q)$ = 'it is possible that (12)'.

In possible world semantics this would be equivalent to ' "if the 'Big Bang' initiated the universe then it will expand forever" is true at some (at least one) possible worlds'. On this basis one is able to combine more complex formulae of deduction. Whether modal alethic logic is the ideal (for) modal logic or just some subtype of it is a debated issue among philosophers, but some common ground seems to be that there are certain relations between possible worlds. Sometimes this is referred to as accessibility or alternativeness between worlds (see McCawley 1981: 276), figuratively how you can 'get' from, say, $w1$ to $w2$, irrespective of the stipulated ontological status of the worlds. That means that the traditional mathematical principles of reflexivity, symmetry and transivity (McCawley 1982: 276) apply to the formulae produced by systems of formal modal (alethic) logic. A further extension of such systems is the production of predicate logic systems for modal logic (see McCawley 1982: 285–96). Lewis (1973) takes up the question of relations between possible world in the context of counterfactuals, that is what is not true at the actual world, and he offers a clarifying account of these relations in that he proposes not an abstract distance – illustrated by closeness in numerical measure – but a three-place predicate notation expressing the relative closeness between three possible worlds (McCawley 1982: 312).

Lewis also defends the idea that possible worlds do in fact exist as entities in some way or other. This is called absolute realism (Schurz 2006: 443) and is a subtype of realism, a metaphysical claim that holds that universals (what can be used as predicates in propositions about more than one entity) are real. An alternative view is reductive realism which says that possible worlds do exist but can be reduced to entities that are more familiar, and this view is the most common among scholars in the field. A third position is anti-realism, and from the meaning of this label one may infer that it denies both the realistic stance (that universals exist) and, accordingly, that possible worlds exist and that possible-world-sentences are meaningful. In this respect Kripke conceived of a possible world as 'a counterfactual course of history' (Kripke 1981: 6), and, in a broader perspective, one may set up a quite impressive number of combinations of different kinds of existence of possible worlds, maybe ending with the mundane view that they are just useful fictions used in logical reasoning.

Kripke made a number of contributions to philosophical logic, notably to the theory of the semantics of names* – which he called rigid designators. He developed an idea now called the causal theory of reference, and he has profoundly changed the common view on the basic logical notions of *a priori* and *a posteriori* relative to analytical and synthetic truths. But in the context of modal logic his major contribution is the solutions he offers to the problems concerning modal logic, possible world semantics and the metaphysical consequences of a number of principles appealed to by logicians. This has to do with, for instance, the above-mentioned realism as one kind of assertion about whether possible things exist or not; another view is actualism, which says that everything that exists is what is actual – that is, what we can say there is a fairly clear consensus about in the real world. Now, the problem is that if one is an actualist and accepts the formal consequences of modal logic in what is called a simplest quantified version, one also has to accept the unattractive outcome that possible things do exist. Kripke's solution to the problem requires a rather technical account but it has to do with the way he handles the semantics (specifically the domains) of individual terms in modal propositions, a theoretical suggestion called 'Kripke Models'. An unpretentious interpretation might say that he claimed that possible things can be said to exist but only, so to speak, in their own worlds, from which it follows that propositions about them put forward in the actual world end up being false. In this way the problem with their truth value, that they seem to be true also in the actual world (which has some unpleasant metaphysical consequences), has been dissolved. Kripke's solution is not undisputed but his intellectual achievements in the field are widely acknowledged.

Possible world semantics presents the linguist and the philosopher with a number of suggestions that may solve some traditional problems. For instance, the apparent problem of circularity in a truth-conditional semantics for linguistic expressions may be solved by rephrasing the question from asking about relations between meanings of sentences in this world to asking about relations between different worlds, called possible worlds, as meanings of sentences. This may also solve the question about the meaning of a false sentence in that a false sentence may be true in some possible world, which thereby presents an intuitively acceptable positive correspondence between the sentence and that particular world. However, this leaves open the question of whether this will make us understand what a false sentence means in our world. It also does not dissolve the relation between sentence, meaning and possible world; it does not solve the correspondence problem. It would not be unfair to say that possible world semantics chooses to ignore such problems concentrating on constructing formal systems that can handle traditional technical problems in other formal systems.

Primary sources

Carnap, R. (1947). *Meaning and Necessity*. Chicago: Chicago University Press.
Kripke, S. (1959). 'A completeness theorem in modal logic'. *Journal of Symbolic Logic* 24: 1–14.
Kripke, S. (1981). *Naming and Necessity*. Oxford: Blackwell.
Lewis, D. K. (1973). *Counterfactuals*. Oxford: Blackwell.
McCawley, J. (1981). *Everything That Linguists Have Always Wanted to Know About Logic, But Were Ashamed to Ask*. Oxford: Blackwell. 273–359.
Menzel, C. (1990). 'Actualism, ontological commitment, and possible world semantics'. *Synthese* 85: 355–89.
Schurz, G. (2006). 'Alethic modal logics and semantics'. In D. Jaquette (ed.), *A Companion to Philosophical Logic*. Oxford: Blackwell. 442–77.

Further reading

Benthem, J. van et al. (2006). 'Part IX. Modal logic and semantics'. In D. Jaquette (ed.), *A Companion to Philosophical Logic*. Oxford: Blackwell. 389–509.
Dancy, J. (1985). *Introduction to Contemporary Epistemology*. Oxford: Blackwell.
Groenendijk J. and M. Stokhof (2002). 'Type-shifting rules and the semantics of interrogatives'. In P. Portner and B. H. Partee (eds), *Formal Semantics*. Oxford: Blackwell.
Kratzer, A. (2002). 'The notational category of modality'. In P. Portner and B. H. Partee (eds), *Formal Semantics*. Oxford: Blackwell.
Martin, R. M. (1987). *The Meaning of Language*. Cambridge, MA: MIT Press.
Robertson, T. (1998). 'Possibilities and the arguments for origin essentialism'. *Mind* 107. 428: 729–49.
Saeed, J. I. (2003). *Semantics*. Second edition. Oxford: Blackwell.
Stalnaker, R. C. (2002). 'Assertion'. In P. Portner and B. H. Partee (eds), *Formal Semantics*. Oxford: Blackwell.

Hans Götzsche

POSTSTRUCTURALISM

Poststructuralism is an outgrowth of structuralism* It is a method of analysis which had a tremendous impact in the last decades of the twentieth century on work done in the fields of linguistics, anthropology, psychology, literary criticism and elsewhere. Arguably, it remains a potent force to reckon with in the early twenty-first century, though it has been at the centre of intense and often acrimonious debates.

See also: Signs and Semiotics; Structuralism; Deconstruction
Key Thinkers: Bourdieu, Pierre; Derrida, Jacques; Lacan, Jacques; Saussure, Ferdinand de

Like so many other terms that take the prefix 'post-', poststructuralism is a complex notion. Part of the difficulty in getting to grips with the term has to do with just how one is supposed to view its relation to structuralism. In one sense, the term does imply that it regards structuralism as a thing of the past (as in 'post-World War Two period'). But equally it also captures the idea that it is an offshoot of structuralism or, alternatively, it is a movement that draws its strength from the legacy of structuralism (as in 'postgraduate student').

In other words, to understand what poststructuralism is about, one needs to have some idea of what constitutes structuralism. Structuralism is a mode of inquiry which looks at the phenomena under its scrutiny as made up solely of the relations among the entities in question, rather than those entities themselves. In other words, the entities themselves are not positively defined, but identified at best as mere place-holders. This has the consequence that all structures are by definition hermetically closed unto themselves. It is only on this condition that a structure can be regarded as composed of pure negativities. To put it differently, the 'structurality' of a given structure is conditional upon the entire space having been taken up by binary relations: the forceful removal of any entity will automatically trigger a rearrangement of the remaining entities. This in turn means that all structures are fully integrated, each with respect to itself, and autonomous with respect to other structures.

Structuralism was a huge success as an idea in the early decades of the twentieth century and it held sway over several academic disciplines well into the second half of that century. It revolutionised linguistics and set it apart from philology and historical linguistics, which dominated the discipline in the nineteenth century. In fact the neat separation between synchrony and diachrony that Ferdinand de Saussure advocated was but a straightforward consequence of the requirement that a structure, in order to function the way it was required to, had to be closed unto itself. But it soon became clear that this was at odds with the further requirement that a structure also had to be resilient, so as to permit 'the rearrangement of its internal units' in order to accommodate eventual structural changes. From a structuralist point of view, all changes were, so to speak, sudden and cataclysmic and, while keeping the overall structure intact, would result in an internal rearrangement of the network of relations within the structure. History, in this world-view, progressed by fits and starts, rather than in a smooth and gradual continuum. In the philosophy of science, Thomas Kuhn famously advocated a view of the progress of science which had all the trappings of structuralism in this sense.

As already noted, the twin requirements of the closure and the resilience of a structure are mutually incompatible. In a ground-breaking essay called 'Structure, Sign, and Play in the Discourse of the Human Sciences', Jacques Derrida (1966) drew attention to this irreconcilable incompatibility and argued that the only way structuralism could be salvaged is by admitting that a structure can have only an imaginary centre. 'The centre cannot be the centre' concluded the French philosopher in what is often cited as one of his most enigmatic statements. Now, this imaginary centre does indeed appear to be either controlling or, contrariwise, being controlled by the structure.

The first alternative results in the positing of an all-powerful subject, Cartesian in its lineage, whose intentions underpin meanings and prevent them from going astray or floating around freely. Humanism, alongside its offshoots existentialism and phenomenology, provides the necessary philosophical backdrop against which such a subject could be envisaged. Intentionality* ('aboutness') would be the hallmark of the subject of language. He/she would constitute the fulcrum around which language turns.

In the late 1960s and early 1970s, however, there was a concerted move among French intellectuals to incorporate into structuralism insights from Marxism and Lacanian psychoanalysis. The speaking subject was unceremoniously dislodged from the high pedestal where he/she had remained safely and majestically ensconced. The subject was decentred and demoted to the status of a marionette. Marxist structuralists like Louis Althusser advocated this second alternative, on the strength of the conviction that the 'mature Marx' had made a crucial break with his own earlier Romantic humanism, whereby what would be left at the centre is an illusory subject, seeming to be in control of him/herself and his/her meanings, while actually being subjected or subjugated by the structure.

Derrida contended that both of the options signalled by structuralism result from a misunderstanding of the function of the absent centre. The structure's absent centre functions rather like the black hole at the centre of a galaxy (a structure like any other). It is here that Derrida recognises the effects of history within the structure, traditionally thought to offer no room for origin or history (whereof the separation of synchrony from diachrony). What this means is that the subject can be neither Cartesian (all-knowing, intending) nor a being at the mercy of forces beyond his/her control. The structuralist subject, in other words, must give way to a poststructuralist agent who must act in history (not independently of it) while, no doubt, constrained by the structure around him/her.

This then can be pointed out as the hallmark of poststructuralism: the emergence of the historical subject within the very entrails of a structure.

This new subject is one who has been empowered to act on his/her own and is endowed with agency. Once the presence of an agent who is in a position to subvert the order of things, thwarting it from within, is recognised, it is but a short step to reject the existence of all pre-ordained, foundationalist, essentialist and totalising conceptual schemes.

Michel Foucault played an important role in the development of poststructuralism. Having been a die-hard structuralist himself, Foucault grew increasingly discontented with two of structuralism's key assumptions. On the one hand, while recognising the pervasiveness of structures in many of human activities, Foucault became sceptical of the idea that structures invariably control and regulate the human condition. On the other hand, he also came to recognise the inevitable 'situatedness' of our gaze and the impossibility of ever attaining a transcendental standpoint from which to contemplate things.

Freeing the subject of language from the shackles of structurally imposed subjugation is key to a politics of identity. But then the escape from the prison-house of structure should not herald a return to liberal individualism whereby the individual determines his/her own destiny through the exercise of a series of rational choices. This is the central thrust of and moving impulse behind the work of Pierre Bourdieu. In his book *Outline of a Theory of Practice* (1977) Bourdieu made a proposal for avoiding both the Scylla of the total subjugation of the subject of language and the Charybdis of navel-gazing individualism, by putting forward the notion of 'habitus'. In Bourdieu's view, social agents develop, over a period of time, a 'feel for the game' which is a kind of eminently practical and bodily knowledge.

Poststructuralism is closely tied to and often confused with postmodernism. While the two indeed share many common concerns, it is important to bear in mind that the latter is concerned to critique, in a way the former is not, the Enlightenment project and the sheer arrogance of those who claimed to be fighting the battle of Reason against Irrationality.

Poststructuralism, alongside postmodernism, opens up an entirely new set of possibilities for thinking about ethical issues. With the metanarratives of foundationalist, essentialist and totalising discourse completely discredited, poststructuralism leaves us no option but that of regarding the path of ethics as an exercise in tight-rope walking, with no safety net in case a false step is taken. In other words, it foregrounds the question of personal responsibility. In the United Kingdom, a specialist group called 'Post-Structuralism and Radical Politics' has been actively engaged in promoting discussion on the political implications of poststructuralism in all walks of life.

Primary sources

Belsey, Catherine (2002). *Poststructuralism: A Very Short Introduction*. Oxford: Oxford University Press.

Bourdieu, Pierre (1977). *Outline of a Theory of Practice*. London: Cambridge University Press.

Derrida, Jacques (1966). 'Structure, sign, and play in the discourse of the human sciences'. In Jacques Derrida (2001),

Writing and Difference. London: Routledge.

Sarup, Madan (1993). *An Introductory Guide to Poststructuralism and Postmodernism*. Second edition. Athens, GA: University of Georgia Press.

Sturrock, John (1979). *Structuralism and Since*. London: Oxford University Press.

West, David. (1996). *An Introduction to Continental Philosophy*. Cambridge: Polity Press.

Williams, James (2006). *Understanding Poststructuralism*. Canada: McGill-Queen's University Press.

Further reading

Valentine, Jeremy and Alan Finlayson (eds) (2002). *Poststructuralism and Politics: An Introduction*. Edinburgh: Edinburgh University Press.

Kanavillil Rajagopalan

PRESUPPOSITION

A type of extra and assumed meaning attached to the basic meaning of utterances or sentences. In a broad sense presupposition can be defined as what must by necessity be assumed to be the case in order to interpret a short ordered sequence of linguistic expressions in a meaningful way. The idea was introduced by Gotlob Frege who said that presuppositions (in German: *Voraussetzung* '(pre)condition') are particular conditions that have to be satisfied for single linguistic expressions to have a denotation (Beaver 1996), but twentieth-century linguistics and philosophy has focused more on the presuppositional meaning associated with sentences and utterances.

See also: Connotation/Denotation; Definite Descriptions; Implicature; Names; Possible World Semantics; Sense/Reference; Speech Act Theory; Truth Value

Key Thinkers: Frege, Gottlob; Grice, H. P.; Russell, Bertrand; Strawson, P. F.; Montague, Richard

The notion of presupposition as a theoretical concept in linguistics and the philosophy of language tries to solve the problem that in discourse utterances may be articulated and fully understood by the interlocutors, while a detached and uninitiated observer may find it hard to understand the meaning of what is being said. Imagine I go to the supermarket together with my wife and, seeing among the amount of goods a certain kind of soup in small plastic bags, I say 'Look, there is this special Italian soup in small plastic bags', and my wife responds 'My Italian language course has no more classes'. The background knowledge assumed by both of us is that I do not cook and therefore I just warm up some prefabricated meal for us when she comes home from her Italian classes. The line of reasoning is that when she has no more Italian classes, I will not have to do this any more and therefore we will not have to buy more plastic bag soup. According to H. P. Grice, this instance of background knowledge and tacit line of reasoning may be called a kind of (conversational) implicature*, or, in later developments, presumptive meaning or preferred interpretation (Levinson 2000), but it might also be considered a kind of presupposition. Which option is chosen depends on whether one sees presupposition as a semantic or as a pragmatic function and furthermore on whether one's concern is natural languages or formal languages. Frege's main objective was to nurture the technical languages of science in the form of formal logic* and mathematics, and the specific linguistic functions of these languages that now are regarded as presuppositional functions were the main interest of the central figures Bertrand Russell and P. F. Strawson.

Working with his famous, and to some scholars notorious, example 'The present king of France is bald' (Russell 1905: 483), Russell claims that the proposition does not fail to have a truth value* (a point of view held by Frege) but has to be broken down into a number of component propositions each of which has to be true for the compound proposition to be true. Since one of the propositions ('there exists a king of France') is false, then the compound proposition is false, and therefore meaningful according to the view that truth conditions are the meaning of sentences. This view was challenged by Strawson (1950) who said that the proposition singled out by Russell – together with the second component proposition, 'there is no more than one king of France' – is not asserted but presupposed since the definite description* 'the [present] king of France' fails to refer (it did in 1950 and has done since then). In this respect Strawson agrees with Frege. Therefore the proposition containing the definite description cannot be used to make an assertion and accordingly it is meaningful but has no truth value. The positions held by Russell and Strawson respectively have given rise to much

heated discussion and controversy among philosophers and linguists, and while later on Strawson modified his views, many twentieth-and twenty-first-century scholars prefer not to commit themselves to any of the standpoints.

However, the philosophical implications of this issue are by no means trivial since, on the one hand, they deal with some aspects of the basic problem of how linguistic expressions can be used to refer to things in the world and, on the other hand, how we can express knowledge of the world in so-called existential sentences like 'there is a [one and only one] queen of Denmark', as opposed to so-called identity sentences like 'a queen is a female monarch' and predications like 'the queen of Denmark is intelligent'. One further concern is how we refer to fictional and abstract entities and, in the present context, how we use such kinds of reference in presuppositions. These are, in the end, epistemological questions, and some of the formal properties of presuppositions have some bearing on deeper philosophical contemplations. One such common property shared by presumably all theories of presuppositions is the way presuppositions work under negation. Consider the following sentence:

(1) The queen of Denmark is intelligent.

Accepting the convention that (1) can be represented by the symbol q, then it follows that the truth value of q as well as its negation ~q depends on the truth value of the presupposition 'there is a queen of Denmark', which can be represented by the symbol p.

Thus, it seems to be a matter of fact that p is the necessary condition of both q and ~q. In this respect a pre-supposition differs from an entailment in that the same does not seem to hold for entailments. Consider the sentence:

(2) Jack the Ripper killed the woman.

It follows from the meaning of the sentence that the woman must be dead, and this has to do with the meaning of the word 'kill'. The basic meaning of 'kill' is that somebody being 'killed' must be dead. This is not the case with, for instance, the word 'shoot'. The sentence 'the policeman shot the murderer' may refer to an incident where the murderer survived. Thus entailments are closely con-nected with the lexical meanings of the words used (verbs like 'kill' and 'shoot') while presupposition is a rela-tion between sentences and between sentences and the world. This can be illustrated by sets of sentences such as the following:

(3a) John has stopped smoking
(3b) John has been smoking
(3c) John has not stopped smoking

If John has stopped smoking (3a), then he must have been smoking in the past, but the same goes for the case in which he has not stopped smoking (3c), and therefore (3b) is a presuppo-sition of both (3a) and (3c). Not so with entailments:

(4a) Jack the Ripper killed the woman.
(4b) The woman is dead.
(4c) Jack the Ripper did not kill the woman.

The denial of (4b) automatically makes (4a) false while the denial of (4a), as in (4c), has no influence on the truth value of (4b) since the woman may have died from other causes. This is opposed to (3a) and (3c) in that if (3b) is denied: 'John has not been smoking', then both (3a) and (3c) become false by necessity, because one cannot stop doing something one has not been doing. This is the basis of what is sometimes called presuppo-sition failure. Imagine somebody is being asked the question:

(5) Have you stopped beating your dog?

Questions like these are much debated in informal logic because the respon-dent is being trapped: he can neither say 'yes' or 'no', because in both cases he will confess to the fact that he has actually beaten his dog in the past, even though he may not have done so, and then the only relevant way to respond is to question the question itself, viz. its presupposition(s). In this case many would feel that the presup-position is disguised by the implicit meaning of the words. It may seem more evident that somebody is dead if one has been killed (4a and 4b), and it may seem even trivial to say of the sentence 'the king of France is bald' that the existential sentence 'there is a (one and only one) king of France' is a presupposition of that sentence, because if somebody mentions a 'king of France' then there must be a king of France.

Nevertheless this was the subject matter of the controversy between Russell and Strawson and of the fol-lowing debates. Russell's interest had to do with the semantics of what he called 'definite descriptions' like 'the (red) car' which he conceived of as what he called 'names*' (that is, not only proper names in our understanding), a stance based on the argument mentioned above, viz. that a phrase like 'the (red) car' formally should be dissolved into the proposition 'there exists a red car'. Accordingly Russell claimed that 'names', which he defined as linguistic expressions being able to be used as logical subjects in propositions, included definite descriptions, and therefore these could be used – as referring expressions in propositions – to refer to things in the world, for instance a red car. This solved the problem that in ordinary predicate logic there are no definite descriptions, only individual or quantitative terms like 'Aristotle', 'he' or 'all dogs', and accordingly Russell was able to justify predicate sentences like 'the (red) car is rusty'.

This has further implications in modern logic but it also presented Russell with the problem that definite descriptions may be empty, at variance with our common-sense view that the use of the definite article implies that there is some well-known entity out there. But as is also well known, definite descriptions may sometimes have no referents – for instance in fictional and abstract contexts – that is, no entities that satisfy their description, such as is the case with the definite noun phrase 'the king of France'. From this it follows that propositions containing them cannot specify truth conditions and accordingly they have no semantics. According to Frege, they were meaningless, while Russell, as mentioned

above, held that propositions picking them up as subjects were false. Strawson, then, said that Russell had got it all wrong in that he ignored the distinction between 'a sentence', 'the use of a sentence' and 'an utterance of a sentence'. In Strawson's view, sentences have no truth value, only the use of a sentence can produce a proposition which is either true or false. As for the definite description 'the king of France' Strawson argued that 'To say "The king of France is wise" is, in some sense of "imply", to *imply* that there is a king of France' (1950 (1971: 12)), and this is the kind of implication that gave rise to the notion of presupposition; the term was coined by Strawson in his 1952 publication. The outcome was the position that certain sentences, like 'the king of France is bald', are seen as having unfulfilled presuppositions and therefore they have no truth value, or they have the truth value zero. One way to go around the problem, if one does not feel at ease with sentences that have the form of predicate propositions but nevertheless seem to lack truth value and semantics, is to adopt a 'possible world' semantics*. In this kind of semantics, propositions can be seen as functions from the set of all possible worlds to the truth values 'true' or 'false' and in this kind of logic, presuppositions can be conceived of as fulfilled in only a restricted set of worlds. Hence the propositional functions can be defined as having value only in the set of these worlds, that is where the presuppositions of a proposition are fulfilled, a set which is sometimes called the domain of that proposition (Allwood et al. 1977: 150).

Apart from these technical and epistemological questions, some issues concerning presuppositions are on the borderline between such basically philosophical problems and the daily use of language. Some of them deal with the formulaic or grammaticalised expressions associated with specific speech acts:

(6) What did Jack the Ripper do?

In (6) the wh-expression connected with the fixed word order (and a certain prosodic contour) signifies the speech act of a question, and it presupposes that Jack the Ripper did something (cf. Lyons 1977: 597). This kind of presupposition is not indifferent to negation because the sentence:

(7) What did Jack the Ripper not do?

presupposes that there was something that Jack the Ripper did not do. Another kind of presupposition (cf. Lyons 1977: 599) is found in sentences expressing so-called propositional attitudes*, for example, sentences containing expressions like 'think', 'believe', 'realise':

(8) The police realised that Jack the Ripper had killed the woman

In (8) it is a presupposition of the compound sentence that Jack the Ripper actually killed the woman and as for the 'historical' Jack the Ripper, of whom little is known, a sentence like (8) does not seem justified.

As pointed out by Lyons (1977: 600), a pre-theoretical notion of presupposition as a verb 'presuppose' means almost the same as the word 'assume', and it may seem a little odd to say that sentences are able to assume something, because a common-sense understanding might claim that only people can assume. The same question may arise when considering the theoretical idea that a sentence like 'the king of France is bald' presupposes the sentence 'there exists a king of France', because it would be counter-intuitive to think otherwise. This has led to the suggestion that there are, at least, two types of presupposition: one is a semantic notion dealt with in modern logic where scholars try to solve the technical problems of formal languages, and another is a pragmatic notion dealing with what people presuppose in their discourse interactions. To contemplate this question is like opening a Pandora's box in linguistics and philosophy. As Levinson puts it, 'there is more literature on presupposition than on almost any other topic in pragmatics (excepting perhaps speech acts)' (1983: 167).

In order to approach the subject we may take the Italian-soup-in-small-plastic-bags scenario described above as an example. A main topic here will be what are in general called presupposition triggers. A presupposition trigger is one or more words, or 'aspects of surface structure in general' (Levinson 1983: 179) that generate a relation of presupposition between what is actually expressed and what must be assumed. At face value only the word 'Italian' seems to be common to the two utterances thereby suggesting there is a connection between them. But this similarity may elicit a rather large number of possible scenarios and it is in fact deceptive. My wife and I may have any kind of fast food after her Italian classes. If, instead of fantasising, we look at the details of what is being said, my utterance was 'Look, there is this special Italian soup in small plastic bags', and this may be interpreted as a man-and-wife convention for the speech act of a question: 'Should we buy some?' Taken as a question, the presupposition is 'either we buy some or we don't buy some'. In this case it is the unspoken but intended question that triggers the presuppositional relation in that the specific clause surface structure of questions – the syntactic inversion and the prosody of questions produced by native speakers of English – will come to my wife's mind when I paraphrase my intended question as the declarative sentence I actually utter. If this reading seems fair enough, the logical response from my wife should be an answer implying either that we should or we should not buy the soup-in-small-plastic-bags, and it actually may be so. The sentence 'My Italian language course has no more classes' may be paraphrased as 'My Italian course has stopped', and the verb 'stop' is a so-called change-of-state verb triggering the necessary presupposition(s) 'I have attended an Italian language course in the past and now I don't attend it any more because there are no more classes'.

In order to establish a connection between my question 'Do we buy or not buy?' and the 'Italian classes', one may speculate what my wife's absence or late home-coming has to do with fast food and one only has to infer that in this family fast food is on the menu when the housewife is away or late, and that my wife's response may boldly

be interpreted as a 'No, we should buy no more soup'. But this is, in a narrow sense, not something presupposed. It may belong to the 'normal' state of affairs in certain cultures or subcultures, but none of the words or other surface aspects can, directly, trigger such presuppositions. Only knowledge about the family and a number of circumstantial facts may yield the information that this has nothing to do with a scenario where, for instance, the students of my wife's language class eat Italian soup every time they meet. However, in a broad sense these inferred assumptions may be called presuppositions. Some scholars have defended radical theories of pragmatic presupposition in which the key concepts are 'appropriateness' or 'felicity' (Levinson 1983: 204) and 'mutual knowledge' or 'common ground', meaning that a presupposition can be 'appropriately used if it is assumed in the context that the propositions indicated by the presupposition-triggers are true' (Levinson 193: 205). The contextual prerequisite is furthermore that this is known by the participants, and consequently what is not mutually known by them will not come up as presuppositions because they are inappropriate. In this framework the chain of inferences assumed in my conversational transactions with my wife on 'Italian soup' may well be called presuppositions, but one problem is just the criterion about mutual knowledge. When examining actual discourse it is fairly hard to make justified claims about what people know – as opposed to claims about what they say.

At the core of theories on presuppositions there are other difficulties, among them the problem of whether presuppositions are compositional relative to the complex clauses they are presuppositions of (Levinson 1983: 191). There is not a consensus among scholars in the field about what constitutes a standard notion of presupposition in linguistics and the philosophy of language.

Primary sources

Asher, N. and A. Lascarides (1998). 'The semantics and pragmatics of presuppositions'. *Journal of Semantics* 15, 3: 239–300.

Beaver, D. I. (1996). 'Presupposition'. In J. van Benthem and A. ter Meulen (eds), *Handbook of Logic and Language*. Amsterdam: Elsevier Science B.V.

Frege, G. (1892). 'Sinn und Bedeutung'. In *Zeitschrift für Philosophie und philosophische Kritik*, NF 100:25–50. English translation, 'On sense and meaning'. In Peter Geach and Max Blach (eds) (1980), *Translations from the Philosophical Writings of Gottlob Frege*. Oxford: Blackwell. 56–78. First edition 1952.

Journal of Semantics Vol. 9 no. 3 1992. Special issue on presupposition.

Journal of Semantics Vol. 9 no. 4 1992. Special issue on presupposition.

McCawley, J. (1981). *Everything That Linguists Have Always Wanted to Know About Logic, But Were Ashamed to Ask*. Oxford: Basil Blackwell.

Portner, P. and B. H. Partee (eds) (2002). *Formal Semantics*. Oxford: Blackwell Publishing.

Reyle, U. (1993). 'Existence presuppositions and background knowledge'. *Journal of Semantics* 10, 2: 113–22.

Russell, B. (1905). 'On denoting'. *Mind* 14: 479–99.

Russell, B. (1957). 'Mr Strawson on referring'. *Mind* 66: 385–89.

Strawson, P. F. (1950). 'On referring'. *Mind* 59: 320–44.

Strawson, P. F. (1952). *Introduction to Logical Theory*. London: Methuen.

Further reading

Allwood, J, L.-G. Andersson and Ö. Dahl (1977). *Logic in Linguistics*. Cambridge: Cambridge University Press.

Levinson, S. C. (1983). *Pragmatics*. Cambridge: Cambridge University Press.

Levinson, S. C. (2000). *Presumptive Meanings. The Theory of Generalized Conversational Implicature*. Cambridge, MA: MIT Press.

Lyons, J. (1977). *Semantics*. Cambridge: Cambridge University Press.

Saeed, J. I. (2003) *Semantics*. Second edition. Oxford: Blackwell Publishing.

Hans Götzsche

PRIVATE LANGUAGE

A private language is a putative language the meaning of whose expressions are essentially grounded in the subjective or private states of the users of the language. The notion was first employed by Ludwig Wittgenstein (*Philosophical Investigations*) in order to refute both classical and contemporary conceptions of linguistic meaning. The notion remains at the centre of Wittgenstein scholarship and has a highly controversial use in philosophy of language and mind more generally.

See also: Deconstruction; Empiricism/Rationalism; Language Games; Logical Positivism; Presupposition

Key Thinkers: Ayer, A. J.; Carnap, Rudolf; Chomsky, Noam; Fodor, Jerry; Frege, Gottlob; Kant, Immanuel; Kripke, Saul; Russell, Bertrand; Wittgenstein, Ludwig

In the first half of the twentieth century, the received understanding of a classical empiricist theory of language was that words are outward signs of private states (ideas or images). Such a position found its contemporary advocates in Bertrand Russell, Rudolf Carnap and A. J. Ayer. Arguably following Immanuel Kant and Gottlob Frege, Ludwig Wittgenstein argued that such an essentially private language was impossible and, therefore, the empiricist conception of meaning is confused. Although the argument has been interpreted in many different ways, its basic structure is as follows. (1) Rule following is constitutive of competent language use. (2) Rule following is a *normative* activity – that is, there are essential conditions on whether one is following the rules correctly or not. (3) If linguistic meaning is private, then the agent must be following private rules. (4) If the rules are private, then there is no difference between following the rules correctly or not; whatever *seems* right will be right. (5) Therefore, there can be no such private language.

In general terms there are two schools of thought on the argument. One school, most prominently represented by Saul Kripke, views the argument as an attempt to show that linguistic meaning is essentially public, in that only a public check by other speakers could establish whether one is following the rules or not. Another school, more diagnostic in approach and associated with John McDowell, takes the argument to be a principled declining of a justification of our normative activity, for the reason that any non-normative basis, such as consensus, would never suffice to establish the kind of correctness involved in meaning.

Wittgenstein's argument has also surfaced in cognitive science. Jerry Fodor and Noam Chomsky have argued that meaning, linguistic and non-linguistic, has an empirical basis in an unconscious system of rules that determine interpretation as opposed to normatively governing it. They defend this approach against the private language argument by pointing out that the rules at issue are not essentially private, but simply not available to first person conscious access; ultimately, whether there are such rules or not is an empirical issue that cannot be *a priori* determined.

Primary sources

Wittgenstein, Ludwig (1953). *Philosophical Investigations*. Oxford: Blackwell.

Kripke, Saul (1984). *Wittgenstein on Rules and Private Language*. Oxford: Blackwell.

McDowell, John (1984). 'Wittgenstein on following a rule'. *Synthese* 58 (3): 325–64.

Fodor, Jerry (1975). *The Language of Thought*. Cambridge, MA: Harvard University Press.

Chomsky, Noam (1986). *Knowledge of Language*. Westport: Praeger.

Further reading

Miller, Alexander, and Crispin Wright (eds) (2002). *Rule-Following and Meaning*. London: Acumen.

John Collins

PROPOSITIONAL ATTITUDES

A propositional attitude is what someone is described as having by a propositional attitude report: for example, by an utterance of 'Jane believes that Fido is barking' or 'Henry wishes his cat would have kittens'. The subtle semantics and pragmatics of propositional attitude reports, as well as the role of propositional attitudes themselves in language use, have made them one of the more controversial topics in linguistics.

> *See also*: Compositionality;
> Definite Descriptions;
> Descriptivism; Intentionality;
> Propositions; Sense/Reference
> *Key Thinkers*: Frege, Gottlob;
> Kripke, Saul; Quine, W. V. O.;
> Russell, Bertrand

A standard route into the topic of propositional attitudes begins with the observation that propositional attitude reports differ from ordinary relational claims. On the face of it, for Jane to believe that Fido is barking is for her to bear a two-place relation to the proposition that Fido is barking – just as for her to stroke Fido is for her to bear a two-place stroking relation to the dog Fido. This surface similarity is deceptive.

One difference can be illustrated by comparing (1) with (2):

> (1)
> a. Jane strokes Fido.
> b. Fido exists.
> c. There is something that Jane stroked.

> (2)
> a. Jane believes that Fido is barking.
> b. Fido exists.
> c. There is something that Jane believes is barking.

Like other ordinary relational claims, (1a) has existential import that (2a) and other attitude reports seem to lack. In particular, (1a) entails both (1b) and (1c) while (2a) apparently entails neither (2b) nor (2c). After all, Jane could have the belief reported in (2a) even if Fido is a figment of her imagination, contrary to (2b); and in that case, contrary to (2c), nothing would have the property of being believed by Jane to be barking, for if there were, that thing would be Fido, and there is no Fido.

Another difference relates to the law of identity. This law, compelling in the context of ordinary relations, is less plausible in the context of attitude reports. Thus, suppose Fido is Rex. This identity and (1a) could not both be true without (1d) also being true. In contrast, the identity and (2a) do not entail (2d). After all, Jane may not realise that Fido and Rex are one and the same dog.

> (1)
> a. Jane strokes Fido.
> d. Jane strokes Rex.
> (2)
> a. Jane believes that Fido is barking.
> d. Jane believes that Rex is barking.

These two distinctive features of propositional attitude reports – apparent lack of existential import and apparent substitution failure – give rise to a range of semantic puzzles. Any solution to these depends on a proper appreciation of the nature of a fundamental notion in the philosophy of language and mind: propositions*, that is the things that attitude reports report us as believing, desiring, intending, and so on. After presenting two such puzzles, one relating to each distinctive feature we will think about how different theories of propositions require differing treatments of the second of these puzzles.

The lack of existential import threatens to sabotage solutions to the already notorious problem of negative existentials. This is the problem of understanding how we can ever correctly deny something's existence when, in order to do so, we would need to refer to it, and hence need it to exist. Various purported solutions are available, but a plausible condition on their acceptability is that they make sense of the legitimacy of inferences with the form in (3):

(3) *a* does not exist, therefore not . . . *a*
. . .

For example, if Saladin never existed, it follows that Saladin could not have fought Richard the Lionheart. But the inference appears to fail when (3) is 'Fido does not exist, therefore Jane does not believe that Fido is barking'. Any theory of negative existentials therefore has an additional burden: to explain exceptions to (3) thrown up by propositional attitude reports.

The second feature, apparent substitution failure, threatens the compositionality thesis, a cornerstone of most approaches to formal semantics. In one form, this thesis holds that the referential or truth conditional properties of complex expressions are a function of the referential or truth

conditional properties of their simpler components. For example, the truth condition stated in (4a) is a derivable consequence of (4b), (4c), and some background semantic principles.

(4)
a. 'Fido is a dog' is true iff Fido is a dog.
b. 'Fido' refers to x iff x = Fido.
c. 'is a dog' is true of x iff x is a dog.

But what about (1a)? Its truth condition, stated in (5a), ought to be derivable from (5b) plus background semantic axioms for the other parts of the sentence.

(5)
a. 'Jane believes that Fido is barking' is true iff Jane believes that Fido is barking.
b. 'Fido' refers to x iff x is Fido.

The problem is that any compositional derivation of (5a) using (5b) seems to license a parallel derivation of the illegitimate (6a) from (6b). Given that Fido is Rex, (6b) follows from (5b), and the derivation of (6a) from (6b) could then mimic that of (5a) from (5b). Yet (6a) seems wrong: Jane's belief that Fido is barking is not enough to make the sentence 'Jane believes that Rex is barking' true, even if Rex is Fido.

(6)
a. 'Jane believes that Rex is barking' is true iff Jane believes that Fido is barking.
b. 'Rex' refers to x iff x is Fido.

Notice that this problem does not arise for 'Rex is a dog', which is true if Fido is a dog and Rex is Fido.

These puzzles may seem like mere technical challenges, but their endurance suggests otherwise. What follows is a summary of two prominent theories of propositions, stressing how each confronts the puzzle of apparent substitution failure. Both theories treat propositions as structured complexes of elements, but they disagree on the nature of these elements.

Followers of Bertrand Russell assume that propositions are structured complexes of real-world entities. Sentences map onto the propositions they express via a mapping that takes individual words onto the real-world entities they refer to. The proposition expressed by a typical utterance of (1a), for example, would be (1e), the first element of which is a two-place relation, and the second element of which is an ordered pair consisting of Jane then Fido.

(1)
e.   <strokes, <Jane, Fido>>

Thus (1e), and hence (1a) itself, will be true just so long as the ordered pair satisfies the two-place relation. More generally, the truth value* of propositions is determined compositionally from its components.

So (2a) expresses the proposition (2e), which breaks down further into (2f). The simple proposition Jane purportedly believes is a component of the more complex proposition expressed by (2a) itself and is represented in (2f) as '<barks, <Fido> '.

(2)
e.   < believes, <Jane, that Fido is barking>>
f.   < believes, <Jane, <barks, <Fido>>>

Since the elements of propositions are actual entities, the referents of the words used, substituting co-referring expressions will alter neither the identity of the proposition expressed nor, therefore, the truth value of the sentence. Russellians must explain the appearance of substitution failure in propositional attitude reports without granting that this appearance is genuine.

Before 1972 the standard way was Russell's own. Ordinary names* like 'Fido' and 'Rex' are not in fact referring expressions at all, he said. They are really disguised definite descriptions*, which have an internal structure of their own but no referents. The contrast between (2a) and (2d) does not, therefore, constitute a case of changing truth value by substituting co-referring expressions.

In more detail, suppose 'Fido' in Jane's idiolect is a disguised version of 'The dog I bought last year' and 'Rex' is a disguised version of 'The dog I ran over two years ago'. In that case, (2a) and (2d) would express the distinct propositions (2g) and (2h) respectively (where $\forall$ can be read as roughly equivalent to 'for every', $\exists$ as 'exists' and $\rightarrow$ as 'entails'; see the entry on 'Logic' for a fuller account of these logical constants).

(2)
g.   <believes, <Jane, $\exists x(x$ is a dog I bought & $\forall y(y$ is a dog I bought $\rightarrow$ $x=y$) & x is barking) >>
h.   <believes, <Jane, $\exists x(x$ is a dog I ran over & $\forall y(y$ is a dog I ran over $\rightarrow$ $x=y$) & x is barking) >>

No actual dog is a component of either proposition, so 'Fido' or 'Rex' lack a shared referent, or indeed any referent.

Russell's defence of Russellianism fell out of favour after Saul Kripke's 1972 criticisms of descriptivism about names. More recent Russellians (for example, Salmon 1986) have instead tried to explain the appearance of substitution failure as a pragmatic effect. While (1a) and (1d) express the same Russellian proposition at the semantic level, the small difference between them carries pragmatic significance easily mistaken for a semantic difference.

The second view of propositions, Fregeanism, is similar to Russellianism save that the elements in a proposition are not objects but perspectives on, or ways of thinking about, or (to use Gottlob Frege's own terminology) 'modes of presentation' of, objects. The mapping from sentences onto the propositions they express is therefore a function from a word onto, not an object, but a specific mode of presentation of an object. Frege calls this function the word's sense*. Two words, such as 'Fido' and 'Rex' (or 'George Orwell' and 'Eric Blair'), can have a common referent but distinct senses. For this reason, substituting one of the words for the other within a sentence will change the proposition expressed. It will not (normally) change the truth value, however. The truth value of Fregean propositions is determined in the same way as Russellian ones, by referents rather than modes of presentation; and Fregean propositions can be converted into Russellian propositions by replacing each perspective on an object with the object itself. Substitution will therefore not (normally) affect truth value.

But Fregeans have a ready explanation for exceptions such as (2a) and (2d): when a word occurs within the scope of a propositional attitude verb, Fregeans say it refers to its customary sense, not its customary referent. Since 'Fido' and 'Rex' have distinct customary senses, the propositions expressed by (2a) and (2d) have different components even after conversion into Russellian propositions, and hence potentially different truth values.

The most pressing question Fregeans must answer is: what is a sense? If a sense is just a disguised definite description, anti-descriptivist objections to Russell carry over. Some take the sense of a word to be the concept it expresses. But concepts are often defined as components of propositions, and if 'the sense of "Fido"' is unpacked merely as 'that component of a proposition which is expressed by "Fido"', Frege's solution seems hollow. More substantial and controversial theories of concepts are available, but at the very least Fregeans must address profound questions in the philosophy of mind before they can claim to have solved the substitutivity puzzle.

To sum up, propositional attitude reports appear to behave differently from sentences devoid of psychological attitude verbs. These differences pose a challenge to semanticists. The compositionality thesis, in particular, is difficult to defend in this context without taking potentially controversial stands on the nature of propositions, a nature whose investigation belongs as much to the philosophy of mind as it does to the philosophy of language.

Primary sources

Frege, G. (1892/1997). 'On *sinn* and *Bedeutung*'. In M. Beaney (ed.), *The Frege Reader*. Oxford: Blackwell.

Kripke, S. (1972/1980). *Naming and Necessity*. Cambridge, MA: Harvard University Press.

Russell, B. (1919). *Introduction to Mathematical Philosophy*. London: George Allen and Unwin.

Salmon, N. (1986). *Frege's Puzzle*. Cambridge, MA: MIT Press.

Further reading

Kripke, S. (1979). 'A puzzle about belief'. In A. Margalit (ed.), *Meaning and Use*. Dordrecht: Reidel. 239–83.

Alex Barber

PROPOSITIONS

A term adopted from philosophy and formal logic*, referring to the language-independent common denominator of the meaning of all the sentences that express the truth of a certain state of affairs, independent of their illocutionary form. Propositions are the central elements used in the investigation of sentence meaning in formal semantics and in speech act theory*.

> *See also*: Artificial Intelligence; Logic; Logical Form; Model-Theoretic Semantics; Possible World Semantics; Speech Act Theory; Truth Theories; Truth Value
> *Key Thinkers*: Austin, J. L.; Montague, Richard; Searle, John; Tarski, Alfred

In the analysis of sentence meaning the application of the concept of propositions has proved to be very fruitful. In formal semantics, truth-conditional semantics and speech act theory sentences are analysed with reference to the underlying propositions that they contain. It is central to these theories that in natural languages propositions are not sentences. 'I am hungry' uttered by different speakers is obviously an instance of the same sentence but as the reference changes with every speaker we have as many different propositions as we have speakers.

In formal semantics mathematical and logical techniques are used to describe the semantic structure of natural languages. Applying propositional calculus, we can deduce how logical operators such as negation, conjunction, disjunction and implications build up complex sentences out of other sentences. Propositions are central to truth-conditional semantics based on Alfred Tarski (1956) and to Montague Grammar, where Richard Montague (Thomason 1974) applies semantic principles developed for artificial languages to natural languages.

In his development of J. L. Austin's (1962) speech act theory, John Searle (1969) divided locutionary acts into utterance acts (uttering noises and words) and propositional acts, by which the speaker is referring and predicating. In uttering the sentences (1) 'Sam smokes habitually'. (2) 'Does Sam smoke habitually?' (3) 'Sam, smoke habitually!' (4) 'Would that Sam smoked habitually' (Searle 1969: 22), the speaker performs an assertion, asks a question, gives an order or expresses a wish. But at the same time she/he refers to a certain person called Sam and expresses the predication 'smokes habitually' with respect to that person. In other words, the reference and the predication are the same in all four sentences, and thus the same proposition is made, regardless of their respective illocutionary acts. This is in opposition to mathematical languages, where every proposition is expressed in the form of a statement.

Logical analysis based on propositions has had a major influence on semantic studies of natural languages. Although the theories are controversial, they can lead to more advanced studies in semantic linguistics, particularly with respect to sentence meaning, and in artificial intelligence.

Primary sources

Searle, John R. (1969). *Speech Acts: An Essay in the Philosophy of Language*. Cambridge: Cambridge University Press.

Thomason, Richmond H. (ed.) (1974). *Formal Philosophy: Selected Papers of Richard Montague*. New Haven: Yale University Press.

Further reading

Austin, John L. (1962). *How to Do Things With Words*. Oxford: Oxford University Press.

Kneale, William (1972). 'Propositions and truth in natural languages' *Mind* 81: 225–43.

Tarski, Alfred (1956). *Logics, Semantics Metamathematics: Papers from 1923 to 1938*. Trans. J. H. Woodger. Oxford: Clarendon Press.

Jürg Strässler

PROTOTYPE

Prototype theory explains how people understand the meaning of a word by reference to the best example of the object indicated by the word. This means that, for example, in identifying an object as belonging to the category of *furniture*, the human mind is geared to thinking in terms of 'chair', that is, the prototype member of that category, rather than with the more marginal ones such as 'lamp' or 'stove'.

See also: Ambiguity/Vagueness; Cognitivism; Intuition; Language Games; Language of Thought
Key Thinkers: Aristotle; Fodor, Jerry; Whorf, Benjamin Lee; Wittgenstein, Ludwig

Every conceivable thing is in principle distinct from every other. In order for them to make sense, people group together exemplars of the same kind into categories. But how precisely the mind works in this respect is not always clear. In the Aristotelian tradition, categorisation is explained as the conjunction of necessary and sufficient features. Hence a bird has to be a winged creature as its necessary feature and possess a beak as its sufficient feature. All members of a category are thought to have an equal status. Once established, a category will separate entities that belong to it from those that do not. No ambiguity or variation is allowed.

In the 1970s Eleanor Rosch conducted a number of cognitive psychological experiments on how people operate with categories and how they learn about things through them. Not all members of a category turned out to be equally representative. Some are more central to the category; others are marginal and even dubious. For example, the people in Rosch's study categorised different kinds of birds according to a graded scale of recognisability ranging from the best exemplar, such as 'robin', to the least likely members like 'ostrich'. Between these opposite ends there is a range of what people will consider as a bird. Very close to 'robin', but already less typical, were birds like 'dove', 'sparrow', 'canary'. Then slightly away from the centre was another group with 'parrot', 'owl', 'pheasant', and 'toucan' in it. Somewhat more distant are 'peacock' and 'duck', then 'penguin', until finally, with some hesitation, the 'ostrich' is considered as belonging to the category. Of all the birds in Rosch's study, 'robin' excelled as the most representative member. It was the prototype of the category.

Similar experiments with other categories such as *vegetables* and *furniture* give the same result. These categories exhibit a graded scale of membership, each with a prototype of its own, in this case, 'pea' and 'chair'. This suggests that people group things together and exclude others according to their similarity to a prototype. Hence the notion of prototype gives a better account of how the mind sets up categories and uses them than the Aristotelian framework. The finding has a strong impact not only in cognitive psychology but also in linguistic research, especially in the works of R.W. Langacker in cognitive grammar and in George Lakoff's semantic studies.

An important notion that links prototype with linguistic meaning is the 'basic level term'. The term 'animal' is a higher, superordinate level in contrast to lower, subordinate level terms such as 'robin', 'canary', 'parrot', and so on. Between these two levels stands the basic level term, in this case, 'bird'. In creating categories, people tend to opt for the basic level terms. Thus when referring to an avian creature, one normally says, 'Look at this bird!' rather than mentioning a specific bird (robin, and so on) or using the superordinate term 'animal'. Basic level terms are the most natural form of categorisation, and for that reason they are said to have the highest degree of cue-validity.

After being shown a word that represents a higher level category, people tend to find it easier to agree that two words representing central members of a category are the same. Thus when primed with the word 'furniture', people generally take less time in deciding that 'chair-chair' are the same words than 'stove-stove'. People are fairly consistent in identifying the best examples of a category. Again, the speed with which people judge whether an object belongs to such and such category also determines the place the object will occupy on the graded scale within the category. The shorter the response time, the more central an exemplar will be. People also seem to rely on the properties of the central members in dealing with other exemplars. This means that attention is normally given first to the central members. It is therefore easier to elicit them than the marginal members.

All these are called prototype effects. They play an important role in the way people mentally organise the outside world. However, these effects are not the same as the cognitive representation itself. The difficulty comes from the role of prototype Though intuitively a robin is the prototypical bird, it cannot be used as a unique criterion for being a bird. Properties of some other birds are also taken into consideration. The question is which properties are to be included and which ones are to be ignored – in other words, how far one can extend the category. While an ostrich may be quite far removed from a typical bird, it is still a bird, not a birdlike creature the way a bat is. A colour is no longer considered to be red as it moves towards being orange or purple. But where are the boundaries of these categories? Such cases show that there are no clear-cut boundaries – in other words, categories are inherently fuzzy.

Furthermore, many words have different meanings, evoking different sets of membership. The word 'jailbird', for example, refers to a criminal who is locked up behind bars like a canary and who may be persuaded to 'sing' (confess) in order to get better treatment. This shows that the word 'bird' is associated not with a single category, namely the avian category, but also with other categories, in this case *prisoner*. Polysemy is the basis for metaphors*. The expression 'he is a fox' to describe a cunning and sly person is an example where the metaphorical use of the word 'fox' gives it a new sense. But obviously slyness is not part of the ordinary sense of the word 'fox'.

In addition to the problems above, a combination of categories can produce a more complex concept without reference to prototypes. People talk about domestic cats and dogs as typical *pets*, allowing for snakes and caimans as less common pets. But 'pet fish' creates some problems. It does not matter whether the fish in question, usually a goldfish, is prototypical fish or not, and it is not relevant either where in the scale of pets the goldfish stands. In fact the combination between 'pet' and 'fish' here is no longer understood in terms of the prototypes of each category.

Prototypes are a mental construction that helps us to understand the world. This construction or model is built upon an immense storage of concepts that can be retrieved to combine with one another in order to form a model to represent reality in the mind. One such powerful model is family resemblance, a notion that goes back to Wittgenstein. This is exemplified by the use of the word 'game'. Although every game has some similarity with other games, there is no single feature that links them all. Instead, there is a complicated network of similarities overlapping and criss-crossing. There is something that makes all members of a category resemble one another even if it cannot be said that they share a common set of properties. What happens is that each member is linked to the others by an intermediate member with which each is in close contact and thus shares some properties. Thus, schematically, it is possible that in a category ABC the members A and C have nothing in common and yet both are part of a family simply because each is in contact with member B.

As synthesised by John R. Taylor, the notion of prototype is very influential in forming grammatical categories. For example, what is prototypical in transitive verbs is the presence of two different participants, namely the agent and the goal. If the agent and the goal are the same, then the verb is transitive-reflexive and is said to be less prototypical of the class of transitive verbs. The notion of prototypes also operates in other areas of linguistics but it is in this cognitive arena that the idea has had its most significant influence.

Primary sources

Lakoff, George (1987). *Women, Fire, and Dangerous Things. What Categories Reveal About the Mind*. Chicago: Chicago University Press.

Langacker, R.W. (1987, 1991). *Foundations of Cognitive Grammar*. Vols 1–II. Stanford: Stanford University Press.

Rosch, Eleanor (1975). 'Cognitive representations of semantic categories'. *Journal of Experimental Psychology: General* Vol. 104: 192–233.

Rosch, Eleanor (1978). 'Principles of Categorization'. In E. Rosch and B. B. Lloyd (eds), *Cognition and Categorization*. Hillsdale; NJ: Lawrence Erlbaum. 27–48.

Rosch, Eleanor and C. B. Mervis (1975). 'Family resemblances: studies in the internal nature of categories'. *Cognitive Psychology* Vol. 7: 573–605.

Taylor, John R. (1995). *Linguistic Categorization. Prototypes in Linguistic Theory*. Second edition. Oxford: Oxford University Press.

Further reading

Aitchison, Jean (2003). *Words in the Mind. An Introduction to the Mental Lexicon*. Third edtion. London: Blackwell. Chapters 4–6.

Löbner, Sebastian (2002). *Understanding Semantics*. London: Arnold. Chapter 9.

Agustinus Gianto

PSYCHOANALYSIS

A method of analysing discourse in order to discover its hidden meanings, originally developed as a cure for various mental disorders, but later extended to become a method of analysing literature, film and other cultural phenomena. Psychoanalysis was developed as a technique by Sigmund Freud from the 1890s to the 1930s; his disciple Jacques Lacan imported structural linguistics into the theory, and extended it into a general philosophy of everyday life that has been influential in the continental tradition.

See also: Signs and Semiotics; Structuralism; Poststructuralism
Key Thinkers: Hegel, G. W. F.; Jakobson, Roman; Kristeva, Julia; Lacan, Jacques; Plato; Saussure, Ferdinand de

Psychoanalysis was founded as a discipline by Sigmund Freud in the 1890s, but it was through the work of Lacan that it took a 'linguistic' turn. Freud, who was contemporary with Frans Boaz, Émile Durkheim and Ferdinand de Saussure, conceived of psychoanalysis as a scientific discipline and his successors typically viewed it as one of the 'human sciences' in the manner of anthropology, sociology or linguistics. The range of conditions which psychoanalysis is used to treat has shrunk since Freud's time, from encompassing psychosis, aphasia, schizophrenia and what Freud and his contemporaries called 'hysteria', to being confined to the relatively minor condition of neurosis and associated personality disorders. Yet psychoanalysis continues to have currency as a tool of cultural critique.

Freud's claim to importance in linguistics comes primarily through Chapter VI of *The Interpretation of Dreams* (1899), 'The Dream-Work'. According to Freud, the 'dream-work' (the work in which the unconscious mind of the dreamer engages in order to create a dream) consists of four stages: condensation, displacement, figurability and secondary revision. Condensation is the process whereby a detailed and seemingly long dream can take place within a very short amount of real time. Displacement is the process of replacing material the dreamer wishes to repress by other elements which apparently have a different meaning. Figurability is the process of turning dream material into pictures – most dreams are pictorial, or are a combination of pictures and language. And finally secondary revision is the process of turning the dream into a 'day-dream', of organising the material so that it may be remembered as a coherent sequence.

The first three of these processes, claims Freud, organise the dream into a series of rebuses. A rebus is a kind of picture-puzzle, whereby pictures symbolise words in an indirect manner. For example, in a 1940s Warner Bros *Merrie Melodies* cartoon, Daffy Duck is shown with a flag attached to his tail, on which are depicted a screw and a baseball. The interpreter puts the two images together to arrive at the single word 'screwball', which as a signifier of Daffy's daffiness partakes of the meaning of neither 'screw' nor 'ball'. In order to arrive at this interpretation, the interpreter must perform a two-stage 'decoding': first he or she must translate each picture into a word – a movement from symbol to signification – and then translate the individual words into a combination that is homophonically, but not semantically, related to them – a movement from signification to meaning. The dreamer, meanwhile, has already performed the same sequence of operations as an encoding process, this constituting the dream-work.

In later works Freud extends the province of psychoanalysis as an interpretive technique from dreams to other, more explicitly linguistic phenomena, such as jokes and flashes of wit, and ultimately to the discourse of the patient more generally. It is this fact, that psychoanalysis takes as its working material the discourse of the patient, that inspires Lacan's 'linguisticisation' of Freud, famously claiming that 'the unconscious is structured as a language' (Lacan 1972: 188). According to Lacan, Freud's 'condensation' corresponds to Roman Jakobson's concept of metaphor*, 'displacement' corresponds to Jakobson's metonymy, while 'figurability' (or 'transposition') corresponds to 'the sliding of the signified under the signifier' (Lacan 2006: 425).

To take the third of these phenomena first, Lacan develops Saussure's theory of the sign, as represented in the Figure 5 (Saussure 1992/1983).

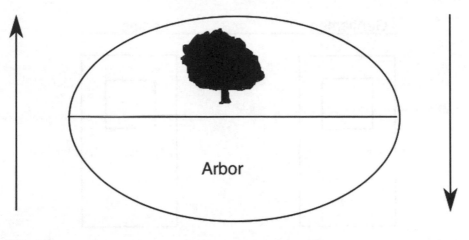

Figure 5

Here, the picture of the tree represents the concept ('signified') of a tree in the speaker's mind, while the word *arbor* represents the 'sound image' ('signifier') of that concept. The horizontal line shows that signifier and signified are discrete manifestations, while the oval shows that nevertheless together they form a psychological unity. The choice of a tree (*arbre* in French) for illustrative purposes is a little joke on Saussure's part, since the relation between signifier and signified is held to be arbitrary (*arbitraire*) – and likewise the signified is separated from the signifier by a *barre* (*barre* being an anagram of *arbre*).

Lacan (2006: 416), meanwhile, replaces Saussure's diagram with the another (see Figure 6).

This both inverts Saussure's diagram and reduplicates it. The signifier is shown to have priority for the subject over the signified, by being placed above it. Meanwhile, the two doors are identical, so that only the signifiers distinguish them. Accordingly, the signifier for Lacan has a material reality, which determines how psychic phenomena are organised, and hence how subjects behave: according to this example, men and women line up before the doors according to the signifiers that label them. In other words, sex is determined socially, rather than biologically. Moreover, the bar separating signifier from signified, which was a relatively minor part of Saussure's theory, assumes a major role in Lacan's: it represents nothing other than the bar of repression. Thus even in everyday life, signifiers do not signify signifieds directly, but rather, they signify, according to Lacan, other signifiers in the signifying chain that constitutes the subject's discourse. It is the task of analysis to uncover the true signifieds of these signifiers, which have been displaced.

This theory of linguistic displacement leads to Lacan's appropriation of Jakobson's theory of metaphor and metonymy. In a series of papers on aphasia, Jakobson defines metaphor as the selection or substitution of terms one for another, while metonymy is

191

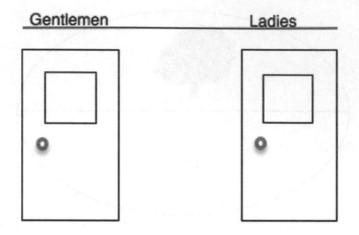

Figure 6

defined as combination of one term with another. Lacan, meanwhile, conceives of Jakobson's distinction between metaphor and metonymy in terms of Hegelian dialectics: his example, 'Your freedom or your life!', is borrowed from Hegel's *Phenomenology of Mind*. Superficially it looks like a Jakobsonian metaphorical equation, freedom=life, where one term can be substituted for another. However, if the slave 'chooses freedom, he loses both [freedom and life] immediately – if he chooses life, he has life deprived of freedom' (Lacan 1979: 212). According to Lacan, insofar as the subject exists as a speaking being, he is subjected to this demand by being as such.

While metaphor is thus equated with demand, metonymy is equated with desire. The formula for the metonymy of desire is, says Lacan, 'desire is the desire of a desire'. This can be read either as 'desire is the desire to desire' (which, following Plato, means that by definition desire can never be fulfilled), or as 'desire is

the desire to be desired'. This latter version introduces the Other into the equation, so that an alternative formulation is 'desire is the desire of the Other', in which the word 'of' can likewise be read as either 'for' or 'by'.

Lacan's theory has always been controversial: as a linguist, Lacan is indebted to his predecessors Jakobson and Saussure, and hence his theory is open to the same criticisms as is structuralist linguistics more generally – for example, that it fails to account for creativity* in language. However, psychoanalysis still has currency as a method of cultural analysis, particularly within literary and film studies, and as exemplified through the work of Slavoj Žižek.

Primary sources

Freud, Sigmund (1976). 'The Dream-Work'. In *The Interpretation of Dreams*. Trans. James Strachey. Harmondsworth: Penguin. 381–651.

Hegel, G. W. F. (1967). *The Phenomenology of Mind*. Trans. J. B. Baillie. New York and Evanston: Harper.

Jakobson, Roman (1971). *Selected Writings II: Word and Language*. The Hague and Paris: Mouton.

Lacan, Jacques (1972). 'Of structure as an inmixing of an otherness prerequisite to any subject whatever'. In Richard Macksey and Eugenio Donato (eds), *The Structuralist Controversy: The Languages of Criticism and the Sciences of Man*. Baltimore and London: Johns Hopkins University Press. 186–200.

Lacan, Jacques (1979). *The Four Fundamental Concepts of Psychoanalysis*. Trans. Alan Sheridan. Harmondsworth: Penguin.

Lacan, Jacques (2006). *Écrits: The First Complete Edition in English*. Trans. Bruce Fink with Héloïse Fink and Russell Grigg. New York and London: Routledge.

Saussure, Ferdinand de (1922/1983). *Course in General Linguistics*. Second edition. Trans. Roy Harris. London: Duckworth.

Further reading

Forrester, John (1980). *Language and the Origins of Psychoanalysis*. Basingstoke: Macmillan.

MacCabe, Colin (ed.) (1981). *The Talking Cure: Essays in Psychoanalysis and Language*. Basingstoke: Macmillan.

Karl Simms

RELEVANCE THEORY

A cognitive theory of pragmatics originally developed in the 1980s by Dan Sperber and Deirdre Wilson. Relevance theory offers a new approach to the study of human communication which is firmly grounded in a general view of human cognitive design. With H. P. Grice, relevance theorists assume that human communication is characteristically intention-based, and so they see verbal comprehension as involving not just the decoding of speech signals, but also the recognition of the speaker's communicative intentions.

See also: Implicature; Logical Form; Presupposition
Key Thinkers: Chomsky, Noam; Fodor, Jerry; Grice, H. P.

Relevance is usually defined as a potential property of inputs (such as assumptions, thoughts, utterances) to cognitive processes. Sperber and Wilson (1995) advance two principles of relevance embodying two central claims about human cognition and communication: a first or 'cognitive' principle of relevance, and a second or 'communicative' principle of relevance. The first of this principles states that: 'Human cognition tends to be geared to the maximisation of relevance' (1995: 260). The second is the statement that '[e]very act of ostensive communication communicates a presumption of its own optimal relevance' (1995: 260). The communicative principle of relevance does not have the same status as Grice's Cooperative Principle and conversational maxims, for it is simply a generalisation about ostensive-inferential communication. This generalisation about communication applies without exception: it is not something that speakers 'follow' or can 'opt out' of, for example.

Relevance theory claims that linguistic communication (and, in fact, all human communication) is relevance driven. Relevance is defined within this framework as a trade-off of two competing factors: cognitive or contextual effects and processing effort. A positive cognitive effect is 'a worthwhile difference to the individual's representation of the world' (Wilson and Sperber 2004: 608), such as a true belief or conclusion. According to relevance theory, an input is relevant to an individual just in case positive cognitive effects result from the processing of that input.

Processing new information in a context may yield three main types of positive cognitive effect. First, it may yield a contextual implication deducible from the combination of new and existing assumptions, but from neither of these alone. Second, it may provide evidence that strengthens an already existing assumption. Third, it may contradict and eliminate information already held. For example, given the contextual assumption 'If the lights are on, then Mary is home', an utterance of the sentence 'The lights are on' as we approach our house may yield the contextual implication 'Mary is home'. Contextual implications are the central type of positive cognitive effect.

Processing effort, on the other hand, is the effort of perception, memory and inference that must be expended in computing cognitive effects. For instance, an utterance of a wordy and syntactically complex sentence would take more effort to process than an utterance of a less wordy and simpler version of that sentence. Likewise, an indirect answer to a question would require more processing effort than a direct one.

On the basis of these two competing factors, the relevance of an input to an individual may be comparatively assessed as follows: (1) other things being equal, the greater the positive cognitive effects achieved by processing an input, the greater the relevance of that input; (2) other things being equal, the greater the effort required in processing an input, the lower the relevance of that input. The following example, adapted from Wilson and Sperber (2004: 609), can be used to illustrate the comparative relevance of alternative inputs to an individual. Suppose that Peter, a friend of ours, asks us who we phoned last night. Let us assume, furthermore, that we phoned Kim and Sandy last night. Each of the following three alternative utterances would constitute a true and relevant answer to Peter's question: 'We phoned Kim and Sandy', 'We phoned Kim', and 'We phoned Kim and Sandy or $2 + 2 = 5$'. However, these answers would not be relevant to the same degree: the first would be comparatively more relevant than the other two. Notice that 'We phoned Kim and Sandy' entails 'We phoned Kim', and so it is a more relevant answer because it yields the positive cognitive effects of the second utterance and more. The first utterance would be a more relevant answer than 'We phoned Kim and Sandy or $2 + 2 = 5$' because, although these two utterances are semantically equivalent, the latter is obviously more costly to process. On the whole, when a similar amount of effort is expended in processing alternative inputs, the more relevant of these inputs is the one that yields more positive cognitive effects. Conversely, when similar positive cognitive effects are derivable from the processing of alternative inputs, the one which is less costly to process is the more relevant.

How much relevance are individuals entitled to expect? According to relevance theory, maximal relevance is an unreasonably high expectation in communication because, for example, our interlocutors might be unwilling or unable to produce information that would yield the most positive cognitive effects for the least processing effort (Higashimori and Wilson 1996). In light of this, Sperber and Wilson (1995) have argued that while cognition tends to be geared to the maximisation of relevance, acts of ostensive communication simply create an expectation of optimal relevance. In other words, for any ostensive stimulus (for example, a verbal utterance) addressees are only entitled to expect a degree of relevance that is sufficient to warrant their effort in processing it, and which is also the highest degree of relevance that their interlocutors are able to achieve given their abilities, goals and preferences.

The presumption of optimal relevance suggests the following general comprehension procedure: 'Check interpretive hypotheses in order of accessibility, that is, follow a path of least effort, until an interpretation which satisfies the expectation of relevance is found; then stop' (Carston 2002: 45). Every utterance gives rise to a number of possible interpretive hypotheses that are compatible with the linguistic meaning of the sentence uttered. According to this general criterion, addressees follow a path of least effort in considering such hypotheses, stopping once they reach one that satisfies their expectations of optimal relevance. Notice that the term 'interpretive hypotheses' as used in the definition above includes not just the proposition the speaker intended to communicate, but also the contextual assumptions, implicatures and attitudes intended by the speaker.

The relevance-theoretic comprehension procedure does not guarantee that communication will always be successful, of course. Misunderstandings do occur from time to time. Rather, this heuristic offers an account of how addressees select the interpretive hypothesis they are entitled to assume is the one overtly intended by their interlocutors.

Relevance theory rejects the traditional assumption that every pragmatically determined aspect of utterance interpretation other than reference assignment and disambiguation must be an implicature*. Central to this framework is the claim that the explicit side of communication should also fall under the scope of a theory of pragmatics (Bach 1994; Carston 2002, 2004b; Sperber and Wilson 1993, 1995). Thus, according to relevance theory, there are two types of communicated 'assumptions' (conceptual representations of the actual world): explicitly communicated assumptions, or 'explicatures', and implicitly communicated ones (implicatures). When is an assumption communicated by an utterance 'explicit'? Sperber and Wilson (1995: 182) suggest that an explicature is an inferential development of the propositional template or 'logical form'* encoded by an utterance. In other words, an explicature involves a combination of linguistically decoded material and pragmatic enrichment. By contrast, implicatures are communicated assumptions resulting from pragmatic inference alone. Let us consider an example of a relevance-theoretic explicature involving the restriction of the domain of a quantificational expression. An utterance of the sentence 'Every cat has white paws' does not make a patently false universal claim about cats, but will typically be used to express a more restricted true proposition – for example, a proposition about cats in our local shelter. Thus, an explicature of this utterance would be 'Every cat in our local shelter has white paws'. As pointed out above, this conceptual representation is a pragmatic development of the propositional schema corresponding to the conventional meaning of the sentence uttered.

The class of explicatures of a given utterance within the relevance-theoretic framework includes not just the proposition expressed by that utterance, but also a range of so-called 'higher-level' explicatures, which are obtained by embedding that proposition under an appropriate propositional attitude* or speech act description (Sperber and Wilson 1993). For example, an utterance of the sentence 'The boss is coming' may be developed inferentially into the higher-level explicature 'The speaker believes that the boss is coming', or even 'The speaker is warning that the boss is coming'.

An interesting distinction is made in relevance theory between strong and weak implicatures (and communication, more generally). The strength of an implicature crucially depends on the manifest strength of the speaker's intention that a specific implication should be recovered. As Sperber and Wilson (1995: 197) put it: 'Some implicatures are made so strongly manifest that the hearer can scarcely avoid recovering them. Others are made less strongly manifest'. Consider, for example, the utterance 'I don't like action thrillers' as an answer to the question 'Have you seen the latest Harrison Ford film?'. It is not difficult to see that such a response can be used to implicitly communicate the assumptions that 'The latest Harrison Ford film is an action thriller' and, in addition, that 'I haven't seen the latest Harrison Ford film'. According to relevance theory, these assumptions are strong implicatures because their recovery is essential to understand the speaker's intended meaning. In other words, the expectation of optimal relevance that an utterance of 'I don't like action thrillers' gives rise to requires that the addressee take these highly salient assumptions (or very similar ones) as being implicitly communicated. The response above may also implicitly communicate the assumption that the speaker has a general dislike for commercial blockbusters, for example. However, this assumption is a weak implicature because it need not be supplied by the addressee in order to satisfy his expectation of optimal relevance. Indeed, there are many other similar implicatures which may have been derived on the basis of the speaker's response, for example that the speaker is not really a film enthusiast, or the speaker frowns upon the use of violence. In general, the more obvious the speaker's communicative intentions, the stronger the communication. Conversely, the wider the range of interpretive possibilities allowed by the speaker, the weaker the communication. The relevance-theoretic approach to the implicit-explicit distinction has led to a significant reassessment of the interface between semantics and pragmatics: the existence of pragmatic aspects of propositional content which do not correspond to items present in the syntactic representation, as argued by relevance theory, strongly suggests that context-sensitivity at this level is widespread.

An important development within relevance theory was the recognition, due to the seminal work of Diane Blakemore (1987, 2002), that linguistic meaning can encode constraints on the inferential phase of utterance comprehension. Thus, linguistic meaning may affect the inferential processes that characterise utterance comprehension in two different ways: while a majority of linguistic expressions encode constituents of conceptual representations, there are also expressions which encode inferential procedures, which we could think of as instructions to increase the salience of a particular type of inferential process.

Blakemore justified the distinction between conceptual and procedural encoding in both cognitive and communicative terms. Since, as it is assumed in relevance theory, the interpretation of utterances involves carrying out computations over conceptual representations, it is reasonable to expect from a cognitive point of view that languages encode information about the inferential procedures in which such conceptual representations enter (and not just the constituents of conceptual representations themselves). From a communicative perspective, using expressions which encode procedures for the identification of intended cognitive effects would obviously reduce the processing cost involved in achieving those effects, a result that is in consonance with the communicative principle of relevance. For example, Blakemore (2002) links the use of the sentential connective 'but' with the cognitive effect of contradiction and elimination. Hence, according to Blakemore, the use of 'but' activates an inferential process resulting in the contradiction and elimination of an assumption which the speaker has reason to believe is accessible to the hearer. For example, an utterance of the sentence 'Kim is rich, but unhappy' activates an inferential process whereby the hearer contradicts and eliminates the accessible assumption that wealth leads to happiness.

Research in relevance theory has also made an important contribution to the study of figurative language. Verbal irony, for example, is analysed in this framework as an 'echoic use' of language in which the speaker dissociates himself tacitly from an attributed utterance or thought (Wilson 2006; Wilson and Sperber 1992). For example, uttering 'You really are good at this!' after a friend has failed to score an easy goal in a quick counter-attack can be construed as an instance of verbal irony because we are tacitly dissociating ourselves from a thought or utterance with a similar content (such as a reassurance that our friend is a skilful footballer) which may have been attributed to us had the circumstances of the game been different. This analysis is a departure from more traditional Gricean accounts,

197

according to which verbal irony constitutes an overt violation of the Quality maxim, thus giving rise to a related true implicature which contradicts the literal meaning of the sentence uttered. The relevance-theoretic approach to verbal irony is in harmony with the framework's assumption that an expectation of relevance, rather than one of truthfulness, is a standard of verbal communication (Wilson and Sperber 2002).

A recent line of research in relevance theory explores in detail the idea that the interpretation of words is also highly context-sensitive, and that lexical context-sensitivity is not restricted to indexical expressions. This line of investigation puts forward the hypothesis that lexical-pragmatic processes such as narrowings, broadenings, approximations and metaphorical extensions are the result of a single pragmatic procedure which fine-tunes the conventional meaning of words in communication (Carston and Powell 2006; Wilson 2003).

In sum, research carried out within the framework of relevance theory has yielded interesting and insightful results (see, for example, Carston 1988, 2002, 2004a, 2004b; Carston and Powell 2006; Sperber and Wilson 1987, 1993, 1995). First, it has provided a cognitive alternative to Gricean and neo-Gricean theories of pragmatics. It has also introduced (or thrown new light into) a number of important theoretical concepts (explicature, echoic uses of language, strength of communicated assumptions) and distinctions (decoding versus inference, explicature versus implicature, conceptual versus procedural meaning, interpretive versus descriptive uses of language, saying versus implicating) in the study of meaning in natural language. Moreover, it has helped to enhance our understanding of the semantics-pragmatics interface by arguing controversially that the contribution of pragmatics to the propositional content of utterances goes far beyond disambiguation and reference assignment.

Primary sources

Blakemore, Diane (1987). *Semantic Constraints on Relevance*. Oxford: Blackwell.

Blakemore, Diane (2002). *Relevance and Linguistic Meaning: The Semantics and Pragmatics of Discourse Markers*. Cambridge: Cambridge University Press.

Carston, Robyn (1988). 'Implicature, explicature and truth-theoretic semantics'. In Ruth Kempson (ed.), *Mental Representations: The Interface between Language and Reality*. Cambridge: Cambridge University Press. 155–81.

Carston, Robyn (2002). *Thoughts and Utterances: The Pragmatics of Explicit Communication*. Oxford: Blackwell Publishing.

Carston, Robyn (2004a). 'Relevance theory and the saying/implicating distinction'. In G. Ward and L. Horn (eds), *The Handbook of Pragmatics*. Oxford: Blackwell. 633–56.

Carston, Robyn (2004b). 'Explicature and semantics'. In S. Davis and B. S. Gillon (eds), *Semantics: A Reader*. Oxford: Oxford University Press. 817–45.

Carston, Robyn and George Powell (2006). 'Relevance theory – new directions and developments'. In E. LePore and B. Smith (eds), *Oxford Handbook of Philosophy of Language*. Oxford: Oxford University Press. 341–60.

Higashimori, Isao and Deirdre Wilson (1996). 'Questions on relevance'. *UCL*

Working Papers in Linguistics 8: 111–24.

Sperber, Dan and Deirdre Wilson (1987). 'Précis of relevance: communication and cognition'. *Behavioral and Brain Sciences* 10: 697–754.

Sperber, Dan and Deirdre Wilson (1993). 'Linguistic form and relevance'. *Lingua* 90: 1–25.

Sperber, Dan and Deirdre Wilson (1995). *Relevance: Communication and Cognition*. Oxford: Blackwell. First edition 1986.

Wilson, Deirdre (2003). 'Relevance theory and lexical pragmatics'. *Italian Journal of Linguistics/Rivista di Linguistica* 15: 273–91.

Wilson, Deirdre (2006). 'The pragmatics of verbal irony: echo or pretence?'. *Lingua* 116: 1722–43.

Wilson, Deirdre and Dan Sperber (1992). 'On verbal irony'. *Lingua* 87: 53–76.

Wilson, Deirdre and Dan Sperber (2002). 'Truthfulness and relevance'. *Mind* 111: 583–632.

Wilson, Deirdre and Dan Sperber (2004). 'Relevance theory'. In G. Ward and L. Horn (eds), *The Handbook of Pragmatics*. Oxford: Blackwell. 607–32.

Further reading

Bach, Kent (1994). 'Conversational impliciture'. *Mind and Language* 9: 124–62.

Blakemore, Diane (1995). 'Relevance theory'. In J. Verschueren, J. Östman and J. Blommaert (eds), *Handbook of Pragmatics*. Amsterdam: Philadelphia. 443–52.

Blakemore, Diane (2002). *Understanding Utterances: An Introduction to Pragmatics*. Oxford: Blackwell.

Huang, Yan (2007). *Pragmatics*. Oxford: Oxford University Press.

Wilson, Deirdre (1999). 'Relevance and relevance theory'. In R. Wilson and F. Keil (eds), *MIT Encyclopaedia of the Cognitive Sciences*. Cambridge, MA: MIT Press. 719–22.

Iván García Álvarez

SENSE DATA

Mental images of physical objects that we perceive directly, with observed properties representing those of the physical object itself. Popular among philosophers through the early twentieth century, the sense data theory has been criticised for its inability to solidly define and recognise sense data as such.

See also: Empiricism/Rationalism; Ideational Theories; Indeterminacy; Mentalism; Sense/Reference

Key Thinkers: Austin, J. L.; Ayer, A. J.; Berkeley, George; Descartes, René; Hume, David; Kant, Immanuel; Locke, John; Moore, G. E.; Russell, Bertrand

Although philosophers as far back as John Locke, George Berkeley and David Hume wrote about human perception and understanding, the term 'sense data' (or its singular form 'sense datum') is more modern, having first appeared in the early twentieth century in the works of such thinkers as G. E. Moore and Bertrand Russell. In the philosophy of perception, the sense data theory argues that properties of mental images directly correlate to those of the physical objects they represent. Growing criticism to the contrary – most notably by J. L. Austin, Frank Jackson and Wilfrid

Sellars – maintains that we form interpretations, not mere mental images, that lack the same properties of those physical objects.

In support of the sense data theory, Hume and Russell use an example of how a table appears differently to us as we physically move alongside it or away from it in order to describe how our sensory experience adjusts to perspectival variation, or changes in our physical relationship to external objects. Because the size and shape of the physical table do not change, our perception is our awareness of the table's corresponding mental image. Other arguments supporting sense data have to do with perception of mental images not directly related to physical objects. This includes optical illusions, hallucinations, double vision and even time delays between the existence of a physical object and our perception of it.

More recently, criticisms of the sense data theory have directly refuted its supporting arguments. For example, sense data theorists would argue that if thing X were made to look exactly like thing Y, what we are directly aware of in our perception is thing Y. This mental image of thing Y is evidence of sense data. Opposing arguments, however, state that this illusion does not change the fact that we are still looking at and perceiving properties of a real (or material) thing X.

Originating from discussions on human knowledge and understanding, the sense data theory is an important component of the philosophy of perception. As the debate continues over whether mental phenomena behind perception exist as mental images or as pure interpretation, critics of sense data receive increasing support in linguistic circles, where words in language trigger direct awareness of internal interpretations, not property-bearing sense data.

Primary sources

Austin, J. L. (1962). *Sense and Sensibilia*. Oxford: Clarendon Press.

Berkeley, George (1998). *Three Dialogues between Hylas and Philonous*. Ed. J. Dancy. New York: Oxford University Press.

Hume, David (2000). *An Enquiry Concerning Human Understanding: A Critical Edition*. Ed. T. Beauchamp. Oxford: Clarendon Press.

Russell, Bertrand (1964). *The Problems of Philosophy*. New York: Oxford University Press.

Further reading

Firth, Roderick (1965). 'Sense data and the percept theory'. In R. Swartz (ed.), *Perceiving, Sensing, and Knowing*. New York: Anchor Books. 204–70.

Chrucky, Andrew (1992). 'The alleged fallacy of the sense datum inference'. *Eastern Pennsylvania Philosophical Association*. Bloomsburg University.

Huemer, Michael (2004). 'Sense data'. *Stanford Encyclopedia of Philosophy* (http://plato.stanford.edu/).

Jennifer A. Baldwin

SENSE/REFERENCE

The distinction between sense and reference (German '*Sinn*' and '*Bedeutung*') goes back to the German logician Gottlob Frege. According to his understanding, sense and reference are two different aspects of meaning of linguistic expressions, reference being the entity to which an expression refers and sense being the way in which that entity is presented. For example, the expressions 'Tom' and 'the prisoner' may well refer to the same person, but they differ in sense. This highly controversial distinction had, and still has, a strong influence on semantics and philosophy of language.

See also: Analytic Philosophy; Compositionality; Connotation/Denotation; Definite Descriptions; Names; Propositional Attitudes; Truth Value
Key Thinkers: Carnap, Rudolf; Dummett, Michael; Frege, Gottlob; Kripke, Saul; Leibniz, Gottfried Wilhelm; Mill, J. S.; Russell, Bertrand; Searle, John; Strawson, P. F.

Gottlob Frege, the father of modern mathematical logic, and also considered one of the founders of analytic philosophy, developed the distinction between sense and reference mainly in his essay '*On Sense and Reference*' ('*Über Sinn und Bedeutung*', 1892). This paper is considered one of the most important historical sources of modern semantics. In it Frege suggested that in order to grasp the meaning of an expression, one must comprehend not only the object it refers to but also the way the object is presented, that is to say the sense of the referring expression.

Frege's theory was opposed to the then common understanding, dating back to John Locke, that identified the meaning of a word with the internal idea connected with it. Frege, in contrast, identified meaning with the reference of the expression. In connection with this denotational conception of meaning, he worked out a theory around two main puzzles about language.

The first puzzle is in dealing with identity statements such as 'the Morning Star is the Evening Star'. Of course this sentence conveys the information that the objects called the Morning Star and the Evening Star (this pair is used by Frege) are physically identical (both are the planet Venus). If we substitute the expression 'Evening Star' with the co-referring expression 'Morning Star' in the example above, it results in 'the Morning Star is the Morning Star'. In contrast to the first statement, this is a tautology. It gives only trivial information and does not tell us anything new because the statement holds *a priori*. It is not possible to comprehend and above all to explain this difference in the meaning of the two sentences solely by the reference of a sign, because this is the same for both expressions.

This observation leads Frege to conclude that there is a second aspect to the meaning of a sign besides the reference, namely the sense ('*Sinn*'). The sense of a sign corresponds to the mode of presentation ('*Art des Gegebenseins*'). In the example the expressions 'Morning Star' and 'Evening Star' present two different ways of characterising the planet Venus, the brightest shining visible celestial body in either the evening or the morning. The difference between them in the example given above lies in a difference in the mode of presentation of the signs since their reference, the planet Venus, is the same.

The direct reference approach – assuming that the meaning of an expression is its referent – was already claimed by Mill but the two problems described above (identity statements and empty names) led Frege and later P. F. Strawson and John Searle to claim that proper names* have sense, and additionally but not necessarily, reference. This view is also referred to as mediated reference theory. Philosophers like Saul Kripke, John McDowell and Gareth Evans have argued against this position, convinced that Frege's treatment of so-called empty names was inconsistent. Kripke attacked Frege's and Bertrand Russell's position in his lectures 'Naming and Necessity' asserting that proper names do not have senses at all. Kripke said that the reference of a proper name is determined by the associated description and he explained that contrary to the descriptive properties a proper name refers to the same object across all possible worlds (counterfactual worlds included).

The terms used by Frege are '*Sinn*' and '*Bedeutung*'. This terminology is confusing. '*Bedeutung*' is generally translated as 'meaning'. But what is commonly understood as meaning, language internal and independent from facts, rather corresponds to Frege's other term '*Sinn*' or sense. Other authors adapt the connotation/denotation or intension/extension distinction. The essay is translated as 'Sense and Reference' by Max Black (1948), but as 'Sense and Meaning' in Frege's *Posthumous Writings* (1979). They are herein after called 'sense' and 'reference'.

According to Frege's theory, a sign has a sense, and this has a reference.

But a referent can correspond to several senses (not necessarily a unique sense), for example in different languages. With 'sign' Frege refers to proper names, under which he widely subsumes all expressions which denote or could denote objects, because a grammatically correct meaningful expression having a sense might lack a reference. For instance, the expression 'the least rapidly convergent series' has no reference because for each convergent series a less rapidly convergent series can be found. Other examples of empty names are figures from mythology like 'Odysseus', as already seen above. This was another reason for Frege to distinguish a second aspect of meaning. Frege holds the view that this inconsistency marks a deficiency of natural language and even of symbolic language of mathematical analysis. For a logically perfect language ('*Begriffsschrift*') he demands that every correctly formed expression has a reference.

Sense and reference need to be distinguished from the associated idea ('*Vorstellung*'), the internal image of an object, which is subjective. It varies from person to person and even for one person it is not always the same. In Frege's theory of meaning the sense lies between the reference of a proper name (the object itself) and the subjective idea. It is neither subjective nor is it the object itself. Frege developed the theory of sense and reference into a philosophy of language. Thus, departing from proper names he generalises the twofold semantic function to entire declarative sentences. The meaning of a sentence (or complex expression) is determined by the meanings of its constituents. This is the principle of compositionality* controversially attributed to Frege. Hence it should be possible to substitute constituents of the sentence with co-referring constituents without affecting the reference of the entire sentence.

Leibniz had formulated this regularity as his law of substitution and in Frege's theory the objective content of a declarative sentence is called a thought ('*Gedanke*') and is understood as the sense of a sentence. Substitution might change the sense or thought as in the example given below.

'The morning star is a body illuminated by the sun.'
'The evening star is a body illuminated by the sun.'

In contrast what remains the same is the truth value of the sentence, which Frege considers the reference. The idea of truth values comes from the discipline of logic or logical semantics. It refers to a function which maps sentences on to the truth values true or false. Corresponding to what is said about proper names, Frege claims that sentences need to have sense but not necessarily reference. This can be shown in the sentence 'Miss Marple investigated the assassination in the Orient Express'. This sentence is meaningful but, as it contains the name 'Miss Marple', a fictional character whose reference is doubtful, it cannot be said to have a reference, that is a truth value*.

The following paragraph highlights several subordinate clauses as exemptions from the substitution principle.

This theory of sense and reference can only be maintained if we assume that in these contexts the expressions do not have their customary reference. In his essay 'Sense and Reference', Frege analyses various types of subordinate clauses in detail.

If we substitute the proper name Charlotte Brontë with her pseudonym Currer Bell in the following true sentence 'Dorothy believes that Charlotte Brontë is the author of *Jane Eyre*', the meaning of the entire sentence is changed because the resulting sentence is not necessarily correct: 'Dorothy believes that Currer Bell is the author of *Jane Eyre*'. Dorothy might not be aware of the fact that Charlotte Brontë at that time published under the assumed masculine name Currer Bell; therefore she might believe that 'Charlotte Brontë is the author of *Jane Eyre*' and at the same time believe that it can not be the case that 'Currer Bell is the author of *Jane Eyre*', despite the fact that they are one and the same person.

The issue described above is also known as Frege's second puzzle about language. How can it be that the principle of substitution fails in the context of propositional attitude* reports (or of indirect quotation)? The answer is that in these cases we talk about the words themselves. Expressions correspondingly do not have their customary reference, but they have their indirect reference, coinciding with what is customarily their sense. Frege introduces the term 'indirect' (German '*ungerade*') reference/sense contrary to the 'customary' ('*gewöhnlich*') reference/sense. This leads to the position that under the given circumstances a clause's reference is not a truth value but a thought. Thus we can only substitute the subordinate clause with another with the same thought (that is, reference) in order to keep the truth value of the complex sentence but not necessarily substitute another with same truth value.

The situation is comparable in sentences with 'it seems that' and 'command', 'ask', 'forbid', or 'doubt whether', to name a few. In all these cases the words in the subordinate clause have an indirect reference and this determines that the reference of the subordinate clause is not a truth value but a thought, a command, a request, a question and so on. According to Frege, the subordinate clause following these expressions may also be understood as proper name of the thought it represents in the compound sentence.

The discussion about sense and reference of propositional attitude reports, initialised by Frege, is still alive. One topic is the question, for example, of how nested quotations or propositional attitudes – leading to a hierarchy of senses – fit into Frege's theory. Apart from cases of indirect reference of words, there are other cases where sense and reference do not correspond to thought and truth value respectively. In the sentence 'whoever invented the ingenious Miss Marple was a fanciful person', the grammatical subject 'whoever' has no independent sense, but only in connection with the main clause. This accounts for the fact that the sense of the subordinate clause is not a complete thought. Besides, the reference is not a truth value but the person Agatha Christie. A further example is conditional sentences. Usually neither the antecedent clause nor the consequent clause qualifies to express an entire thought. It is their combination which expresses one single complete thought. While several types of subordinate clauses are in a way incomplete, others – for example, concessive clauses – are complete in this respect.

The remaining cases of failure of the substitution test are explained with additional subsidiary thoughts not explicitly expressed. One example given by Frege himself is a causal subordinate clause: 'Because ice is less dense than water it floats on water'. Frege argues that the compound expresses more than one thought per clause namely three thoughts altogether:

1. Ice is less dense that water.
2. If anything is less dense that water, it floats on water.
3. Ice floats on water.

The clause 'because ice is less dense than water' does not only express the first but also part of the second thought. This overlapping is the reason why it is not possible to exchange the subordinate clause given above by another one with the same truth value without doing harm to the truth of the entire sentence. It thus does not serve to disqualify the theory of sense and reference of sentences in this view.

Frege's ideas had a significant impact on the development of modern semantic theories. The distinction between sense and reference continues to be the subject of research in philosophy. Besides the topics already mentioned, another issue still discussed in the literature is the questions raised by sentences which contain expressions depending on context, that is deictical terms such as 'today'. As Frege considers a thought to be complete, the question of what is the sense of these expressions arises among Frege's interpreters and is broadened to a general quest for an adequate theory of deixis.

Primary sources

Black, Max and Peter Geach (eds) (1980). *Translations from the Philosophical Writings of Gottlob Frege*. Oxford: Blackwell. First edition 1952.

Church, Alonzo (1956). *Introduction to Mathematical Logic I*. Princeton: Princeton University Press. Revised and enlarged version.

Frege, Gottlob (1879). 'Begriffsschrift, eine der arithmetischen nachgebildete Formelsprache des reinen Denkens'. Halle: Louis Nebert. Trans. J. Van Heijenoort as 'Concept script, a formal language of pure thought modelled upon that of arithmetic'. In J. van Heijenoort (ed.) (1967), *From Frege to Gödel: A Source Book in Mathematical Logic, 1879–1931*. Cambridge, MA: Harvard University Press.

Frege, Gottlob (1892). Über Sinn und Bedeutung'. *Zeitschrift für Philosophie und philosophische Kritik* Vol. 100: 25–50.

Frege, Gottlob (1892/1948). 'Sense and reference'. Trans. Max Black. *The Philosophical Review* Vol. 57, no. 3 (May 1948), 209–30.

Frege, Gottlob (1979). *Posthumous Writings*. Ed. Hans Hermes, Friedrich Kambartel, Friedrich Kaulbach. Trans. Peter Long, Roger White. Chicago: University of Chicago Press.

Kripke, Saul (1972). 'Naming and necessity'. In Donald Davidson, Gilbert Harman (eds), *Semantics of Natural Language*. Dordrecht: Reidel.

Russell, Bertrand (1905). 'On denoting'. *Mind*: 479–99.

Quine, W. V. O. (1980). 'Reference and modality'. In *From a Logical Point of View: Nine Logico-Philosophical Essays*. Cambridge, MA: Harvard University Press. 139–59. First edition 1953.

Further reading

Beaney, Michael and Erich H. Reck (eds) (2005). *Gottlob Frege: Critical Assessments of Leading Philosophers*. Vol. IV: *Frege's Philosophy of Thought and Language*. London: Routledge.

Burge, Tyler (2005). *Truth, Thought, Reason: Essays on Frege*. Oxford: Oxford University Press.

Carl, Wolfgang (1994). *Frege's Theory of Sense and Reference. Its Origin and Scope*. Cambridge: Cambridge University Press.

Dummett, Michael (1973). *Frege: Philosophy of Language*. London: Duckworth.

Ricketts, Thomas (ed.) (forthcoming). *The Cambridge Companion to Frege*. Cambridge: Cambridge University Press.

Sluga, Hans D. (1993). *The Philosophy of Frege*. Four vols. New York: Garland.

Eva Herrmann-Kaliner

SIGNS AND SEMIOTICS

The term Semiotics (*Semiologie*) in the sense that it is understood in the twenty-first century was first used by Ferdinand de Saussure in his 1908 lessons on general linguistics. A sign is any entity representing another entity: smoke as a sign of fire, or a stop signal alerting drivers to come to a halt at a crossroad. To the whole set of signs in human and non-human communication belong different subsets depending on their quality. They can thus be encompassed as visual signs, auditory signs, verbal signs, cloth signs, and the like. As far as linguistics is concerned, semiotics is the science that studies linguistic signs, which is tantamount to saying that linguistics is part of a more general science of semiotics which in turn is a branch of general psychology.

See also: Langue/Parole;
Structuralism
Key Thinkers: Bopp, Franz;
Hjelmslev, Louis; Morris, Charles;
Peirce, C. S.; Saussure, Ferdinand de

The very first mention of the label 'semiotics', spelled 'semeiotics', dates back to 1670 when the English physician Henry Stubbes used it to denote the branch of medicine relating to the interpretation of symptoms. Twenty years later John Locke used the label to discuss his tripartite subdivision of science:

the third branch may be called Semei-otike, or the doctrine of signs; the most usual whereof being words, it is aptly enough termed also Logike, logic: the business whereof is to consider the nature of signs, the mind makes use of for the understanding of things, or conveying its knowledge to others. (Locke 1963: 174)

But we have to wait until the end of the nineteenth century to see the label applied to language.

Ferdinand de Saussure defined what he called *Semiologie* as the science of signs. He conceived of semiotics as part of social psychology and therefore of general psychology. Semiotics is part of psychology because the sign is a twofold psychic entity: such an entity is composed of two sides, the concept and the acoustic image, both of which reside in the 'same psychic site'.

Saussure was introduced to a science of signs by his professor Michel Jules Alfred Bréal, whose course in semantics he attended in 1881. In his lessons, later collected in his famous *Essai de Sémantique* (1897), Bréal claimed that 'les mots sont des signes: ils n'ont pas plus d'existence que les gestes du telegraphe aérien ou que les points et les traits du télégraphe Morse' ('Words are signs: they have no further existence than the movement of the railway semaphore signal or the dots and dashes of Morse code') (Bréal 1897: 835), and departed from the eighteenth-century semiologic tradition in order to show the inconsistency of the organicistic conception of the language. Bréal was influenced by the studies of Franz Bopp and William Dwight Whitney and the notion of sign they utilised in their language investigation, and by the philosophical perspective of Etienne Bonnot de Condillac and the importance he gave to psychology in his philosophical studies. Bréal's semantics is thus based on the psychological laws of the human mind, and traces of John Locke's and Condillac's ideas can be found in his work as well as insights from the studies on psychology and memory sciences like those offered by Hippolite Taine, Théodule-Armand

Ribot and Paul Pierre Broca. To the thirty-year shaping of his theory of sign, Bréal included a strong psychological value that he drew from the studies on the human mind which were so pervasively spreading in the second half of the nineteenth century. He thus attempted to search the cognitive and intellectual features of the human mind which regulate the nature of language.

This aspect of Bréal's semantics is evident in the work of Saussure, who aimed to find a bridge between the psychic essence of the concept and the concrete reality of the word. He came up with the idea of 'sign' as an indivisible pair consisting of abstract concept and concrete realisation. Until one of his 1911 lessons, when he first used the two terms *signifiant* and *signifié*, Saussure generally spoke of sign in the same way as was done by his contemporaries, that is as the phonological counterpart of an entity. Later he developed a more refined theory where the sign is conceived of as a dyadic entity formed by the indivisible combination of a signifier (*signifiant*, the acoustic image) and a signified (*signifié*, the mental representation of reality). The signifier and the signified are intimately linked by an associative link whereby each triggers the other. Hence they stand in a static dyadic relationship which goes under the label of signification. With reference to language, a linguistic sign is not a link between a thing and a name, but between a concept and a sound pattern. This means that language is mainly symbolic, since the relations between the sound sequences and their meanings are conventional, or arbitrary, and have to be learnt. On Whitney's claim of the arbitrary nature of sign, Saussure contended that the meaning of a sign is not contained within it, but arises in its interpretation. This means that meanings do not exist *per se* but are established by the language users in relation to the context of use. In other words, the role of the interpreter must be accounted for, either implicitly as in Saussure, or explicitly as in Peirce.

Saussure's apparatus was followed by Hjelmslev (1943) who substituted the terms *expression* and *content* to refer to the signifier and signified respectively. He also referred to planes of expression and content, each having substance and form. Thus there are four categories which may facilitate analytical distinctions: substance of expression, form of expression, substance of content, and form of content.

In the United States semiotics developed in the second half of the nineteenth century within the field of philosophy where Charles Peirce claimed that semiosis is 'an action, or influence, which is, or involves, a dynamical operation of three subjects, such as sign, its object, and its interpretant, this tri-relative influence not being in any way resolvable into action between pairs' (Hartshorne et al. 1958: 5.484). Whereas in the Saussurean theoretical apparatus, the sign is a bipartite entity, Peirce conceived of it as a dynamic triadic relation:

> a sign or *representamen* is something which stands to somebody for something in some respect or capacity. It addresses somebody, that is, creates in the mind of that person an equivalent sign, or perhaps a more developed sign.

207

The sign which it creates I call the *interpretant* of the first sign. The sign stands for something, its *object*. (Hartshorne et al. 1958: 2.228)

Semiosis is therefore an endless process, something that Eco (1976) defined as 'unlimited semiosis'.

In his investigation of the triadic nature of sign (*Triadism*), Peirce claimed that 'all thought whatsoever is a sign, and is mostly of the nature of language' (Hartshorne et al. 1958: 5.421). In his triadism, Peirce analysed the sign in itself, in relation with the object, and in relation with the interpretant, thus developing a huge number of categories. As far as language is concerned, the most relevant triad is the one which originates from the relation that a sign establishes with itself. The sign-to-sign relation produces three modes, an icon, an index, and a symbol. The icon is a mode in which the signifier is perceived as imitating the signified, as is the case with onomatopoeia. An index is a mode in which the signifier is arbitrary but connected in some way, physically or causally, to the signified, for example in the case of demonstrative pronouns. A symbol is a mode in which the signifier is fundamentally arbitrary. These three modes give rise to three basic principles which are fundamental to investigate linguistic phenomena: the principle of indexicality, of iconicity, and of symbolicity.

Peirce's scientific contribution went almost unknown during his lifetime, and his semiotic approach was spread by Charles Morris who, drawing largely on the Peircean theoretical framework, approached semiotics through the lenses of Mead's behaviourism* and investigated the understanding of the unitary process of semiosis. He proposed to focus on the relation that the sign can establish with the other entities in the semiotic process. Thus the sign-object relation points to the dimension of semantics; the sign-sign relation refers to syntax; and the sign-interpreter relation refers to pragmatics. Such a tripartite division became normalised in linguistics.

Semiotics is a broad discipline which deals with any type of signification and communication. It encompasses branches like social semiotics, visual semiotics, zoosemiotics, music semiology, computational semiotics, and literary semiotics, to mention but a few.

Primary sources

Bréal, Michel (1897). *Essai de sémantique. Science des significations*. Paris: Hachette.

Eco, Umberto (1976). *A Theory of Semiotics*. Bloomington: Indiana University Press/London: Macmillan.

Hartshorne, Charles, Paul Weiss and Arthur W. Burks (eds) (1958). *Collected Papers of Charles Sanders Peirce*. Eight volumes. Cambridge, MA: Harvard University Press.

Hjelmslev, Louis ([1943]1953). *Prolegomena to a Theory of Language*. Baltimore: Indiana University Publications in Anthropology and Linguistics.

Morris, Charles W. (1938/1970). *Foundations of the Theory of Signs*. Chicago: Chicago University Press.

Saussure, Ferdinand de (1916/1983). *Course in General Linguistics*. Trans. Roy Harris. London: Duckworth.

Further reading

Chandler, Daniel (2001). *Semiotics: The Basics*. London: Routledge.

Eco, Umberto (1984). *Semiotics and the Philosophy of Language*. Bloomington: Indiana University Press.

Locke, John (1689/1963). 'Of the division of the sciences'. Book IV, chapter XXI. *An Essay Concerning Human Understanding*. Ed. Peter N. Nidditch. Oxford: Clarendon.

Annalisa Baicchi

SITUATIONAL SEMANTICS

An information-based approach to natural language semantics. Formulated by Jon Barwise and John Perry in their influential book *Situations and Attitudes* (1983), it is built upon the notion of a 'situation' – a limited part of the real world that a cognitive agent can individuate and has access to. A situation represents a lump of information in terms of a collection of facts. It is through the actualist ontology of situations that the meaning of natural language utterances can be elucidated.

> *See also*: Logic; Possible World Semantics
> *Key Thinkers*: Austin, J. L.; Davidson, Donald; Frege, Gottlob; Grice, H. P.; Lewis, David; Montague, Richard; Strawson, P. F.; Tarski, Alfred; Wittgenstein, Ludwig

Situational semantics ('situation semantics' in the sequel) starts with the hypothesis that what is called 'the world' is an inconceivably large totality. Limited parts of the world are called 'situations' and can be individuated by cognitive agents. Thus, people perceive situations, cause them to be brought about, and have all sorts of attitudes toward them. One fact remains: we are at all times in situations (cf. Norbert Hornstein: 'Situations people the world. They are dated and located.').

While the Barwise-Perry volume (1983) is exceptional in its programmatic employment of situations (applied, among others, to naked-infinitive perception and belief reports), historically there was always some interest in situations. Two noteworthy – albeit cryptic – passages in *Zettel* (Wittgenstein 1981: 2, 13) show that Wittgenstein thought that situations a person is embedded in are of key value in making their behaviour intelligible. Authorities of pragmatics like J. L. Austin, H. P. Grice and Peter Strawson could be regarded as friendly to a situational approach, for they try to come to terms with the notion of 'context'. And for some, situations are generalised versions of 'events' as conceived by Donald Davidson and others.

A situation is a rich object consisting of individuals enjoying various properties and standing in a variety of relations. It is a 'small' world. Incidentally, there is a crucial difference between situation-theoretic and mathematical relations. The latter are set-theoretic constructs whereas the former are relations of the kind recognisable by cognitive agents. A situation may extend quite far in space and time. An agent can watch a film about a past assassination, scrutinise the latest videos from the Jupiter mission, or chat with someone who relates their adventures in the Pampas of Argentina.

One of the features of situation semantics is its information-based disposition. Let us define something's being P (a property) or something's having R (a relation) to something else as a 'state of affairs' (Armstrong 1997). In situation semantics, 'infons' are posited as discrete items supplying such bits of information. An infon is shown as an $(n + 2)$-tuple $<R, a_1, \ldots, a_n, p>$, where R is an n-place relation (properties being 1-place relations); $a_1, \ldots, a_n$ are objects appropriate for the respective argument places of R; and p is polarity. If p=yes (respectively, no) then $a_1, \ldots, a_n$ stand (respectively, do not stand) in the relation R.

Abstract situations are proposed to be counterparts of real situations in order to make the latter amenable to formal manipulation. Given a situation s, the set $\{i \mid s \models i\}$, where i stands for an infon, is the corresponding abstract situation. Notice that this set collects all facts (infons that are made true by s). Alternatively, s is said to 'support' (make it the case that) i – denoted as $s \models i$ above – just in case i is true of s.

Devlin (1991: 31) has studied what situations might amount to and how we can 'individuate' them. A scheme of individuation – a way of carving the world into uniformities – is an essential facet of the situational approach. This way we can single out – say, via direct perception or thinking – and treat situations as entities that can later be referred to. When agents individuate a situation, they cannot be expected to give clear-cut descriptions of all that the situation comprises: situations are vague objects. Another

intricacy was cited by Gadamer (1975: 268–9) who saw that the very idea of a situation necessitates that an agent is not located outside of it and hence may be unable to have objective epistemic access to it.

Human beings and lower organisms display a fundamental ability to discern similarities between situations. This is accomplished via regularities, that is individuals, relations, or locations that endure from one situation to another. Thus, I believe that snow makes driving difficult, that doctors are available for medical assistance, that parents care about their offspring, that I will receive a present on Father's Day.

Barwise and Perry note that agents 'must constantly adapt to the course of events in which they find themselves' (1983: 10). This adaptation takes place as an upshot of attunement to similarities between situations ('uniformities'). Thus, a useful uniformity in my life has to do with the milkman. Every morning (a different situation), he brings the milk at about 8 o'clock and leaves it on our doorsteps. By just being attuned to this uniformity, I contribute to my well-being. Violation of a uniformity is possible; there is no milk service on holidays.

Representation of uniformities yields 'types'. Suppose Bob was eating cookies yesterday and is eating cookies now. Both of these situations share the same constituent sequence <eats, Bob, cookies>. These events, occurring at different times, have the same type. In the same vein, consider two 'parametric' infons <embraces, $\hat{g}$, Carol, yes> and <embraces, $\hat{g}$, $\hat{h}$, yes>, where $\hat{g}$ and $\hat{h}$ are placeholders for individuals. Their meaning can be rendered as 'Someone embraces Carol' and 'Someone embraces someone', respectively. Anchoring parameters of an infon yields (parameter-free) infons. For example, given <embraces, ĝ, Carol, yes>, if $F(ĝ)$ = David (F is an anchoring) then we obtain <embraces, David, Carol, yes>.

Networks of abstract links between situation types provide information flow (Dretske 1981). Thus, the statement 'smoke means fire' expresses the law-like relation that links situations where there is smoke to situations where there is a blaze. If a is the type of smoky situations and b is the type of fire situations, then having been attuned to the constraint $a \gg b$ (read 'a involves b') an agent can pick up the information that there is a fire in a particular site by observing that there is smoke.

According to situation semantics, meanings of expressions reside in systematic relations between different types of situations. They can be identified with relations on discourse situations d, connections c, the utterance situation u itself, and the described situation e. Some public facts about u – such as its speaker and time of utterance – are determined by d. The ties of the mental states of the speaker and the hearer with the world constitute c. A discourse situation d involves the expression uttered, its speaker, spatiotemporal location of the utterance, and the addressee. Each of these defines a linguistic role (role of the speaker, of the addressee, and so on). The utterance situation u constrains the world in a certain way, depending on how the roles for discourse situations, connections and described situation are to be filled.

For instance, an utterance of 'I am smiling' defines a meaning relation. Given d, c, and e, this relation holds just in case there is a location l and a speaker s such that s is speaking at l, and, in e, s is smiling at l. In interpreting the utterance of an expression f in context, there is a flow of information, partly from the linguistic form encoded in f and partly from contextual factors provided by the utterance situation u. These are combined to form a set of constraints on the described situation e.

Ideas from situation semantics have been applied to a number of issues in logic*, language, cognition and information. To take three comprehensive projects, Barwise and Etchemendy (1987) analyse self-reference and paradox, Gawron and Peters (1990) deal with pronominal anaphora, and Cooper (1996) focuses on generalised quantifiers. Unlike the classical approaches to meaning (including Fregean senses, Tarskian truth, Montague grammar), there is an ordinary feel to situation semantics; it does not impose human-made assumptions in our conceptual scheme (in contra-distinction to Lewisian possible worlds, for example). It is an archetype of what a naturalised theory of semantics should look like.

Primary sources

Barwise, Jon (1989). *The Situation in Logic*. Stanford, CA: CSLI Publications.

Barwise, Jon and John Etchemendy (1987). *The Liar*. New York: Oxford University Press.

Barwise, Jon and John Perry (1983). *Situations and Attitudes*. Cambridge, MA: MIT Press.

Devlin, Keith (1991). *Logic and Information*. New York: Cambridge University Press.

Devlin, Keith (2006). 'Situation theory and situation semantics'. In Dov Gabbay and John Woods (eds), *Handbook of the History of Logic, vol. 7*. Amsterdam: Elsevier. 601–64.

Seligman, Jerry and Larry Moss (1997). 'Situation theory'. In van Benthem, Johan and Alice ter Meulen (eds), *Handbook of Logic and Language*. Amsterdam: Elsevier. 239–309.

Further reading

Aczel, Peter, David Israel, Yasuhiro Katagiri, and Stanley Peters (eds) (1993). *Situation Theory and Its Applications, vol. 3*. Stanford, CA: CSLI Publications.

Armstrong, D. M. (1997). *A World of States of Affairs*. Cambridge: Cambridge University Press.

Austin, J. L. (1979). *Philosophical Papers*. Ed. J. O. Urmson and G. J. Warnock. Oxford: Oxford University Press.

Barwise, Jon, Jean Mark Gawron, Gordon Plotkin, and Syun Tutiya (eds) (1991). *Situation Theory and Its Applications, vol. 2*. Stanford, CA: CSLI Publications.

Cooper, Robin (1996). 'The role of situations in generalized quantifiers'. In Shalom Lappin (ed.), *The Handbook of Contemporary Semantic Theory*. Cambridge, MA: Blackwell Publishers. 65–86.

Cooper, Robin, Kuniaki Mukai, and John Perry (eds) (1990). *Situation Theory and Its Applications, vol. 1*. Stanford, CA: CSLI Publications.

Davidson, Donald (1980). *Essays on Actions and Events*. Oxford: Clarendon Press.

Dretske, Fred (1981). *Knowledge and the Flow of Information*. Cambridge, MA: MIT Press.

Gadamer, Hans-Georg (1975). *Truth and Method*. Trans. and ed. Garrett Barden and John Cumming. New York: Seabury Press.

Gawron, Jean Mark and Stanley Peters (1990). *Anaphora and Quantification in Situation Semantics*. Stanford, CA: CSLI Publications.

Grice, H. P. (1989). *Studies in the Way of Words*. Cambridge, MA: Harvard University Press.

Strawson, P. F. (1997). *Entity and Identity*. Oxford: Oxford University Press.

Wittgenstein, Ludwig (1981). *Zettel*. Ed. G. E. M. Anscombe and G. H. von Wright. Trans. G. E. M. Anscombe. Oxford: Basil Blackwell.

Varol Akman

SPEECH ACT THEORY

Speech act theory accounts for an act that a speaker performs when pronouncing an utterance, which thus serves a function in communication. Since speech acts are the tools that allow us to interact in real-life situations, uttering a speech act requires knowledge not only of the language but also of its appropriate use within a given culture.

See also: Logical Positivism; Ordinary Language Philosophy; Performative
Key Thinkers: Aristotle; Austin, J. L; Ayer, A. J.; Grice, H. P.; Husserl, Edmund; Kant, Immanuel; Ryle, Gilbert; Searle, John; Wittgenstein, Ludwig

Speech act theory was first developed by J. L. Austin whose seminal Oxford Lectures in 1952–4 marked an important development in the philosophy of language and linguistics. Austin's proposal can be viewed as a reaction to the extreme claims of logical positivists, who argued that the meaning of a sentence is reducible to its verifiability, that is to an analysis which verifies if utterances are true or false. Austin contended that most of our utterances do more than simply making statements: questions and orders are not used to state something, and many declarative sentences do not lend themselves to being analysed in terms of their falsifiability. Instead, they are instruments that allow speakers to change the state of affairs. This is tantamount to saying that we use language mainly as a tool to do things, and we do so by means of performing hundreds of ordinary verbal actions of different types in daily life, such as make telephone calls, baptise children, or fire an employee.

The fact that not all sentences are a matter of truth verifiability was first advanced by Aristotle who, in his *De Interpretatione*, argued that:

> as there are in the mind thoughts which do not involve truth or falsity, and also those which must be either true or false, so it is in speech. [. . .] A sentence is a significant portion of speech [. . .] Yet every sentence is not a proposition; only such are propositions as have in them either truth or falsity. [. . .] Let us therefore dismiss all other types of sentence but the proposition, for this last concerns our present inquiry, whereas the investigation of the others belongs rather to the study of rhetoric or of poetry. (1–4)

Although he explicitly deems the nature of sentences to be uninteresting in his inquiry on apophantic logos, Aristotle represents the first account of language as action.

Aristotle's standpoint influenced the study of language for centuries and paved the way for a tradition of research on verifiability, but several German and British philosophers anticipated a view of language as a tool to change a state of affairs. The issues of language and conversation were addressed by Immanuel Kant who anticipated some concepts like 'context' and 'subjective idealisation', the rules that articulate conversation, and the para-linguistic gestures used in the accomplishment of speech acts. But it was only at the end of the nineteenth century that a more elaborate treatment of language as action was initiated.

The first, although non-systematic, study of the action-like character of language was conducted by Thomas Reid, who described different acts that can be performed through language, and grouped them into two categories: 'solitary acts' like judgements, intentions, deliberations and desiring, which can go unexpressed; and 'social operations' like commanding, promising or warning, which, by their very social nature, must be expressed. Reid's contribution to the inception of a speech act theory can be fully understood if viewed from the wider perspective of the philosophical developments of his time.

Franz Brentano's distinction between physical and psychological phenomena is particularly relevant in this respect because it reintroduced to philosophy the scholastic concept of

213

'intentionality', which allows for a distinction between mental acts and the external world. As far as speech act theory is concerned, suffice it here to say that Brentano argued that every mental, psychological act has a content and is directed at an object (the intentional object), which means that mental phenomena contain an object intentionally within themselves and are thus definable as objectifying acts. The Brentanian approach to intentionality* allows for a distinction between linguistic expressions describing psychological phenomena and linguistic expressions describing non-psychological phenomena. Furthermore, Brentano claimed that speaking is itself an activity through which we can initiate psychic phenomena. Edmund Husserl picked up the importance of what Brentano's psychological investigation could bring to logic*, in particular the contrast between emotional acts and objectifying acts. Husserl tackled the issue of human mental activities ('acts') and how they constitute the 'object' of knowledge through experience. In his *Logical Investigations* (1900/1) he developed a theory of meaning based on 'intentionality' which, for him, meant that consciousness entails 'directedness' towards an object. It is on the notion of 'objectifying acts', that is acts of representation, that Husserl shaped his theory of linguistic meaning, thus emphasising the referential use of language. Collaterally he treated the non-representational uses of language, that is acts like asking questions, commanding or requesting.

Following Brentano and moving within the field of psychology, Anton Marty offered the first account of uses of language meant to direct others' behaviour, like giving an order, requesting, or giving encouragement. Marty stated that sentences may hint at the speaker's psychic processes and argued that 'deliberate speaking is a special kind of acting, whose proper goal is to call forth certain psychic phenomena in other beings' (1908: 284). Stemming from Brentano's tripartite subdivision of mental phenomena into presentation, judgements, and phenomena of love and hate, Marty discriminated linguistic forms into names, statements and emotives (utterances arousing an interest), which is a model that closely resembles Karl Bühler's *Sprachtheorie*. It is precisely to Bühler that we owe the coinage of the label 'speech act theory'. He offered the first thorough study of the functions of language – *Darstellung* (representation), *Kindgabe* (intimation or expression), and *Auslösung* (arousal or appeal) – thus endowing non-representational sentences with their own status.

A more complete treatment we find in the work of Adolf Reinach, who offered the first systematic theory of speech acts. Reinach received a doctorate in philosophy from the University of Munich; his dissertation was on the concept of cause in penal law. It was within the context of legal language that Reinach argued in favour of the relevance of speech acts which he referred to, presumably independently of Reid's work, as 'social acts, that is acts of the mind that are performed in the very act of speaking'. Reinach (1913) provided a detailed taxonomy of social acts as performative* utterances and their modification, and stated very clearly that the utterance (*Äusserung*) of a social act is different from the inner experience of emotions like anger or shame and from statements (*Konstatierungen*) about experiences. It is precisely the recourse to the physical medium, the *Äusserung*, that transforms the philosophical category of action into a social act. Drawing on previous literature, Reinach separated actions from internal experiences. Then he discriminated between external actions like kissing or killing and linguistic actions, and within this class he distinguished between social acts, which are performed in every act of speaking, and actions, where signs are used but no speech act is performed such as in 'solitary asserting' and emotive uses of language. The final distinction refers to the linguistic actions performed in uttering performative formulae and the linguistic and non-linguistic actions whose performance has an effect on the state of affairs and even changes it.

While Reinach's ideas were spreading through the Munich scholars, at Oxford A. J. Ayer, considered the philosophical successor of Bertrand Russell, deemed philosophically interesting only those sentences that can be subject to the truth-condition analysis. In line with the logical positivism* of the Vienna Circle, Ayer developed the verification principle in *Language, Truth and Logic* (1936) where he stated that a sentence is meaningful only if it has verifiable import. Sentences expressing judgements, evaluation and the like were not to be objects of scientific inquiry. This stance, which is now known as the 'descriptive fallacy', led him into conflict with

Oxford linguist philosophers like Gilbert Ryle and J. L. Austin, who instead were greatly influenced by Ludwig Wittgenstein. He claimed that a language consists of a wide multiplicity of structures and usages that logical positivists had neglected to analyse but which encompass the majority of what human beings say in their construction of meaning.

Following Wittgenstein's insights into language and putting himself against the positivist background, Gilbert Ryle rejected the Cartesian mind-body dualism in *The Concept of Mind* (1949), and revived the centrality of the standard uses of language, thus contributing to the development of 'ordinary language philosophy'* in Oxford.

Taking the same veil and influenced by Husserl, Austin rejected the account that only sentences that are meant to describe a state of affairs are worth studying, and he observed that verifiable sentences are only a small part of the large amount of utterances produced by language users. Not all utterances express propositions: many perform actions as, for example, greetings or orders, which resist a truth-conditional analysis. Indeed, most of the sentences uttered by speakers are used in such a way as to perform more fundamental things in verbal interactions, such as naming a ship, marrying a couple, or making a request. In daily life we perform many ordinary verbal actions, and utterances are used in speech events to accomplish all that is achieved through language. Austin's speech act theory was first delineated in the notes he prepared for some lectures interestingly entitled *Words and Deeds* which he delivered at Oxford University from 1952 to 1954. Such notes constituted the basis on which he developed his Harvard lectures in 1955, posthumously published in 1962. In the first phase of development of his theory, Austin retained the Aristotelian distinction between apophantic and non-apophantic logos, and introduced the terms of constative utterances and performative utterances, where the former describe or constate a state of affairs and the latter perform actions. Austin later realised that a clear distinction between the two types of utterances is unsustainable. If, for example, we say 'There is a rat under your chair', we do more than assert a state of affairs: we warn someone about a possible danger. Assertions can thus be used to perform such acts as to warn, to apologise, and many more. Austin then abandoned the dichotomy and contended that to say something equals to perform something.

According to Austin, when we say something, we perform three acts simultaneously: a locutionary act, an illocutionary act, and a perlocutionary act. At the locutionary level, a speaker produces sounds (phonetic act) which are well ordered with respect to the phonological system and grammar of a particular language (phatic act), and carry some sense with respect to the semantic and pragmatic rules of that language (rhetic act). At the illocutionary level, he is expressing his intention by virtue of conventions shared in his speech community. At the perlocutionary level, he performs a third act which includes the consequences of his speaking, and he has only limited control over them. In order for the speech

act to be successful, it must fulfil some appropriateness conditions, or 'felicity' conditions: locution is successful if words and sounds are correctly produced; illocution is appropriate if it meets the conditions for its realisation; perlocution may be effective when it produces consequences desired by the producer. The notion of illocutionary force embodies the philosophical notion of intentionality, which can be expressed by performing a speech act through three modalities: (1) directly or indirectly through the performance of another speech act ('Pass me the salt' versus 'Can you pass me the salt?'); literally or non-literally depending on the way words are used ('Stick it in your head'); (3) explicitly or inexplicitly when meaning is spelled out fully or incompletely ('I'll be back later, Mary's ready'). Indirectness and nonliterality are disambiguated by way of a conversational implicature*, whereas explicitation is achieved through expansion or completion of what one says.

John Searle, one of Austin's students, contributed widely to developing speech act theory, which he addressed from the viewpoint of intentionality. Specifically he conceived of linguistic intentionality as derived from mental intentionality. In his *Speech Acts* (1969) Searle claimed that Austin's 'felicity conditions' are constitutive rules of speech acts to the extent that to perform a speech act means to meet the conventional rules which constitute a specific speech act. Moving from this approach and analysing the act of promising, Searle proposed a classification of speech acts into four categories: (1) propositional content (what the speech act is about); (2) preparatory condition, which states the prerequisites for the speech act; (3) sincerity condition (the speaker has to sincerely intend to keep a promise); and (4) essential condition (the speaker's intention that the utterance counts as an act and as such is to be recognised by the hearer). One of Searle's major contributions to the theory refers to indirectness, that is the mismatch between an utterance and an illocutionary force.

The interpretation of indirect speech acts has drawn a great deal of attention. Drawing on H. P. Grice's pragmatics, most scholars assume that some inferential work on the part of the hearer is required in order to identify the speaker's communicative intention and the core question is how such inference can be computed. Searle (1975) assumes that the hearer recognises both a direct-literal force, which he understands as the secondary force, and an indirect-nonliteral force, which is the primary force. Similarly Dan Gordon and George Lakoff (1975) argue that inference rules that they label 'conversational postulates' reduce the amount of inferential computing necessary to disambiguate an indirect speech act. Jerrold Sadock (1974) departs from the inferential hypothesis and proposes 'the idiom model' by claiming that a speech act like 'Can you pass me the salt?' is promptly interpreted as a request and needs no inference.

Speech act theory is now receiving great attention and valid theoretical proposals from cognitive linguists. Klaus Panther and Linda Thornburg (1998) claim that our knowledge of illocutionary meaning may be systematically organised in the form of what they call 'illocutionary scenarios'. They are formed by a before, a core, and an after component. If a person wants someone to bring him his pen, he can utter a direct speech act like 'Bring me my pen', which exploits the core component, or he can make his request indirectly exploiting either the before component ('Can you bring me my pen?') where the modal verb 'can' points to the hearer's ability to perform the action, or the after component ('You will bring me my pen, won't you?') where the auxiliary 'will' instantiates the after component of the request scenario. Panther (2005) makes the point that metonymies provide natural 'inference schemas' which are constantly used by speakers in meaning construction and interpretation. Scenarios may be accessed metonymically by invoking relevant parts of them. Indirect requests like 'Can you open the door?', 'Will you close the window?', 'Do you have hot chocolate?' exploit all pre-conditions for the performance of a request, that is, the ability and willingness of the hearer, and his possession of the required object. Such pre-conditions are used to stand for the whole speech act category. By means of the explicit mention of one of the components of the scenario, it is possible for the speaker to afford access to the hearer to the whole illocutionary category of 'requesting' in such a way that the utterance is effortlessly interpreted as a request. With a view to improving Panther's proposal, Francisco Ruiz de Mendoza (2007) contends that illocutionary meaning is directly tied to the notion of *Idealised Cognitive Models* (ICMs), which are principle-governed cognitive structures. Illocutionary scenarios represent the way in which language users construct interactional meaning representations abstracted away from a number of stereotypical illocutionary situations. In an indirect request like 'I fancy going out for dinner' the hearer understands the implicated meaning by relying on high-level situational ICMs – that is, on the generic knowledge that expressing a wish indirectly corresponds to asking for its fulfillment. Thus, it is exactly the quick and easy retrieval from our long-term memory of a stored illocutionary scenario that allows us to identify the nature of indirectness.

Speech act theory is a thought-provoking issue which has attracted the interest of philosophers of language and linguists from diverse theoretical persuasions. Manifold aspects of the theory are being debated such as the classification of speech acts, the relationship between speech acts and culture, and the acquisition of speech acts by children, which proves how this area of language research still provides room for developments and new insights.

Primary sources

Aristotle (1941). *De Interpretatione.* New York: Random House. 38–61.

Austin, J. L. (1962). *How to Do Things with Words.* Oxford: Oxford University Press.

Gordon D. and G. Lakoff (1975). 'Conversational postulates'. In P. Cole and J. L. Morgan (eds), *Syntax and Semantics, Speech Acts.* New York: Academic Press. 83–106.

Husserl, E. (1900/1). *Logische Untersuchungen.* Halle: Nyemeier.

Panther, K. U. and L. Thornburg (1998). 'A cognitive approach to inferencing in conversation'. *Journal of Pragmatics* 30: 755–69.

Panther K. U. (2005). 'The role of conceptual metonymy in meaning construction'. In F. Ruiz de Mendoza and S.Peña (eds), *Cognitive Linguistics. Internal Dynamics and Interdisciplinary Interaction.* Berlin: Mouton de Gruyter. 353–86.

Reinach, A. (1913). 'Die apriorischen Grundlagen des bürgerlichen Rechtes'. In *Jahrbuch für Philosophie und phänomenologische Forschung* 1: 685–847.

Ruiz de Mendoza, F. (2007). 'High level cognitive models: in search of a unified framework for inferential and grammatical behavior'. In Krzysztof Kosecki (ed.), *Perspectives on Metonymy.* Frankfurt: Peter Lang. 1130.

Ryle G. (1949). *The Concept of Mind.* London: Hutchinson.

Sadock J. (1974). *Toward a Linguistic Theory of Speech Acts.* New York: Academic Press.

Searle J. R. (1969). *Speech Acts.* Cambridge: Cambridge University Press.

Searle J. R. (1975). 'Indirect speech acts'. In P. Cole and J. L. Morgan (eds), *Syntax and Semantics 3: Speech Acts.* New York: Academic Press. 59–82.

Wittgenstein L. (1953). *Philosophical Investigations.* Oxford: Blackwell.

Further reading

Ayer, A. J. (1936). *Language, Truth and Logic.* London: Gollancz.

Brentano, F. (1874). *Psychologie vom empirischen Standpunkt.* Leipzig: Duncke and Humbolt.

Marty, A. (1908). *Untersuchungen zur Grundlegung der allgemeinen Grammatik und Sprachphilosophie.* Halle: Nyemeier.

Reid, T. (1894). *The Works of Thomas Reid*. Edinburgh: Maclachlan and Stewart.

Annalisa Baicchi

STRUCTURALISM

A theoretical and methodological approach in linguistics and other human (including social) sciences that attempts to gain insights into its subject matter by assuming that everything to do with human beings is built of more or less autonomous systems as relations of oppositions. These oppositions may be of different types but in general are binary relations. The Swiss linguist Ferdinand de Saussure is often said to have initiated a structuralist movement, school or intellectual world view, rather than developing a coherent theory, and in linguistics a distinction is traditionally made between (Saussurean) European structuralism and American structuralism, the main figure of which is the linguist Leonard Bloomfield. Structuralism in a broad sense has mainly been applied in anthropology, especially by the French anthropologist Claude Lévi-Strauss and other French thinkers, and in literary studies.

See also: Distinctive Features; Glossematics; Langue/Parole; Poststructuralism; Sense/Reference; Signs and Semiotics; Transformational-Generative Grammar
Key Thinkers: Barthes, Roland; Boas, Franz; Bloomfield, Leonard; Derrida, Jacques; Hjelmslev, Louis; Jakobson, Roman; Sapir, Edward; Saussure, Ferdinand de; Whorf, Benjamin Lee

The term structure is derived from Latin *structura* (from *struere*, 'to build') and just as human beings build houses, so structuralism contends that human existence – the physiological and mental set-up of individuals and their social life – is also built from structures in a way that more or less governs what people are able to think and do. In addition to the limitations of the laws of physics and rules of social behaviour, structuralism also maintains that less overt structures restrict psychological and behavioural alternatives by controlling individuals' preferences. In linguistics structuralism is affiliated with the so-called Saussurean ideas about language and other sign-systems (dealt with in 'semiology', later 'semiotics') and it may be most easily understood in the conceptual framework that is attributed to Saussure.

As opposed to the use of language (French *parole*), there is a system of languages and language (*langue*) that is a set of inherent relations that build a structure. In order to arrive at an exhaustive and consistent description of this system, one has to assert that the description is historically specific: characteristic of an abstraction from language use at a certain time and place. In other words, it produces what was labelled a synchronic description of the system. This is opposed to the view prevalent in the nineteenth century that the history and the genealogy of languages was the only (legitimate) theme in the language sciences; the results yielded in this tradition was labelled by structuralists as diachronic description. It is a general experience that words are put together in chains, and a basic notion in structural linguistics is that of syntagm. But since this is a matter of language use, the corresponding notion of paradigm is often more interesting for structuralists. A paradigm is not a discernible and evident entity like a syntagm because we can only identify a paradigm by abstraction and experiment: by playing with the words of a sentence by substituting them. In that way we learn that paradigms can be said to be sets of words that can replace each other on certain positions in chains of words, words that accordingly must be different in one respect and similar in some other respect. This potential of words is said by structuralists to be a matter of how their properties are structural and can be described as such.

The basic opposition, then, is that between the form of a word, the signifier (*signifiant*), and its meaning, the signified (*signifié*). According to Saussure, this relation is arbitrary, a claim that has caused some controversy. But one might say that the relation is, in principle, arbitrary while it is, evidently, not historically arbitrary since we use words in – almost – the same way as we have experienced them when acquiring our mother tongue. From this point of departure, both form and meaning can be subject to structural scrutiny. The extremes of such scrutiny are, on the one hand, phonology and, on the other, semantic orderings of the sense and meanings of words and their mutual relations within the whole of the language system. Phonology is the study of phonemes*: that is, abstract entities identified as generalisations of speech sounds and building a mental system of oppositions that makes the individual language user able to decode the sound chains as words in a language. The enterprise of setting up such phonological systems is often a fairly straightforward project, but the analysis of word meanings is a more challenging task. Some approaches in semantics can be regarded as conceived within the framework of structuralism, for instance the notions of semantic fields and semantic components describing the features creating the basis of semantic oppositions.

The methods of structuralism make no consistent conceptual framework. Phonology investigates the sound systems of a language or a dialect in order to find the distinctive sound features that separate words. But some linguists take different methodological approaches. For example, Louis Hjelmslev, the inventor of glossematics*, started out by dividing a text into two and he continued like this until he ended up with the phonemes. One of the basic problems of structuralism is what answers are given to the question about the nature of meaning. There is obviously a difference between word meaning and the meaning of life, even though appeal to word meanings as oppositional relations may not be unequivocally convincing and even though the question of the meaning of general, abstract and fictional expressions may not be straightforwardly answered. This vagueness in what meaning is may be the background of the diffusion of the concept of structuralism into other academic fields such as anthropology and literature, and its popularity in semiotics.

Although it is often stated as fact, the attribution of the idea of structuralism in linguistics to Saussure may not be totally justified. The source of what we know about his thoughts is *Cours de Linguistique Générale* (*Course in General Linguistics*) from 1916, a work that is based on the lecture notes of some of his students. Furthermore, Saussure may be considered only part of an emerging movement in linguistics that could not reconcile itself to nineteenth-century positivism. Finally, the term structuralism had been used by psychologists in the nineteenth century but it was not used by linguists before the end of the 1920s; Roman Jakobson probably was the first to offer a definition of the theoretical concept. The expressions 'structure' and 'structural' in discussing linguistic phenomena were also used in the first half of twentieth century.

Nevertheless Saussure is usually considered the founding father of linguistic structuralism, and his thoughts as they are presented in *Cours* have had a considerable impact on general structuralist thinking; structuralism reached its peak as an -ism between 1930 and 1960. The broad movement of structuralism was not a unified endeavour but rather a patchwork of different groupings with different goals, different basic assumptions and different kinds of subject matter. In retrospect, European structuralism can be said to encompass some more important groups of people and some more peripheral groupings and individuals, while one person in particular is a travelling herald of the structuralist message: Roman Jakobson.

It may seem ironical that Jakobson, a linguist and passionate reader of Russian poetry, with a background affiliation with Russian formalism, was to become the main inspiring force of European structuralism, the Prague School (which was, with the Geneva School, the centre of European structuralism), and of American structuralism. Passing through Europe and ending up in the United States, he and other Russians contributed significantly to what has become known as the Prague School of structuralism. Fleeing from World War Two, he visited Denmark and influenced the glossematic version of structuralism, and in the United States he inspired anthropology and other sciences, at the same time more or less directly influencing Chomsky's ideas about linguistic universals.

European structuralism was not only a countermovement with respect to positivism but after World War One it was also an opportunity to find an alternative to the dominance of the nineteenth-century German neogrammarians and their 'sound laws'. Most of the characteristics of structuralism mentioned above apply to European structuralism, and a number of other features can be mentioned. Structuralism deals with systems (a word that can, in this context, be taken as a synonym for structure; structuralists who talk about 'structured systems' use a pleonastic term), and knowledge about these systems (the entities of which are considered at least as real as observable entities) are arrived at through abstraction and analysis. The systems are also regarded as social. Even though Saussure's basic assumption about the linguistic sign was that it is a *entité psychique* (Saussure 1916: 99), or psychological entity, in general structuralists maintain that they talk about social phenomena, albeit studied through analysis of what people say. Indeed this may be a necessary theoretical prerequisite if one wishes to avoid philosophical inquiry into the problem of what is private, what is public, and what role language plays in making the private public.

European structuralism has had wide-ranging consequences for the sometimes not particularly explicit basic assumptions of all disciplines of modern European linguistics. This is especially true in phonology, where any textbook on pronunciation and speech sounds takes up the phoneme system of the language in question. This involves ascertaining the distinctive, contrastive features of minimal pairs (of words) in order to identify single phonemes, and, following this procedure, the objective of the process is to find all the phonemes of a single language. This *modus operandi* is now almost a standard method in phonology, whether phonologists perceive themselves as structuralists or not.

Phonology is a fairly technical discipline in linguistics, but structuralist ideas have not confined themselves to intricate linguistic phenomena: they have also been adopted by scholars in fields outside linguistics. In anthropology, one of the main figures is Claude Lévi-Strauss, who met Jakobson in New York, and who attempted to show that the myths and rituals of tribal cultures work as regulating kinship systems and other social institutions. He also analysed them in line with structural linguistic analysis

conceiving of them as 'grammars' intrinsic to the human mind. Whereas Lévi-Strauss studied the built-in meaning of tribal behaviour, other French structuralists like Roland Barthes and Jacques Derrida have applied structuralist thought to literature; the French intellectual Jacques Lacan did the same to psychoanalysis and the French philosopher Louis Althusser founded a 'Marxist structuralism'. In Europe, therefore, structuralism as a broad notion is nowadays mostly associated with French structuralism, and while the structural mind in twenty-first century Europe is most likely not a member of a club named 'structuralism', structuralist beliefs are almost common sense in many theoretical, often implicit, basic assumptions.

In contrast to the European structuralistic vein – which was linguistic in its outset and all the time concerned at some level with linguistic meaning – American structuralism tended to ignore meaning and focus on linguistic form, while also in general maintaining so-called linguistic relativity*. Both attitudes can be explained in terms of the background of American linguistics. The United States was built on a mixture of immigrants and their descendants whose cultures had long philological traditions, while also comprising the ethnic Native American cultures, the anthropological and linguistic documentation of which was an immense task. It may therefore seem natural that describing each language on its own terms would be a reasonable goal, and this view, in combination with the low priority given to semantics, logically gave rise to the fairly extreme idea that the way people think depends on the structure of their language, the so-called Sapir-Whorf hypothesis.

Franz Boas is regarded as the founder of American structuralism. An anthropologist untrained in linguistics, he contributed notably to the description of the phonological and grammatical structures of Native American languages. Boas incremented the prestige of language studies as a part of anthropological studies, which traditionally included archaeology and cultural and physical anthropology. But he was also an advocate of relativism, a view that he passed on to his students and followers, and, in line with this, one of his main concerns was to promote the basic methods of fieldwork. If languages are more or less self-contained entities, it sounds reasonable to call for careful and detailed investigation into each particular language in order to offer exhaustive descriptions. And this may be one of the only reasons for the predicate structuralism to this stage of American structuralism: what was accounted for through linguistic fieldwork were the internal structures of particular languages.

The same characteristic may be attributed to the most prominent American structuralist, Leonard Bloomfield. In his principal theoretical work, *Language* (1935), the words 'structure' and 'structural' are not frequently found. The book offers more of a methodological account of categories and their hierarchies than an all-encompassing and consistent theory, but there are two features that are worth mentioning. In opposition to European structuralism, Bloomfield and American structuralism emphasise sentences as linguistic units, a bias that goes back to Boas and the (basically pragmatic) idea that human beings communicate in sentences, not by using words in isolation. The other thing is the fact that, contrary to general opinion, Bloomfield did not totally abandon linguistic semantics from his linguistic approach. For instance, he appeals to a special kind of meaning:

> Since our study ordinarily concerns only the distinctive features of form and meaning, I shall henceforth usually omit the qualification linguistic or distinctive, and speak simply of forms and meanings, ignoring the existence of non-distinctive features. A form is often said to express its meaning. (Bloomfield 1935: 141)

This is also by necessity consistent with his hierarchy of categories which would otherwise have been impractical because the notions 'meaningful' and 'meaningless' are necessary theoretical concepts for the distinctions between the classes of linguistic units, for instance in the expression the 'smallest meaningful unit . . .'.

But some of Bloomfield's followers in American structuralism took it further away from semantics and linguistic meaning, one of them being Zellig Harris, whose principal work actually has the word 'structural' in its title. And these two themes, the meanings of the words 'structuralism, structural and structure', and the question of whether semantics can be disposed of, are being transferred to the modern world's most famous linguist, Noam Chomsky. It may seem ironical that Chomsky's programmatic work, *Syntactic Structures* (1957), dealt with formal (mathematical in a broad sense) descriptions of phrase structures, accordingly using the term 'structure' while explicitly abandoning the idea of meaning having any role to play in this formal approach to linguistics. The position is repeated in *New Horizons in the Study of Language and Mind*:

> As soon as the first attempts were made to provide actual descriptions of languages forty years ago, it was discovered that the intricacy of structure is far beyond anything that had been imagined, that traditional descriptions of form and meaning merely skimmed the surface while structuralist ones were almost irrelevant. (2000: 122)

The outcome of the structuralist project will find its place (cf. Chomsky 2000: 5) in this the latest theoretical paradigm, labelled generative grammar, in which the term 'structure' is a basic and axiomatic one, and in which the unearthed structures are assumed to be mental, but have nothing to do with meaning. On the one hand, Chomsky seems to carry further some of tenets of American structuralism and, on the other, he dissociates himself from its basic theoretical ideas and methods. In a way he is back at the starting point of Saussure (maybe not as a historical figure but as the icon of European structuralism), and in another way he is not. He says, like Saussure, that he studies mental (what Saussure calls psychological) phenomena, and, like Saussure, he does so as abstractions from mental products: words. In this respect they put forward comparable ideas. Where they part is the question of which

phenomena they study. Saussure and his followers see language as words, primarily their phoneme structure and their semantics, while Chomsky sees language as phrase structures.

One of the distinctions set up by some structuralists in linguistics is that between form and substance, meaning that, for instance, the physical nature of speech sounds studied in phonetics is interesting but secondary to the important effort of finding and modelling the phonemes – as mental and material entities – as the form of language systems. This illustrates a fundamental problem with structuralism, that some of its theoretical notions are extremely general, almost universal. Likewise, there is a certain kind of vagueness in the terms 'form' and 'structure'. From their classical origin they are the heirs of words that did not have different meanings. 'Form' and 'structure' meant almost the same, and in some contexts they still do. In formal logic, for instance, the *raison d'être* of arguments is that they have a certain structure, while in other contexts, for instance in architecture, it may be reasonable to distinguish between the form (shape and surface) of a building and its inner structure. So basically, the proposal of structuralism seems to be no more than the idea that things in the world are ordered in ways that make them more than silhouettes in a nebulous landscape. As such, structuralism has pervaded modern Western civilisation.

Primary sources

Benveniste, Emile (1939). 'Nature du signe linguistique'. *Acta Linguistica* Vol. I, fasc. 1: 23–9.

Bloomfield, Leonard (US 1933, UK 1935). *Language*. London: George Allen and Unwin.

Boas, Franz (ed.) (1911, 1922, 1934). *Handbook of American Indian Languages, Parts 1, 2, 3*. Washington, DC: Smithsonian Institution, Bureau of American Ethnology.

Bröndal, Viggo (1939). 'Linguistique structurale'. *Acta Linguistica* Vol. I, fasc. 1: 2–10.

Chomsky, Noam (1957). *Syntactic Structures*. The Hague. Paris: Mouton.

Chomsky, Noam (2000). *New Horizons in the Study of Language and Mind*. Cambridge: Cambridge University Press.

Harris, Zellig (1951). *Methods in Structural Linguistics*. Chicago: University of Chicago Press.

Jakobson, Roman (2002). *Selected Writings* Vol. I–VIII. Third edition. Berlin/New York: Mouton de Gruyter, 1962–88.

Lévi-Strauss, Claude (1958). *Anthropologie structurale*. Paris: Plon.

Saussure, Ferdinand de (1916). *Cours de Linguistique Generale*. Paris: Payot.

Zwirner, Eberhard (1939). 'Phonologie und Phonetik'. *Acta Linguistica* Vol. I, fasc. 1: 29–47.

Further reading

de Beaugrande, Robert (1991). *Linguistic Theory: The Discourse of Fundamental Works*. New York: Longman.

Huck, Geoffrey J. (1995). *Ideology and Linguistic Theory. Noam Chomsky and the Deep Structure Debates*. London and New York: Routledge.

Koerner, E. F. K. and R. E. Asher (eds) (1955). *Concise History of the Language Sciences. From the Sumerians to the Cognitivists*. Oxford: Elsevier Science, Pergamon.

Newmeyer, Frederick J. (1998). *Language Form and Language Function*. Cambridge, MA: MIT Press.

Hans Götzsche

SYSTEMIC-FUNCTIONAL GRAMMAR

An approach to linguistic description which aims to provide a comprehensive account of how language is used in context for communication. The approach views language as a resource that is fundamentally shaped by the uses that people make of it; it therefore aims to explain the forms of language in terms of the meanings that they express, and to develop a grammar which is designed to 'make it possible to say sensible and useful things about any text, spoken or written' (Halliday 1994: xv).

See also: Corpora; (Critical) Discourse Analysis; Integrationism; Langue/Parole; Metaphor; Modality; Transformational-Generative Grammar
Key Thinkers: Halliday, M. A. K.; Bernstein, Basil; Firth, J. R.; Hjelmslev, Louis; Malinowsky, Bronislaw; Sinclair, John; Whorf, Benjamin Lee

Systemic-functional grammar (SFG) originated with M. A. K. Halliday, building especially on the ideas of his tutor J. R. Firth, in publications from the 1960s on, with major contributions by other scholars such as Ruqaiya Hasan and, in more recent years, Jim

Martin and Christian Matthiessen among many others. From early in its development, SFG has had two main distinguishing features, which are reflected in the name. First, whereas many approaches focus on the syntagmatic, 'horizontal' dimension of how constituents may be combined with other constituents in a well-formed structure, SFG prioritises the choices that are open to the speaker at any particular point in an utterance – the paradigmatic, 'vertical' dimension. The grammatical structures are then seen as the outcome of choices from those available (the technical term in SFG is that structures 'realise' choices). Sets of choices between options can most economically be shown in the form of systems: for example, 'if A is the case, there is a choice between B and C; if B is chosen, there is then a choice between D, E and F; but if C is chosen, there is then a choice between G and H'. Systems embody the Saussurean concept of *valeur*: a linguistic form has meaning by virtue of the other possible forms that could have been chosen instead. Hence this is a 'systemic' grammar. Second, the model is oriented primarily towards meaning rather than form: that is, its aim is to describe how wordings are used in expressing meanings. What a linguistic form consists of is seen as less important than the function that it performs in the clause: hence, this is a 'functional' grammar. The following paragraphs expand on these distinguishing features in turn.

The systemic nature of the grammar can be illustrated with a relatively simple example. The choices at nominal group level between different kinds of determiner (such as 'the' and 'a') can

be represented as a system, labelled determination (names of systems are traditionally written in small capitals in SFG). The entry condition (the linguistic context in which the choices apply) is 'nominal group'; the first choice (at least in English) is between 'specific' ('the [cat]') and 'non-specific' ('a [cat]'). Each option taken opens up a further set of choices until a formal realisation is reached: for example, selecting 'specific: personal: interactant: addressee' leads to the deictic (determiner) form 'your [cat]', whereas selecting 'specific: demonstrative: selective: near + plural' leads to 'these [cats]'. As this last instance shows, some sets of choices in the system may be simultaneous: that is, rather than only choosing one of two or more mutually exclusive options, the speaker chooses from two sub-systems at the same level. Thus, taking the 'selective' option means choosing both between 'near' and 'far' and between 'plural' and 'non-plural'. Part of the system is shown in Figure 7 (three dots indicates where more delicate choices have been omitted). Simultaneous choices are enclosed by a curly bracket; and the formal realisations (in this case specific words rather than general structures) are signalled by downward-slanting arrows. A complete version of the system can be found as Figure 6-2 in Halliday and Matthiessen (2006: 313).

Systems do not operate in isolation: they interact with each other. For example, the system of polarity (positive/negative) interacts with a number of other systems, including determination: here, a combination of 'negative' with 'non-specific: total' gives the deictic 'no' as in 'no [cats]'.

As relatively simple systems build up into system networks in this way, the complexity increases, but that reflects faithfully the complexity of the meaning choices that are realised in any utterance.

The other key feature of the grammar is its functional nature. In contrast to form-oriented approaches which concentrate more or less exclusively on how clauses are constructed, with meaning excluded and dealt with separately in a semantics component, SFG is designed to map the relationships between forms and meanings in a consistent way. This has a number of important implications. First, the most important labels are functional, or semantic (telling us what the elements mean), rather than formal (telling us what they consist of). This can be seen in the terms used in Figure 7: they indicate what meaning choice is being made: for example, whether the nominal group is being determined, or specified, in terms of possession or of location in relation to the speaker. Even traditional labels such as subject are reinterpreted in SFG as not being purely syntactic ('controlling' agreement with the verb) but as having meaning: the subject expresses the entity which is represented as responsible for the validity of the proposition expressed in the clause (that is, the proposition is represented as true for, or applicable to, this entity).

This connects with a second implication: whereas many approaches are parsimonious in that they place great value on achieving maximally economical descriptions of grammar, SFG is 'extravagant' in Halliday's term. In order to capture the multivariate relations between meaning and structure, the grammatical model has to allow for different perspectives on the clause, providing a much richer and

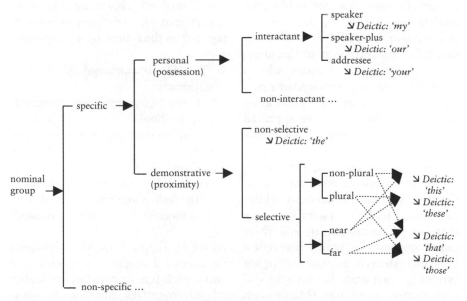

Figure 7 Part of the system of DETERMINATION in English

227

more informative set of descriptions. This then leads on to a third important implication: since the communicative function of utterances can only be fully understood in relation to their meaning in context, the grammar has to be designed in such a way that the analyst can 'shunt' between specific choices at clause level or below and the context within which the utterance is used. For example, an interrogative such as 'Why aren't you leaving?' may function as a question, but in certain contexts it may instead function as a command. The 'context' here would include who the interactants are, what their relationship is, how power is distributed in the culture (who has the right to give commands to whom in particular circumstances), and so on. In many approaches, the use of the interrogative as a command would be treated as in some way an extension of its 'literal' decontextualised use as a question and dealt with separately as a matter of pragmatics; but, in SFG, the analyst would take all these factors into account in arriving at a full grammatical characterisation of the utterance, exploring the reasons why a particular meaning expressed in a particular way at a particular point in an interaction is likely to have appeared appropriate to the speaker in a particular situation.

The two key bases of the model, system and function, come together in the concept of metafunctions. Halliday argues that the system networks that can be identified fall into three main groupings, with interaction between systems in any one group, but little or no interaction between the systems across groupings (Matthiessen 2006 provides corpus-based evidence to support this claim). Thus, mood (declarative, interrogative, imperative) interacts with polarity in that, for example, the position of the negative particle 'n't' varies in relation to the subject with different mood choices; but transitivity roles (see below) are unaffected by whether the clause is declarative or interrogative. The three groupings of systems make up what Halliday calls three metafunctions, each of which realise different broad types of meaning.

The interpersonal metafunction comprises those systems which function to enact social relations between addressers and addressees, to express the speaker's viewpoint on events and things in the world, and to influence the addressee's behaviour or views. Apart from mood and polarity, some of the main systems are modality*, mood tag, and, at the semantic level, speech function (whether the clause functions as statement, question, command or offer). This is the area of the grammar in which differences in meaning such as the following are captured:

The flight is confirmed. (declarative, statement)

Is the flight confirmed? (interrogative, question)

Confirm the flight. (imperative, command)

Would you confirm the flight? (modalised interrogative, command)

The flight mustn't be confirmed. (negative modalised declarative, command)

As the examples show, SFG highlights the crucial distinction between mood and speech function: for example, not all interrogatives function as questions. The choice of forms may seem to be imposed naturally by the context. For example, if you want information you use an interrogative question; but in fact speakers in different contexts consistently exploit choices. There is, for instance, an important difference between expressing a command through the imperative or the modalised interrogative wordings shown above; and there is also a choice between the interrogative question 'Is the flight confirmed' and the declarative question 'The flight is confirmed?'. These choices depend on, and simultaneously reflect the speaker's view of, the context of utterance. A basic tenet of SFG is that any difference in wordings is the result of meaningful choice.

The second metafunction is the experiential. This is language seen from the perspective of how it is used to talk about events, states and entities in the world, to construe the speaker's view of the world. This kind of meaning is traditionally taken – even in many linguistic approaches – as 'real' meaning. In SFG, however, it is only one kind of meaning: in simple terms, why something is said (the interpersonal angle) and how it is said (the textual – see below) is as important as what is said (the experiential). An experiential analysis of a clause focuses on the process (realised by the verb), the participants in that process (typically, but not always, realised by nominal groups), and the circumstance(s) in which the process happens (typically realised by adverbial groups or prepositional phrases). Processes can be divided into six main types, which reflect the cognitive categories that we use to make sense of the events around us (Halliday and Matthiessen 2006 expand on this relation between grammar and cognition): material (processes of action), mental (processes of sensing, which construe our interior worlds), relational (processes of being and having), verbal (processes of conveying messages, by saying, and so on.), behavioural (characteristically human physiological processes), and existential (processes of existing). Each of these types can be further subdivided into more delicate options: for example, one subdivision of material processes, the largest group with the greatest number of cross-cutting options, is between 'creative' (a process which results in a new entity, such as 'build') and transformative (a process which involves a pre-existing entity, such as 'cut'). The participants in each process type are given different labels which reflect their relation to the process. There is no space to give a full account, but Table 2 gives a flavour of transitivity analysis.

It is worth highlighting that transitivity may be 'blind' to certain parts of the clause. The clause in Table 3 has the same transitivity configuration as the first example in Table 2.

The unlabelled constituents are dealt with in another part of the grammar (in the example above, they are interpersonal in nature). Transitivity labels are semantic, but it is important to note that each corresponds to different grammatical possibilities. Halliday (1994: xx) stresses that 'all the categories employed must be clearly "there" in the grammar of the language'. There is only space to mention two of these grammatical reflexes as examples: material processes cannot project (that is have a 'that' clause as

The man	drove	the car	fast
Actor	Process: material, transformative	Goal	Circumstance

I	recognised	the driver
Senser	Process: mental, cognition	Phenomenon

The man	was	a fast driver
Carrier	Process: relational, attributive	Attribute

Table 2

Might	the man	have	driven	the car	too fast	perhaps	?
-	Actor	-	Process: material	Goal	Circumstance		

Table 3

their complement), whereas mental and verbal processes can; mental and behavioural processes must normally have human sensers/behavers, whereas material processes have no such restriction.

The third metafunction is the textual. This is the part of the grammar which is concerned with how the meanings in the clause are organised to fit in with the co-text of the surrounding messages and with the wider context of the utterance. The textual system that has been most fully explored is that of theme: the theme of a clause is the initial experiential constituent, which has a special role in signalling how the current clause relates to clauses around it. Very broadly, there is a choice between unmarked themes (where theme and subject are the same), which typically signal continuity of some kind in the topic, and marked themes (where something other than subject, such as an adverbial adjunct,

is theme), which signal that there is some kind of specific contextual pressure at work, often associated with a change of textual frame. For example, in the following extract from a guide to a historical monument, the choice of themes (underlined) is designed to help the reader to follow the text organisation. The marked themes (in italics) signal that the text is moving on to deal with a different part of the church, whereas the unmarked themes signal that the text is, for the moment, continuing to focus on the same part of the church introduced in the preceding marked theme.

On the northern side of the church was a porch ... Further east, on the west side of the north transept was a room ... The east wall of the room was divided into three parts ... Its use is not known for certain, but it may have been a vestry and sacristy ...

Rise in radiation exposure	leads	to warning
Actor	*Process: material*	*Circumstance*

Table 4

One factor which complicates the already complex three-dimensional picture above is grammatical metaphor, which has been identified in SFG as a crucial mechanism by which language can expand the potential meanings that can be expressed. Grammatical metaphor* involves the use of wordings which do not map in a straightforward way onto the meanings that they express. This can be seen in the following newspaper headline: 'Rise in radiation exposure leads to warning'. A transitivity analysis of this clause is in Table 4.

This captures part of the meaning as it is expressed; but it is clearly possible to unpack the clause into more 'congruent' wordings which reflect more naturally the events in the world that are being represented. One possible wording (some of the 'missing' information is supplied from the newspaper article itself) would be 'Because [= 'leads to'] doctors are exposing [= 'exposure'] patients to radiation [= 'radiation'] more often [= 'rise'], researchers are warning [= 'warning'] that . . .'. This is a much less economical way of representing the meaning, but it is also more natural, in that it is easier to process in speech and easier for a non-specialist to understand. Grammatical metaphor of this kind is particularly associated with formal technical writing. It is not just an impressive-sounding way of saying simple things (though it is certainly used in that way in some texts); it allows new kinds of meanings to be made. In the headline, 'radiation' is an instance of metaphor, but it is extremely difficult to unpack it: it has become an accepted term for referring in a condensed form to a complex phenomenon. Grammatical metaphor is often ignored in other grammatical approaches; but, since SFG is a grammar of discourse, it has a central place in the model.

SFG is the most fully-developed alternative to what was, for much of the twentieth century, the main linguistic paradigm, which aimed to split the problem of describing language into separate areas such as syntax, semantics, sociolinguistics, and so on. SFG rejects that kind of 'divide-and-conquer' solution, on the grounds that language is a resource for social communication and can only be properly understood if that whole picture is taken into account at all stages of investigation. Its orientation to language in use means that it has been widely adopted in discourse analysis* and corpus linguistics and in a range of other areas, most notably education, natural language generation and language acquisition studies.

Primary sources

Halliday, M. A. K. (1978). *Language as Social Semiotic: The Social Interpretation of Language and Meaning.* London: Arnold.

Halliday, M. A. K. (1985, second edition 1994, third edition, with Christian Matthiessen, 2004). *An Introduction to Functional Grammar*. London: Arnold.

Halliday, M. A. K and Ruqaiya Hasan (1976). *Cohesion in English*. (English Language Series 9). London: Longman.

Halliday, M. A. K. and Christian M. I. M. Matthiessen (2006). *Construing Experience Through Meaning: A Language-based Approach to Cognition*. Second edition. London and New York: Continuum.

Halliday, M. A. K. (2002–). *Collected Works of M. A. K. Halliday*. Ed. Jonathan Webster. Ten vols. London and New York: Continuum.

Martin, J. R. (1992). *English Text: System and Structure*. Amsterdam and Philadelphia: John Benjamins.

Matthiessen, Christian M. I. M. (1995). *Lexicogrammatical Cartography: English Systems*. Tokyo: International Language Sciences Publishers.

Further reading

Butler, Christopher S. (2003). *Structure and Function: A Guide to Three Major Structural-Functional Theories*. Two vols. Amsterdam: John Benjamins.

Eggins, Suzanne (2004). *An Introduction to Systemic Functional Linguistics*. Second edition. London: Pinter.

Matthiessen, Christian M. I. M. (2006). 'Frequency profiles of some basic grammatical systems: an interim report'. In Geoff Thompson and Susan Hunston (eds), *System and Corpus: Exploring Connections*. London: Equinox. 103–42

Thompson, Geoff (2004). *Introducing Functional Grammar*. Second edition. London: Arnold.

Geoff Thompson

TRANSFORMATIONAL-GENERATIVE GRAMMAR

Any formal description of language consisting of an algorithm which generates sentence structures and of a set of transformations which modify them systematically. In particular the theory developed by Noam Chomsky, whose goal it is to account for the implicit knowledge of language inherent in the human mind by means of a formalised system of rules. Transformational-generative grammar claims to produce all and only the possible sentences of a language determined by intuition* and the evaluation by competent native speakers and to account for language acquisition and speakers' knowledge of language.

See also: Acceptability/
Grammaticality; Behaviourism;
Empiricism/Rationalism;
Innateness; Language of Thought;
Logical Form; Minimalism;
Universal Grammar
Key Thinkers: Chomsky, Noam;
Fodor, Jerry; Katz, J. J.; Montague,
Richard

Transformational-generative grammar has been one of the most influential linguistic theories since the publication of Chomsky's (1957) *Syntactic Structures*. It is a systematic, objective, scientific formalisation of grammar, based on the belief that the structure of language is determined by the structure of the human mind, that all languages share some common, universal characteristics and that the species-specific creativity* of human language – that is, the capacity of all native speakers to produce and understand an infinite number of sentences that they have never heard before – must be accounted for. Furthermore, such a theory should also reflect processes of language acquisition and language use. Transformational-generative grammar has been constantly developed into more powerful theories, mainly by Chomsky himself, based on suggestions and criticism from many scholars, perhaps the best known of whom are Jerry Fodor, J. J. Katz, and Richard Montague. Chomsky's views have always been controversial, but they cannot be ignored.

In *Syntactic Structures*, the first of Chomsky's continually developing models, Chomsky declared that syntax is a completely autonomous part of language, independent of semantics and the phonological system. Furthermore he proclaimed that the syntax of a language can be formalised in a mathematically precise way by means of different rules operating on different levels. His programme was revolutionary in two ways. First, it was an attempt to formalise at least some of the features of language; and, second, Chomsky dissociated himself from the prevailing idea that a grammatical description of a language can only be derived from the observation and analysis of actually occurring data. For Chomsky '[s]yntax is the study of the principles and processes by which sentences are constructed in particular languages. Syntactic investigation of a given language has as its goal the construction of a grammar that can be viewed as a device of some sort for producing the sentences of the language under analysis' (1957: 11). Furthermore such a theory 'is to provide a general method for selecting a grammar for each language'. In order to achieve this aim, Chomsky relied heavily on features that are important for the success of theories in physics, and thus arguably established linguistics as a science.

After rejecting linear finite state grammars and after showing the limitations of phrase-structure (PS) descriptions, a formalised version of immediate constituent analysis, Chomsky developed a grammar with a tripartite structure. It consisted of a set of phrase-structure rules, a set of morphophonemic rules that convert sequences of morphemes into sequences of phonemes, and an intermediate level of transformations modifying the output strings of elements generated by the PS-rules into strings that can serve as the input to the morphophonemic rules. With a generative component generating the underlying structures and a transformational component modifying them into surface structures, this approach was the birth of what was to be known as transformational-generative grammar.

The PS-rules given in Chomsky (1957: 111), which generate the underlying structures, are the following (slightly modified): (1) $\Sigma \to$ NP + VP, (2) VP $\to$ Verb + NP, (3) NP $\to$ {NP$_{sing}$ / NP$_{pl}$}, (4) NP$_{sing} \to$ T + N, (5) NP$_{pl} \to$ T + N + S, (6) T $\to$ *the*, (7) N $\to$ {*man, ball*, etc.}, (8) Verb $\to$ Aux + V, (9) V $\to$ {*hit, take, walk, read*, etc.}, (10) Aux $\to$ C(M) (*have + en*) (*be + ing*), (11) $\to$ {*will, can, may, shall, must*}. Σ stands for sentence, NP for noun phrase, VP for verb phrase, Θ

233

for zero, T for the definite article, N for noun, V for verb, S for the plural morpheme, Aux for auxiliaries, M for modals, and C is the element that will later be interpreted by a transformational rule as concord; *en* stands for the past participle morpheme and *ing* accounts for the progressive form. Wavy brackets indicate a set of possibilities from which one must be chosen, and round brackets stand for optionality. Thus rule (10) states that C must be chosen and that we may choose zero or more of the parenthesised elements in the given order, resulting in eight different possibilities to rewrite Aux.

Phrase-structure rules are re-write rules which formalise immediate constituent structures of sentences on an abstract level. All the elements to the right of the arrow are the proper constituents of the single element to the left. In other words, rule (1) formalises the fact that in the sentence "The man hit the ball" 'the man' and 'hit the ball' are proper constituents of the sentence, whereas 'the man hit' is not. The output of the PS-rules are kernel strings, that is the underlying structures of kernel sentences. In order to arrive at the surface structure of the kernel sentences we have to apply all the obligatory transformations which regulate the morphological processes, for example, concord.

Transformations were first introduced in linguistics by Zellig Harris (1952) as a means to account for the relationship between linguistic expressions at surface structure. In Chomsky's terminology, transformations are re-write rules applied on the output of the PS-rules, the underlying structure, in order to arrive at the sur-

face structure. In contrast to PS-rules, transformations are not applied to single elements but to phrase markers, the structural description of the underlying structure generated by the PS-rules. In other words, a transformational rule takes one structure as its input and modifies it into another structure.

Formally, transformations consist of two components: the structural description, which serves as the condition for the transformation to be applicable, and the structural change, which describes the output. As an example of an optional transformation, consider the structural analysis NP – Aux – V – NP. In a formal approach these four elements are numbered linearly from left to right as X1 – X2 – X3 – X4. The structural change now gives the precise instruction X1 – X2 – X3 – X4 $\Rightarrow$ X4 – X2 + be + en – X3 – by + X1 , that is, in a less formal way, to re-write the input string NP1 – Aux – V – NP2 as NP2 – Aux + be + en – V – by + NP1. It can easily be seen that this transformation turns the underlying structure of an active sentence such as 'The man hit the ball' into the passive 'The ball was hit by the man'.

It must be noted that in the theory of *Syntactic Structures*, the PS-rules, together with the obligatory transformations, only generate simple, active, affirmative, declarative sentences, so-called kernel sentences, and that all other sentences are generated by applying optional transformations. Though it would not be impossible to generate all the interrogative, negative, passive sentences, and so on by a set of PS-rules alone, the obvious relationship between, for example, passive and active sentences would be lost. All transformations are based on deletion or insertion of elements resulting in substitutions or permutations and are either obligatory or optional. Whereas the obligatory transformations account for the necessary morphological processes needed to arrive at the actual sentences, optional transformations such as negation, passivisation, question formation and so on change the meaning by introducing new semantic information. Note that sentences such as (a) 'The man didn't hit the ball' (b) 'The ball was hit by the man' (c) 'Did the man hit the ball?' and so on, are not derived from (d) 'The man hit the ball' but that the kernel sentence (d) is generated by means of obligatory transformations and sentences (a) to (c) by optional transformations from the same underlying kernel string.

Furthermore Chomsky distinguishes between singular and generalised transformations. Singular transformations operate on individual strings of elements, whereas generalised transformations combine two different strings into one, resulting in embedding and conjunction and thus accounting for the possibility of recursive constructions and the infinite capacity of the grammar.

The model proposed in *Syntactic Structures* had some major drawbacks: the growing complexity of the transformational component, particularly with respect to the generalised transformations, the covert relationship between, for instance, affirmative and negative sentences, and above all the fact that it was a purely syntactic theory.

As the generalised transformations were responsible for the recursiveness of language, another solution to handling this vital feature of a comprehensive theory had to be found. So, instead of taking two sentence structures and conjoining them, it was proposed that by integrating a rule of the type NP + N + (S) the task could be shifted into the PS-rules and the generalised transformations could be discarded. Similarly, instead of having a negative or interrogative transformation, inserting the necessary element into the respective affirmative or declarative kernel string, it was suggested that an abstract marker (neg) or (Qu), or both of them, is inserted in the underlying structure as an optional element, yielding the rule S (Qu) (neg) + NP + VP. If these markers are chosen in the generative process, the respective obligatory transformations are triggered off by these markers to produce negative, interrogative or negative-interrogative sentences.

J. J. Katz and Paul M. Postal suggested in their seminal book *An Integrated Theory of Linguistic Descriptions* (1964) that the underlying structure already contained all the necessary elements for the semantic interpretation of sentences, and that transformations only account for the necessary adjustments in order to arrive at the surface structure and thus are obligatory. Furthermore as the meaning of the sentences is stated by means of PS-rules, these transformations must also be meaning-preserving.

Based on these suggestions, Chomsky proposed in *Aspects of the Theory of Syntax* (1965) a much stronger transformational-generative model than his original one. The base component of the *Aspects* Theory still consisted of a set of PS-rules and a lexicon to create the deep structure. But in contrast to the 1957 model, the base not only contained syntactic information but also all the semantic elements, and could thus serve as the input for the semantic component, on the one hand, and the transformational and phonological component, on the other, to account for semantic interpretation, that is meaning and phonological form respectively. The syntactic part still consisted of a generative and a transformational part, but their functions were different. It was now the base component that accounted for recursiveness and for all the semantically relevant options, and therefore there was no need for optional transformations anymore. In the 1960s and 1970s this theory was so important that it became known as the Standard Theory, and there was hardly any syntactic research done that was not based on this model by either accepting and developing it or by rejecting and replacing it by other theories.

Major criticism of the Standard Theory came from within generative grammar itself. Some of Chomsky's students felt that the scope of grammar was too narrow and should be extended into other areas of language, particularly into semantics. They called their approach generative semantics*. Observing that the grammaticality of a sentence is not independent of the beliefs of the speaker or that it has a lot to do with the lexemes actually chosen, they suggested that syntactic and semantic processes could not be separated and thus discarded the notion of deep structure. They claimed that all aspects of meaning could be captured in a form similar to Chomsky's phrase markers as semantic representations from which the surface structures are generated by transformations. However, by trying to include more and more phenomena into their theory, they had to widen the range of rules so drastically that the model lost its explanatory power. Furthermore, such a theory cannot account for universal features of language and is a move away from explanation back to descriptivism*.

Apart from generative semantics there were a very large number of post-Chomskyan models, the most important of which were Charles Fillmore's (1968) Case Grammar, operating with logical cases such as agent, instrument, experiencer, victim, place and so on, as constituents in the base component; Valency Grammars, which considered the verb as the only governing element from which all other expressions are dependent; and Montague Grammar, as an attempt to formalise the semantic structure of natural languages.

Insights from these approaches led to a continuous development of the Standard Theory to what were to be known as the Extended Standard Theory and the Revised Extended Standard Theory. The major change in the Extended Standard Theory was that semantic interpretation could not be based on the deep structure alone, but that it is determined by the deep structure as well as by the surface structure. However, the deep structure keeps its important syntactic role. In the Revised Extended Standard Theory we have a strict delimitation of the different grammatical components, that is syntax, semantics, as well as phonology, stylistics and pragmatics, the introduction of marked elements and above all the reduction of the number of transformations to a single, heavily constrained move-α rule. This development led to the Government and Binding Theory (GB-Theory) advocated in Chomsky (1981).

In GB-Theory, sentence descriptions are simultaneously created on the four interdependent levels of syntax (or D-structure), S-structure, phonetic form and logical form, each of which is concerned with specific aspects of the description of the sentence under consideration. It is based on the principles and parameters theory, which states that there is a finite set of fundamental principles common to all natural languages and a finite set of binary parameters that determine the range of permissible variability in language, language acquisition and language understanding. A major difference from the Aspects model is the fact that logical form is now derived from the S-structure and not from the D-structure.

The principles that constrain the range of possible sentence structures are contained in closely related subsystems as formulated in Chomsky (1981: 5–6):

> Binding theory poses locality conditions on certain processes and related items. The central notion of government theory is the relation between the head of a construction and categories dependent on it. θ-theory is concerned with the assignment of thematic roles such as agent-of-action, etc. (henceforth: θ-roles). Binding theory is concerned with relations of anaphors, pronouns, names and variables to possible antecedents. Case theory deals with assignment of abstract Case and its morphological realization. Control theory determines the potential for reference of the abstract pronominal element PRO.

It is the aim of GB-theory to find the principles and parameters common to all languages so that the syntax of a particular language can be explained along these lines. Evidence and counter-evidence from specific languages has led to continual refinement of the theory, so that as much variation in human language as possible can be accounted for.

In *The Minimalist Program* (1995), the latest step in the continuous development of transformational-generative grammar, Chomsky provided a radically new approach to the implementation of his underlying ideas. The well-established concepts of D-structure and S-structure have been discarded as well as government, the central element in GB-theory. Even the ubiquitous phrase-structure rules have been eliminated from the theory to a large degree. The only conceptually necessary categories left are the lexicon and the two levels of phonetic form and logical form* and it is the role of a grammar to map them onto each other. It is suggested that all the other categories be dealt with in externally specified systems outside the actual grammar. Using conceptions of economy, assuming that humans use as economic a system as possible, it is suggested that an optimal solution of relating phonological form and logical form can be found.

As suggested by the title of Chomsky's book, minimalism* has not yet been fully developed into a comprehensive theory, but is a program, according to which a theory of the language faculty could be developed. Although the minimalist program is well established in linguistics, it is severely criticised by developmental psychologists, cognitive scientists and neuroscientists, particularly because of its claims with respect to language acquisition and innateness*.

Transformational-generative grammar has influenced the study of syntax more than any other theory, but it also had an impact on other fields within linguistics, such as phonetics and phonology, sociolinguistics, pragmatics, discourse analysis and politeness theory. Furthermore Chomsky's innovative approach to the study of language and his methodology have influenced anthropology, philosophy, psychology and sociology, as well as computer science, neuroscience, literary criticism, music theory, and other fields. They have provided new insights for second-language teaching and learning and speech pathology, and above all, they have changed our conception of the mind.

Primary sources

Bach, Emmon W. (1974). *Syntactic Theory*. New York: University Press of America.

Chomsky, Noam (1957). *Syntactic Structures*. The Hague: Mouton.

Chomsky, Noam (1965). *Aspects of the Theory of Syntax*. Cambridge, MA: MIT Press.

Chomsky, Noam (1975). *Reflections on Language*. New York: Pantheon Books.

Chomsky, Noam (1981). *Lectures on Government and Binding*. Dordrecht: Foris Publications.

Chomsky, Noam (1995). *The Minimalist Program*. Cambridge, MA: MIT Press.

Fodor, Jerry A. (1964). *The Structure of Language. Readings in the Philosophy of Language*. Englewood Cliffs: Prentice Hall.

Jackendoff, Ray S. (2007). *Language, Consciousness, Culture: Essays on Mental Structure (Jean Nicod Lectures)*. Cambridge, MA: MIT Press.

Lyons, John (1970). *Noam Chomsky*. Glasgow: Fontana/Collins.

Otero, Carlos (1994). *Noam Chomsky: Critical Assessments*. Four vols. London: Routledge.

Smith, Neil (1999). *Chomsky Ideas and Ideals*. Cambridge: Cambridge University Press.

Further reading

Fillmore, Charles J. (1968). 'The case for case'. In E. Bach and R. T. Harms, *Universals in Linguistic Theory*. New York: Holt, Rinehart and Winston.

Harris, Zellig S. (1952). 'Discourse analysis'. *Language* 28: 1–30.

Katz, Jerrold J. and Paul M. Postal (1964). *An Integrated Theory of Linguistic Descriptions*. (Research Monographs, 26). Cambridge, MA: MIT Press.

Lakoff, George; and John R. Ross (1976). 'Is deep structure necessary?'. In James D. McCawley (ed.), *Syntax and Semantics* 7: 159–64.

Salkie, Raphael (1990). *The Chomsky Update. Linguistics and Politics*. London: Routledge.

Jürg Strässler

TRUTH THEORIES

Truth theories are philosophical attempts to pin down the concept of truth. Truth is arguably one of the most central issues in philosophy and truth theories vary a great deal from one another in terms of what they claim as well as what they take for granted, that is, their metaphysical baggage. Philosophers have always been at pains to define truth and suggest ways of ascertaining when something is true and when it is not.

See also: Analytic/Synthetic; Correspondence Theory; Definite Descriptions; Logic; Presupposition; Propositions; Truth Value
Key Thinkers: Aristotle; Ayer, A. J.; Davidson, Donald; Frege, Gottlob; Kant, Immanuel; Peirce, C. S.; Quine, W. V. O.; Ramsey, F. P.; Russell, Bertrand; Strawson, P. F.; Tarski Alfred; Wittgenstein, Ludwig

Ever since Pontius Pilate asked the question 'What is truth?' and, as the saying goes, preferred not to wait for an answer, the issue has been posed and intensely probed time and time again by philosophers. But truth has proved to be evasive. Over the centuries, philosophers have proposed competing theories of truth, but this is an area of investigation where new problems keep cropping up faster than they are able to tackle them. In philosophy, the predicate 'true' is always in contrast with 'false', unlike popular usage where it is often opposed to 'fictitious', 'fake' or 'spurious'.

Philosophers have long contended with a mind-boggler referred to generically as the 'liar paradox'. The liar paradox illustrates an early conundrum which any theory of truth worth

the name should avoid. Consider the sentence, 'I am lying'. If one asks whether this sentence is true or false, one is soon confronted with a paradox. If it is true, then the speaker is admitting that he/she is lying or that what he/she is saying is false. On the other hand, if it is false, then we have the speaker's word that he/she is not lying or that what he/she is saying is true. So, either way, the question as to the truth or falsity of the sentence 'I am lying' leads one to an intellectual quagmire. There are many variants of the liar paradox that produce similar results. Among these are 'Epimenides the Cretan says all Cretans are liars' (is Epimenides lying or telling the truth?) or 'The barber of Seville is one who, while continuing to live in Seville, decides to shave every man in Seville who does not shave himself' (does the barber shave himself?). It is clear that, irrespective of the definition of truth one works with, one has to make sure that the paradox produced in each of these cases must somehow be skirted.

The solutions proposed by philosophers for the liar paradox and its variants differ considerably. Some recommend that we regard such sentences as meaningless on the grounds that one part of a sentence cannot sensibly refer to the sentence as a whole and therefore predicate of it that it is true or false. Others concede that such sentences do make sense (how else do we know that they are odd?) but are neither true nor false. Others decree that such sentences are ill-formed because they violate a ban on self-reference. Still others decree that all paradoxical sentences, being outright contradictions, are false and argue further that any attempt to derive the truth of part of a paradoxical sentence by logical means is doomed to fail. Bertrand Russell identified a version of the 'liar paradox' in set theory by asking us to imagine 'a set of sets that are not members of themselves' and wondering, apropos of this larger set, if it is a member of itself. What Russell successfully showed by his discussion of this antinomy was the importance of weeding out the threat of contradiction from a mathematically sound theory of truth, or for that matter, any theory whatsoever.

Anyone setting out to propose a theory of truth has to sort out a number of initial questions. To begin with, it is important to know what it is of which we may sensibly predicate truth or, to put it technically, what sorts of entities can be said to be truth-apt. For instance, the sentence 'It will rain tomorrow' is bound to be either true or false – we will soon discover whether it is one or the other – whereas 'Will it rain tomorrow?' or 'If only it rained tomorrow/Would that it rained tomorrow' is not considered to be a candidate for truth ascription. On the other hand, *'Il pleuvra demain'*, *'Vai chover amanhã'*, *'kal pani barsega'*, which are the French, Portuguese and Hindi translation-equivalents of 'It will rain tomorrow' respectively, are just as true or false under the same set of circumstances as the English sentence. This means that what is true or false is not the sentence 'It will rain tomorrow' (which, of course, belongs only to the English language). In other words, truth has to do with what a sentence says or what we may call its meaning.

Many philosophers use the technical term *proposition**, which they distinguish from a *sentence* (a syntactic entity) and a *statement* (a unit of pragmatics). Another property of truth is that a sentence, once true, will always be true no matter what the specific circumstances of its utterance, making due allowances for such elements as 'tomorrow' that, as it were, date the sentence. In other words, truth is not only a universal but also an eternal property. Furthermore, it is an inalienable property. With reference to the specific example above, it must be pointed out that what is being considered truth-apt is neither the sentence per se nor the proposition expressed by it, but a dated instantiation of it, that is to say, a token of that sentence as produced on a certain date and at a precise time. This caveat is absolutely necessary because, unless we are further told when/on which day the sentence was uttered, it would be impossible to verify its truth, for the simple reason that this can only be done retrospectively – a day after it is uttered.

The philosophers who broadly subscribe to the view of truth adumbrated in the foregoing paragraphs are working within what is referred to as the correspondence theory* of truth. This is a way of conceiving of truth that dates back to at least as far back as Aristotle, who famously claimed in his *Metaphysics* (1011b25): 'to say of what is that it is not, or of what is not that it is, is false, while to say of what is that it is, and of what is not that it is not, is true'. Underlying the correspondence theory is the assumption that truth is a matter of correspondence between what one says on the one hand and what there is out there in the world (say, a fact or a state of affairs) on the other. It is perhaps the most satisfactory theory from a purely intuitive point of view and is certainly the oldest. It is implicit in such routine practices as a police investigation into a possible crime in which a witness account is checked and double-checked by comparing it to every single detail of the crime scene, or the police coming up with an artist's sketch of the physiognomy of the suspect on the basis of details furnished by persons who claim they witnessed the crime.

The correspondence theory is underwritten by metaphysical realism, which is a claim for the existence of things independently of what anybody might say or believe about them. It also posits, as in Ludwig Wittgenstein's celebrated analysis in *Tractatus Logico-Philosophicus*, a world consisting entirely of facts which can be truthfully and exhaustively mirrored by language. Furthermore, every proposition is either true or false and none can be both simultaneously or neither. Now, there can be no doubt that correspondence theory and its underlying metaphysical realism, whether or not explicitly spelt out or thought through, informs most of what laypersons believe about these issues. Incidentally, when it comes to the layperson, philosophers are wont to distinguish epistemic truth (what one knows) and doxastic truth (what one believes) from aletheutic or alethic truth (truth *ipsis*).

But the time-honoured claim of classical, two-valued logic* to the effect that between truth and falsity there could be no third value was thrown into disarray when Gottlob

Frege claimed in a paper published toward the end of the nineteenth century that the truth of the sentence 'the present king of France is bald' was conditional upon there being a king of France. In other words, the sentence (or proposition, if you will; note that Frege had in mind an undated version) would be neither true nor false if put forward at a time when France was no longer a monarchy. To control the damage such a claim represented to binary logic, Bertrand Russell presented his famous Theory of Descriptions, under which what appears to be a reference to the putative king of France turns out to be a claim to the effect there is a king of France at the time the sentence is produced and which, thanks to its declarative mood, can be adjudged true or false, depending on the facts of the matter.

The Frege-Russell dispute over the need or otherwise to posit presupposition* as a condition for a sentence to be either true or false impacted on work done in linguistic semantics in the 1970s and the first half of the 1980s. The initial enthusiasm in favour of the Fregean approach soon gave way to the Russellian alternative of reinterpreting the putative presuppositions as straightforward entailments, thanks to the work of scholars such as Deirdre Wilson and Ruth Kempson.

There are exceptions to the correspondence theory's claim that truth is a matter of correspondence between a linguistic object and a language external reality. These are so-called 'analytic' sentences, first identified by Immanuel Kant, following in the footsteps of John Locke and Gottfried Wilhelm Leibniz. For Kant, analytic statements are those in the declarative mood, where the predicate is contained in the concept of the subject, as in 'All bachelors are unmarried'. By contrast, synthetic statements such as 'The dog barked at the stranger' can be adjudged true or false, only on the basis of whether or not they faithfully report something that actually occurred in the real world. All synthetic statements are thus claimed to fall between the limiting cases of tautology and contradiction (true and false, respectively, regardless of what happens to be the case in the world).

There are many other theories of truth that, in one way or another, challenge the correspondence theory. Coherence theory is one such. Coherence theorists hold that truth is a matter of internal consistency within a whole system of propositions. In other words, truth is to be predicated primarily of the system as a whole and only secondarily and derivatively of individual propositions, based on whether or not they cohere with one another. Under such a generous definition, a system comprised entirely of false propositions (that is, false under the correspondence theory) may nevertheless receive the certificate of truth, thanks to the fact they cohere with (do not contradict) one another and thanks also to the fact that the coherence theory does not require validation by any factor external to the system. The popular saying 'Truth knows no contradiction' may be seen as drawing on the key insight of coherence theory. So too the practice of cross-examination of a suspect by the police or of a defendant by a prosecutor, where the attempt is to catch the respondent contradicting himself/ herself, may be seen as putting to practical use the central principle of coherence theory–the assumption behind the practice being that, if the respondent is telling all the truth, only the truth, and nothing but the truth, he/she will not give an answer that contradicts any other during the same cross-examination.

In the nineteenth century, Charles Sanders Peirce, William James and John Dewey defended a theory of truth that, despite differences among these thinkers on details, claimed that truth is that which effectively works. This is called the pragmatic (or pragmatist) theory of truth. Peirce added the further requirement that truth is 'the opinion which is fated to be ultimately agreed by all who investigate', thus emphasising the public character of truth. William James replaced that with an emphasis on the process of belief-formation by the individual rather than the product and pointing to the utility of holding something as true as the criterion for judging it to be true. John Dewey, agreeing with Peirce that truth is the conclusion to be arrived down the end of the road, went on to define it in terms of his favourite concept of *warranted assertibility*. One might say that pragmatism, with its steadfast opposition to the Cartesian dogma, realism, Continental rationalism and its emphasis on instrumentalism, is opposed to correspondence theory. But it has also been argued that pragmatism incorporates – or at the very least is not averse to – certain elements of both correspondence and coherence theories.

There are other versions of coherence theory that concede that, although individual propositions have nothing do with a language-external reality or the way we experience it, the system as a whole does, at least at its fringes. For instance, W. V. O. Quine held that, in talking about the world, we typically move from talking *in* certain terms to talking *about* them, that is to say, from the material mode to the formal mode, in what he famously referred to as a 'semantic ascent'. At the other extreme of the spectrum is the American neopragmatist philosopher Richard Rorty who flatly denies that there is any relation whatsoever between language on the one hand and the external world on the other, so that all talk of correspondence is philosophical balderdash.

That truth itself might be definable only by means of a sort of semantic ascent was what led the Polish logician Alfred Tarski to develop his semantic theory of truth – a theory of truth in formal or artificial (not natural) languages. He captured the insight in the formula: ' "p" is true if and only if p' (Tarski 1933*)*. The key to interpreting the formula lies in admitting a neat separation between *object language* (the language under investigation) and *metalanguage* (the language employed to say things about the object language). Tarski's central idea was that truth in a given (object) language can only be explicated by means of a sentence in the corresponding metalanguage or, equivalently, truth is invariably a metalinguistic predicate.

Thus, in the formula above, 'p' is a sentence in the object language in the sense that it is about this sentence that one predicates truth or whatever. The occurrence of p (the one without the inverted commas) is part of the met-

alinguistic observation concerning the truth of that sentence in the object language. In other words, the truth of 'p' is claimed to be guaranteed by the truth of p. This means that one can predicate truth only in a language other than the one in which the sentence for truth ascription is presented or, alternatively, 'p' and p belong, as it were, to two different languages. Evidently, as Tarski himself was the first to admit, his definition of truth does not work for natural languages, where self-referential sentences of the form 'This sentence is not true' are permitted, in spite of the difficulty in assigning to it a meaning. In a formal language, such troublesome cases can be blocked by fiat. Tarski's theory of truth is a version – albeit a very sophisticated one – of the correspondence theory.

In 1927, Frank Ramsey published a paper in which he defended the idea, originally entertained by Frege, that to say of a sentence that it is true is not to say anything else about it. That is to say, someone who says 'p' is thereby already saying, as it were, 'p is true'. In other words, the only difference between the statements 'p' and 'p is true' is that the latter makes explicit what the former says implicitly. Thus was born so-called 'redundancy' or 'deflationary' or 'disquotational' theory of truth. A. J. Ayer took Ramsey's thesis to its obvious conclusion, namely that truth is an empty predicate. This has been called the 'disappearance theory' or the 'no truth theory of truth'. P. F. Strawson used Ramsey's thesis to come to an equally interesting conclusion, by arguing that to say of a sentence that it is true is to endorse it or give it a stamp of approval. Strawson's thesis

243

has received the name of the 'performative* theory of truth' because it draws on J. L. Austin's speech act theory* which initially posited an important distinction between saying and doing. Quine, to whom the disquotational theory of truth is generally attributed, interpreted Tarski's semantic theory in the light of Ramsey's insight and argued that Tarski's was, at bottom, a deflationary theory to the extent that, in Tarski's approach, the predicate 'is true' only made sense in a metalanguage, not in the object language.

Truth theories, dedicated to answering the deceptively simple-looking question of what it is to say that a sentence, statement or proposition is 'true', have dominated the work of some of the most eminent thinkers, and have touched on many of the major issues in the philosophy of language.

Primary sources

Aristotle (350 BCE). *Metaphysics*. Trans. W. D. Ross. Available at http://classics.mit.edu/Aristotle/metaphysics.html (accessed 4 October 2007).

Ayer, Alfred J. (1952). *Language, Truth and Logic*. New York: Dover Publications.

Frege, Gottlob (1892). 'On sense and meaning'. In Peter Geach and Max Black (eds) (1980). *Translations from the Philosophical Writings of Gottlob Frege*. Oxford: Blackwell. First edition, 1952. 56–78.

Quine, Willard V. O. (1970). *Philosophy of Logic*. Englewood Cliffs, NJ: Prentice Hall.

Ramsey, Frank P. (1927). 'Facts and propositions'. *Aristotelian Society Supplementary Volume 7*: 153–70.

Rorty, Richard (1979). *Philosophy and the Mirror of Nature*. Princeton: Princeton University Press.

Russell, Bertrand (1905). 'On denoting'. *Mind* 14: 479–44.

Strawson, Peter. F. (1949). 'Truth'. *Analysis*: 83–97.

Tarski, Alfred (1933). 'The concept of truth in formalized languages'. Reprinted in Alfred Tarski (1956), *Logic, Semantics, Metamathematius*. Trans. J. H. Woodger. Oxfurd: Clarendon Press. 152–78.

Further reading

Alston, William P. (1996). *A Realistic Conception of Truth*. Ithaca, NY: Cornell University Press.

Davidson, Donald (1984). *Inquiries into Truth and Interpretation*. Oxford: Oxford University Press.

Dummett, Michael (1978). *Truth and Other Enigmas*. Cambridge, MA: Harvard University Press.

Horwich, Paul (1990). *Truth*. London: Basil Blackwell.

Kirkham, Richard (1992). *Theories of Truth: A Critical Introduction*. Cambridge, MA: MIT Press.

Rescher, Nicholas (1973). *The Coherence Theory of Truth*. Oxford: Oxford University Press.

Kanavillil Rajagopalan

TRUTH VALUE

At their simplest, truth values are often thought to be governed by the principle of bivalence, in which any declarative sentence's truth value can be either true (when what the sentence states is the case) or false (when what the sentence states is not the case). There is debate in logic and the philosophy of language about the appropriateness of the principle of bivalence and hence, about the nature of truth value.

See also: Definite Descriptions; Logic; Logical Form; Logical Positivism; Propositions
Key Thinkers: Aristotle; Dummett, Michael; Frege, Gottlob; Strawson, P. F.

Though problems about truth and falsity are discussed in ancient logic, for example by Aristotle, the phrase 'truth value' as we use it in modern philosophy comes from Gottlob Frege. He defined the truth value of a sentence as its being true or false, and claimed that there are no other truth values in declarative sentences, which normally refer to 'the True' or 'the False'. Though Frege's further view that truth values are objects is disputable, the main controversies about truth value concern what it is that has truth value (see Kneale and Kneale 1962; Haack 1978: chapter 6) and whether every declarative sentence is either true or false.

A sentence must be declarative, rather than, for example, interrogative or imperative, if it is to be a candidate for having a truth value. Thus, 'London is in England' and 'Torture is wrong' are candidates; 'Where is London?' and 'Don't go there' are not. Declarative sentences are usually called 'statements'. By the principle of bivalence, each statement is either true or false, but not both. Bivalent semantics, then, recognises only two truth values; the semantics of classical logic* is bivalent.

In contrast, in a non-bivalent approach to semantics a statement's falsehood does not follow from its being not true. For example, suppose our truth values are: true, false, and indeterminate. Then from the suppo-

sition that a given statement is not true, we can conclude merely that it is either false or indeterminate. Using bivalent semantics it could only be false.

Non-bivalent semantics has been motivated by 'empty terms', lacking any truth value at all (Strawson 1950); 'semantic presupposition'* in which a logically resolvable sentence presupposes something impossible (Strawson 1952; see Allwood, Andersson and Dahl 1977: 149–55); 'semantic paradoxes', such as the sentence 'This statement is untrue' (see Read 1995: chapter 6; Haack 1978: chapters 8, 11); 'future contingents', in which a statement refers to events that have not yet occurred (see Haack 1978: chapter 11); and mathematical statements, which in some approaches are always false because they refer to non-existent entities (see *Key Thinkers*: Dummett, Michael; Read 1995: chapter 8). While truth value in bivalent semantics may appear straightforward, wider investigation by philosophers of language and by logicians suggests that truth value is both a complex and a contestable idea.

Primary sources

Frege, Gottlob (1892). 'On sense and reference'. In Max Black and Peter Geach (eds) (1960), *Translations from the Philosophical Writings of Gottlob Frege*. Second edition. Oxford: Blackwell. 56–78.

Further reading

Allwood, Jens, Lars-Gunnar Andersson and Östen Dahl (1977). *Logic in Linguistics*. Cambridge: Cambridge University Press.

Haack, Susan (1978). *Philosophy of Logics*. Cambridge: Cambridge University Press.

Kneale, William and Martha Kneale (1962). *The Development of Logic*. Oxford: Clarendon. Chapters 8 and 10, especially 576–93.

Read, Stephen (1995). *Thinking about Logic*. Oxford: Oxford University Press.

Strawson, P. F. (1950). 'On referring'. *Mind* 59: 320–44.

Strawson, P. F. (1952). *An Introduction to Logical Theory*. London: Methuen.

Stephen McLeod

TYPE/TOKEN

At its most intuitive, the distinction between types and tokens is a distinction between two different ways of counting linguistic entities. One reason for paying attention to the distinction is the ease with which failure to do so causes confusion in discussions of language.

See also: Language of Thought
Key Thinkers: Peirce, C. S.

Suppose you are asked how many cars there are in a car park. You could count by type or by token. For example, if there are five Fords, one Fiat and three Toyotas, that gives three types of car but nine tokens of car. The terminology of 'type' and 'token' was coined by C. S. Peirce (1966: 4.537), but the distinction it marks has been known under different labels for far longer. Indeed, the distinction is arguably a primitive component of everyone's mental apparatus. The contrast between type and token maps quite closely onto the contrast between universals and particulars or onto that between properties and their instances. Most uses of the words 'type' or 'token' by linguists or philosophers operate broadly along these lines.

Most appeals to the type/token distinction in a linguistic context belong to one or other of two kinds. For the first, consider how many letters there are in the word 'London'. Counting by letter type, there are four: 'L', 'O', 'N', and 'D'. Counting by letter token, there are six: one 'L', two 'O's, two 'N's, and a 'D'. This contrast also applies at the level of whole expressions. There are, for example, nine word tokens in (1) but only seven word types:

(1) 'The blue cat ran circles around the green cat.'

This manifestation of the type-token distinction clearly generalises to many other linguistic categories. Think, for example, of how many phonemes* there are in 'Mississippi'.

The second manifestation of the distinction crops up when authors mark the contrast between sentences and utterances of sentences by describing the latter as tokens of the former. As with the first use, this also helps to eliminate ambiguity*. Suppose Jane and John both utter the sentence 'London is in England'. Have they performed the same utterance? The answer is affirmative if we mean the same utterance type, where the type is defined as the sentence produced, but negative if we mean the same utterance token.

This second usage may seem at odds with the first. To obtain two tokens of the word 'Alfred' in the second usage of the type/token distinction would require two utterances of the word. But in the first usage there are two tokens of this word in the sentence 'Alfred Brendel was named after Alfred the Great', even if that sentence is not uttered even once.

The relation between the first and second usages can be understood if we return to our non-linguistic example. The vehicles in a car park can be typed according to manufacturer, to colour, to engine size, or to age, and so on. Similarly, the utterances produced at a particular party can be typed in different ways: by the identity of the utterer, for example, or by loudness, pitch, time of occurrence,and so on. But the most useful way of typing utterances in linguistics is usually by the expression produced. So dominant is this way of comparing and contrasting utterances that it has become normal to talk as though sentences themselves *are* the type, while utterances are tokens of them. Though this use is, arguably, erroneous, it is simple enough to understand what an author has in mind in writing this way. The practice has even given rise to talk of a sentence's being 'tokened', by which is meant its being uttered. A related practice is to describe the indexicality of expressions such as 'I', 'now', and so on as 'token reflexivity', since indexicals depend for their referential properties on features of the context of their utterance.

A further factor driving this second use of 'token' derives from the philosophy of mind. It makes little sense to talk of sentences of the language of thought* as having been uttered, and 'tokened' is a useful alternative. To token a sentence of the language of thought is for that sentence to occur explicitly in one's brain. Philosophers of mind also make a related distinction between types and tokens of actions (where only the latter are specific events) and types and tokens of mental state (such as the belief that London is in England, which anyone might have, versus Jane's belief that London is in England).

The type/token distinction admits, then, of several different manifestations in linguistics. Using the label to mark the contrast between a sentence and a particular utterance of it may be slightly out of kilter with other uses but it has become dominant and is at least comprehensible in context.

Primary sources

Peirce, Charles S. (1966). *Collected Papers of Charles Sanders Peirce*. Cambridge, MA: Harvard University Press.

Further reading

Wetzel, Linda (2006). *Types and Tokens: An Essay on Universals*. Cambridge, MA: MIT Press.

Alex Barber

UNIVERSAL GRAMMAR

In Noam Chomsky's theory of human natural language, the genetically determined initial state of the linguistic competence in the individual human mind/brain, which is the starting point of the linguistic development of the individual into a mature user of a natural language.

See also: Acceptability/
Grammaticality; Continuity;
Empiricism/Rationalism;
Generative Phonology; Generative
Semantics; Innateness; Mentalism;
Transformational-Generative
Grammar
Key Thinkers: Chomsky, Noam;
Kant, Immanuel.

The linguistic development of every human being is amazing. When a baby is born, it does not speak, nor does it understand the language of its parents. But some years later, every child understands much of what is being said in the natural language used at home and uses parts of it in its spontaneous speech. After some additional years, the boy or girl is a fluent user of the same natural language and seems to share his or her linguistic competence with adult, mature users of it.

Such a development is amazing on several accounts. First, it apparently requires no learning, in the sense used when we describe the child as having learnt to use a spoon or a pencil properly and regularly. Second, it apparently requires no effort–neither on the part of the baby or the child, nor on the part of the parents. What is required is that the latter use the language in the presence of the former. Third, it takes place independently of other facets of human development, such as spatial orientation or face recognition. Fourth, and most importantly, the product of development is very complex, as is easily realised by anyone who tries to describe in full the linguistic competence of a child, beyond the lexical dimension.

Amazement is often a plea for explanation. What enables the human mind/brain to move from a seemingly poor initial state to an obviously complex mature state? This is the fundamental question of language acquisition, dubbed by Chomsky 'Plato's problem'. Within the spectrum of answers given to that question, there are two extreme and commonly rejected positions and then two intermediate ones, both of which are related to rich philosophical traditions that have been in rivalry for many years. One of these intermediate answers is the idea of universal grammar.

All the different answers are positions with respect to the role played in language acquisition by the human mind/brain and by human experience. One extreme position portrays the whole process of language acquisition as resting solely on human experience; in the initial state of the process the baby's mind/brain is a blank tablet. The opposite extreme position portrays the whole process as resting solely on innate human knowledge. Both of these positions are obviously untenable. The former cannot explain the fact that different children, whose experiences, in terms of the utterances made in their vicinity, are quite different from each other, turn out to speak the same natural language. The later cannot explain the fact that there are many different natural languages. Thus, conceptions of language acquisition that have the form 'either nature or nurture' are wrong. Accordingly, the intermediate positions see both nature and nurture as offering essential contributions to the language acquisition process. However, they involve different views of the contribution of the human mind/brain to the process, and consequently, also of the contribution made by human experience to the process.

A position that reflects the philosophical tradition of empiricism takes the mind/brain of the baby when born to include a general learning device, one that processes what is observed during experience and gradually develops all human cognitive competencies, including language, but also face recognition and calculation, for example. The mind/brain of the baby knows nothing about language but acquires it by applying the general learning device to the linguistic experience.

It is important to understand that such a position is actually a research programme. To hold such a position within the framework of scientific research is to be committed to an investigative effort to propose a theory that specifies the structure and operation of the general learning device and to put it to empirical test in a variety of areas of human cognitive competency, including language.

The major argument that has been raised against that position is called 'the poverty-of-the-stimulus argument'. It has been argued by Chomsky and many of his followers that the natural language acquired by the child has highly abstract properties that cannot be the product of any general learning device, especially since the input received consists only of utterances made in its presence. For example, each sentence of a natural language has a syntactic structure. Those structures have abstract properties that cannot be formulated by inductive learning functions from the utterances babies and children hear. An example of such an abstract property would be the very idea of structure. A mature speaker's linguistic competence induces a distinction between what counts as a proper sentence in one's natural language and what does not count as such. A general learning device has to capture this distinction, simply by processing utterances of sentences or other linguistic expressions. Such a general device would have to reach the conclusion that the distinction does not involve numerical calculation but rather structural processing. There is no reason to assume that general learning devices will have the ability to reach such a conclusion and also do it quickly. This is especially so in the context of the limited linguistic database of a small child.

The major alternative to the idea of a 'general learning device' in language acquisition is that of universal grammar. Here the position is that the mind/brain of a new-born baby includes an innate concept of natural language. That is a system of properties shared by all human languages, historically actual, or psychologically possible, which constitutes the essence of human language. Thus, for example, the fact that the syntax of a human natural language is structural rather than numerical is a fact about language that is included in the universal grammar. It is not learnt by a general learning device from experience, but innately given to human beings as a feature of the mind/brain.

It should be noted that universal grammar is not a grammar in the ordinary sense. It is a system of conditions that every natural language fulfills precisely because every natural language is an end-product of an acquisition process that begins with the universal grammar. Universal grammar is uniquely linguistic. It is what the human mind/brain knows, by genetic endowment, about natural language. This is one facet of the modularity of language: its cognitive independence of the rest of the mind/brain. Universal grammar is generic, in the sense of serving as the initial state of different acquisition processes that lead to different natural languages.

The unique linguistic nature of the universal grammar and its generic property are manifest in a theory of principles and parameters that has been developed within the research programme of universal grammar. Universal grammar includes a class of parameters that have to be set, on grounds of linguistic experience. When the parameters are set, much of the nature of the natural language to be acquired has been determined. An example is the head parameter: the head of a noun phrase is a noun, the head of a verb phrase is a verb, and so on. In a language, all heads appear on the same side of the phrase. Some natural languages are head-first ones: English is an example. Some are head-last ones: Japanese is an example. In order to set the head parameter, the child does not have to hear more than a few examples of appropriate expressions or sentences.

The universal grammar research programme emerged from the philosophical tradition of rationalism. The related conception of innateness, though ancient, is particularly related to seventeenth-century philosophy of language and cognition. Its generic nature is *related* to Kant's conception of the mind. Much of generative linguistics should be viewed as taking place within the research programme of universal grammar.

Primary sources

Chomsky, Noam (1966). *Cartesian Linguistics: A Chapter in the History of Rationalist Thought*. New York and London: Harper and Row.

Piattelli-Palmarini, Massimo (ed.) (1980). *Language and Learning: The Debate between Jean Piaget and Noam Chomsky*. Cambridge, MA: Harvard University Press.

Chomsky, Noam (1986). *Knowledge of Language: Its Nature, Origin, and Use*. New York, Westport, CT and London: Praeger.

Chomsky, Noam (1982). *The Generative Enterprise*. A discussion with Riny Huybregts and Henk van Riemsdijk. Dordrecht: Foris; *The Generative Enterprise Revisited* (2004). Discussions with Riny Huybregts, Henk van Riemsdijk, Naoki Fukui and Mihoko Zushi, with a new Foreword by Noam Chomsky. Berlin and New York: Mouton de Gruyter.

Chomsky, Noam (1988). *Language and Problems of Knowledge: The Managua Lectures*. Cambridge, MA and London: MIT Press.

Chomsky, Noam (2002). *On Nature and Language*. Ed. Adriana Belletti and Luigi Rizzi. Cambridge: Cambridge University Press.

Further reading

Cook, Vivian and Mark Newson (1996). *Chomsky's Universal Grammar: An*

Introduction. Second edition. Oxford: Blackwell.

McGilvray, James (ed.) (2005). *The Cambridge Companion to Chomsky.* Cambridge: Cambridge University Press.

Asa Kasher

USE/MENTION

To utter the word 'Paris', for example, while referring to the French city, is to use that word. To utter the word while referring to the word itself is to mention the word. The distinction matters to those investigating language because they are required to talk sometimes about a word and sometimes about what that word refers to, giving rise to potential confusion over which they are doing.

See also: Propositional Attitudes; Sense/Reference
Key Thinkers: Frege, Gottlob; Leibniz, Gottfried Wilhelm; Quine, W. V. O.

In spoken language the distinction between the use of a word and the mention of a word is often difficult to work out. In most languages there is no convention for indicating through pronunciation which is being employed. Speakers and hearers rely on the context in which a word is used in order to convey and understand what is meant. Yet the distinction has a significant effect on meaning to the extent that it can make the difference between sense and nonsense. For example, here are two plausible claims:

(1) Paris is a bustling metropolis.
(2) 'Paris' begins with the sixteenth letter of the English alphabet.

Here are two implausible claims:

(3) 'Paris' is a bustling metropolis.
(4) Paris begins with the sixteenth letter of the English alphabet.

(1) and (3), while differing in accuracy, sound the same when spoken aloud. The same goes for (2) and (4). This is why failure to be clear on whether one is talking about what a word refers to or about the word itself can cause confusion.

In writing various conventions allow for easy disambiguation between use and mention. Mentionings are often enclosed within single inverted commas; under another convention, they are italicised. In speech, context usually suffices to make clear which interpretation is intended. If that is not possible, speakers sometimes make a deliberate effort to highlight the distinction by explaining that they mean 'the word "Paris"' or 'Paris the city'.

For an example of where confusion might occur, consider the contrast between (5a) and (5b):

(5) (a) What does 'citizenship' mean?
    (b) What does citizenship mean?

An utterance of (5a) would typically be inviting a simple definition of the word, such as might be given in a dictionary. (5b), though it sounds the same, is more plausibly asking for someone's view on the broader implications of citizenship as a status.

Several factors make the use/mention contrast difficult to define precisely.

One is that the very label for the contrast is misleading: to mention a word often is to use it, albeit to refer to itself. Another is that one can mention a word without actually using it, as with (6):

(6) The five letter word that refers to the capital of the largest French-speaking European country has two syllables.

Since such cases do not give rise to confusion, they are not what people would have in mind as typical mentionings, but mentionings they nevertheless are. Yet another complication is that non-mentioning uses of a word have little in common beyond being non-mentionings. They are certainly not all cases of using the word to refer to a standard referent. Think of 'the' or 'Santa Claus', for example, or the use of words to refer to a non-standard referent in malapropisms.

Anaphora – in which one word or expression is referentially dependent on another – introduces yet more complexity. In (7), the final word is anaphoric to the fifth word, even though the fifth word refers to itself while the final word refers to a city. With the 'it' in (8) the situation is reversed. Following W.V.O. Quine's work on propositional attitudes*, example (9) is still more complex. The 'so' in 'so-called' refers to the name 'Giorgione' (which means 'tall George') while 'his' refers to the Renaissance artist himself, making it unclear whether the name to which both are tied anaphorically should be in quotation marks or not.

(7) The final letter in 'Paris' is left unvoiced by the people who live there.

(8) The people of Paris do not pronounce it that way.

(9) 'Giorgione' was so-called because of his size.

The use/mention distinction can be difficult for language users to negotiate, yet it is important in discussions of language precisely because it exists at the interface between expression and meaning. The fact that for speakers and hearers the distinction is often imperceptible without additional communicative actions, including gestures and intonation, has made use/mention a central problem in pragmatics as well as in the philosophy of language more generally.

Primary sources

Frege, Gottlob (1892). 'On sense and reference'. In P. Geach and M. Black (eds) (1980), Translations for the Philosophical Writings of Gottlob Frege. Third edition. Oxford: Blackwell.

Quine, W. V. (1956). 'Quantifiers and propositional attitudes'. Journal of Philosophy 53, 177–87.

Further reading

Davidson, Donald (1979). 'Quotation'. In Donald Davidson (2001), Inquiries into Truth and Interpretation. Oxford: Oxford University Press.

Devitt, Michael and Kim Sterelny (1987). Language and Reality. Oxford: Blackwell. 34–5.

Alex Barber

Index

Entries are indicated in **bold**.